The Specification
of Computer
Programs

INTERNATIONAL COMPUTER SCIENCE SERIES

Consulting editors   **A D McGettrick**   University of Strathclyde

J van Leeuwen   University of Utrecht

OTHER TITLES IN THE SERIES

UNIX™ is a trademark of AT & T

The Specification of Computer Programs

Władysław M. Turski
University of Warsaw/
Imperial College of Science and Technology

Thomas S. E. Maibaum
Imperial College of Science and Technology

ADDISON-WESLEY
PUBLISHING
COMPANY

Wokingham, England · Reading, Massachusetts · Menlo Park, California
New York · Don Mills, Ontario · Amsterdam · Bonn · Sydney
Singapore · Tokyo · Madrid · Bogota · Santiago · San Juan

Cover graphic by kind permission of Apollo Computer, Inc.
Typeset by Setrite of Hong Kong.
Printed and bound in Great Britain by R.J. Acford

First printed 1987.

British Library Cataloguing in Publication Data

Turski, Władysław M.
    The specification of computer programs.—
    (International computer science series)
    1. Electronic digital computers—
    Programming
    I. Title   II. Maibaum, Thomas S.E.
    III. Series
    005.1'2   QA76.6

    ISBN 0−201−14226−0

Library of Congress Cataloging in Publication Data

Turski, Władysław.
    The specification of computer programs.

    (International computer science series)
    Bibliography: p.
    Includes index.
    1. Computer software—Development.   2. Electronic
digital computers—Programming.   I. Maibaum, Thomas
S. E., 1947−   . II. Title.   III. Series.
    QA76.76.D47T87   1987   005.1   86−28900
    ISBN 0−201−14226−0

Preface

This book is about specifications of computer programs, but it is not a book about a specification method, a specification language or a specification technique currently available on the market. It is not even about any of these things as they may become available in the future. The main purpose of this book is to *explain the nature* of specifications. Thus it is a book about such aspects of specifications as are inherently there, even if a particular presentation chooses to ignore them.

The main ideas covered by the book, the notion of canonical step and software development by linguistic transformations, may seem at first glance too broad to fit the title. The authors firmly believe that there is no point in talking about specifications in isolation from the rôle they play in software development, just as there is no point in talking about software development without discussing specifications. Hence we have tried to show not only what specifications *are* but also how they serve to direct and constrain the software/design/development/implementation process.

Although this book is on specification of computer programs, we have tried not to forget that ultimately the software must be expressed in a way that admits an unambiguous mechanical interpretation. This observation leads to an important question that must be answered at the very beginning: is the mechanical interpretation a constraint on an intended meaning or a substance of it? In other words, is software development, from specification to program, tantamount to replacement of mechanically non-interpretable detail, or does it preserve the totality of meaning associated with the specification, adding − if necessary and/or expedient − details which, while not contradicting the specification, make the mechanical interpretation unambiguous, easier or more efficient? Crudely said, does the specification say more, or less, than the corresponding program? We find it philosophically more acceptable and technically more fruitful to choose the view that the software development process *preserves the meaning* of a specification while adding execution-oriented details. Hence our emphasis on computability throughout the process, and our insistence on making quite clear the principal difference between the computability (effectiveness) of a statement and the efficiency of its execution.

This distinction is indeed a very profound one. In many instances, although by no means always, we know how to improve the execution efficiency of a statement while preserving its intended meaning. The actual interpretation of the term 'meaning' adopted in this book is described in its body. We are fully aware that there are other perfectly good interpretations. However, with no known exegesis of the term 'meaning' could a transformation of an ineffective (non-computable) statement into an effective one be seen to preserve its meaning.

We try to approach the nature of specifications in several different ways. There is a software engineer's way and a mathematician's way to talk about specifications. In the current literature these two ways are not always convergent; indeed, they often appear so discrepant that one is led to believe that people are talking about quite different things. We think they are not. They just use widely different languages. They also differ in their education, experience and tastes. The reader of this book will judge it for himself, but we have tried not to invent yet another language to confuse everybody. Instead we have made a conscious attempt to adopt, as far as we were capable, terminological and semantic notions of both software engineers and mathematicians. Hence two preliminary chapters: we believe all readers could enjoy reading both, but we hope no software engineer reading this book will yield to the temptation to skip the mathematical preliminaries, nor a mathematician the software engineering ones.

We know from experience that books, certainly technical ones, are seldom read sequentially. Readers, especially the casual browsers (to whom our expressions of deepest sympathy: we are browsers too!), like to pick a chapter, a section, or even just a couple of paragraphs. This is fine with us. We hope to seduce even a most casual reader to read a little more, but we have imbedded so many repetitions and paraphrases throughout the body of the book that the main ideas have a fair chance of being picked up from almost any continuous selection of a dozen or so pages. The conscientious reader, the ideal − but who knows if still extant − consumer of all courses prepared by the authors, may feel slightly bemused by frequent repetitions. We would be honoured to have such readers. The repetitions are not verbatim, of course. If they are detected, we gained a friend who really cares for what he reads! The lengthy Appendix is not merely another repetition of the mathematical notions relied upon in the main body of the book. It is a skeletal form of a textbook on mathematical logic for software engineers. It may be a good idea to read it before the rest of the book and then consult it each time the need to pin down a notion is felt.

This book is not a textbook in the widely accepted sense. There are no exercises or other easily noticeable features of a good textbook. Neither is this book a monograph, as it does not develop a monolithic view of a subject. It is much closer to the idea of a reading book, or collection of essays, on the subject of specifications. In writing the book we did not pursue any single technical development; on the contrary, as much as possible we tried to draw upon the very rich body of available literature — books as well as papers and research reports. We did not attempt to rewrite the material we borrowed (with thanks!) in a single style, although some changes here and there were necessary. We felt that the field was not consolidated enough to warrant an attempt at notational or stylistic unification. The example of programming languages tells us that such attempts may remain futile in the future. Hence, the reader should neither seek notational guidance from us, nor be surprised by the diversity of notational devices we use.

The subject matter of most examples in the book is very simple; with few exceptions, the illustrative examples refer to integers or even natural numbers. Of course we realize that software is written for much more complicated application domains! There are even some examples which have richer stories as their real world interpretations. But for the most part we needed an example to illustrate a technical point, not to teach some new facts about the reality. Quite apart from obvious difficulties arising from the sheer volume of 'real life' examples, there is an added problem of not being sure if the 'real world' phenomena chosen for illustrative purposes would be sufficiently familiar to all readers to allow them to concentrate on the technical point rather than on the story employed to make this point. This, incidentally, also explains why if an example has a story to it, almost invariably the story is in some way facetious: we did not wish the readers to take the story itself too seriously.

For neither of this book's authors is English their native tongue. In neither of the author's native tongues is there the slightest chance that a speaker will mistake the grammatical gender of a noun for the sex of a person denoted by this noun. In both native tongues of the authors the nouns denoting neutral professional roles are of masculine gender. Both authors of this book appreciate the advantages of using English for scientific communication but neither of them wishes to engage in the faintly ridiculous dispute about the sex of nouns. Thus, in this book, the personal pronouns agree with the gender of nouns and not with the sex of persons, even if the notion of the nouns' gender seems alien to a substantial portion of the people who learned English (or American, or Australian, etc.) outside a school. To make it quite explicit: when we refer to a programmer we shall use the pronoun 'he'.

Władysław M. Turski
Thomas S.E. Maibaum

Contents

Chapter 1 Software Engineering Preliminaries

1.1 Why specifications are needed

If there is one thing on which all software experts agree, it is the necessity to establish the correctness of every program and system that is delivered to customers or intended to be otherwise used. A program may have many attributes of quality: it may be efficient in some sense, e.g. using a minimal amount of storage or consuming no more than a necessary amount of CPU time when run alone; it may be robust, i.e. designed so that its execution will not be substantially impaired under adverse conditions, such as less than perfect data; it may be portable, i.e. its execution will not be restricted to a single type of computer; it may be easy to modify to suit a somewhat changed application request, etc. But if it is incorrect, its value is nil.

Of course, much of the consensus about the necessity to ascertain program correctness obtains from the vagueness of the notion of correctness. Surely, when the term 'correctness' denotes only the intuitive (common sense) notion, no-one can object: who would be willing to accept an incorrect program? The intuitive meaning of the attribute 'correct' is − unfortunately − emotionally loaded. Correctness is good, lack of it is bad.

There is a definite danger in using emotionally charged terms in technical contexts: we are constrained to consider only such situations to which terms with positive emotional connotations are obviously applicable; we are not really free to consider cases in which the appropriateness of applying such attributes could be seriously questioned[†].

Thus, if we are to make any technical use of the commonly shared belief that 'software should be first of all correct', we must strip this

---

† One can easily verify this statement by a number of psychological experiments. Consider any emotionally positive attribute name: complete, efficient, reliable, etc. Regardless of what technical meaning is attached to these terms (and there is seldom an obvious and generally accepted interpretation of these attribute names in the context of computer programs), indeed without paying much attention to the definitions of these attributes, most people intuitively reject developments in which the negated attribute names could apply. No one seems to accept that, with specific definitions of the term, incompleteness, inefficiency or unreliability could be desirable!

attribute of its emotionally loaded name, or, to be more precise, analyse the technical context of the assertion 'program P is correct' to such an extent that it would be the technical ramifications of the assertion which would come to one's mind rather than the general (and vague) sense of approval.

A moment's reflection suffices to convince oneself that whatever else we wish to convey by saying that such and such a thing is correct, we certainly admit that in addition to the thing we consider there exists some entity separate from it with respect to which we are proclaiming its correctness (or, indeed, incorrectness). Thus a statement about correctness always presupposes an external frame of reference, explicit or implicit. (This is a very general observation, certainly not limited to software issues. 'Correct translation' presupposes a context: without it, one cannot 'correctly translate' even simple expressions like 'light beam'. 'Correct behaviour' presupposes a known code: people in mourning dress in black in some cultures, in white in some others.)

There are several possible frames of reference in which correctness of a program may be considered. Two most important ones are referred to when we speak of syntactic correctness and of semantic correctness. A program is said to be *syntactically correct* when it satisfies the grammatical rules of whatever language is employed for its expression. Thus, if the chosen language is FORTRAN,

```
DO I = 1,100
A(I) = 0
CONTINUE
```

is not a syntactically correct program, nor a part of a syntactically correct program, because the grammar of FORTRAN requires that the DO statement contains a label.

```
DO 125 I = 1,100
A(I) = 0
CONTINUE
```

is not a correct program, but may be a part of one: each of the three statements by itself obeys the grammatical rules of FORTRAN; the required 'matching' label 125 may be attached to a statement in the unlisted part of the program.

```
DO 125 I = 1,100
A(J) = 0
125 CONTINUE
```

is a syntactically correct FORTRAN program even if it would be hard to explain its meaning.

Depending on the kind of grammar employed to define the particular programming language, the question whether or not a given inscription is a syntactically correct program may or may not be algorithmically decidable. Similarly, depending on the kind of grammar, the question of syntactic correctness may extend to issues which with some other grammars would not be considered syntactic. For instance, in the so-called strongly typed languages, purely grammatic rules impose strict constraints on types of operands participating in an operation. In some other languages the types of operands are not constrained, indeed, often cannot be constrained by syntactic rules. While no degree of type constraints can guarantee meaningfulness of an operation, strong typing prevents many nonsensical combinations of operands. This illustrates an interplay between syntactic and semantic correctness: the actual borderline between the two is not universal, some problems that can be resolved on purely syntactic grounds in one language may require a semantic analysis in another.

It is not known in general how far one can extend the scope of issues covered by syntactic correctness: using the so-called two-level (VW or Van Wijngaarden) grammars one can push into a programming language syntax quite a bit of logical inference mechanism (Deussen, 1975) which most of the uninitiated would unhesitatingly consider a semantic matter. If, however, a grammar is fixed, so is − automatically − the extent of syntactic correctness, even if no algorithm to determine correctness of arbitrary constructs over the language alphabet is readily available (or even when such an algorithm is known to be impossible).

Since we shall always assume that the grammar of the language is fixed before we write any expression, we are justified in assuming that all expressions we are dealing with are syntactically correct. (Whether we are actually able to establish syntactic correctness of a given expression by applying an algorithmic test is an altogether different issue, which we shall simply ignore. We are justified in doing so if we insist that all expressions we shall ever be interested in are constructed in such a way as to guarantee their syntactic correctness. An inquisitive reader will be pleased to observe that we are placing relatively mild restrictions on the kind of grammars we are willing to admit, while imposing rather strict discipline on the way in which we are going to use them. We believe that such an approach is methodologically sound: if the discipline cannot be enforced we may relax it and tighten the restrictions on admissible grammars. Whenever such trade-offs are possible, one can do worse than assume the most liberal attitude towards the rules.)

After the syntactic correctness of a program is established, either by an analysis or by actual construction, we are faced with the problem of its *semantic correctness*. The first issue to decide upon becomes: what to take for the external frame of reference?

Basically we can take two approaches: either we would accept the program, try to derive its meaning and then ponder the question 'does it make sense?', or we assume that we know the intended sense of the program and must then establish whether or not the program indeed expresses the intended sense.

The first approach is not without a philosophical charm. One could elaborate on it by referring to a truly Platonic world of ideal programs, or support it by a strict fundamentalism, insisting that only programs which express consistent ideas are semantically correct, the latter being *eo ipso* realizable. Lest the reader fall into the trap of judging us frivolous, let us hasten to add that this is basically the approach taken by a large computer company who, having sold umpteen copies of their communication software system, hired a team of academics, asking them to determine the exact meaning of the software.

The second approach seems more promising from an applied point of view: it does admit the primacy of the intended purpose for which a program is written. It should be noted immediately that the way in which this approach has been introduced is not the way in which we would like to see it actually taken: literally checking if a program indeed expresses the intended meaning is hopelessly inefficient. The actual implementation of the philosophical principles of this approach should proceed differently: given an intended meaning of a program, execute its construction in a way which guarantees that upon completion it will express the intended meaning. At this stage of our discussion, however, we may consider such pragmatic remarks a little premature; let us therefore return to the original, intellectually simpler, statement of intent.

Thus we are inclined to declare a program semantically correct if it can be established that the program expresses an *a priori* stated meaning.

Two points deserve special attention: we expect programs to be capable of expressing a meaning and we want to be able to compare meanings. Unless we are very careful, we may very soon be forced to consider an endless chain of questions: what is the meaning of ...? what is the meaning of the meaning of ...? etc. Without going into a philosophical discussion of issues certainly transgressing any reasonable interpretation of the title of this book, we shall accept that *the meaning of A is the set of sentences S true because of A*. The set S may also be called the set of consequences of A; we are therefore equating the meaning of A with the consequences of A. Calling sentences of S consequences of A underscores the fact that there is an underlying logic which allows one to deduce that a sentence is a consequence of A.

Usually the A itself is a set of sentences, thus we are saying in fact that the meaning of a set of sentences is the set of consequences that are deducible from it. Can we consider a program to be a set of sentences (the A that is to have a meaning)? Perhaps not directly; that is why we insist merely on the program's capability to convey a meaning. But there are ways of looking at a program which make it appear as a set of sentences. Let us consider an example:

```
begin
var x: integer;
    input x;
```

$$(1.1)$$

```
   x:= x + 1;
   output x
end
```

This program (clearly) expresses the same meaning as the sentence:

> If the input value is an integer number x then the output value is also an integer value x' such that $x' = x + 1$.

Or, more compactly,

$$(\mathbf{A}\ x:\mathbf{integer})(\mathbf{E}\ x':\mathbf{integer})(x' = x + 1) \qquad (1.2)$$

Among the consequences of (1.2) we may list

$$x = 4 \Rightarrow x' = 5$$

and

$$x = 0 \Rightarrow x' = 1$$

and, of course, many others, all obtained by the same reasoning:

X is an integer, $x = X$
$(\mathbf{A}\ x:\mathbf{integer})(\mathbf{E}\ x':\mathbf{integer})(x' = x + 1)$

---

therefore $Y = x'$ is an integer and $Y = X + 1$

Sentence (1.2) establishes a relation in the cartesian product

integer $\times$ integer

Figure 1.1 presents its conventional diagram: the locus of pairs satisfying $x' = x + 1$ lies in the straight line passing through $(0, 1)$ and forming the angle of 45° with the x-axis.

Consider another relation in the same product:

$$(\mathbf{A}\ x:\mathbf{integer})(\mathbf{E}\ x':\mathbf{integer})(x' > x) \qquad (1.3)$$

The diagram of this relation is presented in Figure 1.2. (It will be observed that relation (1.3) most certainly is not a function, whereas relation (1.2) is!)

Does program (1.1) express the same meaning as relation (1.3)? Not quite! While all consequences of program (1.1) — obtained if we wish so via consequences of the equivalent relation (1.2) — are indeed consequences of (1.3), there are consequences of (1.3), e.g. $x = -1 \Rightarrow x' = 2$, which are not among the consequences of program (1.1).

A program

```
begin
var x: integer;
   input x;                                              (1.4)
   x:= x + random;
```

    output x
end

may be considered as expressing the same meaning as relation (1.3) provided we can prove that *random* assumes an arbitrary positive integer value. (In fact we may have to prove a slightly stronger statement about *random*, viz. that no positive integer can be excluded as a possible value of *random*. With this stronger statement about *random* we may claim that program (1.4) not only expresses the same meaning as relation (1.3) but also that it does so fairly.)

    These examples demonstrate at least one way in which programs may be viewed as expressing a meaning, certainly not less so than, say, relations. There are other ways of attributing a meaning to a program; the point we wanted to make now, however, was to stress a possibility of viewing a program entirely without any reference to execution. (This is not to say that we shall be totally insensitive to executability concerns; quite the contrary — there are many contexts in which concern with various program execution issues is legitimate and, indeed, most important. We wanted merely to demonstrate that an execution-oriented interpretation is neither necessary nor in any sense the most natural one.)

    One way or another, a program can be seen as expressing a meaning. This makes feasible our proposal to consider the problem of semantic correctness of programs as the problem of comparison of two meanings: one expressed by the program, another explicitly stated *a priori*.

    Moreover, with the adopted interpretation of 'meaning of' as the set of consequences, we see how, in principle, one can compare meanings. Of course, the required comparisons need not always be algorithmic; depending on particular circumstances the comparison may be much more difficult a task than a mere identity check for two lists of statements. In the following we shall consider many technical devices making comparisons of meanings as easy as possible; certainly the main idea of the proposed approach to semantic correctness is to make the necessary checks calculable. In fact, we shall insist as much as possible on such methods of program development which, by adhering to principles of design and implementation which guarantee semantic correctness by construction, avoid the actual comparison.

    Whichever approach is taken — correctness by construction or correctness checking — the first thing we must be sure of is the *a priori* stated, intended meaning of the program. Traditionally, the statement of intended program meaning is known as *program specification*.

    Thus we have reduced our concern for semantic correctness of programs to the following pattern: first we must have a specification, then we construct a program. The specification expresses our intended meaning, which either serves as the paradigm against which the meaning expressed by the program is checked, or is used to guide the program construction

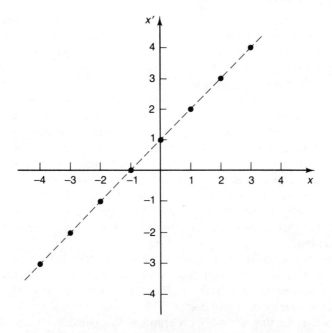

Figure 1.1   Diagram of relation $x' = x + 1$.

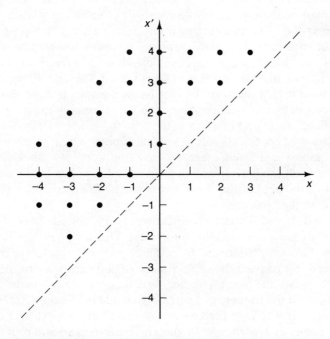

Figure 1.2   Diagram of relation $x' > x$.

process in a way which guarantees that the final product expresses the same meaning as the specification. In either case (and also in any case that may arise by the application of a mixed design/implementation strategy) the meaning of the specification conveys all that we may legitimately expect the program to express.

Naturally, a semantically correct program may possess many attributes which under suitable interpretation may be considered as its meaning. Some, or even all, such attributes may be deemed important or significant under particular circumstances or from a specific point of view. It may be advantageous to analyse a set of program attributes in order to select the best program from this or that point of view if we have more than one semantically correct program. But if we do not wish to get hopelessly confused, we should always remember that semantic correctness is a property that a program possesses (or not) with respect to a given specification.

To serve as the frame of reference for semantic correctness analysis is the main function of specifications in the process of program design/ implementation and verification. But this is not the only rôle in which specifications may be found useful.

If we agree that the only programs worth considering are those that are semantically correct, in many contexts we may find it simpler to discuss specifications rather than programs. Indeed, if the meanings of a specification and of the corresponding program coincide under suitable interpretation, the only reason to construct programs at all is that we wish to express the same meaning in a different way, e.g. by using different linguistic constructs. (Roughly speaking, programming may be seen as the process of translation of specifications into constructs of a different linguistic system. More on this in Chapter 4.) The underlying pragmatic observation is that the form of specification makes it more amenable to some sorts of mental manipulation than the corresponding programs. It is not unlikely to expect, for instance, that the concepts employed in the formulation of specifications are less machine-oriented, more abstract, or indeed more application-oriented than the concepts employed in the formulation of the corresponding program. Should this be the case, in the context of the application domain it is much easier to discuss the specification than the program.

As a rule, we expect specifications to be considerably shorter (as texts) than the corresponding programs. This again makes them more attractive in many contexts, for example when a change is being contemplated. Of course, changing a piece of software without at the same time changing the corresponding specification destroys the semantic correctness of the former, and therefore should be discouraged as strongly as possible. If a change is to be considered at all, it must be a change to specifications and a change to the corresponding program at the same time. But to discuss the change may be (and often is) easier when the text to be changed is more succinct.

Finally, let us consider a traditional distinction. It is very frequently stated that whereas specifications say 'what', corresponding programs say 'how'. We do not particularly like this distinction, as under scrutiny and with the proviso that the specification and program both express the same meaning there is not much difference left between the what and the how. But there is a particular instance in which this distinction is very helpful. Consider a very large piece of software, well documented in every respect but one: there is no comprehensive specification available. We know how this software system executes on a computer, we even know enough about it to attempt a modification. But without knowing what it is that our large program expresses, we do not really dare to modify the software. Seen from this point of view, *ex post* specification writing is not such an absurd activity as it may appear.

1.2 How specifications arise

At the end of the preceding section we described one way in which specifications may arise: as a (hopefully, precise) succinct description of an existing program. While under special circumstances it may be a proper and useful thing to do, we should not consider this particular origin of specifications as typical. Intuitively − and there does not seem much wrong in following one's intuition now and again − specifications arise before corresponding programs; indeed, we are inclined to view them as prescriptions for eventual programs.

Before trying to answer the question of the origin of specifications in general, let us consider a simple view of three entities: an application domain, a programming language domain and a specification.

An application domain (a bank, an industrial plant, a telecommunications network, etc.) can be seen as a number of objects, perhaps hierarchically arranged into compound ones, together with relations and functions that exist between these objects. Such is the nature of real-life domains that there is no single view, no universally best way of looking at them.

For example, when we consider a telecommunications network, we may wish to disregard the make of individual subscriber stations as long as they have certain technical characteristics, but there are points of view (e.g. a telephone set manufacturer's) in which not only the make but also the colour of the sets is important. Similarly, we may consider the relations established by dial-up connections, but choose to disregard those following from the charging policy. Alternatively, we may wish to concentrate on patterns established by reduced charge times and zones, etc.

The choice of a viewpoint dictates how we see an application domain, just as in any scientific study the choice of concerns dictates which aspects we decide to disregard. We may consider planets as material points, disregarding their actual shapes and mass distributions, or we may choose to consider Lunar mascons[†]. Usually, in scientific study the choice of the point of view itself is in turn dictated by the choice of phenomena we want to investigate, or by the capacity of the available techniques (intellectual or laboratory) to handle the observations. Thus, to a certain degree, the view of a domain may be determined by an *a priori* knowledge or intention. We shall return to this remark in a little while. At the moment let us just note that a study of a domain presupposes a choice of the point of view, and that there is no guarantee that with a different point of view we would get the same picture of the domain, let alone the same results from the subsequent study.

A programming language domain, being by definition formal rather than natural, does not admit arbitrary views. Although each program written in the given language may be justly considered as a domain of its own, with particular objects, relations and functions defined by appropriate programming constructs, all such individual programs − domains that can be created within the overall domain of a programming language − share certain structural and other generic features.

Let us assume that we have chosen (and fixed) a particular view of the application domain and written a suitable program. (We do not explain at the moment what is implied by 'suitable'; intuition may suggest here some interpretation of this term, but no satisfactory concise expression of these vague ideas that may hide behind 'suitable' has ever been put forward, nor have we found one of our own.)

A pleasing (i.e. intellectually satisfying) description of the relationship that exists between a fixed view of the application domain and a suitably composed program obtains from the assumption that it is the specification that 'binds' the program to its application domain. (In fact, it would have been much closer to our intended description to say 'binds together' a program and its application.)

In Section 1.1 we have demonstrated the need for specifications as the frame of reference against which program correctness can be defined as a notion, and, in practical terms, against which a program may be verified, or, preferably, guided by which it can be correctly constructed. Regardless of the actual use we make of the relationship between specification and program, we agree that it is an instance of a calculable[‡] relation defined on specifications and programs. We may call this relation 'satisfaction'[§] and write *P*sat*S* whenever program *P* satisfies specification *S*.

[†] Mass concentrations irregularly distributed throughout the Moon's body otherwise considered as homogeneous.

[‡] When we say that a relation R, defined on $X \times Y$, say, is calculable we understand that there are precisely stated rules, which, given $x \in X$ and $y \in Y$, allow one to determine, in a finite time, if xRy holds.

[§] For more on the relation of satisfaction see Section 3.3.

Can we think of a similar relation that would reflect the nature of the relationship between a (view of the) application domain and the specification? We suggest considering the relation of abstraction. It neatly captures our intuitive notion that the specification should represent in abstract terms the view we hold of the application domain. We do not, however, have the slightest idea how to make the relation of abstraction into a calculable one; at least, how to do so directly.

Consider again the relationship between the specification and program. We agreed to call the corresponding relation 'satisfaction', and we know that to be of any use it must be a calculable relation. What about the inverse relation, i.e. the relation that exists between a program and the specification that this program satisfies? Is it not really a kind of abstraction? Recall that some specifications are written after the program is not only created but also actually applied over and over again. Is not writing the specification *a posteriori* for an existing program in fact creating an abstraction of the program? Since this seems to agree with our intuition, let us apply the same principle − in reverse − to the other side: let us assume that the relation between the specification and the chosen view of the application domain is also that of satisfaction, viz. that the chosen view of the application domain satisfies the specification.

In Figure 1.3, solid arcs correspond to primary relations, dotted ones to inverse relations. We feel that the natural order of creation in this case proceeds from the application via an abstraction process to specification (hence we could have written *SabstrA* meaning that specification *S* 'abstracts' application *A*, if we could only define the rules by which the relation **abstr** could be computed!) and via a program construction process from specification to program so that *PsatS*. Leaving aside for the

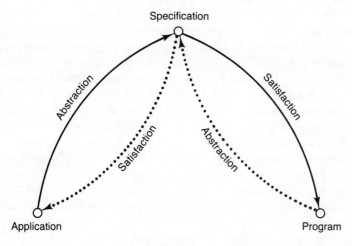

Figure 1.3 Relations between specification, program and application.

moment the perplexing question of whether we can make this relation calculable, let us observe that now we have obtained a complete symmetry of relationships between specification, application and program (Figure 1.3).

Given A, S and P we know (or at least we assume that we know) how to compute $P\,\text{sat}\,S$. The principle of evaluation is based on our definition of correctness: P should express the same meaning as S; thus $P\,\text{sat}\,S$ if and only if P expresses the same meaning as S. If both P and S are formal expressions (or sets of expressions) the notion of their consequence sets is well defined and whilst the comparison of the two sets of consequences may cause some technical difficulties, in principle it entails no problem.

If we allow that at least in some cases specification is extracted from an existing program (by an abstraction process!) we can use the same relation **sat** to check if our abstraction is formulated correctly. This suggests that we may try to employ the same trick in the left-hand side of Figure 1.3. Namely, having obtained a specification S for an application A, we may check if $A\,\text{sat}\,S$. The trouble is that whereas S is a formal expression (well, we may insist on its being formal!), A is a view of a real-life domain, and we do not have much control over its form. If A happens to be formal, of course, there is not much difference between the left- and right-hand sides as far as verification of the **sat** relation is concerned.

In Section 1.3 we shall consider a pragmatic approach to application programming in which one does not assume that A is a formal expression. For the time being, however, let us concentrate on the ontological aspects of program specification.

A general scientific paradigm applicable to the situation depicted in Figure 1.3 is that of theory formation. In natural sciences, theories are formulated as abstractions of observed facts. In the process of theory formation a view of a natural domain is first adopted. Planets are represented by material points, a physical pendulum by the mathematical one, telephone conversations are represented by an Erlangen distribution, life-cycles of individuals by birth, procreation period and death, etc. A theory is then expressed as a set of formal expressions, and consequences of the theory are obtained that can be compared with observations of Nature (again suitably filtered by the adopted view: it does not make sense to accuse Newton's theory of planetary motion with the fact that the specific reddish tinge of Mars cannot be deduced as its consequence). Of course, when the consequences of theory do not agree with suitably filtered observations we change the theory, as happened with Newtonian mechanics when the drift of Mercury's perihelion was observed.

Based on a theory, we may construct a mathematical model of it — in the domain of, say, real numbers. Thus, based on Newton's theory of planetary motions and a theory of ordinary differential equations, we may construct the model of planetary movements in Cartesian coordinates or in orbital elements. If the model is constructed correctly, i.e. if whatever follows from (is a consequence of) the theory also follows from the model (a fact which we establish or reject not by observations but by reasoning and calculations!), if, in a word, the model satisfies the theory, we may — when convenient — use the model rather than the theory for validation experiments, viz., roughly speaking, for comparisons with observations (not forgetting about the required filtering of the latter!). This is done pretty frequently in natural sciences; so often, in fact, that the literally meaningless but insiduously catchy phrase about mathematical models of reality has been coined and repeated *ad nauseam* by assorted science-column journalists.

(A good part of the confusion can be attributed to the perverse nature of the noun 'model' in many ethnic languages. For example, in English it is perfectly natural to use the phrase 'to be a model of' in two exactly opposite meanings: on the one hand, a concrete exemplification of generally stated principles, and, on the other hand, principles of concrete phenomena freed from irrelevant detail are both called 'models'. In this book we shall meticulously observe the convention that 'to be a model of' is unidirectional; a model is in some respect more concrete than whatever it is a model of. Thus the ephemeris of a planet (its predicted positions on the firmament) are a part of a model of whatever theory of the planetary motions was used as the specification for the calculational scheme (the scheme as a whole being a model of the theory composed of the theory of the planetary motions and necessary mathematical theories, such as the theory of differential equations, Euclidean geometry, etc.). The Copernican system is not a model of the solar system: it is its theory, and, if anything, it is the observations of the real solar system — suitably filtered! — which need to satisfy Copernican theory. If the observations do not satisfy a theory we may prefer to reject it and look for a better one, viz. for such a theory which the observations would satisfy.)

Theories are not only built in natural sciences. Interesting examples of a somewhat different approach to theory construction are to be found in mathematics. Mathematics, let us recall, does not study real-world domains. Its objects of interest are formal: numbers, relations, functions, abstractly defined lines, surfaces, spaces and various structures of such objects (relations between functions, spaces of transformations, etc.). Many mathematical domains had been quite well investigated long before their concise definitions were available. For instance, integer numbers and a huge body of fascinating properties thereof were very well known indeed before an Italian mathematician (Peano, 1858–1932) formulated his famous axiomatic theory of integers. Why should mathematicians be so anxious to produce a formal theory of — after all — formal domains? Well, the answer is simple, really. It is interesting to see how little one needs to say axiomatically (thus asking other people to accept it without question) in order to be able to derive all other known facts as consequences. Or, putting it somewhat differently, what are the irreducible principles of, say, integer arithmetic, from which all properties of integers and all theorems about integer numbers would follow?

This motivation is not only intellectually very appealing; it is also very practical (of course to the extent that anything mathematical can be considered practical − but we should not assume this condescending attitude; mathematicians do set a very good example of intellectual efficiency). Indeed, if we have a small set of principles from which everything else follows, we are able to build models of 'everything that follows' quite inexpensively: we just need to make sure that our model satisfies the principles and that the rules of 'following from' either are copied, or can themselves be consistently modelled by (combinations of) model-specific rules.

(Unfortunately, it turns out that such a simple approach does not work for integer arithmetic: the famous Peano axioms turned out to be satisfied not only in the domains which behaved as conventional integers should, but also by domains containing such unusual objects as transfinite integers − integers larger than any natural number. This discovery led to a much more restrictive notion of *categoric theory* and *standard models* (Grzegorczyk, 1974). Another discovery was made by the brilliant Austrian mathematician, Gödel (1906−1978), who proved that there are arithmetic theorems about integers that can be neither proven nor refuted within normal logic. Gödel's undecidability principle establishes an ontological limit on logic's power to deduce formally all facts from any single set of axioms. Important as it is for the philosophy of mathematics, it should not concern us too much. Usually the decidable part of any mathematical domain is sufficiently large for any practical purpose. Indeed, it took mathematicians quite a long time and quite a large effort to find an arithmetic theorem that would be independent, and thus neither provable nor disprovable from Peano axioms.)

Another well known example of an axiomatic theory of a well understood domain is Euclidean geometry, axiomatized in ancient times, but certainly well developed long before Euclid.

The subtle difference between theories in natural sciences and those in mathematics is two-fold. First, because there is no real domain explicitly underlying mathematical ones, there is no filtering involved in forming a view of reality. A mathematical domain is its only reality, therefore we are never in danger of having to redo a theory because an aspect of reality, heretofore disregarded (filtered out), must now be taken into consideration. Second, while in the natural sciences the exploration of a domain progresses more or less in step with the development of the theory, in mathematics the domains are usually pretty fully investigated (explored) before their theories are required and their construction is attempted.

Now, if we consider specification-building as an activity similar in nature to theory construction, we immediately see in it a measure of both natural-scientific and mathematical approach; the main features, however, are quite different.

The principal reason that makes specification-building unique among other theory-creation activities is the duality of the specification's role. A specification is rather like a natural science theory of the application domain, but seen as a theory of the corresponding program it enjoys an unmatched status: it is a truly postulative theory, the program is nothing but an exact embodiment of the specification. Thus, if we limit our considerations, as software engineers are often told to, to the software design/development process that starts with a given specification, we admit that all application-related issues have already been satisfactorily resolved, and that as a theory of the application field the specification is fully accepted.

Two pragmatic observations seem in order. First, if the assumption about the specification being an acceptable theory of the application domain is, let us say, premature, we may expect a totally non-systematic and hard-to-justify validation of the program against the application domain to be used in lieu of, or as an extension of, the natural-scientific process of theory verification. Second, a software engineer being excluded from the abstraction process leading to the formulation of a specification, the only criteria of quality he can apply to the specification are purely formal, such as consistency or calculational completeness of a sort.

If we consider the right-hand side of Figure 1.3, we can observe that the dotted line represents a process familiar from mathematics: abstraction from a well defined domain to its succinct theory, subject to rigorous verification techniques (represented in this interpretation of Figure 1.3 by the solid line on the right-hand side). This is exactly the path taken by the academic community, both in theoretical work − when abstract data types are being defined (concise, formal definitions − theories of stack, queue, monitors, etc.) − and also in applied work (ranging from academic specifications of application software, such as editors and file management systems, to *ex post* written specifications for commercially available software). In all such cases the primary domain is formal (artificial), well investigated and thoroughly familiar to the specifier. Even better examples of such an approach are provided by numerous publications on software development, where the application domain is purely mathematical or even purely 'programmatical': when a specifier has a full command of all relevant domain-related facts, such as properties of integer numbers when specifying and developing a prime number generating routine, the specifier may use this knowledge at any stage of the design/development process.

Under such circumstances, the actual program design is little more than an exercise in elegant proof construction (syntactic ambiguity intended!).

In a typical application problem the domain is known − at best −

only pragmatically, and often not at all, apart from isolated observations. Most frequently, the attempts to provide a computerized service for an application domain are at the same time first attempts to provide a workable theory of the application. This is true even if some pragmatic knowledge about the domain is available: experience teaches that some phenomena in the domain are related in such and such a way, that there are such and such constraints that must be observed, or else. Thus it is known, for example, that landing permission at airport X must not be issued more frequently than in 240 second intervals, or that accepting a credit card payment in excess of £N.00 at the ABC store should not be allowed without special sanction from the management.

Such pragmatic knowledge usually reflects some deeper relations between more fundamental notions, but neither the relevant relations nor even the fundamental notions themselves are known. Thus, in the process of specification building, a very large number of isolated, surface phenomena are elevated to the status of axioms. This entails two very substantial risks: (1) that the sheer number of such pragmatically justified dos and don'ts precludes their verification, if not for consistency (whether or not they contradict each other), then certainly for completeness (have we collected them all?), and (2) that having elevated the surface phenomena to the status of axioms, we have forsaken the option to provide a concise, generic axiom set from which the individual constraints would follow and which would be much easier to model – in general – in the program domain. Quite often when the specification theory is a collection of separate pragmatic rules, the corresponding (and correct!) program tends to be a laborious case analysis, with complex control structure and an unpleasantly large number of exceptions.

Considering this aspect of specification building, one cannot help mentioning that a very large class of computer applications, the so-called real-time applications, is almost entirely dominated by specifications constructed from pragmatic observations. The very fact that explicit time constraints are mentioned in the specifications usually indicates that no analytic study of the application domain was successfully completed, that primitives of the domain are unknown, or that the nature of relations between the primitives has eluded the investigators. Indeed, it is very strange why the absolute time intervals (i.e. a measure of the Earth's rotational progress) should be at all related to, or appear in, relations between phenomena occurring in a chemical reaction tank or over an airfield. One suspects that in most real-time application systems a much more concise and general theory would arise from the study of relations and functional dependencies between events than from the registration of absolute time intervals. Unfortunately, the heritage of the non-digital control era is that universal clock-based control systems provide a unified approach to the problems arising in their application domain (an event-dependent control system in non-digital implementation being much too hard to realize and implement). Thus we are very probably faced with the classical example of an approach, in its time necessitated by the available tools, now being followed in a doctrinaire fashion even though the tool that necessitated it no longer dominates the application field.

When the attempts to write a specification are indeed the first study of a given field, or at least the first study aimed at deriving a concise, normative description, there arises a very hard-to-resist temptation to consider the outcome of such attempts as more important than it is; often as more important than the reality itself. A not infrequent consequence, particularly in the field of so-called Management Information Systems, was evident in almost desperate attempts to shape the reality so that it would conform with whatever the specification said. In other words, a specification was treated as a prescriptive theory for *both* sides of our diagram in Figure 1.3! That such an approach leads to spectacular disasters is only to be expected, and, indeed, the almost universal failure of the much advertised MIS projects of the 1970s provides ample evidence of this methodological misconception.

How, then, should a prudent software engineer proceed when faced with a problem of designing and implementing a software system for a poorly investigated application area for which no sufficiently trustworthy descriptive theory exists, i.e. when he lacks the true foundation for his work? (We assume that if a sound descriptive theory of the application domain is available, it can be converted into a prescriptive theory − a specification for software − relatively easily. While this is not necessarily a trivial task, it does not appear to be an impossibly difficult one. Certainly it is an entirely different situation from that which obtains when no descriptive theory is available.)

There are two major ramifications of the question posed in the preceding paragraph:

1. To what extent should a software engineer get involved in the descriptive theory building for an application domain?
2. To what extent is it a software engineer's duty to convince himself that a specification he is given is a sound descriptive theory of the application?

A purist may find it possible to answer both these problems by a very short statement: a software engineer's task starts with a specification. His only duty is to check its quality as a prescriptive theory for a program (consistency and sufficient completeness, see Chapter 3). We should not like to quarrel with the purist's view: it certainly is a sound one, and when made into a professional motto may even help in a court of law. But we would also like to be a little more pragmatic, as the strict adherence to the purist's view may cause a loss of business for professional software engineers and push too many potential clients to seek semi-professional or altogether quacky help.

Let us then take the two problems one by one:

1. The variety of application domains is truly staggering. It would be presumptuous to assume that software engineers may gain − as individuals − sufficient subject expertise in many domains. (In fact, as the proportion of software engineers educated as such grows with time, the happy coincidence of finding an application expert turned software engineer will be rarer and rarer.) Thus, if a software engineer is to get at all involved in the abstraction process (leading to the formulation of an application domain theory), his participation must be that of a partner collaborating with an application domain expert. The rôle of the software engineer in this partnership is not to become an application expert, but to assist the application expert in the theory building. The expertise a software engineer brings into the cooperative effort is mainly methodological, the methodology in question being one oriented at obtaining a specification that possesses such qualities that make the subsequent program design and implementation as well based as possible. (As an example, the software engineer should try to steer the abstraction process away from all forms of detail-canonization, should insist on looking for primitives and general forms of relationships instantiated by observable surface phenomena, etc.)

2. The more firmly we believe that the specification is the *ultima ratio* of software design/implementation, the more effort we should be willing to put into validation of the specification against the application domain. Quite apart from ethical considerations (which ask us not to waste the client's money on design and implementation of something he does not really need or want), getting the specification validated in the application domain is a prudent thing to do. A well thought out validation procedure may (and usually will) identify many weaknesses of the specification at a very early stage of the software writing process. Unpleasant as the thus necessitated corrective actions may be, they are incomparably less unpleasant and a lot less expensive to take than the alternative: improvements and/or changes to the already implemented software. When we write a software system for a client, it is eventually going to be used. When used, it will be confronted with the application area. Assuming that the software is correct with respect to the specification, its confrontation with the application domain may be viewed as the validation of the specification, but this would be very likely the least efficient and the costliest method of validation.

Any validation of the specification against the application domain must involve an expert judgement: we cannot rely on fully formal, calculable verification in the way we do when we check that a program satisfies the specification, because in most cases the application domain would not be a formal system, and therefore the question of whether the specification and the (filtered view of) an application domain express the same meaning cannot be resolved in the same fashion as for the two formal systems: specification and program. We want to check if this is so, but we cannot resort to calculations. Hence we must rely on an expert judgement. (Note that had we delayed the validation of a specification until the implementation was completed, we would have relied on the user's expert judgement anyhow!) Thus, again, the validation of a specification appears as a cooperative venture and should be performed jointly by the software engineer and the application domain expert.

1.3   The customer's rôle

In an ideal world the customer for software services will be capable of, and willing to, analyse the application domain, write a consistent and sufficiently complete descriptive theory of it and also prove to his eternal satisfaction that this theory is a correct abstraction of the application domain. Incidentally, the vision of such an ideal world is not so unrealistic as it may appear at first glance. A large class of computer users live in such a world: physicists, astronomers, many engineers and some mathematicians indeed do themselves formulate the descriptive theories of domains of interest. They also transform the descriptive theories into specifications (sometimes, unfortunately, rather implicitly) and write their own programs. The trouble is, such people seldom become customers of software firms.

For most application areas, however, the vision of the ideal world is little more than a pipe-dream. (Even if we are tempted at this point to make a few acid remarks about the lamentable state of affairs, we would not gain much by restricting our attention to the situation that would arise when the deplorable trend towards removing vestigial traces of the scientific method from general education is reversed. First, we doubt it will ever be reversed; second, even if reversed, it would take so long for the reversed trend to bear fruit that we shall not live to see them.)

Thus we envisage the practical situation in which the customer cannot provide a good descriptive theory, let alone a specification, all by himself. As pointed out in the preceding section, we expect the descriptive theory to be the product of cooperation between the software engineer and his client. Similarly, we insist that the semantic verification of the specification is to be done cooperatively by the software engineer and his client.

We assume the customer to possess a fair pragmatic knowledge of his domain of interest and at least a preliminary notion of what he wants the eventual computerized system to achieve. In trying to convert this knowledge into a descriptive theory and program specification we would like to achieve the following:

1. to catalogue all notions in terms of which the domain-specific knowledge is expressed;

2. to categorize the catalogued notions with respect to their functionality (find out which ones are constants, relations and functions);

3. to establish structural and hierarchical dependencies between the categorized notions;

4. to discover which notions are primitive and which are derived (especially important if we suspect that some of the catalogued relations are in fact consequences of more fundamental, primitive ones);

5. to check if all primitive notions are indeed included in our catalogue (often the catalogue will include relations that are consequences of unlisted rules);

6. to check the consistency of the emerging descriptive theory and, as far as possible, its completeness.

The terminology used in the above six points is obviously biased towards one particular kind of formalism − that which we use the most in the following chapters of this book. It should be stressed, however, that just as it is impossible to avoid using a formalism (all communication between people, except perhaps telepathy, depends on the use of a formalism!), no particular formalism should be *a priori* taken as the best for all cases. In fact, a formalism (say) tainted with algebraic expressions, may be a very poor vehicle for expressing the descriptive theory of an application domain; it may also raise totally unnecessary barriers between the software engineer and his client-partner. The apparent success of semi-formal system design techniques[†], such as SADT (Ross, 1977), indicates that the dialogue between application area expert and software engineer may be greatly facilitated by using a neutral terminology of graphical forms.

Predefined forms (Figure 1.4) have two practical advantages: they are relatively easy to process by automated tools and they tend to impose certain structural rigour on the description process without assaulting their user with a verbally oriented grammar. The first advantage is amplified when the forms are not printed (or drawn) on paper, but directly displayed on the computer screen. In fact, when the forms are displayed on a screen to be completed by user-supplied information, one can easily see their duality: on one side they appear as 'language independent abstractions' of hierarchy, composition and dependence, on the other as an input medium to linguistically well defined formulae (viz. those that accept the user-supplied parameters).

The significance of having at one's disposal automated tools to process the emerging domain descriptive theory and its constituents becomes quite clear when we consider the amount of exceedingly boring work

---

[†] In this context, 'system design' probably means the same as 'system specification' and, in fact, is just another expression for the name of the process we are considering, i.e. for descriptive-theory building.

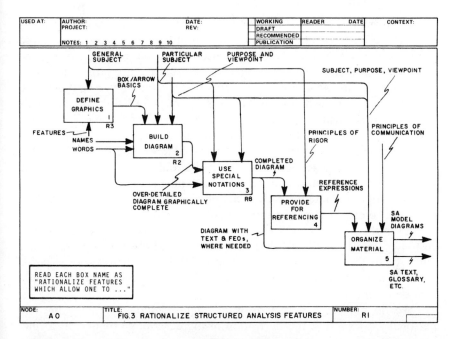

Figure 1.4　An example of a SADT™ form (© SofTech Inc., and reproduced with permission).

needed to verify consistency (i.e. to find possible inconsistencies, such as missing definitions of components listed as constituents of compound notions, missing definitions of objects appearing as arguments in listed functions, type conflicts, etc.).

The second advantage has two aspects. One, methodological, obtains from the innate structure of graphical forms. Of course the significance of this aspect critically depends on the quality of the form design. One can easily envisage designs which would be too restrictive, more like stencils than linguistic constructs. But if the forms are carefully designed they can preserve almost intact the flexibility of a language: the ability to combine unrestricted number of forms into a form of the same type; the ability to represent decomposition into constituents, the number and kind of which are not necessarily fixed in advance; the ability to represent a hierarchy, the depth of which would not be fixed in advance either, etc. Usually such freedom of composition rules is associated with a language of suitably flexible grammar, but it can be achieved by means of well thought out graphical forms not only without losing the ability to express structured-ness of description, but actually enhancing its appearance if not presence. That this goal can be achieved without using any form of verbalization may be considered as advantageous on psychological grounds.

The second aspect is of a didactic nature. To achieve the ability to express structure, a verbal-like language must rely on a strict and usually formally defined grammar. Such a grammar must be learned and mastered pretty well (as a whole) before the user can even start describing the application domain. The grammar itself is usually quite large and, more importantly, bears no relation to the area that is ultimately to be described. The need to learn such grammar often puts off potential users, especially as it initially seems totally unrewarding. The use of predesigned forms or, better still, of form-editing software tools, allows one to bypass this seemingly pointless exercise and start immediately on matters close to the user's interests. As mentioned above, if the tool is sufficiently flexible, a graphic form editor may be as powerful a means of expressing a theory as a verbally oriented language; thus, not much is lost if this kind of formalism is used for creation of a descriptive theory.

From the preceding discussion it transpires that software engineer — customer cooperation in this stage of the specification process is rather impersonal, viz. through the set of tools provided by software experts. While this is certainly the most important aspect of cooperation, it is not its total extent.

We do not think that a software engineer should actually become personally involved in the derivation of the descriptive theory: as a rule, his expertise in the application area is nil, and we cannot condone unprofessional involvement of well meaning amateurs in matters that require solid knowledge and understanding. But a software engineer may assist the client in the best possible use of the tools (by tutoring and technical guidance), and in questions of methodology. These arise quite naturally when the process of building a descriptive theory comes to a halt, either as a result of an error (say, an inconsistency is discovered) or because there is nothing more to do. In the latter case it is claimed that the abstraction process (see Figure 1.3 again) is completed; in the former, that the process runs into a cul-de-sac and is to be somehow put back on the right (well, at least on a different) track. A software engineer may be able to understand deeper reasons for the halt in the abstraction process, as the observed manifestations may be quite superficial. Thus it is advisable that any errors discovered in the process of theory building be brought to a software analyst's attention. (This is especially important if an automated tool was used in the process: the available fault diagnostics would often mean more to a programmer than to an application specialist.)

When the abstraction process seems completed (runs out of steam) the software expert may start using its outcome as the specification (perhaps, after some meaning-preserving transformations if the descriptive and prescriptive forms of a theory differ in formalisms). We strongly advise against such practice, however. First, the completion of the abstraction process, as any other major step, must be subject to a validation procedure. Second, the obtained descriptive theory may and should be subject to a thorough analysis. Postponing a little the discussion of the validation procedure, let us consider the analysis of a supposedly finished descriptive theory.

A software expert (and now we really mean an expert!) may be able to recognize weaknesses of a theory even if it passes all formally defined tests, such as consistency and sufficient completeness. A major kind of weakness a formally acceptable theory may have is its size. A very large (i.e. voluminous) theory is always suspect; so is a very complex one. (A software expert may have questioned the Ptolemaic theory of the Solar system purely on these grounds: the number of epicycles thought necessary to describe the planetary motions surely looks suspicious!) This is not to say that all descriptive theories have the simplicity and conciseness of Maxwell's equations for electromagnetic fields. Certainly there are domains which need a lot more equations, and need not fit onto the proverbial back of an envelope, but there are some easily recognizable symptoms of theory unhealthiness. Here are some:

- a very large number of individual axioms, usually in the absence of, or accompanied by, only a few generic axioms;
- relations and functions which admit many exceptions, usually to be handled differently, often each exception requiring special treatment;
- occurrence of notions used very infrequently or very often, the latter case usually accompanied by the phenomenon known as flat hierarchies (a very often used notion does not participate in constructs that in turn participate in other constructs, but tends to enter the highest-level constructs directly);
- lack of a visible, well balanced overall structure: concepts unequally removed from primitive notions often appear side by side in the expressions, such as relations and functions;
- duplications or near duplications, i.e. presence of constructs which differ only in name or other insignificant aspects (an aspect can be considered insignificant if it plays no rôle in the way the construct is being applied).

The above list does not pretend to be exhaustive, none of the listed symptoms is by itself critical, nor should the symptoms be interpreted literally: there may be very good reasons, for instance, why almost identical concepts are named differently. If, however, symptoms such as listed above are indeed present, we should at least investigate whether or not their presence is justified.

Let us now turn our attention to the validation procedure for a descriptive theory.

The criterion we would like to apply is that of satisfaction: we need to verify if the application domain satisfies the theory. It will be recalled that crucial in such verification is the comparison of consequences, a relatively easy issue for two formal systems, a much harder one when either one or both systems are not formal or at least not generative (in the sense that a theory consisting of a set of axioms with suitable rules of inference is generative).

An application domain, even after the details deemed insignificant are filtered out, can hardly be considered as a generative formal system. Thus the comparison of consequences in the left-hand side of Figure 1.3 must be a process principally different from that envisaged for the right-hand side. We recommend that this process should involve the customer's judgement.

The assumption we make is that the user knows all consequences that follow from his view of the application domain. While it is certainly impractical (if not impossible) to ask the user to list all statements that constitute the set of consequences, we believe that an application domain expert can recognize valid consequences or, at least, can point out consequences that are invalid (or, to be more precise, can state that a presented statement is not a valid consequence).

Thus the general plan for validation of a theory against the application domain is as follows. A stream of consequences from the theory is generated. Statements from the stream are interpreted in terms of the application domain and shown to the user. If he accepts them as valid consequences of his view of the application domain, fine. If he discovers some statements that in his opinion are not valid consequences, the theory is wrong, or at least imperfect. (For simplicity, we disregard the possibility of poor interpretation: while a danger of misinterpretation cannot be ruled out, it is very likely that an inappropriate interpretation will result in consequences of the theory being consistently rejected by the client.)

Of course, the plan outlined above has a very serious methodological defect: the stream of consequences of a theory is usually infinite (even if, for finite theories and finite sets of rules of reasoning, the sets of consequences are always countable).

Thus the outlined validation procedure cannot be considered a proof of theory appropriateness, just as testing cannot be considered a proof of program correctness. (It may show presence of bugs, but not their absence, as Edsger W. Dijkstra's immortal dictum says.) We are quite pessimistic about the fundamental possibility of improving the situation in this respect: a calculable proof may replace an exhaustive comparison process only if both infinite sets to be compared can be represented by their generators, and the generators − being finite − can be 'compared' by suitable calculations (for instance, by inductive reasoning). While there is no question that we may insist on intellectual artefacts − such as theories and programs − possessing the qualities necessary for application of proof rather than test procedures, it is not only unrealistic but also philosophically inadmissible to assume the real application domains to follow suit.

Thus, just as mathematical theories can be proved appropriate for mathematical domains (themselves artefacts!) but no physical theory can ever be *proved* appropriate for the real world, the descriptive theories of application areas can merely be tested for their appropriateness. The validity of a descriptive theory of an application domain can be ascertained only up to a point, under the proviso that no consequence has been derived from it that would contradict an observation (or perception of an observation) in the application domain. It may sound a bit minimalistic, but we do not think a better principle can be found.

Even agreeing on the 'minimalistic' criterion of theory validation against a view of the application domain does not make the validation procedure very simple. A straightforward inspection by the client, who is often the author of the theory, is not likely to be very relevant; similar inspection by a software engineer may yield some observations on the quality of the theory (as mentioned before) but is not illuminating with respect to the appropriateness of the theory for the application domain either. In order to seek relevant observations, we must obtain consequences of the theory which could be interpreted in terms of the adopted view of the application domain.

There are two main ways to obtain consequences of a descriptive theory:

- by direct inference,
- by simulated execution.

If the theory of the application domain is formulated in such a way that rules of inference can be directly applied, we may use them to generate statements that follow from the theory. Applying our interpretation in terms of the domain, we convert the derived statements into statements about the domain. A competent customer may now study a stream of thus generated statements and check if they conform to his idea of the application domain properties. This approach uses, on the software engineer's side, techniques very similar to 'reverse theorem provers', i.e. theorem generators. On the part of the customer, the approach reduces to straightforward checking of whether or not a number of statements make sense.

If, as we expect in most cases, the descriptive theory obtained by abstraction is not presented in a form amenable to direct generation of consequences, we must first convert the descriptive theory into a prescriptive one. (For example, a descriptive theory presented in a collection of graphical forms is unlikely to allow direct generation of consequences, apart from purely syntactic ones.)

Such conversion is necessary in any case, since it is the prescriptive form of the theory that is going to be used as the basis of software design and implementation. The conversion is clearly a software engineer's job, as it is directed towards providing the most convenient starting point for his subsequent work. Under these circumstances the validation of the converted theory becomes even more important: there is always a danger that in the process of conversion the meaning of the theory has been corrupted. Thus if the prescriptive theory is validated and found acceptable by the user, the software engineer gains confidence not only in the descriptive theory (perhaps supplied by the client) but also in the validity of the conversion.

Since the conversion is very much a software engineer's task and its result, as a rule, is not intended for use outside his sphere of activity (indeed, the conversion may be justifiably considered as the first step in software design), he is free to choose for the prescriptive theory the formalism most suitable for his purposes. The most important issue at hand being validation, the software engineer may decide to opt for a formalism that allows simulated execution of specifications. (A number of specification languages allow direct execution of specifications written in these languages; some programming languages may be used as formalisms in which write specifications − see Section 3.4, where we consider programs as specifications.) An execution of the specification − a test run of an instance of the prescriptive theory − after interpretation in terms of the accepted view of the application domain, yields an observation to be judged by the customer.

1.4 Specifications and software contracts

Having illustrated the customer's rôle in obtaining and validating the specifications, we should like to consider the issue of software contracts in the light of our understanding of cooperation between the software engineer and his client.

The traditional view of a software contract, slightly simplified for didactic purposes, holds that the client formulates a document known as the requirements specification, the software engineer either accepts this document and agrees to deliver a product conforming to it by a given date or writes another document, known as the technical specification, gets the client to approve it, and only then enters the contractual agreement to deliver a product. Additional clauses of the contract may specify the software engineer's responsibility for continuing support of the delivered system (mostly, repair of errors discovered in the first N months; less frequently, small improvements and modifications, primarily in case the client would wish to operate the software system on a slightly changed hardware configuration or for slightly modified purposes). The larger the expected volume of work required to complete the original assignment, the vaguer are the clauses about the criteria of final acceptance (usually some period of on site testing is mentioned) and about continuing support (a not unusual practice being to describe it in terms of a period of time and some motherhood statement like 'shall make every reasonable effort').

We believe such contracts are quite unique in that they are potentially unfair to both parties, and more often than not it is sheer luck which determines the party that loses more. Indeed: requirements specifications being usually a huge collection of heterogeneous details structured according to some irrelevant principle (alphabetic, for instance, or patterned after the organization chart of the client's firm), they represent little more than just a catalogue of 'wouldn't it be nice' desiderata, often mixing up things related to such disparate aspects as what is to be achieved, how it is to be achieved and what hardware is to be preferred. It is often well nigh impossible to check if requirements specifications are consistent, as the very notion of consistency cannot be uniformly applied to such a mixed bag of requests.

A software engineer accepts the thus 'specified' task mostly on the basis of intuition, sometimes supported by prior experience with 'similar' systems (the notion of similarity being again very, very informal!). When he constructs a design specification – unless it is validated by the customer, as described in the preceding section – he starts his work from his and only his view of what he *thinks* is most important in the requirements specification.

During a considerable period of ensuing design and programming, up to the testing phase, both parties live in a state of great expectations and hopes: the customer hopes for a system that will be right, the software engineer hopes that the delivered system will be what the customer expected.

When the delivery date comes, there is very little that either party can do: there is just this one system, and the customer, if he does not like it, can refuse the payment (or a portion thereof), or even sue for damages, but nothing will change the fact that after waiting for N months (or years!) he is still without the system of his dreams. If the system does not meet the customer's approval, the software engineer may have to forfeit his revenue, or may sue for a partial payment (he worked in good faith). Nothing can change the fact that he has an unwanted system on his hands.

The unfairness of traditional software contracts (the fact that both parties are treated unfairly does not make it fair!) obtains from the mutual lack of real communication: the parties agree on something, neither party really knowing what the other one understands by 'something'.

Insisting that the specifications be made formal is not going to change the situation very much: if the customer agrees and accepts formal specifications as the basis of a contractual agreement without fully realizing their consequences, he may be bound legally to pay for a program provably correct with respect to those specifications, but he may be severely disappointed with the program he gets.

The key to a mutually fair contract is two-fold: precision and understanding. Slightly oversimplifying, we may say that precision is the software engineer's forte, while understanding is the customer's. As there does not seem to exist any magic that would instantly transfer either precision or understanding to the other party, achieving an acceptable level of precision and understanding by both parties must be a process.

Roughly speaking, the process of achieving common understanding at a sufficient level of precision encompasses a top part of the abstraction and a top part of the satisfaction process of Figure 1.3, i.e. those parts during which the software engineer and the customer should actively cooperate, as described in Section 1.3.

Thus we recommend that the software contract itself should be an evolving structure: from an initial form written at the first cooperative meeting, until its final form, written at the last cooperative meeting, at which the decision to implement the fully specified software is taken. We further suggest that the contract's validity during its evolution be limited to the period between signing its current version until the next version is prepared, the next version being explicitly foreseen by the currently valid one.

In fact, we are recommending that big software contracts be abandoned and replaced by a series of much smaller ones, each covering a well defined step in the crucial phase of an application software formation. Thus neither of the two parties will be obliged to accept a risk larger than a few week's engagement. The customer will be at all times fully aware of what he is getting, and the software engineer will be always paid for what he has actually done. Each party will be able to cancel the project at the completion of a small step. The customer will never be more than one short step away from an acceptable (for him) idea of the ultimate system and the software engineer will never engage for a long time on a task the acceptance of which may be questioned.

From a software engineer's point of view, such a policy entails one danger: he will not be able to draw large sums in the form of advance payment just because he is engaged in a project. We believe that the possibility of being paid just because one is engaged in a project (with the ensuing risk that one has been paid for work never completed or completed unsatisfactorily) contributes quite appreciably to the bad reputation some software organizations are earning for the whole profession.

In practical terms, the staged contract scenario may run as follows:

Act I
(Customer, Software Engineer)

Customer: Dear Software Engineer, I have this Rubber Shoe Sole Moulding business, and I would like to put some computers in, you know, to do some melting pot control, and invoicing, and scheduling, and well — to keep track of things, so that I could save a few pennies here and there. Would you do it for me?

Software Engineer: Well, let's see. Can you say a bit more about what it is that you want your computer system to do?

Customer: Well, I have this chap, young Smith. He is quite a lad, you know, and he keeps nagging that our RSSM is terribly old-fashioned, management-wise. Why don't you talk to him, eh?

Software Engineer: Be delighted, could you let me have his phone number so that I could arrange a meeting?

Customer: But of course, here it is . . . . Incidentally, I don't let young Smith make financial commitments, you know, so please report to me if you want anything in terms of, eh, expenses and fees.

Software Engineer: All right, sir. We will submit an estimate soon.

(*Exit Customer*)

Act II
(Young Smith, Software Engineer. Small talk, *ad lib*)

Software Engineer: So you want some computers at your RSSM...

Young Smith: Yes, oh yes. You see we have this melting pot into which we put India rubber, and charcoal and. . .we heat the stuff until it melts and we want to get a pretty good paste. The problem is that the rubber we get these days is very unsatisfactory: almost every shipment has different dirt in it. It can be corrected, of course, but the analysis is frightfully expensive, and the lab that makes them is always late, and we can avoid all this if we could change the stirring rate in the pot and the heating program while the pulp melts into the paste, but this must be done quickly. Also, we are shipping our moulded soles to several customers and we never seem to be able to keep track of their orders and our shipments and. . .

Software Engineer: OK, OK — I'm already lost. Can we put some order into your requirements? Here is a form some of our clients found useful. It is really very simple, you see. . . . I'll leave a supply of them with you and let's make a date for next week. If you have written your requirements on the forms by then, we can move a bit further.

(*Exit Software Engineer*)

Act III
(Customer, Software Engineer. No small talk)

Software Engineer: Sir, we are engaging in the formal requirements abstraction process.

Customer: Eh, well, I mean...

Software Engineer: Mr Smith fully agrees and is actively cooperating. The first stage shall be completed by next Thursday. The total fee for this stage will be...

Customer: You don't mean...

Software Engineer: Yes, I do, but it is only for the first stage.

Customer: And how many, pray, stages are there going to be?

Software Engineer: I cannot tell; no more than necessary, and you can always say 'stop'. We shall not insist that RSSM continues paying for services that you do not wish us to provide.

Customer: All right, all right, here is your cheque.

. . .

Act 2M
(Young Smith, Software Engineer)

Software Engineer: I have run your specification through the syntax checker, there are no type inconsistencies, but Colour-Index generated by Inspection-at-the-Pot does not seem to be used by any other function, nor is it an output. Are you sure you need it?

Young Smith: Well, lets see.... Oh, silly me: Colour-Index should be an argument for Visual-Quality-Estimate, here.... It makes it a quinary relation, right?

Software Engineer: Yes, it does, but that's OK. We can handle them just as easily. I think it will be the last syntactic check. Usually we test now for semantic consistency, you know, to find out if you do not want a thing to be simultaneously red and not red, this sort of stuff.

Young Smith: But of course, do.

Software Engineer: See you next week then.

(*Exit Software Engineer*)

. . .

Act 2N
(Young Smith, Software Engineer)

Software Engineer: ...You will be getting reports R1 each day, R2 each week...values of input parameters were specified.

Young Smith: I rather like them. But could we also have another report, giving percentages of rejects for each customer?

Software Engineer: OK, I'll make a note of it. Now if you would like to follow the process control subsystem, here are some simulated protocols of event sequences. Would you care to study them?

Young Smith: ...Sorry, but this sequence cannot happen in reality. Perhaps I forgot to tell you that we never put in coals before India rubber − it makes an awful smell, you see...

Software Engineer: Dammit, this means...well, never mind, I think I can change the specification to reflect this constraint. Are there any other things of this nature you did not mention?

Act $(2N + 1)$
(Customer, Software Engineer)

Software Engineer: Sir, we have performed some dynamic testing of the specification, and run into errors.

Customer: I know, I know, Mr Smith told me it was his mistake really.

Software Engineer: You know, these things happen. That is precisely why we pay so much attention to the specification building and validation. I think we can redesign the process synchronization part − that is, the part responsible for the discovered errors − but it will take about two weeks. Let me remind you, sir, that you can stop our cooperation at any time, at any of our pleasant conversations.

Customer: Not on your life! the two weeks' worth of extra work is nothing now, when I am thoroughly satisfied with everything that has gone on so far. Here is your new cheque.

(*Exit happy Software Engineer*)

. . .

(As many acts as necessary to follow)

Chapter 2 Mathematical Preliminaries

2.1 Linguistic systems

2.1.1 Pragmatics

Whenever we express our thoughts, we use a linguistic system to do so. It may appear unnecessarily snobbish to employ an expression like 'linguistic system' in the preceding sentence, when a much simpler one, 'language', would do almost as well. But would it? In a sense, yes. After all, 'language' is the name we usually give to a collection of means by which a communication is effected: English, Latin, Swahili, etc., are often referred to as natural languages; there is a plethora of sign languages, from chess notation to markings on garment labels; there is body language and the bee-dance language; there are PROLOG, BASIC and other programming languages. Some languages are primitive while others are powerful. As a term, 'language' is so general that, apart from contexts in which its meaning is constrained by previous discussion, it seldom occurs by itself: usually the term needs a constraining qualifier, as in the expressions 'programming language' or 'Shakespearian language'. On the other hand, the very generality of the term leaves open the question of how much of its very rich contents we are actually referring to. Is it the vocabulary, grammar or both? Is it the general idioms or peculiarities of an author? Is it 'just the language' or also the historic memory embedded in its phrases? Finally, is it only the descriptive power or also the accepted patterns of reasoning within the language that are being referred to when we mention a language?

All these and similar questions may seem unduly pedantic, and there certainly are many occasions in which one is perfectly justified in using the term 'language' without stopping to ponder them. But there are many pragmatic reasons to be concerned with such questions; reasons not restricted to our particular field of interest − specification of computer programs.

A person translating a document from Chinese into Finnish must be concerned with much more than just a dictionary translation of words. The problem of correctness of such a translation critically depends on the chosen attitude: is grammatical correctness enough? Does the translator wish to convey deeper meaning and, if so, how much of Chinese literary (and cultural) tradition can he expect his Finnish readers to possess? Is he entitled to substitute Finnish proverbs for Chinese, or should he rely on footnotes explicating the (translated but not very meaningful) Chinese ones?

Since we want to be quite explicit about how much (or rather how little) implicit general meaning is associated with our technical vocabulary, rather than relying on shared understanding of the terms, we use the slightly pompous expression 'linguistic system' instead of 'language'.

By a linguistic system we mean a system consisting of two parts:

- a collection of sentences,
- a code of reasoning.

Basically, there are two ways in which a collection of anything may be defined. A simpler but quite inefficient (in most cases of practical interest) method is to list all elements of the collection. This way works fine for small collections, where the exact size of 'small' may depend to a certain extent on the machinery at one's disposal. With paper and pencil, enumeration is practical for several hundred elements, perhaps for some thousands – if one can devote one's life to it. With the assistance of a word processor the number may be several million. If we want to use an explicitly listed collection for any purpose, its size imposes strict limits on the practicality of its use. Even a trivially simple question 'is a given object an element of our collection' becomes expensive to answer with a very large collection of explicitly listed (but otherwise unstructured) elements.

The naïve approach to list all members of our collection becomes, of course, totally useless if the collection is known to be infinite, unless we can rely on some devices like 'etc.' or '...' which, appended to the list of enumerated elements, indicate a possibly infinite tail. Naturally enough, if such devices are to be meaningful, the collection cannot be really quite unstructured – an extension rule must be either given or inferred from the enumerated head of the collection.

Thus a mathematician may 'write' an infinite collection of numbers as:

0, 2, 4, 6, ...

counting on his readers to infer that the collection consists of all non-negative even integers; or another collection as

$t_0 = 1$
$t_1 = 1$
$t_i = t_{i-1} + t_{i-2}$ for $i \geq 2$

where the rule for computing the elements is explicitly given.

The second example illustrates the other way in which a collection can be defined. One lists some elements of the collection explicitly and provides a rule (or a set of rules) by which all remaining elements can be obtained. In following this route one has to bear in mind two complementary questions: are the rules sufficient to obtain all elements of the collection and do they exclude all unwanted objects from the collection? (These questions need not always arise. If we postulate that the collection of interest is defined by such-and-such rules, that all these rules lead to members of the collection and that nothing else is in the collection, we are of course quite safe. In practice, however, it happens very often that we have a pretty good idea of what constitutes our collection and try to capture this idea by means of, hopefully, suitable rules.)

For example, if we defined the set of prime numbers to be all numbers obtained from the formula

$$p = 2i + 1 \quad \text{where } i \text{ is a natural number}$$

we would have in fact defined a collection of numbers containing, in addition to most prime numbers, also numbers such as 9 (obtained when $i = 4$) and 15 (obtained when $i = 7$).

In fact, no closed form formula[†] to define all prime numbers is known. This illustrates a restriction on the second way of defining collections: it is not always possible (or at least it is not always known whether it is possible) to provide a closed form formula yielding all elements of a collection. The restriction is not very severe, however, if we extend the notion of 'formula' to cover not only closed formulae, but also algorithms (such as the famous 'sieve of Eratosthenes' algorithm for obtaining all primes). While it is true that with any reasonable definition of 'executable algorithm' there always will be collections which cannot be defined as all results yielded by all possible executions of an algorithm, we are not limiting ourselves too severely if we say that all collections we shall consider in this book are computable, i.e. there is always an algorithm (or, as a special case, a closed formula) which generates all elements of the collection. (The justification for this statement will be given somewhat later when we discuss in detail the notion of computability.)

The considered examples of collections may appear much too simple for our purposes; we certainly want our 'sentences' to be objects far more expressive than just even or prime numbers. It would be possible to dismiss this observation. From Chapter 1 it ought to be quite evident that we shall be concerned primarily with the linguistic systems in which one formulates theories. It is known from the mathematical study of theories and models that any consistent theory has a countable model, i.e. a model in the domain constituted by objects that can be uniquely identified by natural numbers. Thus we can make all our considerations appear as if relating to natural numbers. This argument − no matter how strict in the

---

[†] Intuitively: a self contained prescription to define a set.

mathematical sense — is not a very good one from a pragmatic point of view: the expressibility of a theory in terms of functions and relations on natural numbers is scarcely related to any application domain concepts and/or properties. It is a nice general principle, useful in so far as it provides a common ground for discussion about theories and for comparative studies thereof, but for any particular application, hardly ever illuminating. (It is rather like the universality of Turing machines. Everything that can ever be computed can be computed by a Turing machine, yet nothing ever is computed on a Turing machine, which exists but as a mental implement.)

Thus we shall consider linguistic systems whose sentence collections are much richer than just statements about natural numbers.

As a rule, sentences in the linguistic systems we shall be concerned with will be defined inductively from simpler linguistic constructs, the constituent constructs being in turn defined by syntactic equations, often in the so-called Backus—Naur Form (BNF).

The BNF equations allow us to introduce names for classes of objects and define linguistic constructs as structures consisting of elements of named classes. For instance

$$\langle digit \rangle ::= 0|1|2|3|4|5|6|7|8|9$$

introduces a name *digit* for the class consisting of ten symbols: 0, 1, 2, 3, 4, 5, 6, 7, 8 and 9.

$$\langle unsigned\ number \rangle ::= \langle digit \rangle | \langle unsigned\ number \rangle \langle digit \rangle$$

defines *unsigned number* to be either a *digit* (i.e. an element of the *digit* class) or any *unsigned number* extended on the right by a *digit*. Thus 7, 71, 315, 0000, and 31415926 are all *unsigned numbers*.

Similarly,

$$\langle letter \rangle ::= a|b|c|d|e|f|g|h|i|j|k|l|m|n|o|p|q|r|s|t|u|v|w|x|y|z$$
$$\langle identifier \rangle ::= \langle letter \rangle | \langle identifier \rangle \langle letter \rangle | \langle identifier \rangle \langle digit \rangle$$

define an *identifier* to be an arbitrarily long (but not empty!) sequence of juxtaposed *letters* and *digits* always starting with a *letter*. Thus a, a1, a127, pi, r2d2 are all examples of an *identifier*, whereas 3a is not.

Note that equations for *digit* and *letter* classes are in fact finite enumerations, whereas equations for *unsigned number* and *identifier* define infinite collections of (finite!) objects.

Often it is important to classify (or categorize) linguistic constructs into narrower groups. It may be, for instance, important to differentiate between identifiers referring to integer numbers and those referring to strings. We may do so quite easily by means of BNF equations.

$$\langle integer\ identifier \rangle ::= \textbf{integer}\ \langle identifier \rangle \tag{2.1}$$
$$\langle string\ identifier \rangle ::= \textbf{string}\ \langle identifier \rangle \tag{2.2}$$

(In the above equations the boldfaced inscriptions are to be understood as special symbols; thus **integer** is not the sequence consisting of **i**, **n**, **t**, **e**, **g**, **e**, **r** but a single symbol.) With these equations **integer** a is an *identifier* referring to an integer (or an integer valued variable), whereas **string** a is an *identifier* referring to a string. If in the equation for a linguistic construct we find

$$\ldots \langle integer\ identifier \rangle \ldots$$

an instantiation of this part of the equation by **integer** a is correct, while the instantiation by **string** a would be syntactically incorrect.

Observe that if *integer identifier* and *string indentifier* are defined by equations (2.1) and (2.2) respectively, they are not instances of any more general notion. (It is illegal to instantiate an occurrence of *identifier* by either *integer identifier* or *string identifier* as the equation for *identifier* does not allow for special symbols **integer** and **string**.) Such a more general notion can be introduced by

$$\langle integer\ or\ string\ identifier \rangle ::= \langle integer\ identifier \rangle | \langle string\ identifier \rangle \tag{2.3}$$

but this would introduce an indiscriminate union of the two notions: wherever *integer or string identifier* occurs it can be instantiated by any one of the two. While this may sometimes be useful, we are probably more interested in a mechanism that allows only consistent instantiation by a selected alternative. One such mechanism is known as two-level or Van Wijngaarden grammars which we illustrate by a brief example[†].

In addition to 'normal' BNF equations, let us consider the so-called meta-equations which define classes of linguistic construct names. (We shall use capital letters to differentiate between meta and non-meta notions and equations.)

$$\langle TYPE \rangle ::= \textbf{integer}|\textbf{string}$$
$$\langle TYPE\ identifier \rangle ::= \langle TYPE \rangle \langle identifier \rangle$$

With these equations we have two instances for *TYPE identifier*, viz. **integer** $\langle identifier \rangle$ and **string** $\langle identifier \rangle$ (and infinitely many when *identifier* is also instantiated). The *TYPE identifier* is, of course, a more general notion than either of the two. Assume that we have an equation which defines a linguistic construct in which either an **integer** *identifier* or a **string** *identifier* may occur, but which ought to preserve cognisance of which one did occur, e.g.

$$\langle TYPE\ expression \rangle ::= \langle TYPE\ identifier \rangle | \ldots \tag{2.4}$$

[†] In this example some very important aspects of Van Wijngaarden grammars are totally ignored.

With the convention that instantiation of meta-notions must be consistent throughout the equation, (2.4) is in fact equivalent to two equations

$\langle$ **integer** *expression* $\rangle ::=$ **integer** $\langle$ *identifier* $\rangle | \ldots$

and

$\langle$ **string** *expression* $\rangle ::=$ **string** $\langle$ *identifier* $\rangle | \ldots$

in which the consistency of classification of linguistic objects is preserved. With an indiscriminate union, e.g. as defined by equation (2.3) and with a similar equation for *expression*:

$\langle$ *integer or string expression* $\rangle ::= \langle$ *integer or string identifier* $\rangle | \ldots$

it would be impossible to discriminate between intended, correct instantiations:

$\langle$ *integer expression* $\rangle ::= \langle$ *integer identifier* $\rangle | \ldots$
$\langle$ *string expression* $\rangle ::= \langle$ *string identifier* $\rangle | \ldots$

and unintended ones:

$\langle$ *integer expression* $\rangle ::= \langle$ *string identifier* $\rangle | \ldots$
$\langle$ *string expression* $\rangle ::= \langle$ *integer identifier* $\rangle | \ldots$

While BNF with modifications is probably the most widely used formalism for defining grammars of linguistic systems, it is by no means the only one. The advantage of BNF consists in the fact that it lends itself readily to automatic processing, i.e. it is relatively easy (and in many instances automatic) to construct an algorithm which, given an inscription in the alphabet of our linguistic system, will compute the answer to the question of whether or not this inscription is a sentence (i.e. satisfies equations which define this linguistic construct). In fact, such algorithms not only produce the desired answer but, in the case of a positive answer, also construct a derivation tree, i.e. a trace of the parsing analysis which establishes the answer.

The ability to parse a sentence in a linguistic system under consideration, i.e. the ability to distinguish in an inscription the nameable linguistic constructs and recognize that they are structurally assembled in a fashion prescribed for sentences, is quite important. First of all, it is the most readily available and the most direct proof that an inscription is indeed a sentence. (The converse is not necessarily true. A grammar may be such that the inability to establish that an inscription is a sentence does not necessarily mean that it is not one.) Equally important, however, is the use of parsing in subsequent processing of a sentence. For instance, when translating between languages, we often find a better translation if we proceed not in the word-by-word fashion, but translate constituent idiomatic phrases, which may have corresponding phrases in the other language not necessarily obtainable by glueing together correspondents of individual words. Clearly, in order to adopt the phrase-by-phrase translation technique, we need the ability to delineate phrases in a sentence. This need is even more acute in translating programming languages, when, as in interpretive mode translation, certain actions are to be taken immediately on recognition of an instance of any of a number of linguistic constituents of a sentence (often called a 'statement' in the context of programming languages).

Since the subject of this book is not translation, nor a study of programming languages, we shall not dwell on the subject of sentence recognition any further. Suffice it to say that the collection of sentences of a linguistic system may be defined so that:

1. given an inscription consisting of symbols of an agreed alphabet it is possible to decide with certainty if this inscription is a sentence, and the decision itself may be computed in a finite number of well defined steps;
2. if an inscription is a sentence, its parsing into linguistic constituents defined in the grammar under consideration is also an algorithmic, terminating process;
3. if so desired, the linguistic constituents may be categorized into types, and rules of grammar may be constructed so that correct sentences can be built only in such ways that type constraints are respected. Should this be the case, it is also possible to extract type information about linguistic constituents from the parse of the sentence.

The second part of a linguistic system we called a *code of reasoning*. In most general terms, this is a collection of rules which allows one to reason, i.e. to draw conclusions. Probably the most widely accepted pattern of reasoning is represented by the following:

if sentences $S_0, \ldots, S_{n-1}$ are true, so is sentence S_n (2.5)

Note that the above pattern makes no assumption with respect to whether sentences $S_0, \ldots, S_{n-1}$ are really true. The rules of reasoning generally avoid such assumptions: it is recognized that ultimately the truth or falsity of sentences, apart from the so-called *tautologies*, depends on assumption or assumptions which cannot be verified by pure reasoning within a linguistic system. In particular, when a linguistic system is used for the description of a 'real-life' domain, the truth of at least some of the sentences must be established in that domain. We are convinced that this must be so by an analysis of a simple example. The sentence

For any x and y satisfying $x < y$ there exists z satisfying $x < z < y$ (2.6)

is one that may be formulated easily in any linguistic system employed to describe properties of numbers. If the 'numbers' in question are reals, the sentence is true; if they are integers, it is false, as there is no integer z that would satisfy $3 < z < 4$, for example. Thus the truth or falsity of sentence (2.6) depends on the domain to which it refers.

The domain to which the sentences of a linguistic system refer is known as a *valuation domain*. It must be observed that for a given linguistic system one can consider many valuation domains and that, at least in general, the various valuation domains need not be very similar. The converse observation is equally important; if we take a domain, there may be many linguistic systems for which it could be used as a valuation domain. This is particularly true if the domain is taken to be a view of a part of a real world, such as a bank or a railway network. There may be, and usually are, many languages in which one could talk about the chosen part of the real world. The chosen language is a linguistic system for which the selected view of a part of the real world is a valuation domain.

To valuate sentences of the linguistic system it is not enough to indicate a valuation domain. We must also indicate how the references are established; in fact, we must clearly say which objects of the domain are accepted values for variables, which function names from the linguistic system are to be valuated by which sets in the valuation domain, etc. In a word, we must establish a whole *valuation structure*.

Some sentences of our linguistic system may be regarded as necessarily true in any admissible valuation structure. These sentences are variously known as *tautologies* or *logical axioms*. Thus a tautology is a sentence whose truth does not depend on the choice of a valuation structure.

Usually a small number of tautologies are listed as the kernel of the particular logic accepted for the linguistic structure. Repeated application of the rules of reasoning expands the kernel into the set of all tautologies. If the term 'logical axioms' is reserved for the sentences of the kernel, we may say that tautologies are sentences whose truth value follows only from the logical axioms and rules of reasoning.

Naturally, tautologies do not say very much about any domain that may be described in the linguistic system − any admissible valuation structures will preserve their truthfulness. On the other hand, if a domain could be found in which a tautology of a linguistic system would be falsified, we would know for sure that the valuation structure was not admissible. In practice, this does not happen often: the logical axioms as sentences usually do not refer to individual nameable objects, they describe the kind of logic that is being used and, therefore, without a profound change in logics any domain would meet the requirement of preserving the truthfulness of tautologies. This is true even in cases when we do change the logic; we do so in a way which conservatively extends the logic of the linguistic system: all old rules are preserved although some new ones are (not contradictorily) added.

We shall discuss the properties of linguistic systems in relation to valuation domains in the next section, when we consider the notion of a linguistic level, i.e. a linguistic system with extralogical axioms. Let us now investigate what kind of general properties may be expected to be found in a linguistic system.

2.1.2 Deducibility

Assuming that we know how to tell sentences from non-sentences (which is purely a syntactic matter) and assuming that we know some sentences to be true, we want to be able to solve two problems:

1. given a sentence A, establish whether or not A is true;
2. obtain consequences of a set of sentences G, i.e. all sentences true on the strength of sentences in set G being true.

We shall use a notational device to describe the fact that sentence A is a consequence of sentences contained in G: $G \vdash A$. Thus the first problem may be written as 'given G and A, check $G \vdash A$', the second as 'given G, generate all A such that $G \vdash A$'.

In general, these two problems are not necessarily related. If nothing is known about the set G and its rôle in the linguistic system under consideration, it may turn out that the set G is too weak to establish truthfulness of A. This may be the case even if the set G is rich enough to generate a lot of interesting consequences. The question of whether the set G is powerful enough to generate all true sentences is treated a little later, under the heading of completeness.

Thus, pondering the first problem, we are concerned with its literal statement: is the set G enough to establish that A is true? Observe that if we succeed in establishing the truth of A based on sentences in G, A may be safely considered to be true (at least as safely as sentences of G are, provided that G is consistent — see below). The failure to establish this fact, however, says nothing about A being false, or 'untrue'. The cases of A being false and G being too weak to establish the truth of A cannot be told apart.

Thus even if we have a means to solve the second problem, i.e. to generate all consequences of G, we cannot always solve problem (1).

Our ability to solve problem (2) depends on the rules of reasoning adopted in the linguistic system. We can assume that these are chosen to meet two objectives: to be in some agreement with intuitively acceptable patterns of reasoning and to be sufficiently systematic to allow as easy as possible a solution to problem (2) and as close as possible an approach to the solution of problem (1).

Without making any assumptions about the set G, apart from its finiteness, can we describe any general deduction procedure, applicable whenever the rules of reasoning fit the pattern (2.5)?

The sentences $S_0, \ldots, S_{n-1}$ in (2.5) are known as *premises*, the sentence S_n as the *conclusion* of the rule. Generally, there is some structural kinship between the set of premises and the conclusion for a rule of reasoning, in which case it is not explicit sentences which are listed as premises and conclusions but generic variables which can be instantiated by sentences. (Strictly speaking the rule should then be called a meta-rule, but we shall disregard such subtleties here.) For instance, the famous rule of detachment, or *modus ponens*, of Aristotelian logic, has the form

If X and X **implies** Y are true sentences, Y is a true sentence   (2.7)

In (2.7) there are two premises:

X is a true sentence

and

X **implies** Y is a true sentence.

The conclusion is

Y is a true sentence.

Thus, if we know that in our linguistic system the two sentences

cat eats mice

and

cat eats mice **implies** it never rains

are both true then, assuming our linguistic system includes the rule of detachment (2.7), we are allowed to conclude that

it never rains

is a true sentence; indeed on substituting 'cat eats mice' for X and 'it never rains' for Y in (2.7) we get:

If 'cat eats mice' and 'cat eats mice **implies** it never rains' are true sentences, 'it never rains' is a true sentence.

Let us repeat once more that in establishing the truthfulness of the conclusion 'it never rains' from premises 'cat eats mice' and 'cat eats mice **implies** it never rains' by *modus ponens* we are not allowed to question whether or not the premises are 'in fact' true: they are assumed. Thus, if the given set of true sentences G contains 'cat eats mice' and 'cat eats mice **implies** it never rains', in formulae: $G = \{$cat eats mice, cat eats mice **implies** it never rains$\}$, and the rules of reasoning include *modus ponens* (2.7), then

1. sentence 'it never rains' is true
2. set of consequences of G includes 'it never rains'; in formulae:
   $\{$cat eats mice, cat eats mice **implies** it never rains$\} \vdash$ it never rains.

Observe that 'it never rains' was not included in G (at least in its listed part) and therefore we concluded a new true sentence. (That G included 'cat eats mice **implies** it never rains' does not mean that any part of the implication by itself is a member of G: to draw the conclusion both premises must be known to be true independently!) Observe also that we have used a logical connective **implies** in one of the premises. Usually the patterns of rules of reasoning use a number of logical connectives which combine sentences into 'larger' sentences, or primitive sentences into compound ones. The meaning of such logical connectives is usually defined in terms of the so-called truth-value tables, which determine the truthfulness or falseness of a compound sentence as the function of truthfulness or falseness of primitive sentences joined by the connective.

Thus for instance the meaning of the connective **and** is given by the table

S_1	true	true	false	false
S_2	true	false	true	false
S_1 **and** S_2	true	false	false	false

In other words, the connective **and** makes the compound sentence S_1 **and** S_2 out of two primitive sentences S_1 and S_2, such that S_1 **and** S_2 is true if and only if both sentences S_1 and S_2 are true (i.e. false for all other combinations of truth values of S_1 and S_2).

The truth value for the connective **implies** is given by

S_1	true	true	false	false
S_2	true	false	true	false
S_1 **implies** S_2	true	false	true	true

Since truth-value tables for most logical connectives are well known, we are not listing any more examples; just in case it may be forgotten we mention that in addition to diadic connectives (such as **and**, **implies**, **or**, etc.) there is also a unary connective, **not**, which has a very simple defining truth-value table:

S	true	false
not S	false	true

Thus **not** S is a sentence which is true when sentence S is false, and false when sentence S is true. The logical connectives are usually written by means of special symbols, different from any other symbols used in the linguistic system. Hence, for example, **implies** is often written as $\supset$ or $\Rightarrow$; **and** as $\wedge$ or &; **or** as $\vee$ or $|$; **not** as $\neg$ or as a bar over the sentence that is negated ($\bar{S}$).

One logical connective is a bit awkward because of writers' propensity to make notational shortcuts. Consider the truth-value table

S_1	true	true	false	false
S_2	true	false	true	false
$S_1 \Leftrightarrow S_2$	true	false	false	true

Thus $S_1 \Leftrightarrow S_2$ is true if and only if both its components are simultaneously true or simultaneously false. This connective is often written as $\equiv$ or **equivalent**. The difficulty arises when the same symbol is used for a logical connective employed as a sentence generating functor (i.e. just as we have been using all other connectives) and for the metastatement that it has been established that sentences S_1 and S_2 have the same truth values. We shall restrict the use of $\equiv$ to the latter case; for the former we shall use **equivalent** or, if a shorter form is preferred, $\Leftrightarrow$.

Returning now to the problem of deriving the consequences of a given set of true sentences G, we observe that the rules of reasoning may be ordered by the number of premises: first the rules with no premises, then the rules with a single premise, then the rules with two premises (such as *modus ponens*), and so on.

Within a class (class being defined as all rules with the same number of premises), rules may be ordered by any applicable principle. As a result, we get an ordered sequence of rules of reasoning $R_0, \ldots, R_k$. (In fact, a very popular system has but one rule − *modus ponens*!)

We take now the first rule, say R_0, and apply it to all sentences of G admissible as its premises. The obtained conclusions are added to G (if they are not already there). Thus we obtain set G_0 of sentences that contains all possible consequences of G under rule R_0. Since R_0 may again be applicable to some sentences in G_0, this process may continue *ad infinitum*. If it stops, we may try to apply the next rule, etc.

Consider an example:

> $G = \{0$ is a natural number, x is a natural number $\Rightarrow x + 1$ is a natural number,$\ldots\}$

> R_0: if S is a true sentence containing a natural number variable then S obtained by substituting a natural number for this variable is also a true sentence.

Applying R_0 to 'x is a natural number $\Rightarrow x + 1$ is a natural number' with 0 substituted for x (we can do so on the strength of the first sentence in G) we get '0 is a natural number $\Rightarrow 0 + 1$ is a natural number', and so

> $G_0 = G \cup \{0$ is a natural number $\Rightarrow 0 + 1$ is a natural number$\}$

where $\cup$ denotes the set union operation.

If the set of rules also includes *modus ponens*, we may apply it to the sentences

> 0 is a natural number

and

> 0 is a natural number $\Rightarrow 0 + 1$ is a natural number

which yields the conclusion

> 0 + 1 is a natural number

which should be included into the set of true sentences $G_1 = G_0 \cup \{0 + 1$ is a natural number$\}$. Now the rule R_0 is applicable again, yielding the sentence '$0 + 1$ is a natural number $\Rightarrow 0 + 1 + 1$ is a natural number', the rule of detachment can be applied again, after which we get $G_2 = G_1 \cup \{0 + 1 + 1$ is a natural number$\}$ etc.

Thus, even a very simple set of axioms with very few rules of reasoning may lead to an infinite set of consequences. In most cases this infinite set of consequences can be structured. This can be achieved, for example, by labelling each deduced consequence by the sequence of identifiers of the rules applied in its deduction; in our example '$0 + 1$ is a natural number' will be labelled by $R_0 M$, and '$0 + 1 + 1$ is a natural number' by $R_0 M R_0 M$, with M standing for the identifier of *modus ponens*. Since we are applying the rules of reasoning in a systematic way, the consequences derived from an initial axiom set can be categorized into classes labelled by the same chain of rules applied. The classes will, of course, contain different sentences, depending on which sentences of the already established set of consequences are used as actual premises, but all sentences of a class will share the same deduction pattern. The classes may be mapped onto a hierarchy, such as a tree structure, by a standard technique: classes labelled by a single rule form the roots, classes labelled by two rules are sons of roots, classes labelled by three rules are sons of nodes labelled by two rules, etc., under the proviso that all sibling nodes labelled by n rules $r_1 r_2, r_{n-1} r_n$ differ in the last rule but share the $n - 1$ rule prefix (which labels their common father node). Note that although the height (depth) of the tree may be infinite, no node has more than N sons, where N is the number of rules of reasoning in our linguistic system. If we admit empty classes corresponding to the situations where no combination of already deduced sentences forms an admissible combination of premises for the last rule in the class label, the tree is exactly an N-ary one and each class contains no more than a finite number of conclusions.

Thus a hierarchical arrangement of consequences deducible by application of fixed rules of reasoning to a finite set of axioms, while possibly containing an infinite number of consequences, can always be made regular. Therefore a computer program can be constructed which would generate an ever larger set of consequences according to some principles, e.g. according to the 'length' of deduction, measured in the number of rules applied to obtain a given sentence. Of course, such a program need not terminate; indeed, it will not terminate if the set of consequences is infinite (which is the most likely situation).

Having such a program in one's possession is not an answer to the first problem we posed, viz. 'is the sentence A a consequence of a given set G'. If we find sentence A in the stream of consequences generated after the first hour, ten hours, etc., of our program execution, fine − we have the positive answer. But we cannot draw any conclusion from the absence of this sentence. Without additional intelligence it is just as likely that the sentence A has not yet come up as that it is not deducible.

There are many much more sophisticated programs in existence which try to compute a deduction pattern for an input sentence A. Known as *theorem provers*, these programs attempt to find a sequence of rules which would deduce a given sentence from axioms via auxiliary sentences deducible from the axioms. As a rule such programs do not progress by blind application of rules of reasoning, but try to discover structural properties of the sentence in question and direct the search for the deduction chain by thus discovered properties. In addition to syntactic properties obtained from the parse of the sentence, these programs also apply heuristic rules and are often influenced by hints provided by the human operator. For details about some such programs see Boyer and Moore (1979).

In the following considerations, unless otherwise stated, we shall assume that the rules of reasoning of the linguistic system are those of classical predicate calculus with *modus ponens* (see Appendix).

The fundamental theorem (Herbrand−Tarski)[†] on deduction in such linguistic systems states that if a sentence A is deducible from the (finite or infinite) set G of sentences, then there exists a finite set of sentences $\{X_1, \ldots, X_n\} \subset G$ such that the sentence $(X_1 \ \& \ \ldots \ \& \ X_n) \Rightarrow A$ is deducible from logical axioms alone. In a somewhat vaguer formulation the deduction theorem says that any sentence deducible from G is implied by the conjunction of at most a finite number of elements of G. Yet another formulation of the same theorem states that if a sentence can be proved at all, it can be proven from a finite number of premises by a finite number of applications of rules of deduction; the conjuncts $X_1, \ldots, X_n$ represent all specific (rather than just general logical) information needed to establish A.

2.1.3 Consistency

Even if the set of consequences of a given set of statements under given rules of reasoning is infinite, we are definitely interested in certain global properties of such a set. One of these is the property of consistency. We say that a set of sentences G is *consistent* if and only if there is no sentence A such that $G \vdash A$ and $G \vdash \neg A$ at the same time. (Note that the consistency of G is fully compatible with neither $G \vdash A$ nor $G \vdash \neg A$ being the case.) In other words, we say that G is consistent if *at most* one of the sentences A or $\neg A$ can be deduced from G; that is, that no contradictory

---

[†] The precise formulations and full proofs of all mathematical results mentioned in Sections 2.1 and 2.2 are to be found in Grzegorczyk (1974), a classic textbook upon which we have extensively relied.

sentences can be deduced. A set G which is not consistent is called *inconsistent*.

The notion of consistency also covers, of course, the set G itself; in order to convince oneself that it is so, it suffices to observe that any sentence $A \in G$ satisfies $G \vdash A$; thus if both $A \in G$ and $\neg A \in G$, the set G is inconsistent by the adopted definition.

In the following text we shall often refer to the set of consequences of a given set of sentences G, i.e. to the set of sentences deducible from G. We shall use the notation $Cn(G)$ to denote this set.

A sentence A such that neither $A \in Cn(G)$ nor $\neg A \in Cn(G)$ is said to be *independent* of G. If a set G is consistent, so is any of its subsets.

Indeed, assume that set G is consistent and set $H \subset G$ is not. By the definition of inconsistency there must exist a sentence A such that $A \in Cn(H)$ and $\neg A \in Cn(H)$. But obviously $Cn(H) \subset Cn(G)$ for $H \subset G$, therefore $A \in Cn(H)$ implies $A \in Cn(G)$ and $\neg A \in Cn(H)$ implies $\neg A \in Cn(G)$ which contradicts our assumption of G being consistent.

If set G is consistent and sentence A is such that $\neg A \notin Cn(G)$ then the set $G \cup \{A\}$ is consistent, regardless of whether $G \vdash A$ or not.

Indeed, assume that $G \cup \{A\}$ is inconsistent. This means that there is a sentence X such that both $X \in Cn(G \cup \{A\})$ and $\neg X \in Cn(G \cup \{A\})$, thus $(X \& \neg X \in Cn(G \cup \{A\}))$. By the deduction theorem we have then $(A \Rightarrow (X \& \neg X)) \in Cn(G)$. From the definition of implication, negation and conjunction by truth-value tables it follows that $((A \Rightarrow (X \& \neg X)) \Rightarrow \neg A) \in Cn(G)$ from which by detachment we get $\neg A \in Cn(G)$ which contradicts our assumption.

Thus if sentence A is independent of G we can extend G by A and still get a consistent set of sentences (the just proved result assumed that $\neg A \notin Cn(G)$); if $A \in Cn(G)$ the extension of G by A is still consistence-preserving; but A not being independent of G it is not so interesting: intuitively speaking, extending a set of sentences by its consequences is not augmenting its descriptive power.

Is there a limit to which a consistent set of sentences can be (interestingly) extended without violating its consistency? We can answer this question better using another concept.

2.1.4 Completeness

A set of sentences G is said to be *complete* if for any sentence A either $A \in G$ or $\neg A \in G$.

A set of sentences which is not complete is known as an *incomplete* set of sentences.

Consider now a special case when a set of sentences is closed under the rules of reasoning, i.e. when $G = Cn(G)$. Such sets of sentences are known as *theories* (see the Appendix). Any consistent, incomplete theory can be slightly extended without losing its consistency. Indeed if a theory is incomplete there is a sentence A such that neither $A \in \text{Cn}(G)$ nor $\neg A \in \text{Cn}(G)$. Thus by virtue of the last proved result on consistent sets of sentences, G can be extended by A (or, alternatively, $\neg A$), forming a set $G \cup \{A\}$ (resp. $G \cup \{\neg A\}$) which is consistent.

Such extensions cannot, however, go on infinitely: a consistent theory is complete if and only if every other set of sentences larger than G is inconsistent. Indeed, let H be such a larger set of sentences, $G \subset H$, $G \neq H$. This means that there is a sentence X, such that $X \in H$ and $X \notin G$. If the set G is complete, then (since $X \notin G$) $\neg X \in G \subset H$ and, therefore, the set H contains both X and $\neg X$, which makes it inconsistent. If the set G is incomplete, there is a sentence $\neg X \notin G = \text{Cn}(G)$ and therefore the set $H = G \cup \{X\}$ is both larger than G (as incompleteness of G guarantees that X can be chosen so that $X \notin G$) and consistent by virtue of the extension theorem. Thus a theory is complete if and only if any larger set of sentences in the considered linguistic system is inconsistent.

It is an easy exercise (one that in the Appendix is recommended to readers) to prove that every inconsistent theory is complete and every incomplete theory is consistent. Thus the very existence of a sentence independent of a theory assures us of its consistency. This observation makes the assumption of G's consistency in the theorem on extension quite superfluous: if a sentence $\neg A$ cannot be deduced from the set G, the latter cannot be inconsistent. (As from an inconsistent set of premises anything follows, so should $\neg A$!)

The completeness resulting from inconsistency is quite unhealthy. Indeed, it suffices to take any sentence and its negation, and we can formally deduce all other sentences of the language. The very important observation, or moral, to be drawn from the possibility of this kind of trivial completeness is that we should always first insist on consistency and worry about completeness (if at all) afterwards.

On the other hand, we should realize that when we are dealing with consistent theories which are not trivial there are always sentences not deducible from them (if the theory in addition to being consistent is also complete then either the sentence or its negation is, of course, deducible).

In the preceding several paragraphs we have restricted our attention to theories rather than any sets of sentences. The nice agreement of formal results that follow from such a restriction with intuitive expectations of the terms 'consistency' and 'completeness' suggests that the maximality of the complete consistent sets of sentences, proved for theories, could be used as the definition of completeness for arbitrary sets of statements:

A consistent set of sentences G is *complete* if and only if every other set of sentences larger than G is inconsistent. This definition nicely captures the intuition that a consistent set of sentences cannot be expanded indefinitely other than by including into it its own consequences.

In the preceding considerations of deducibility, consistency and completeness we did not pay much attention to the fact that the linguistic system, through its grammar, may introduce constant symbols interpreted in a valuation system as referring to 'concrete' objects (and objects of different types, too); our all-encompassing notion of a sentence did not reflect any concern with this aspect of the linguistic system. In doing so we have followed the logician's tradition that 'logic does not recognize individual constants'.

In practice, the linguistic systems employed for program specification will have constants of different categories and variables restricted to categories of constants. Similarly, the various expressions and formulae that constitute sentences will not have the symbols occurring in them drawn at random from the whole vocabulary of the linguistic system. The symbols in sentences will be related in so far as a sentence is meant to refer to a particular aspect of the domain being described. In this sense, sets of sentences will also probably consist of related sentences, i.e. of sentences which employ similar vocabularies.

If the sentences of a set chosen for consideration use only a portion of the whole available vocabulary it is only natural to expect all sentences built exclusively from other parts of the vocabulary to be independent of the considered set. Such 'logical' independence agrees, of course, with the notion of independence introduced above. The theorem on extension also applies, although from the pragmatic point of view it is hard to imagine what useful purpose can be served by joining together a set of sentences written in one part of the vocabulary with a sentence written with totally different symbols (i.e. probably referring to totally different objects and relationships under any reasonable valuation). While such an extended set of sentences is formally consistent, it may be difficult to see any useful concept being captured by this set of sentences.

As an illustration consider a possible theory of the solar system, i.e. a consistent set of sentences in which terms such as planet, orbit, angular momentum, radial velocity, etc., are employed. (Under an interpretation in a valuation system consisting of, say, equatorial coordinates of planets of our solar system, these variables will have their natural counterparts.) The sentence 'goat's milk contains traces of heavy metals' will almost certainly be independent of the theory of the solar system. (If the vocabulary used in this sentence is indeed totally separate from the vocabulary employed in the solar system theory, this sentence *must* be independent.) Thus, by the extension theorem, the theory consisting of all sentences of the 'old' solar system theory and of the sentence 'goat's milk is free of traces of heavy metals' will be consistent, although it may prove difficult to build its model not only in terms of equatorial coordinates of planets but also in any other realistically conceived domain.

While with separated vocabulary of the linguistic system the notions of independence and consequence cause no trouble with our intuition (in some instances they may lead to the absurdly obvious, but never to the objectionable), the notion of completeness presents a somewhat deeper problem.

Consider once more our illustration. Since we presume that the sentences about chemical composition of goat's milk are correctly expressible in the linguistic system, their independence of the theory of the solar system makes the latter formally incomplete. This hardly upsets anybody but the driest formalists among the readers of this book. Why should a theory of the solar system be branded incomplete just because nothing about goat's milk can be deduced from it?

A moment's reflection suffices to convince us that we are falling into a trap set and baited when we agreed to have a heterogeneous vocabulary for linguistic systems without somehow reflecting this fact in the definition of completeness. One way of solving this problem is to restrict the notion of completeness to sentences using the same terminology. To express this restriction in a more precise way requires a somewhat less general concept of 'sentence' and 'terminology'; thus we would have to adopt some grammar. Since we intend to make this section as general as possible and not subscribe to any particular syntax, we must try to overcome this difficulty without actually fixing our attention on any particular syntax.

How, in general, are sentences built? They consist of function and relation symbols (in natural languages these correspond, roughly speaking, to verbs, verbal clauses and their equivalents) applied to variables and constants (objects, subjects, corresponding equivalent clauses, in general; noun-like structures), joined by connectives and subject to quantifications (i.e. qualified by expressions such as 'always', 'sometimes', 'for all', 'at least for one', 'it is necessary', 'it is possible').

Now, if any categorization is introduced into our linguistic system, it is more than likely that the reason for its introduction is the envisaged heterogeneity of objects of the intended valuation domain. Thus it is primarily the constants which are categorized, or, more precisely, it is the categorization of constants that is the primary objective of having the categorization at all. The categorization of variables is a natural consequence — they are restricted to a particular type of constant, or to a particular combination of types. Similarly, relations and functions will be categorized with respect to types of their arguments and results. Even the quantifiers may be thought of as being categorized by, ultimately, the types of constants: 'for all integers' is different from 'for all reals'[†].

Thus we may characterize the 'type' of sentence by associating with it

---

[†] Categorization of quantifiers may always be avoided at the expense of adding a suitable qualifier. Instead of saying 'for all integers x: $\phi(x)$' we may say 'for all x: $integer(x) \Rightarrow \phi(x)$ where $integer(x)$ is a predicate true if its argument is an integer and false otherwise.

the set of all type-categories of constants and variables that occur in it (and therefore to which all relations and functions are restricted).

A set of sentences will then be characterized by the union of sets characterizing the individual sentences occurring in it.

A set G of sentences characterized by type-categories $T_1, \ldots, T_n$ is called a *complete* set of sentences characterized by these type-categories if and only if for every sentence A characterized by type categories $t_1, \ldots, t_k$, such that $\{t_1, \ldots, t_k\} \subset \{T_1, \ldots, T_n\}$, it is true that $A \in G$ or $\neg\, A \in G$.

The basic properties of consistent and/or complete sets of sentences that we discussed above without paying attention to the categorization of the linguistic system remain valid after suitable changes in formulation.

As an example we restate the theorem on maximality of complete sets of sentences: a consistent set G of sentences characterized by type-categories $T_1, \ldots, T_n$ is complete if and only if every set of sentences characterized by no other type-categories and larger than G is inconsistent.

Note that, since the notion of consistency is based on that of consequence and thus deducibility, we do not have to guard the statements about consistency with caveats related to categorization: we are certainly entitled to expect that rules of reasoning in a categorized linguistic system pay attention to categorization. The caveats in statements about completeness had to be introduced exactly because the notion of independence covers two basically different cases: that of non-deducibility caused by mismatch of categories and that of non-deducibility due to insufficiency of information contained in the set of sentences on which the deduction was based.

We shall conclude this section with a fundamental theorem about sets of sentences true in a non-empty domain. First, however, we need some auxiliary definitions.

A formula (i.e. an expression in the linguistic system that may contain free variables) is said to be *satisfiable in a domain under the considered interpretation* if and only if there exists a sequence of domain objects which upon consistent substitution into the interpreted formula turn it into a statement of fact in the domain. By 'consistent substitution' we mean the substitution of the same domain value for all different free occurrences of the same variable.

The interpretation mentioned in this definition respects categorization − if any − of our linguistic system and establishes correspondence between predicate and function symbols of the linguistic system with relations and functions in the domain.

For example, the formula

$$\textbf{integer } i, j\colon i > j \tag{2.8}$$

is satisfiable in the domain of integers when $>$ is interpreted as the usual 'greater than' relation because one can find a sequence of objects (integers) in the domain that upon substitution would turn this formula into a true statement of fact: **integer** 3, 2: 3 > 2.

A formula is *true* in a domain under the considered interpretation if it is satisfiable in this domain under the same interpretation by *any* sequence of objects.

Naturally, formula (2.8) is not true in the domain of integers since, for instance, **integer** 3, 5: 3 > 5 is not a statement of fact and therefore the sequence 3, 5 does not satisfy the formula.

Since a sentence is a formula without free variables, the notions of satisfiability and truth in a domain coincide for sentences, provided the domain is not empty. (The exclusion of empty domains may seem pedantic: 'any sequence' and 'all sequences' of objects in an empty domain may easily exhibit some particular property but there will be no sequence which actually has this property. Actually, the exclusion is important in so far as artificially created domains may 'accidentally' happen to be empty; such as, for example, the domain of bug-free software. Having then established properties of such a domain does not yet mean that anything that enjoys these properties actually exists.)

Two simple ways of converting formula (2.8) into a sentence

$$A \textbf{ integer } i, j: i > j \tag{2.9}$$

$$E \textbf{ integer } i, j: i > j \tag{2.10}$$

result in a sentence true in the domain of integers under the considered interpretation (2.10) and in a sentence not true under the same interpretation (2.9).

For a given domain D, let us denote by $E(D)$ the collection of all facts; let also $I(A)$ denote the result of the 'considered interpretation' of the sentence A. Then $I(A) \in E(D)$ expresses the same information as saying that sentence A is true in domain D under the considered interpretation.

It is easy to see that $I(A) \notin E(D)$ is the same as $I(\neg A) \in E(D)$. Indeed, if A is not satisfiable by any sequence of objects, there must be a sequence of objects that does not satisfy it, this sequence of objects then satisfies $\neg A$ and, since $\neg A$ is a formula without free variables (as A is a sentence, so is $\neg A$), if a sequence satisfies $\neg A$ then any sequence does so, thus $\neg A$ is true in the domain. In other words, under a fixed interpretation any sentence is either true or non-true (i.e. false) in a domain. The main theorem follows rather directly: for a fixed interpretation, the set of all sentences true in the non-empty domain D is complete and consistent.

Indeed, the just proved alternative (that any sentence is either true or false) establishes the completeness of the set of interpreted sentences which are true in a domain. Its consistency follows from the following reasoning. Assume $E(D)$ were inconsistent. That would mean that there exists a sentence A, such that both $I(A) \in \mathrm{Cn}(E(D))$ and $I(\neg A) \in \mathrm{Cn}(E(D))$. Now $E(D)$ obviously enjoys the property $\mathrm{Cn}(E(D)) \subset E(D)$: a fact deducible from facts observable in a domain must be considered a fact in this domain[†]. Therefore, inconsistency of $E(D)$ would amount to both $I(A) \in E(D)$ and $I(\neg A) \in E(D)$, but we have just proved that these two are mutually exclusive.

Thus, under a given interpretation of a linguistic system the collection of all sentences true in a domain constitutes a consistent and complete theory of the domain. This theory may be very different from what is normally expected of a theory; it may, for instance, not be axiomatic at all (see the Appendix). But the fundamental theorem conforms with our intuition that stating all facts about a domain amounts to providing a consistent and complete theory of that domain.

The fundamental theorem, together with the monotonic property of consistent sets of sentences (if $G \subset H$ and H is consistent then G is consistent too), provides the tool most frequently used by logicians to prove consistency of a theory. Indeed if we want to prove a theory consistent it is enough to show that, under a suitable interpretation, the theory is included in the collection of facts about some non-empty domain, D. Such a domain is then known as a *model* of the theory. It is worth pointing out that while possession of a model guarantees consistency of the theory, nothing is said about how completely this theory describes the domain, i.e. how large a part of the collection of facts about the model domain is captured by interpreted sentences of the theory.

2.2 Linguistic levels

2.2.1 Pragmatics

Having decided upon a language, or having a language selected for us, we can describe the object of our interest. Naturally, the description may be done at various levels of detail. In fact, there are numerous circumstances in which descriptions at different levels of detail are needed side by side. These circumstances are not limited to situations arising naturally in design, where one is likely to have a general description, a decomposition scheme, a close-up view of each constituent, an assembly schema and blueprints for all details, not to mention various calculations ascertaining that 'things fit together'. Most manuals for home appliances and mechanical equipment, such as cars, electronic entertainment gadgets, etc., also describe the piece in question at various levels of detail (not always neatly

---

[†] The inclusion $\mathrm{Cn}(E(D)) \subset E(D)$ may be proved quite rigorously.

separated!). It is also trivially true that computer programs are described
at different levels of detail.

The same program is described by its library label, external (user)
specification, listing in source language, assembly code version and
hexadecimal memory dump. The label describes the program by its unique
(in a given environment) name; the user specification describes the
(possible) intended use of the program, its limitations and particular
applicability, lists and describes inputs, and explains expected outputs and
possible error messages; the source language listing provides a description
of input/output transformations with a degree of detail presupposed by
the particular programming language; assembly code gives details relevant at the level of detail envisaged by the operating system; the
hexadecimal dump displays detail normally hidden: the settings of various
unnamed flags and toggles. Of course we could take the description to
even finer details: we can look into the microcode version to learn how
gates are switched and pulses counted and synchronized, or into the
service engineer's interpretation of the same, this time expressed in
voltages and currents at pins and junctions. There is no need to stop there
− a description at the solid-state physicist's level is also possible, this time
in terms of charges, potential barriers, etc. In fact, we could go into even
finer detail − first into statistical physics and then into the realm of
particle physics; at least in theory, as the transition between the latter two
is not an obvious matter.

On the one hand, we hope that no matter which level we have
chosen, we are describing the same program. On the other, we are
certain that each time we change levels, we do not merely change the
granularity of description − we are adding terms and phenomena not
describable on a less detailed level. As the domains in which we model
our specification/theory become more and more detailed, there are more
and more facts not captured by sentences constituting the description
given at a higher level. (The last sentence employs terminology introduced
at the end of the preceding section, but the diversity of detail, granularity
and the phenomenon of a higher level not capturing all details present in
a lower level description of the 'same thing' are facts of life.)

As we provide more detailed descriptions, we are guided by two
needs: primarily, to establish a model of the higher level theory, and then
to do so in the 'best' way on a given level. The freedom that we exploit
when attempting to optimize the description at a given level arises from
the fact that our obligation is merely to ensure that under suitable interpretation all sentences of the higher-level theory are included among true
sentences about the current domain. There may be many ways to achieve
this − ways differing by 'unused' sentences, i.e. sentences which are not
used in establishing satisfaction of the higher level theory.

Even if a theory on a higher level is complete (and we do not really
believe that any specification is ever complete − see below), only a part

of all facts on a lower level will be necessary to support this theory — the rest is irrelevant as far as the specification is concerned and, consequently, may be arranged so as to obtain whatever additional benefits may seem desirable.

Formally speaking, the term *linguistic level* will be used in this book to refer to a linguistic system with a set of extralogical axioms.

Extralogical axioms are axioms (i.e. sentences assumed to be true without a proof) which need not be satisfied by all valuation structures. In other words, it is the extralogical axioms which capture specific properties of the domain being described. Since we are at the moment discussing means of description, it is immaterial whether the domain in question already exists (and then the extralogical axioms express, hopefully in a succinct way, its main properties) or is yet to be constructed (in which case the extralogical axioms may be thought of as a concise expression of the requirements). In either case the relationship between the domain and the theory deducible from the axioms is the same (that of satisfaction in the logical sense of the word). The structure of the linguistic level itself does not recognize at all what specific purpose it serves in the design/implementation process.

Also formally, observe that the notion of a linguistic level subsumes the notion of a linguistic system. Thus with the same linguistic system we may have many different linguistic levels, just as the change of the linguistic system even without a change in extralogical axioms results in a change of linguistic level. Of course, any extralogical axioms in a linguistic system must conform to the rules of grammar of that system and must be its sentences. Thus a change of a linguistic system that involves a modification of its syntax rules must be reflected in a corresponding change of axioms. If, on the other hand, the change of the linguistic system is restricted to a change in rules of reasoning (preserving the syntax, we change the logic) the extralogical axioms may remain unchanged as formulae of the language but their meaning may change considerably.

Actually, both the changes in syntax and the changes in rules may necessitate cosmetic changes in the write-up of extralogical axioms; formally such changes are quite necessary and very important. In practice, while necessary in order to ensure the proper construction of axioms, many are not very instructive and we shall often disregard them.

2.2.2 Level of computable functions and relations

Although we were making no assumptions with respect to *what* we want to describe in the linguistic system under consideration, it is very likely that we will want to include descriptions of computable functions and relations. Thus we are going to present now a linguistic level in which computable functions and relations can be described. We shall start with a linguistic system the rules of reasoning of which encompass all axioms of classical sentential calculus and the rules of generalization and *modus ponens* (see the Appendix). (This choice of logic is dictated by its familiarity.)

First let us observe that there is a close relationship between computability of a function and that of a relation. Intuitively, a function is 'computable' if a prescription is known such that given the function argument (or set of arguments) which meets the type restriction, if any, one can obtain the corresponding value merely by following the prescription and that 'to follow the prescription' does not involve repeating an operation (or a set of operations) an infinite number of times. Thus, in fact we are concerned only with *effective computability*.

Given a relation R of n arguments, any function f of n arguments such that $R(x_1, \ldots, x_n) \Leftrightarrow f(x_1, \ldots, x_n) = 0$ is known as the characteristic function of the relation R. Observe that a relation may have many characteristic functions; for instance, the relation of equality on two integers has many characteristic functions, some of which are listed below.

$$f_1(x, y) = x - y$$
$$f_2(x, y) = (5x - 3y) - (3x - y)$$
$$f_3(x, y) = (x - y) + (7x - 7y)$$

A relation is said to be *computable* if and only if there exists a computable characteristic function of this relation.

Assume that we are given an initial set of computable functions. Which linguistic constructions are certain not to lead outside the class of computable functions?

Definition by superposition

If functions $f(\ldots, x, \ldots, y, \ldots)$ and $g(\ldots, z, \ldots)$ are computable (the elisions standing for other arguments), then the function h, defined by

$$h(\ldots, x, \ldots, z, \ldots) = f(\ldots, x, \ldots, g(\ldots, z, \ldots), \ldots)$$

is also computable. Indeed, given $\ldots, z, \ldots$ we compute the value of $g(\ldots, z, \ldots)$ and substitute it for y in $f(\ldots, x, \ldots, y, \ldots)$.

Observe that using a particular kind of superposition, the identification of arguments, one can reduce the number of arguments of a function. For instance, identifying y with x (that is, substituting $y = x$) reduces the number of arguments in the multiplication function, $x \cdot y$, from two to one, $x \cdot x$, yielding the 'square of' function.

Definition by cases

We are all familiar with definitions by cases, such as

$$sgn(x) = \begin{cases} -1 \text{ if } x < 0 \\ 0 \text{ if } x = 0 \\ 1 \text{ if } x > 0 \end{cases}$$

In general

$$f(x_1, \ldots, x_n) = \begin{cases} g_1(x_1, \ldots, x_n) \text{ iff } r_1(x_1, \ldots, x_n) \\ \vdots \qquad\qquad\qquad \vdots \\ g_k(x_1, \ldots, x_n) \text{ iff } r_k(x_1, \ldots, x_n) \end{cases}$$

If functions $g_1(x_1, \ldots, x_n), \ldots, g_k(x_1, \ldots, x_n)$ and relations $r_1(x_1, \ldots, x_n), \ldots, r_k(x_1, \ldots, x_n)$ are all computable, so is the function $f(x_1, \ldots, x_n)$. Indeed, we compute the conditions $r_1, \ldots, r_k$ and, depending on which one is satisfied, we compute the corresponding g_i. For this schema to work without any difficulties the conditions $r_1, \ldots, r_k$ should be mutually exclusive:

$$r_i(x_1, \ldots, x_n) \,\&\, r_j(x_1, \ldots, x_n) \Leftrightarrow \textit{false} \text{ for any } i \neq j$$

and form a complete set of conditions

$$r_1(x_1, \ldots, x_n) | \ldots | r_k(x_1, \ldots, x_n) \Leftrightarrow \textit{true}.$$

Inductive definitions of functions

The general schema for inductively defining functions of many arguments is pretty cumbersome. We give two fairly general schemata for one- and two-argument functions:

$$f(0) = k$$
$$f(n + 1) = h(n, f(n))$$

and

$$f(0, x) = g(x)$$
$$f(n + 1, x) = h(x, n, f(n, x))$$

These schemata are called schemata of simple recursion or schemata of recursion with respect to a single argument. More complicated schemata of general recursion will not be considered here. In many instances a multiple recursion and even mutual recursion can be reduced to simple recursion. (See footnote on p. 45.) For instance:

- conditional recursion

$$f(0, u) = g(u)$$
$$f(x + 1, u) = \begin{cases} h_1(x, u, f(x, u)) \text{ if } R_1(x, u) \\ h_2(x, u, f(x, u)) \text{ if } R_2(x, u) \\ \vdots \qquad\qquad\qquad \vdots \\ h_l(x, u, f(x, u)) \text{ if } R_l(x, u) \end{cases}$$

with mutually exclusive and exhaustive R_i's;

- recursion with more than one initial value

$$f(0, u) = g_0(u)$$
$$f(1, u) = g_1(u)$$

$\vdots$

$f(l, u) = g_l(u)$
$f(x + 1, u) = h(x, u, f(x, u))$ if $x \geq l$

- mutual recursion

$f_1(0, u) = g_1(u)$
$f_2(0, u) = g_2(u)$
$f_1(x + 1, u) = h_1(x, u, f_1(x, u), f_2(x, u))$
$f_2(x + 1, u) = h_2(x, u, f_1(x, u), f_2(x, u))$

can all be reduced to simple recursion. (The schema for mutual recursion may have more than just two functions.)

On the other hand, the simple recursion schema can often be reduced to a simpler form. For example, the simple recursion schema involving a function of one argument only reduces to iteration

$f(0) = 0$
$f(n + 1) = g(f(n))$

or, less precisely,

$$f(n + 1) = g(g(\ldots g(0))..) = g^n(0)$$
$$\underbrace{}_{n \text{ times}}$$

Schemata of simple recursion obviously do not lead outside the class of computable functions.

Observe that schemata of simple recursion permit us to define many useful functions which do not seem to have a 'recursive nature'. For example, in the domain of natural numbers the predecessor function may be defined by

$P(0) = 0$
$P(n + 1) = n$

and the subtraction function in the same domain may be defined by

$x \doteq 0 = x$
$x \doteq (n + 1) = P(x \doteq n)$

We shall restrict our considerations to computability in the domain of natural numbers. There are two good reasons for doing this. First of all, as pointed out in Section 2.1.1, any theory that has a model, i.e. *any* consistent theory, has a countable model, i.e. can be interpreted in the domain of natural numbers. Secondly, no considerations seriously related to digital computing can depend on the considered domain not being the one of natural numbers (or, to be more precise, finite subsets of natural numbers).

Minimization

The fourth method of defining functions is based on the minimization operation. This operation can be applied to any relation $R(\ldots, x, \ldots)$ yielding a function or, in the particular case of a one-argument relation, a number. Symbolically, the operation is denoted by $(\mu x) [R(\ldots, x, \quad)]$ and its meaning can be expressed in words as 'the smallest natural value of x such that the relation R is satisfied'.

We have, for instance,

$$(\mu x)[x > 3] = 4$$
$$(\mu x)[x \text{ is odd and prime}] = 3$$
$$(\mu x)[(x + 1)^2 > y] = \sqrt{y}$$
$$(\mu x)[(x + 1)y > z] = entier(z/y)$$

The minimization does not always yield a number or a computable function even if the relation to which the minimization operator is applied is computable. If the relation to which the minimization is applied satisfies the condition

$$(Ay)(Ex)R(x, y) \tag{2.11}$$

then the function obtained is computable. (A similar condition guarantees computability of functions obtained by minimization of relations of arity higher than two.)

Observe that condition (2.11) is not met in the definition of $entier(z/y)$ as it is not true that for $y = 0$ and any z there exists an x such that $(x + 1) \cdot 0 > z$. The instances of minimization which satisfy (2.11) are known as *effective minimization*. If (2.11) is not met, the minimization is applied *ineffectively*. An effective minimization that defines $entier(z/y)$ is given by

$$entier(z/y) = (\mu x)[y = 0 \mid (x + 1) y > z]$$

If the minimization is applied effectively to a computable relation we get a computable function. Indeed, assuming that $R(x, y)$ is computable, there exists a function $g(x, y)$ which is its characteristic computable function. This means that by evaluating $g(x, y)$ we can check if $R(x, y)$ holds. The function $f(y) = (\mu x)[R(x, y)]$ can then be computed as follows. Consider all natural numbers $0, 1, 2, \ldots$ (in that order). For a given y, check if $R(0, y)$ holds. If yes, $f(y) = 0$; if not, check if $R(1, y)$ holds, etc. The effectiveness condition guarantees that sooner or later a number x will be found for which $R(x, y)$ holds. This number is then taken as the value of $f(y)$. Thus for any y, $f(y)$ can be computed effectively, provided (2.11) holds.

If (2.11) does not hold, i.e. if there exists at least one y_0 such that no x satisfying $R(x, y_0)$ exists, the outlined procedure for evaluating $(\mu x)[R(x, y)]$ at y_0 fails because having unsuccessfully tried to satisfy

$R(x, y_0)$ by $(0, y_0)$, $(1, y_0)$,...,(n, y_0) we still would have no indication whether to stop trying or not. Even if we extend the definition of the function obtained by application of the minimization operator (μx) to read

$$(\mu x)[R(x, y)] = \begin{cases} \text{the least number } x \text{ that satisfies } R(x, y) \text{ if} \\ \text{such a number exists, i.e. if (2.11) is met;} \\ 0 \text{ if (2.11) is not met} \end{cases}$$

that is, even if we accept the definition of a function by minimization that is not effectively applied, we do not obtain a *calculable* function from an ineffective minimization of a computable relation.

This point is very worthwhile to ponder as it clearly demonstrates two important observations:

1. that starting from a computable relation and applying a well defined operator we may get a well defined function which would nevertheless be non-computable;

2. that the proof of the effectiveness of the minimization operation is an additional obligation that must be fulfilled before we may safely consider any linguistic level which relies upon definitions by application of the minimization operator.

The class of computable functions in the domain of natural numbers, *Comp*, can be defined inductively:

1. The successor function, $suc(x) = x + 1$, the two 'select one argument' functions, $I(x, y) = x$, $J(x, y) = y$, and the constant function $0(x) = 0$ are in *Comp*.

2. If two functions, f and g, are in *Comp*, so is the function h, obtained by superposition:

    $$h(\ldots, x, \ldots, y, \ldots) = f(\ldots, x, \ldots, g(\ldots, y, \ldots), \ldots)$$

3. If two functions, f and g, are in *Comp*, so is the function h obtained by induction under the schema of simple recursion:

    $$h(0, x) = f(x)$$
    $$h(suc(n), x) = g(x, n, h(n, x))$$

4. If a function f is in *Comp* and the effectiveness condition

    $$(\mathbf{A}u)(\mathbf{E}x)f(u, x) = 0$$

    is satisfied, then the function h defined by the minimization

    $$h(u) = (\mu x)[f(u, x) = 0]$$

    is also in *Comp*.

A relation R is computable ($R \in Comp$) if and only if there exists a function $f \in Comp$ such that

$$(\mathbf{A}x_1 \ldots \mathbf{A}x_n)(R(x_1, \ldots, x_n) \Leftrightarrow f(x_1, \ldots, x_n) = 0).$$

This definition of computable functions includes all functions for which there exist effective, algorithmic means of computing results from given arguments.

For example, let us prove that addition is a computable function. For simplicity, we shall not use the prefix notation, such as $add(x, y)$, but a more conventional one, $x + y$.

Define first two auxiliary functions

$$S_1(n, y) = J(n, suc(y))$$
$$S_2(x, n, y) = J(x, S_1(n, y))$$

both computable as they are obtained by superposition from 'base' computable functions suc and J.

Addition can now be defined by simple recursive schema

$$0 + x = J(0, x) = x$$
$$suc(n) + x = S_2(x, n, n + x)$$

strictly following point (3) above.

Similarly one can define functions: multiplication, exponentiation, etc.

Using the definition of computable relations one can obtain computable functional expressions for union, intersection, negation, and other operations on relations. Assuming that

$$Q(x, y) \Leftrightarrow f(x, y) = 0$$
$$R(x, y) \Leftrightarrow g(x, y) = 0$$

we can define

$$Q(x, y) \,\&\, R(x, y) \Leftrightarrow (f(x, y) + g(x, y)) = 0$$
$$Q(x, y) \mid R(x, y) \Leftrightarrow (f(x, y) \cdot g(x, y)) = 0$$
$$\neg Q(x, y) \Leftrightarrow (1 - f(x, y)) = 0$$
etc.

Universal bounded quantification ('for all x not exceeding n'), a logical operation of great use in describing properties of domains, can also be defined easily in a computable fashion via effective minimization. Indeed:

$$(\mathbf{A}x : x < n)(R(\ldots, x, \ldots) \,\&\, \neg R(\ldots, n, \ldots)) \Leftrightarrow$$
$$n = (\mu x)[\neg R(\ldots, x, \ldots)]$$

and, therefore, since $\neg R(\ldots, x, \ldots)$ is computable, so is bounded universal quantification. If the collection of operations allowed in extending the base functions does not include effective minimization, the class of computable functions obtained is known as the *primitive recursive* ones. For some time it was thought that any function that can be effectively computed was primitive recursive. The set of all functions that can be effectively computed is known as the class of general recursive functions. The above given inductive definition of the class of computable functions contains functions that are not primitive recursive.

The essential extension of the notion of computability over that associated with simple recursion (and, in some structurally simple cases, iteration) is due to the effective minimization operation. Indeed, it can be proved that every computable function can be defined using at most one effective minimization operation (Kleene's theorem on normal form). It can also be proved, however, that for any class of functions, closed under superposition and containing the successor function, there exists a function that is outside this class.

The last-mentioned result deserves a little thought. It states that if we have a class of functions, if only the syntax of its construction rules is such that superposition of functions of this class yields functions of the same class (the requirement of *suc* being a member of their class is trivial, it is difficult to imagine any class of useful functions without *suc*), then a function can be defined that would not be in this class. Of course it is perfectly legitimate to apply this result to the class of computable functions. We get then the statement that there exist functions that are not in the class of computable ones, therefore which are not (effectively) computable. This result seems so striking that a sketch of a proof is in order.

Consider a class of functions F and a function of two arguments $g(n, x)$, not necessarily $g \in F$, such that for any function $f \in F$ of one argument

$$(\mathbf{E}n)(\mathbf{A}x)(g(n, x) = f(x))$$

Such a function g is referred to as a *universal function* for the class F. Assume now that F contains the successor function and is closed under superposition. Suppose that the universal function $g \in F$. As a result of our assumptions, $g(x, x) + 1$ must also be in F (as obtained by superposition of successor, $+1$, on $g(x, x)$, itself easily obtained from $g(n, x)$ by identification of arguments, a particular case of superposition). By definition of the universal function there must be an n such that $(\mathbf{A}x)g(n, x) = g(x, x) + 1$ (since $g(x, x) + 1$ is a function of one argument!). But substitution of x for n in the last formula yields its instance $g(x, x) = g(x, x) + 1$ which is patently false. Therefore the universal function cannot be in F, as assumed.

The above proof being non-constructive, we cannot yet be certain that for the class of computable functions there exists a function that does not belong to it. We must actually produce a universal function first and only then, by virtue of the proved result, can we assert that it does not belong to the class of computable functions, i.e. that it is non-computable.

It turns out that we can explicitly construct a universal function for the class of primitive recursive functions. This function − not primitive recursive itself! − can be proved to be computable, thus establishing, incidentally, that the class of computable functions is indeed larger than that of primitive recursive functions. It can also be proved that a function obtained by minimization of a universal function for the class of primitive recursive functions is universal for that of computable functions. This function provides the sought-after example of a universal function for the class of computable functions.

Since the universal function in question is obtained by minimization and is not computable, the minimization must be non-effective. This points out the danger of unbounded quantification used in definitions of functions (and relations). In fact, every essential use of an unbounded quantifier (existential or universal, it does not matter), *unless it can be proved to be effective*, creates a function of a higher class of non-computability.

We have allocated so much space to the seemingly esoteric problem of computability just in order to be able to make the observation that when describing a domain (i.e. specifying or portraying it) in a linguistic system that admits quantifiers (and one without them would be a very poor language indeed) we must be extremely cautious with their use. Any use of an unbounded quantifier, such as a universal quantifier over an infinite set, or an existential but ineffective one, increases the non-computability class of the construct thus defined.

Finally, let us observe that the notion of computability we discussed so far was that referring to *effectiveness*, but not necessarily to *efficiency* of actual computations. In fact, the very core of the arguments put forward, the effectiveness of minimization, taken literally, would only guarantee that computations of a 'sequential search' variety terminate. This may be sufficient for purely qualitative reasoning. For practical cases involving millions of possibilities, the sequential search is seldom good enough.

2.2.3 Definability

Broadly speaking, when we construct a linguistic level, we start with a set of axiomatically stated properties and then define other properties in terms of the axiomatic kernel. Quite naturally there arises a question of what concepts are definable by means of this or that kind of linguistic constructs. This question has two distinct portents: one related to deducibility, the other to computability. The first aspect of definability is concerned with the consequences of a set of axioms, its minimality in a sense. Formulating the axioms of a theory, we may be, for instance, concerned with the problem of whether we have not, by chance, included axioms that are deducible from others, also included. (This is by no means to be understood as a judgment against introducing superfluous axioms — their didactic value may easily outweigh any penalty for redundancy!)

The notion of definability in this sense is closely related to syntactic properties of the linguistic system, as is the twin notion of deducibility.

A term is said to be *definable* in a theory if its definition is a theorem in this theory (i.e. a sentence deducible from the axioms).

For instance, the term $<$ is definable in the theory of natural numbers by successor and addition symbols since it can be proved that

$$x < y \Leftrightarrow (\mathbf{E}z)(x + suc(z) = y)$$

In general, a predicate P is definable in the theory T by extralogical symbols $q_1, \ldots, q_n$ if the equivalence

$$(\mathbf{A}x)(P(x) \Leftrightarrow A) \tag{2.12}$$

can be proved in the theory T with formula A containing no other extralogical symbols than those from the sequence $q_1, \ldots, q_n$, all its free variables bound by the universal quantifier in front of (2.12).

Observe that if we are defining a previously unused term (or predicate symbol) by means of other, previously used symbols, then the essential part of the proof of (2.12) is to establish that A holds for all x, or to find exact restrictions on the validity of A. The equivalence part of (2.12) is easy to prove in these circumstances: $P(x)$ has no inherent meaning as yet, it is defined to mean the same as A, i.e. to hold whenever A holds and nowhere else. On the other hand, it may very well be that both P and the symbols used in A are already equipped with some meaning (e.g. they are all employed in axioms of the theory). In this case we must indeed prove the equivalence of the two sides.

There are several important and useful theorems about terms defined by other terms.

If a term P is definable in a theory T by terms $Q_1, \ldots, Q_m$, then for every two models of this theory, M_1 and M_2, if submodels in which terms $Q_1, \ldots, Q_m$ can be interpreted are isomorphic, then the isomorphism covers also the relations p_1 and p_2 which are assigned to P by the interpretation of T in M_1 and M_2 correspondingly.

This theorem assures us that the term defined by means of other terms 'behaves' in all models that are isomorphic to each other in an isomorphic fashion. Even less precisely said, if we have two models which are isomorphic as far as basic terms are concerned, the isomorphism of terms defined by means of these terms is guaranteed.

In particular, since identity is a special case of isomorphism, we can infer that if a term P is definable by terms $Q_1, \ldots, Q_m$ then in a model where $Q_1, \ldots, Q_m$ are interpreted as names of relations $q_1, \ldots, q_m$ there is only one interpretation of P as a name of relation p.

Thus if we have a model of a theory, in which model the terms $Q_1, \ldots, Q_m$ are interpreted as names of relations $q_1, \ldots, q_m$ and a certain term P can be interpreted as a name of two *different* relations p_1 and p_2, then P is not definable by terms $Q_1, \ldots, Q_m$. This observation is often used as the basis for proving that a term is not definable by specified other terms: it is sufficient to find a model in which the term in question could be interpreted as a name of two different relations.

The converse is also true. If we have a domain D with relations p_1,

$p_2, q_1, \ldots, q_m$ and a theory T such that $T \subset E$ (D without p_1) & $T \subset E(D$ without $p_2) \Rightarrow p_1 = p_2$ then the term P is definable by the terms $Q_1, \ldots, Q_m$, where of course $Q_1, \ldots, Q_m$ are interpreted as names of relations $q_1, \ldots, q_m$ and P is interpreted as the name of relation p_1 or relation p_2, respectively.

The other aspect of definability concerns relations defined by formulae. Consider a domain D and let X stand for a sequence of objects from that domain. Consider also a formula A in which the terms $Q_1, \ldots, Q_m$ occur: under an interpretation of T in D these terms are interpreted as names of relations $q_1, \ldots, q_m$. We shall say that the formula A defines a relation r in D iff $(\mathbf{A}x)(r(x) \Leftrightarrow (x$ satisfies A in D under the considered interpretation$))$.

This means that the relation r consists of those and only those sequences of objects in D which under given interpretation of terms included in A satisfy A. In the linguistic level the relation r may be named by any unused identifier, say, R.

Another formulation of the same concept is given by the definition: formula A defines relation r in D if and only if the sentence $(\mathbf{A}x)(R(x) \Leftrightarrow A)$ is in $E(D)$.

Since we have pointed out the importance of including quantification in formulae defining functions, let us discuss the relations defined by formulae with quantifiers.

A relation $P(x_1, \ldots, x_n)$ is called *recursively enumerable* if there exists a computable relation $R(x_1, \ldots, x_n, y)$ such that for any natural $x_1, \ldots, x_n$ it is true that

$$P(x_1, \ldots, x_n) \Leftrightarrow (\mathbf{E}y\text{:natural}) R(x, \ldots, x_n, y)$$

A set Z is recursively enumerable if the one argument relation $x \in Z$ is recursively enumerable.

Recursively enumerable sets differ in an important way from computable ones. Indeed, whereas the question whether an element x belongs to a computable set can always be settled by a finite number of tests, for a merely recursively enumerable one the negative result of any finite number of tests does not tell us much: the element x is just as likely to be a not-yet-checked member of the set as to be a non-member.

It is sometimes easier to prove that a set is recursively enumerable than to establish its computability (every computable set is of course recursively enumerable).

If a set C and its complement $N - C$ are both recursively enumerable, then they are also computable. Similarly, if two disjoint sets C and D are recursively enumerable and their union $C \cup D$ turns out to be computable, then both C and D are themselves computable.

Every recursively enumerable non-empty set C can be presented as a set of values of a primitive recursive function

$$x \in C \Leftrightarrow (\mathbf{E}n)(x = f(n))$$

It is from this relationship that the class of recursively enumerable sets gets its name: such sets are sets of values of recursive functions.

2.2.4 Some practical considerations

A linguistic level is seldom defined from scratch. Usually a linguistic level is presupposed; often a part of the level is just brought in by reference to a well understood and unambiguously identifiable theory.

When describing a domain of practical interest, say a banking system or a guidance system for an aircraft, one is unlikely to list explicitly the axioms of natural arithmetic or even more fundamental rules of reasoning. The linguistic system may be assumed quite silently; similarly, the basic theories that are relied upon. It would be utterly unrealistic to expect that people writing specifications for computer programs will always specify, with all necessary details, the formal theories they are implicitly relying upon. Even in mathematics no-one ever lists explicitly all relevent basic axioms; no-one goes explicitly through all the deduction steps. When a mathematician says that he is considering a continuous function or a particular form of partial differential equation, he is expressing himself on a linguistic level very far removed from the level of natural arithmetic. He can do so safely because there is an established tradition of a layered mathematical language, in which individual levels are identified by the use of specific terms. The relationships between levels are investigated separately from any work carried out within a level and the detailed proofs can be omitted because of two factors: (1) critical steps are ex-hibited and analysed by many mathematicians, many are even named (thus a mathematician may say 'this follows by application of forcing' or 'proof by *reductio ad absurdum*'), and the knowledge of established patterns of reasoning constitutes a necessary part of a working math-ematician's tools of trade; (2) if needed, any step can be reconstructed and minutely investigated.

In development of software for practical applications we are faced with a situation which differs from that encountered in mathematics in several very important respects.

Probably the most important difference is the lack of established linguistic levels. The terminology being used is often chaotic, basic pre-mises unlisted, assumptions not checked for consistency, etc.

Secondly, there is no established tradition for deductive reasoning. Facts are discovered by empirical means (or are assumed), often without paying any attention to the question of whether they are primitive (on a given linguistic level) or could be derived as consequences of others. There being no (or very few) established patterns of reasoning, very little use is being made of 'canned' trains of premise—conclusion chains. It is left to individuals to present their justification of statements made in a convincing manner. Only too often 'convincing' means here not necessarily 'verifiable by application of well defined rules' but all sorts of very poor substitutes, from 'on my authority' to plain '*fiat*'.

Thirdly, it is not only linguistic levels that are poorly or not at all defined. It is the very linguistic system that is confusingly used, including its simplest, grammatical aspects.

Fourthly, while a mathematician usually works within a single linguistic level, a software designer (programmer) almost invariably has to deal with several *essentially different* linguistic levels. The previous statement is to be understood as applying not so much to the macro time scale as to the micro one. A mathematician during his working life may switch linguistic levels as his interests change, say from set theory to analytic functions. A programmer uses several distinct linguistic levels when working on nearly every single problem in his professional career. Indeed, we will show in Chapter 4 that the transitions between linguistic levels constitute the most universally applicable technique of software development. (This technique is so ubiquitous in program development that its actual application is often quite subconscious (see Maibaum and Turski, 1984). Naïve attempts to alleviate the difficulties attendant on working in several linguistic levels either by stratifying the population of programmers into system analysts, programmers and coders, or by splitting the software design/implementation process into several *a priori* fixed stages (the so-called 'waterfall' approach), much as they bear witness to the fact of the multilevel nature of software work, were not very successful.)

If the specification and subsequent development of software is to be made rigorous, there is no way that present confusion could be preserved. On the other hand it is unthinkable that specification writing and software development for millions of applications could be more demanding of the people involved in these activities than mathematics.

One way out of this contradiction may seem attractive: if the application domains are as well analysed as mathematical domains, suitable theories will be formulated and the work on a banking system could rely on various existing theories, just as in working on a problem in algebraic topology one relies on many mathematical theories and results therein established. This way has one fatal shortcoming – its time scale is utterly impractical. It took several thousand years to develop mathematical theories. True, there was little public demand and even less reward for this kind of work, but to expect that the beneficial activities of funding agencies can accelerate the natural development by a factor of several hundred is a bit over-optimistic. The necessary theories will not develop independently of software construction in time to be of much use in software construction.

The other way is the one we hinted at in Chapter 1. The software specification for application domains is the process of theory formation for these domains. It is precisely because of this that this process is so difficult and so exciting.

If, however, specification construction is in fact theory-making, we must think about means which would make this task manageable. There are several such means of sufficient generality.

Combining theories

Given two theories in the same linguistic system, T_1 and T_2, we want to consider a theory T that would be the sum of T_1 and T_2.

From a purely formal point of view, this is a rather simple operation. If both theories are axiomatized with $Ax(T_1)$, $Ax(T_2)$ standing for their respective sets of axioms, we are considering a theory with $G = Ax(T_1) \cup Ax(T_2)$ as the set of axioms. The sentences that constitute this theory are $Cn(G)$ and we expect $Cn(G)$ to be closed under the rules of inference of the linguistic system. One hopes, of course, that each of the theories T_1 and T_2 by itself is at least consistent, but this does not guarantee yet the consistency of G in the general case (see Robinson's Theorem in the Appendix). The case when theories T_1 and T_2 have no shared terms, and rules of the syntax ensure that in G there will be no sentences containing terms from both T_1 and T_2, even if guaranteed to be consistent, is not very appealing. In most cases, when we combine theories, it is just because we are interested in sentences which have terms from both constituent theories. The thus combined theory must be investigated as to its consistency. It is encouraging that the possible inconsistency could be due only to the sentences combining terms of both theories.

If we associate the notion of a consistent theory with that of a module in a programming language, the set of sentences that use terms from both theories may be seen as the shared interface between the two modules.

Generic theories

A theory T may be constructed so that its sentences contain place-holders for constructs to be defined by some other theory, X. When such a theory is instantiated by a concrete theory, we get an instance of the generic theory $T(X)$. The use of generic theories is obvious: rather than building separate theories for stacks of integers, stacks of arrays, stacks of strings, etc., we build a generic theory of stacks of somethings and then instantiate 'something' in it to be integers, arrays or strings, each itself described by a theory.

Observe that there is no risk of inconsistency arising from the proper[†] use of instantiated generic theories. The sentences of T must be consistent for any valuation of terms; if they are consistent for 'somethings' they will be consistent for integers, arrays or strings. In principle, theories T and X

[†] Proper use of instantiation presupposes that the concrete theory intended to be substituted for X conforms with any restrictions imposed on X in $T(X)$. Thus, for example, if $T(X)$ requires values in X to be totally ordered, we cannot properly instantiate X by a theory of ancestral relations.

need not be in the same linguistic system as long as the theory T does not contain operations that 'go inside' the instantiating objects, even though we are not aware of examples exploiting this idea.

Extensions of a theory

Sometimes we may be interested in extending a theory T by some axioms. This means that theory T is incomplete (otherwise any non-trivial extension would lead to inconsistency). We have shown how any consistent theory may be enlarged by adding to it sentence by sentence; under the provision that the negations of sentences being added are not deducible from the sentences already in, such an extension preserves consistency. Of course, if a sentence being added can itself be deduced from the sentences already in the theory, the resulting extension does not really enrich the theory; it may, however, have a didactic value. An essential extension takes place only if the sentence being added is independent of the theory.

There exist specification languages which make the operations on theories explicitly accessible to their users. The motivation behind such languages is quite obvious. The specification of a fairly large system as a single set of axioms being an unrealistic undertaking, one has to follow the most general mental technique available in human conquest of complexity, to wit, that of rational separation of concerns, or modularization. Each identifiable 'concern' should be specifiable by means of a theory: if it is not, then either the 'concern' is still too large or so badly identified that its description cannot be given by means of a relatively small, consistent set of axioms. Once a satisfactory specification of a 'concern' by means of a suitable theory is available, it can be combined with other, similar descriptions, to form a theory of a larger 'concern'. Since the various 'enlarging' operations on theories are expected to be a very common practice in specification building, a language intended for presentation of this process should provide well defined means of recording such operations.

We can hope that with this approach gaining practical recognition an armoury of useful specifications will be built, either as a textbook or, preferably, as a library from which the specification building bricks can be taken. When such a library is indeed available, there is no need explicitly to copy all details of a theory being employed; it can be referred to by its name, and a detailed record used only when the final write-up is required, or, more likely, when it must be decided whether the result of a particular operation yields a theory that has defined qualities − first of all, whether it is consistent or not.

It is not expected that the availability of any fixed (or extensible) library of theories will solve all specification-writing problems. Any practically significant domain will require not only a combination of off-the-shelf theories but a number of particular theories as well. Also, the actual selection of ready-made theories and their particular combination will, of course, depend on the domain being described, on particular aspects of it selected as being important, and − last but not least − on the skills and knowledge possessed by the specifier.

An early example of a language specifically designed along these methodological lines is provided by Clear.

In designing Clear, Burstall and Goguen had in mind a language to express theories of algebraic type. The relevant part of a linguistic level − axioms of the type − take the form of *equations* in which *operators* of the type act on variables, implicitly universally quantified to range over suitable *sorts*, i.e. sets of objects. The vocabulary of operators, together with their arities and indications of which sorts are suitable as which operands for a given operator, constitutes the *signature* part of a theory presentation.

Thus, a theory of natural numbers may be given a Clear presentation as follows[†]:

Sorts nat, bool
  Operations *zero*:   → **nat**
            suc: **nat**   → **nat**
          iszero: **nat**   → **bool**
            true: → **bool**
           false: → **bool**
            not: **bool**   → **bool**
             or: **bool, bool** → **bool**
  Variables *m, n:* **nat**
  Equations *iszero*(*zero*) = *true*
          iszero(*suc*(*n*)) = *false*
            not(*true*) = *false*
            not(*false*) = *true*

Writing explicit presentations for largish theories would be, of course, exceedingly tedious, and therefore error prone. Thus Clear provides theory-building operations. First a small theory that is explicitly presented may be converted into a theory-constant, for example:

Nat0: **theory sorts nat**
  opns *0*:   → **nat**
     suc: **nat** → **nat**
        eqns endth
Bool0: **theory sorts bool**
  opns *true*:   → **bool**
        false: → **bool**
          ¬ : **bool**   → **bool**
          & : **bool, bool** → **bool**

[†] All examples on Clear are taken from Burstall and Goguen (1977).

> **eqns** ¬*true* = *false*
> ¬*false* = *true*
> *false* & *p* = *false*
> *true* & *p* = *p* **endth**

Note that the variable *p*, ranging − obviously − over sort **bool** is left undeclared.

The simplest operation on theories is *combine*, denoted by + standing between two theory names. The sorts of a combined theory are the union of sorts of the constituents; the set of operators is also the union of the sets of the constituents' operators, similarly for the equations. Thus *Nat0* + *Bool0* denotes the same theory as:

> **theory sorts bool, nat**
> **opns** *true*:   → **bool**
>   *false*:   → **bool**
>   ¬ : **bool**   → **bool**
>   & : **bool, bool** → **bool**
>   *0*:   → **nat**
>   *suc*: **nat**   → **nat**
> **eqns** ¬*true* = *false*
>   ¬*false* = *true*
> *false* & *p* = *false*
>   *true* & *p* = *p* **endth**

A specified theory may be *enriched* by including in it additional operators and corresponding axioms, for example we may enrich *Bool0* + *Nat0* by operators ≤ and *eq* by means of the following definition:

> *Nat1*:
>   **enrich** *Bool0* + *Nat0* **by**
>   **opns** ≤: **nat, nat** → **bool**
>   *eq*: **nat, nat** → **bool**
>   **eqns** $0 \leq n = true$
> $suc(n) \leq 0 = false$
> $suc(m) \leq suc(n) = m \leq n$
> $eq(m, n) = m \leq n \ \& \ n \leq m$ **enden**

Note that operators ≤ and *eq* do not belong to *Bool0*, nor to *Nat0*, they are a 'part' of *Nat1*. (In Clear, one may enrich a theory by adding not only operators, but also sorts.)

When the axioms of a theory take the form of equations, the natural rules of inference are *reflexivity* ($x = x$), *transitivity* ($x = y \ \& \ y = z \Rightarrow x = z$) and *symmetry* ($x = y \Rightarrow y = x$), constituting the usual meaning of equality, and *substitutivity* ($f(a) = g(a) \Rightarrow f(expression) = g(expression)$ if *expression* is systematically substituted for *a* in $f(a)$ and in $g(a)$). Thus, the theory consists of the set of all equations derivable from the equations part of a theory presentation by means of the above-listed rules of inference (and closed under these rules). Thus, from the *Nat1* presentation, it follows that:

$$eq(0, 0) = true$$
$$eq(suc(0), suc(0)) = true$$
$$\vdots$$

are all in the theory *Nat1*. The equation

$$eq(n, n) = true \quad \text{(for all } n \in Nat1)$$

cannot be established, however, by substitutivity, reflexivity, transitivity and symmetry alone. Thus $eq(n, n) = true$ is not a part of *Nat1*!

In order to include such equations into a theory, an operation of *induction* on theories is included in Clear. This operation, denoted by **induce**, **induce** *Nat1*, say, includes in a theory all equations containing a universally quantified variable that are equiform to such equations which, by virtue of the axioms listed in the presentation, can be proved to hold for any (i.e. arbitrary) variable free term.

Hence, because $eq(n, n) = true$ can be proved in *Nat1* for any fixed (constant) n, $(An: \textbf{nat})$ $(eq(n, n) = true)$ is in **induce** *Nat1*. (In Clear, the universal quantification An: **nat** is usually skipped!) Similarly, in *Nat* = **induce** *Nat1*, the following equations:

$$eq(m, n) = eq(n, m)$$
$$eq(l, m) \,\&\, eq(m, n) \,\&\, \neg eq(l, n) = false$$

hold, establishing symmetry and transitivity for general equations.

Finally, Clear introduces a fourth operation on theories, **derive**, which allows one to extract from a richer theory sorts and operations that are of interest for the job in hand. (By combining, enriching and inducing theories we may have created a theory with too many bells and whistles; derivation allows us to extract the core of the thus constructed theory, whatever meaning of 'core' we have in mind.)

For example, if we do not need 0 and $\leqslant$ from *Nat*, but wish to preserve *eq*, we may write

    Natequal:
        derive sorts element, bool
        opns *equal, true, false*
      from *Nat* **by**
        element is nat
          bool is bool
       equal **is** *eq*
        true **is** *true*
        false **is** *false* **endde**

Note that the theory building operation **enrich** makes it possible to dispense with explicit denotation for theories altogether if we have a standard denotation for an *empty* theory. Indeed, if Φ is the empty theory, an explicit definition yields precisely the same as **enrich** Φ **by**...**enden**, where the ellipsis covers the same ground as an explicit definition.

Theories obtained by enrichment, combination, induction and derivation, are, in a sense, constant theories. Clear also makes provisions for defining 'generic' theories by means of theory procedures that take theories as their parameters and produce a theory as a result. Bodies of such procedures are, of course, built from the theory-constructing operations introduced earlier.

Often, the formal parameters of a theory procedure definition are referred to as metasorts, to avoid confusion with actual sorts employed in procedure body and/or call. The theory of sort *Triv* is just one example of such a formal metasort.

> **const** *Triv* = **theory sorts element endth**
>
> **proc** *Strings* $(X\colon Triv)$ = **induce enrich** X **by**
>   **sorts string**
>   **opns** *unit*: **element** $\rightarrow$ **string**
> Λ: $\rightarrow$ **string**
>   @: **string, string** $\rightarrow$ **string**
>   **eqns** Λ @ $s = s$
> s @ $\Lambda = s$
> $(s$ @ $t)$ @ $u = s$ @ $(t$ @ $u)$**enden**

introduces a procedure for producing a theory of strings of a sort whose theory will be supplied as the actual parameter of a call of this procedure. An added technicality is that in a procedure call we have to associate operations and sorts of the metasort (formal parameter) with those of the actual parameter sort. Thus we need sort-to-sort and operator-to-operator mappings; they are presented exactly as in the case of **derive** operations. For example, the theory of strings of natural numbers is obtained by calling *Strings* with *Nat*, thus *Strings*(*Nat*[**element is nat**]); since the formal parameter sort, *Triv*, had no operators, the operator part of the mapping is left out in the procedure call.

More details about Clear can be found in Burstall and Goguen (1977). Another example of a specification language firmly based on the 'specification as a theory' principle, fully implemented and supported by suitable verification techniques, is the ι language described by Nakajima *et al.* (1980). This language is used in some examples contained in Section 3.5.

Recently, Guttag *et al.* (1985) have proposed a family of specification languages, Larch. Each language has a component common to all Larch languages and a component particular to a specific language in the family. The shared language is used to specify algebraic abstractions, types (sorts) and operators and their properties. The particular component of each member of the Larch family, known as the interface language, is used to specify program modules and thus relies on notions specific to a programming language. Thus the Larch shared language provides a linguistic level and each particular interface language is an extension of this level.

It is very instructive to quote from the original authors' list of the most important aspects of the Larch family of specification languages:

- The shared language is used to specify a theory, the interface languages are built around the predicate calculus.

- Specifications written in Larch are composable (i.e. can be used to construct other specifications incrementally).

- Larch is designed to be used with a powerful theorem-prover for semantic checking (validation).

2.3 Calculus of extensions and translations

2.3.1 Extensions revisited

As we observed in the preceding section, specifications (i.e. axiomatic theories) are not given whole, *deus ex machina*; they have to be constructed to suit the purpose at hand. One might claim that the subject matter of software engineering is the study and practice of theory construction (and, as we shall see later, a variant of it, translation). Even management of software projects can be seen in terms of theory construction: how can one control the construction of very large theories?[†]

Now, extension is an 'adding to' operation. Given a first-order language L, with (set of) constant symbols, C, function symbols F, and relation symbols R, we may wish to add a new symbol to L to facilitate some aspect of the description which L is being used to construct. For example, if we have a language for the natural numbers ($zero$, suc, $=_{nat}$), we may subsequently decide that we will need an ordering relation le on natural numbers. The language L' obtained by adding le to the set of (diadic) relation symbols of L is said to be an *extension* of L. We denote this relationship by $L \subseteq L'$ or $L' \supseteq L$. For many-sorted languages $\langle S, L \rangle$, where S is a set of sorts and L is an indexed family of constant symbols, an indexed family of function symbols, and an indexed family of relation symbols, we may add new symbols and/or new sorts to our language. Thus, if we had $\langle S, L_{nat} \rangle = \langle \{ \mathbf{nat} \}, \{ zero: \rightarrow \mathbf{nat}, suc: \mathbf{nat} \rightarrow \mathbf{nat}, =_{nat}: \mathbf{nat} \times \mathbf{nat} \rightarrow \{ true, false \}, le: \mathbf{nat} \times \mathbf{nat} \rightarrow \{ true, false \} \} \rangle$ as a many

---

[†] An interesting aside at this point is the observation by Harlan Mills, of the Federal Systems Division of IBM, that a very large proportion of his best managers on software projects had a background in mathematics.

sorted language for natural numbers (technically different from the first-order language mentioned before), we might wish to extend $\langle S, L_{nat} \rangle$ by adding a sort called **set** as a first step in allowing us to describe sets of natural numbers. We would then have $\langle S', L'_{nat} \rangle$, with set of sorts $S' = \{\text{nat, set}\}$ and symbols as for L_{nat}. We again denote such an extension as $\langle S, L_{nat} \rangle \subseteq \langle S', L'_{nat} \rangle$.

Language extension is an aspect of linguistic systems. The grammar defining the language of a linguistic system distinguishes a number of categories of linguistic constructs and provides rules for determining the well formed constructs obtainable from basic symbols (both logical and extralogical) within each of the categories. Given two (extralogical) languages, both within the same linguistic system, the relationship of extension between the two languages reduces to set theoretic containment of corresponding sets of basic symbols in the two languages.

Because the inductive properties of the grammar are used to define the various categories of the linguistic system, the sets of constructs obtainable from the basic symbols will observe the appropriate containment relationships.

Just as we might wish to add new symbols (or sorts) to a language, we might wish to attribute additional properties to (extralogical) symbols of the language. For instance, if L'_{nat} is the first-order language with a diadic relation symbol le, we may have started by asserting the following properties for natural numbers with an ordering relation:

$$\vdash \neg(suc(n) =_{nat} zero) \tag{2.13}$$
$$\vdash suc(m) =_{nat} suc(n) \Rightarrow m =_{nat} n \tag{2.14}$$
$$\vdash le(n, n) \tag{2.15}$$
$$\vdash le(m, n) \,\&\, le(n, m) \Rightarrow m =_{nat} n \tag{2.16}$$
$$\vdash le(m, n) \,\&\, le(n, p) \Rightarrow le(m, p) \tag{2.17}$$

The axioms (2.15), (2.16) and (2.17) define le to be a partial order. Denote by G_{npo} the axioms (2.13)–(2.17). Then we have a specification of natural numbers with a partial order which we will denote NATPO = $\langle L'_{nat}, G_{npo} \rangle$.

Now, in a model of the natural numbers, say 0, 1, 2,...with *zero* interpreted as 0 and *suc* as 'add one', one could interpret le as the usual ordering relation $\geq$ (i.e. greater than or equal to). Worse, one could interpret $le(m, n)$ as 'm divides n evenly' (i.e. without remainder)! This is probably not what we intended, and if we were interested in using a sorting algorithm on natural numbers which used (an implementation of) le as the pairwise comparison operation, we might not get the output we expect! Clearly, one problem is that we have not specified ordering on natural numbers tightly enough – the 'divides' relation is not a total ordering, whereas the ordering we had in mind was.

Thus, we would like to extend NATPO to a theory, NATTO, that would eliminate as models those structures which did not interpret le as a total ordering. Having noted that $\neg(Am\,An\,(le(m, n)|le(n, m)))$ is not a consequence of G_{npo}, we can achieve our goal by adding to G_{npo} the axiom

$$\vdash Am\,An\,(le(m, n)|le(n, m)) \tag{2.18}$$

obtaining G_{nto} and the theory NATTO $= \langle L'_{nat}, .G_{nto} \rangle$. Any interpretation of *le* as 'divides evenly' is now impossible as it is not the case that for every pair of natural numbers, one of them divides the other. (Take two primes as an example.)

We say that NATTO is an *extension* of NATPO, denoted NATPO $\subseteq$ NATTO, because the language of the latter is included in the language of the former — in our example they are the same — and for any formula A we have that

if $G_{npo} \vdash A$ then $G_{nto} \vdash A$

Thus we have not lost any properties (consequences) of our theory but we might have gained some. In first-order logic (PC) and in many-sorted first-order logics (MPC) it is easy to show that if all we do is add extra axioms to our theory we do not lose any results. After all, a proof from G_{npo} is a proof from G_{nto} — we just do not use some of the axioms newly available to us. Proving that we have a proper extension, i.e. that we have introduced new properties, is somewhat more difficult. Assuming a consistent extension, one way we can be sure that a new property has indeed been introduced is to show that it is not the case that

$$G_{npo} \vdash Am\,An\,(le(m, n)|le(n, m))$$

i.e. we must show that it is impossible to prove that (2.18) is a consequence of (2.13)–(2.17). Such 'meta'-proofs are generally very difficult to do.

We have not yet finished our task of specifying an ordering which could be used by a sorting routine as, for example, $\leq$ and $\geq$ can both still be used to interpret *le*. To eliminate the latter, we could posit

$$\vdash An\,(le(zero, suc(n))) \tag{2.19}$$

which would have the desired effect. Letting NATLE $= \langle L'_{nat}, G_{nle} \rangle$ with G_{nle} being G_{nto} plus (2.19), we now have

NATPO $\subseteq$ NATTO $\subseteq$ NATLE

which leads to a nice property of extensions: their composability.

2.3.2 Composability of extensions

If T_1, T_2, T_3 are theories of PC (or MPC) such that we have $T_1 \subseteq T_2$ and $T_2 \subseteq T_3$, then $T_1 \subseteq T_3$.

Thus building by adding new properties bit by bit is technically sound (see the caveat below, however) and accomplishes, in toto, what we expect. For a fuller treatment, see Enderton (1972).

There is just one problem with extensions − we might be adding more properties than we intended, in a special sense. If we try to add to NATLE the axiom

$$\vdash \neg le(n, n) \tag{2.20}$$

to reflect the idea that we really want the strict ordering $<$ on natural numbers, we would have a problem because (2.20) contradicts (2.15).

Technically, we have an inconsistency, and we are now able to show that any formula A can be deduced from axioms (2.13)−(2.20). (Recall that an inconsistent theory can be used to prove anything!) So, some care must be taken in building extensions to ensure that no contradictory requirements are introduced. (The reader is referred back to Section 2.1 for a discussion of the relationship between extension, consistency and completeness.)

One further note about extensions before we move on. Consider the following axioms:

$$\vdash le(zero, suc(n)) \tag{2.21}$$
$$\vdash le(zero, zero) \tag{2.22}$$
$$\vdash le(suc(m), suc(n)) \Leftrightarrow le(m, n) \tag{2.23}$$
$$\vdash \neg le(suc(n), zero) \tag{2.24}$$

If we let G'_{nle} be composed of (2.13), (2.14) and (2.21)−(2.24), it can be demonstrated that

$$\langle L'_{nat}, G_{npo} \rangle \subseteq \langle L'_{nat}, G'_{nle} \rangle$$

This is not an obvious fact, as $G_{npo} \not\subseteq G'_{nle}$, contrary to the situation we had in previous examples. Despite the absence of direct inclusion of the axiom set G_{npo} in G'_{nle}, we do have the property that

$$\text{if } G_{npo} \vdash A \text{ then } G'_{nle} \vdash A$$

To demonstrate this, it suffices to show that each of (2.15)−(2.17) is a consequence of G'_{nle} (an exercise we leave to the reader).

The important point to note is that extension is a relationship between theories and not between axiomatic presentations of theories[†].

2.3.3 Conservative extension

One of the most important concepts in software engineering is that of modularity. It is the main tool in the arsenal of the engineer wanting to

---

[†] The reader may at this point like to ask himself what is the relationship between NATLE and $\langle L'_{nat}, G'_{nle} \rangle$. Are they the same (as theories)? Does one contain the other? Are they incomparable?

tackle extremely large problems and to make them tractable. In particular, if specification is to become useful in software engineering terms, it must rely on appropriate modularity principles[†]. We do not propose to provide here the 'right' notion of modularity for specifications, but discuss the main technical idea on which it must be based.

Suppose that we have some specification of the natural numbers, NAT, say, with (many sorted) language $\langle \{\mathbf{nat}\}, L_{\mathrm{nat}} \rangle$ and axioms G_{nat}, (2.13)−(2.19) (taken to be stated using the many-sorted language). Assume that we wish now to build a description of sets of natural numbers. We would probably proceed by extending the language $\langle \{\mathbf{nat}\}, L_{\mathrm{nat}} \rangle$ to the language $\langle \{\mathbf{nat}, \mathbf{set}\}, L_{\mathrm{nat}} \cup L_{\mathrm{set}} \rangle$ where L_{set} is:

empty:	$\rightarrow$ **set**
insert: **nat** × **set**	$\rightarrow$ **set**
remove: **nat** × **set**	$\rightarrow$ **set**
ismember: **nat** × **set** $\rightarrow$ {*true, false*}	
choose: **set**	$\rightarrow$ **nat**

We now want to extend the axioms for natural numbers by adding some axioms about the new symbols just introduced. However, aside from not wanting to lose any properties of natural numbers (as guaranteed by the defining properties of extensions), we might also expect in this situation that adding symbols for sets and ascribing properties to them should not allow us to infer new properties of natural numbers (i.e. consequences which are not deducible already from axioms (2.13)−(2.19))[‡].

Letting G_{set} be:

$$\vdash \neg ismember(n, empty) \tag{2.25}$$

$$\vdash (\mathbf{A}n(ismember(n, s) \Leftrightarrow ismember(n, t))) \Rightarrow s =_{\mathrm{set}} t \tag{2.26}$$

$$\vdash ismember(m, insert(n, s)) \Leftrightarrow ((m =_{\mathrm{nat}} n) | ismember(m, s)) \tag{2.27}$$

$$\vdash ismember(m, remove(n, s)) \Leftrightarrow (\neg (m =_{\mathrm{nat}} n) \,\&\, ismember(m, s)) \tag{2.28}$$

$$\vdash \neg (s =_{\mathrm{set}} empty) \Rightarrow ismember(choose(s), s) \tag{2.29}$$

we denote by SETOFNAT the theory

$$\langle \langle \{\mathbf{set}, \mathbf{nat}\}, L_{\mathrm{nat}} \cup L_{\mathrm{set}} \rangle, G_{\mathrm{nat}} \cup G_{\mathrm{set}} \rangle$$

[†] Recent experience has shown that the number of axioms in a specification of a system and the number of lines of code needed to implement it differ by *at most* one order of magnitude. If we also include axioms from linguistic levels between the original specification and final implementation, the relationship could very well be reversed. No-one to-day would accept unmodularized (unstructured) programs of more than a few dozen lines of code. Their expectations about specifications will be the same and justifiably so.

[‡] This property is sometimes called *protection* in the abstract data type literature, and the kind of extension we have just been describing is called an *enrichment* (see the description of Clear in Section 2.2).

Clearly NAT $\subseteq$ SETOFNAT as for any formula A over the language of NAT (i.e. using only sorts and symbols from $\langle \{\mathbf{nat}\}, L_{\mathrm{nat}} \rangle$) we have

$$\text{if } G_{\mathrm{nat}} \vdash A \text{ then } G_{\mathrm{nat}} \cup G_{\mathrm{set}} \vdash A \tag{E}$$

The additional property we want is in fact the converse of E:

$$\text{if } G_{\mathrm{nat}} \cup G_{\mathrm{set}} \vdash A \text{ then } G_{\mathrm{nat}} \vdash A \tag{CE}$$

Note that the premise of (E), viz. that the formula A is over the language of natural numbers (employs no set symbols!), is still meant to hold. (If A were allowed to include new set symbols, we would clearly be able to derive new consequences − at least the axioms in G_{set}.) If we have both (E) and (CE), we say that the extension is conservative.

We denote by $T_1 \leq T_2$ the fact that T_2 conservatively extends T_1.

The fact that $T_1 \leq T_2$ has an important practical consequence: given a correct implementation of T_1, we may use it as a basis for implementing the extension T_2 without danger of introducing inconsistencies[†]. Hence the reference to modularity.

This observation forces us to confront a practical problem of deciding when extensions are conservative. Clearly, if we have a theory, $T_1 = \langle \langle S_1, L_1 \rangle, G_1 \rangle \subseteq T_2 = \langle \langle S_2, L_2 \rangle, G_2 \rangle$, then to show that T_2 conservatively extends T_1, i.e. $T_1 \leq T_2$, we must have a (meta)-proof that for all formulae A over $\langle S_1, L_1 \rangle$ we have

$$G_2 \vdash A \text{ implies } G_1 \vdash A$$

Such general proofs *about* theories (as opposed to proofs of consequences within a linguistic system) are not easy.

The situation is akin to the problems associated with an *ex post* verification of programs − a very difficult job in general. It is a lot easier to construct the program to be correct in the first place. Similarly, theories should be extended in a way which guarantees the conservativeness of extensions. This approach has been explored by logicians, and to some extent by computer scientists. Below we consider some procedures whose application ensures the conservativeness of extensions.

As for extensions, we have the following important step-by-step property for conservative extensions.

2.3.4 Composability of conservative extensions

If T_1, T_2, T_3 are theories of PC (or MPC) and we have $T_1 \leq T_2$ and $T_2 \leq T_3$, then $T_1 \leq T_3$.

[†] This would clearly not have been the case with non-conservative extension. Take the example of $G_{\mathrm{npo}} \subseteq G_{\mathrm{nto}}$. If we had implemented G_{npo} with *le* implemented in terms of the 'divides evenly' relation, there would be no way of extending this implementation to be an implementation of G_{nto}.

This result is important in justifying the construction of specifications in a modular manner.

2.3.5   Extension by definition

Suppose that we start with the theory NATLE $= \langle L'_{nat}, G'_{nle} \rangle$ and want to introduce a new relation symbol to abbreviate the formula

$$le(m, n) \; \& \; \neg(m = n)$$

for the 'less than' relationship. This diadic relation symbol, which we will denote by lt is an auxiliary, or defined, symbol and we may introduce it by definition, i.e. by adding lt to L'_{nat} and the following defining axiom:

$$\vdash lt(m, n) \Leftrightarrow (le(m, n) \; \& \; \neg(m =_{nat} n)) \tag{2.30}$$

to G'_{nle}.

Denoting[†] the new theory $\langle L'_{nat} \cup \{lt\}, G'_{nat} \cup \{(2.30)\} \rangle$ by NATLT, we see that we can translate any formula of NATLT to one of NATLE by replacing occurrences of lt in formulae of the former by the definiens of lt (i.e. by the right-hand side of the formula (2.30)) to obtain an equivalent formula of NATLE.

As an example, in the formula

$$Ak(\neg(k = zero) \Rightarrow lt(zero, k)) \tag{2.31}$$

we can replace the occurrence of $lt(zero, k)$ by the corresponding instance of the definiens $le(m, n) \; \& \; \neg(m =_{nat} n)$.

The latter is obtained by substituting the term $zero$ for the variable m, and the term k (just a variable in this case) for the variable n. This yields

$$le(zero, k) \; \& \; \neg(zero = k)$$

which upon substitution in (2.31) gives

$$Ak(\neg(k = zero) \Rightarrow (le(zero, k) \; \& \; \neg(zero = k))) \tag{2.32}$$

So, given a formula A of NATLT, there is a formula A^c of NATLE such that

$$G'_{nat} \vdash A^c \text{ if and only if } G'_{nat}, (2.30) \vdash A$$

and, moreover, we have that

$$\text{NATLE} \leq \text{NATLT}$$

[†] We beg the readers' pardon for the loose use of notation in defining NATLT. However, we are working on the principle that a slight misuse of notation is worth a thousand words and the intention is much clearer.

Looking at the general situation, let $T = \langle L, G \rangle$ be a theory, suppose $x_1, \ldots, x_n$ are distinct variables and let A be a formula over L in which no variables other than $x_1, \ldots, x_n$ are free. Form the extension e: $T \subseteq T'$ by adding a new n-adic predicate symbol r to L (to obtain L') and adding a new axiom

$$\vdash r(x_1, \ldots, x_n) \Leftrightarrow A \tag{2.33}$$

to G (to obtain G'). (2.33) is called the *defining axiom* for r.

Now, given a formula B over the language L', we can translate it to a formula B^e over L as follows. Obtain from A the formula A' by substituting new variables for those of A which are bound (in A) and appear in B. (We do not want accidental bindings of variables on translation.) Finally, replace every occurrence of $r(t_1, \ldots, t_n)$ in B by the corresponding instance of A', namely:

$$A'[x_1/t_1, \ldots, x_n/t_n]$$

One can prove the following:

Theorem

With e: $T \subseteq T'$ and B as above,

1. $G' \vdash B \Leftrightarrow B^e$ (i.e. from G' we can prove that B and the formula B^e we obtain from B by eliminating the defined symbol r are logically equivalent);
2. $T \leq T'$ (i.e. T' is a conservative extension of T);
3. $G \vdash B^e$ if and only if $G' \vdash B$.

To define extensions, we may introduce function symbols analogously to relations symbols. Suppose that $T = \langle L, G \rangle$ is a theory; $x_1, \ldots, x_n, y, y'$ are distinct variables and A is a formula in which no variable other than $x_1, \ldots, x_n, y$ is free. Assume that we can prove the following:

$$G \vdash \mathbf{E}\, y\, A \tag{2.34}$$
$$G \vdash (A \,\&\, A[y/y']) \Rightarrow (y = y') \tag{2.35}$$

$T' = \langle L', G' \rangle$ is built from T by adding a new n-adic function symbol, say f, to L (to obtain L') and adding the new axiom

$$\vdash y = f(x_1, \ldots, x_n) \Leftrightarrow A \tag{2.36}$$

to G (to obtain G'). We call (2.36) the *defining axiom* for f, (2.34) the *existence condition* for f, and (2.35) the *uniqueness condition* for f. The properties (2.34) and (2.35) ensure that the function we are trying to define is in fact well defined. (2.34) ensures that for each $x_1, \ldots, x_n$ there is at least one y which satisfies A and is thus a potential value for (an interpretation of) f, while (2.35) ensures that this value is unique (our functions are deterministic).

Again, corresponding to a formula B over L', we can find a formula

B^e where e: $T \subseteq T'$ is the extension just defined. Suppose B is an atomic formula (i.e. a formula of the form $r(t'_1, \ldots, t'_n)$ for relation symbol r and terms $t'_1, \ldots, t'_n$). If B has no occurrences of f then $B^e = B$. Otherwise, we can write B as $C[z/f(t_1, \ldots, t_n)]$ where the $t_1, \ldots, t_n$ do not contain any occurrences of f and C is an atomic formula with one less occurrence of f than B. (Clearly, by assumption, there must be some term of the form $f(t_1, \ldots, t_n)$ in B and we just look for a minimal such occurrence in the sense that none of the t_i should contain an occurrence of f.) Again, rename variables in A, obtaining A', so that no variable of B is bound in A' and let

$$B^e = \mathbf{E}z\, (A'[x_1/t_1, \ldots, x_n/t_n, y/z] \,\&\, C^e) \qquad (2.37)$$

Now C has one less occurrence of f than B and so the recursion terminates with formulae being finite strings of symbols. The generalization to non-atomic formulae is straightforward. We again have:

Theorem

With e: $T \subseteq T'$ and B as above,

1. $G' \vdash B \Leftrightarrow B^e$;
2. $T \leq T'$;
3. $G \vdash B^e$ if and only if $G' \vdash B$.

We say that T' is an extension of T by definitions if there exist theories $T = T_0, T_1, \ldots, T_n = T'$ such that T_{i+1} is obtained from T_i ($i = 0, \ldots, n-1$) by introducing a defined (relation or function) symbol. Then $T \leq T'$ by using the composability of conservative extensions. Moreover, by composing, in the obvious way, the translations corresponding to the individual definitions, we can translate formulae of T' to corresponding formulae of T.

Definitions are not, however, the most common form of conservative extension used in building specifications. For example, earlier in this section we extended a specification of natural numbers to one for (finite) sets of natural numbers. Although the extension is conservative, it is not an extension by definitions. Thus there is no way of translating a formula containing function and relation symbols from L_{set} (and L_{nat}) to one containing only symbols from L_{nat}. We would be very surprised if we could! A very important research topic of major practical importance is the characterization of various forms of extension which are guaranteed to be conservative.

2.3.6 Translation

Extension and, particularly, conservative extension, as discussed so far in this section, is one of the two main tools we have for building logical descriptions. The other is a property-preserving translation between logical descriptions (theories), i.e. *interpretations between theories*. We are all familiar with the structure-preserving mappings (homomorphisms) which are used in translating from one mathematical structure (a group, say) to another structure of the same kind. What is meant in these cases is that the properties of the structure being mapped are preserved (or extended) as a result of representing (via the homomorphism) the original structure as a substructure of the resulting one.

What corresponds to 'structure' in a given linguistic system is theory and what corresponds to structure-preserving mapping is interpretation between theories. Property preservation will correspond to maintaining or preserving under translation the provability of formulae stated in the original (domain) theory. To define interpretations between theories, we will proceed in stages, defining interpretations (or translations) between two (extralogical) languages L and L' of PC, between a language L of PC and a theory T' of PC, and finally between theories T and T' of PC. We then extend these ideas to MPC, many sorted first-order logic.

An *interpretation I* of L in L', denoted

$$I: L \to L'$$

consists of

1. a unary relation symbol N of L', called the *relativization predicate* for I;
2. a mapping π from the function and relation symbols of L to those of L' which preserves the rank of the symbols, so n-adic function symbols of L are mapped to n-adic symbols of L' and n-adic relation symbols are mapped to n-adic relation symbols.

Given such an interpretation I, we may define a translation of terms of L to those of L', also denoted by I, as in

$$I: Term(L) \to Term(L')$$

We can extend I to map formulae of L to those of L', again denoting this translation by I as in

$$I: Form(L) \to Form(L')$$

Given an n-adic formula A of L, we have

$$A^{\mathrm{I}} = ((N(x_1) \& \ldots \& N(x_n)) \Rightarrow A^{\mathrm{trI}}) \tag{2.38}$$

where *trI* maps formulae of L to those of L' and $x_1, \ldots, x_n$ are the (distinct) variables free in the formula A.

$$trI: Form(L) \to Form(L')$$

is defined recursively as in the Appendix, Section A.7.

I maps symbols (including variables) of L to corresponding symbols of L', 'commutes' with the logical connectives, and relativizes the existential and universal quantifiers (rules (4) and (5) defining *trI* in the Appendix) as well as the ranges of the free variables appearing in formulae being translated (as in 2.38).

The relativization of the quantifiers and ranges of free variables referred to in the paragraph above requires some explanation. As usual in logic, variables are place holders for which we substitute values. 'Syntactic' values are terms and 'semantic' values are objects from underlying sets in logical structures. Suppose we have an interpretation $I: L \to L'$. We will refer to L as the *abstract* language and L' as the *concrete* language[†].

Given I, we can translate a term t over L to t^I over L', where variables appearing in t are translated to variables appearing in t'. Suppose that we want to substitute a term tI for some variable in t. We could get the same effect by substituting tI^I for the corresponding variable in t^I. So substitution involving terms of L can be simulated by substitution involving the translated formula[‡].

However, should we be allowed to substitute any term over L' into t^I, i.e. into a translated formula? The definition of substitution certainly allows us to do this, but, if using L' we want to mirror what we were doing using L, then clearly we have to somehow *relativize* (i.e. restrict) the range of variables appearing in translated formulae, such as t^I, to those terms which are also translations. The relativization predicate is meant to play this rôle.

The same considerations apply to the translation of formulae. Furthermore, when we translate quantified formulae, the range of the variables being quantified should also be relativized when translated. More on this later, when we discuss interpretations between theories.

Now, an *interpretation* $I: L \to T'$ of a language L in a theory $T' = \langle L', G' \rangle$ is an interpretation

$$I: L \to L'$$

from the language L to the language L' of the theory T' such that

$$G' \vdash \mathbf{E}xN(x) \tag{2.39}$$

and

$$G' \vdash (N(x_1) \& \ldots \& N(x_n)) \Rightarrow N(\pi(f)(x_1, \ldots, x_n)) \tag{2.40}$$

for each function symbol f in L.

The condition (2.39) requires that the domain defined by the relativization predicate (i.e. the set of those values which satisfy the relation

---

[†] Note, however, that these adjectives are relative in that L' may also then be translated to L'' and thus become the abstract language in a translation.

[‡] The reader may like to formulate this as a theorem and try to prove it.

defined by it) should be non-empty, and that this fact should be provable in T'. The second condition, (2.40), requires that the application of the translated function, $\pi(f)$, to values satisfying the relativization predicate (as assured by the antecedent of the implication) results in a value which also satisfies the relativization predicate. In short, (2.40) says that the domain of values defined by the relativization predicate is closed under *translated* functions.

As a final stage of our development we define an *interpretation between theories*

$$I: T \rightarrow T'$$

as an interpretation $I: L \rightarrow T'$ (with L being the language of T) such that for each A with $G \vdash A$ (G being the axioms that define T), we have

$$G' \vdash A^{I}$$

In particular, the translation of each of the axioms defining T is itself a consequence of the axioms defining the target theory T'.

As an example, consider the following. Let L be the language of natural numbers (with somewhat non-standard syntax): *nought* is a constant (i.e. a function of no arguments), *addone* is a monadic function and $=_L$ is a diadic relation symbol. Let G be:

$$\vdash \neg(addone(x) =_L nought) \tag{2.41}$$
$$\vdash (addone(x) =_L addone(y)) \Rightarrow x =_L y \tag{2.42}$$

together with the usual axioms defining equality. Let $T = \langle L, G \rangle$. Now consider L' with *zero* a constant, *suc* and *pred* monadic function symbols, *nonneg* a monadic relation symbol, and $=_{L'}$ a diadic relation symbol. Let G' be:

$$\vdash (suc(x) =_{L'} suc(y)) \Rightarrow x =_{L'} y \tag{2.43}$$
$$\vdash (pred(x) =_{L'} pred(y)) \Rightarrow x =_{L'} y \tag{2.44}$$
$$\vdash pred(suc(x)) =_{L'} x \tag{2.45}$$
$$\vdash suc(pred(x)) =_{L'} x \tag{2.46}$$
$$\vdash nonneg(x) \Rightarrow nonneg(suc(x)) \tag{2.47}$$
$$\vdash nonneg(zero) \tag{2.48}$$
$$\vdash \neg nonneg(pred(zero)) \tag{2.49}$$

and the usual axioms for $=_{L'}$.

Let $T' = \langle L', G' \rangle$. Define

$$I: L \rightarrow T'$$

by:

1. The relativization predicate is *nonneg*;

2. π is defined by the table:

symbol	π(symbol)
nought	*zero*
addone	*suc*
$=_L$	$=_{L'}$

To demonstrate that I defines an interpretation from L to T', we must verify (2.39) and (2.40). For the former, we must show that

$G' \vdash \textbf{Ex}\,(nonneg(x))$

In view of (2.48)

$G' \vdash nonneg(zero)$

the result clearly follows. For the latter, we must demonstrate (2.40) for both the image of *nought* and *addone*. For the former, remembering that *nought* is a constant, we must show

$G' \vdash nonneg(\pi(nought))$

i.e.

$G' \vdash nonneg(zero)$

which is the axiom (2.48). For *addone*, we must show

$G' \vdash nonneg(x) \Rightarrow nonneg(\pi(addone)(x))$

which is

$G' \vdash nonneg(x) \Rightarrow nonneg(suc(x))$

This is again an axiom, (2.47).

Thus

$I \colon L \to T'$

is an interpretation of the language L in the theory T'.

We said earlier that interpretations between theories are property-preserving translations; the example considered above will be used to illustrate the meaning of this statement. Before proceeding, we present the following methodologically interesting result.

Interpretation theorem

If $I \colon L \to T'$ is an interpretation of L in T' and $T = \langle L, G \rangle$, then I is an interpretation of T in T' if and only if for each A in G, $G' \vdash A^I$.

Thus, to check if $I \colon T \to T'$ is an interpretation between theories, it is sufficient to check that for each A in G, $G' \vdash A^I$ holds. In our example, we have to show that the translations of (2.41) and (2.42) (and of the axioms defining equality in G) follow from G'.

Consider (2.41):

$(\neg(addone(x) =_{\mathrm{L}} nought))^{I}$
$= nonneg(x) \Rightarrow (\neg((\pi(addone)(x)) \pi(=_{\mathrm{L}}) (\pi(nought))))$
$= nonneg(x) \Rightarrow (\neg(suc(x) =_{\mathrm{L}'} zero))$

We must show

$$G' \vdash nonneg(x) \Rightarrow (\neg(suc(x) =_{\mathrm{L}'} zero)) \qquad (2.50)$$

As for (2.42), after applying I, we must show

$$G' \vdash nonneg(x) \Rightarrow (nonneg(y) \Rightarrow ((suc(x) =_{\mathrm{L}'} suc(y)) \Rightarrow (x =_{\mathrm{L}'} y)))$$

This clearly follows from (2.43). We leave to the reader the proof of (2.50) (and the proofs involving the axioms for equality).

2.3.7 Composability

We now come to a very crucial property of interpretations between theories, which permits the building of translations bit by bit, using small 'steps', and the composing of the steps to get the 'big' translation we want. Our notion of stepwise refinement (see Sections 4.2 and 4.3) will depend crucially on this result.

Consider two interpretations between theories

$$I: T \to T'$$

and

$$I': T' \to T''$$

with $T = \langle L, G \rangle$, $T' = \langle L', G' \rangle$, $T'' = \langle L'', G'' \rangle$; I defined in terms of the relativization predicate N and mapping π; and I' defined in terms of relativization predicate N' and mapping π'. Then, we define the composition $I \cdot I'$ of I and I' as follows:

1. The relativization predicate for $I \cdot I'$ is $N'(x)$ & $\pi(N)$ (x).

2. The map from symbols of L to those of L'' is $\pi \cdot \pi'$ (the obvious composition of π and π').

First of all, let us admit that (1) is a bit of a cheat. We originally defined an interpretation in terms of a monadic relation symbol, called the *relativization predicate*. Here, we use a formula, $N'(x)$ & $\pi(N)(x)$, in the rôle of the relativization predicate. In fact, we want to loosen our definition of relativization predicate to accept a formula with a single free variable.

To justify the choice of the relativization predicate for the composed interpretation, consider the translation of $\mathrm{Ex}A$ — a formula of L:

$$((\mathbf{E}xA)^I)^{I'} = (\mathbf{E}x(N(x) \mathbin{\&} A^{trI}))^{I'}$$
$$= \mathbf{E}x(N'(x) \mathbin{\&} (\pi(N)(x) \mathbin{\&} (A^{trI})^{trI'}))$$
$$\Leftrightarrow \mathbf{E}x((N'(x) \mathbin{\&} \pi(N)(x)) \mathbin{\&} (A^{trI})^{trI'})$$

Now consider translating $\mathbf{A}xA$:

$$((\mathbf{A}xA)^I)^{I'} = (\mathbf{A}x(N(x) \Rightarrow A^{trI}))^{I'}$$
$$= \mathbf{A}x(N'(x) \Rightarrow (\pi(N)(x) \Rightarrow (A^{trI})^{trI'}))$$
$$\Leftrightarrow \mathbf{A}x((N'(x) \mathbin{\&} \pi(N)(x)) \Rightarrow (A^{trI})^{trI'})$$

Thus, in both cases we arrive at formulae of the appropriate form with $N'(x) \mathbin{\&} \pi(N)(x)$ playing the rôle of relativization predicate[†].

We can now state results concerning composition of interpretations between theories, such as:

Theorem on associativity

Given $Ii: Ti \to Ti + 1$, for $i = 0, 1, 2,$

$$I0 \cdot (I1 \cdot I2) = (I0 \cdot I1) \cdot I2$$

i.e. composition of interpretations is associative.

If $N1, N2, N3$ are the relativization predicates corresponding to $I0$, $I1$, $I2$, respectively, then the relativization predicate corresponding to either way of composing the three interpretations is

$$N3(x) \mathbin{\&} \pi2(N2)(x) \mathbin{\&} \pi2(\pi1(N1))(x)$$

where $\pi1$ and $\pi2$ are the maps from symbols to symbols corresponding to the interpretations $I1$ and $I2$ respectively. The fact that this is so, of course, depends crucially on the fact that the logical connective & itself is associative.

2.3.8 Extension to MPC

Finally, we need an extension of our definition of interpretations between theories to many sorted first-order logic, MPC. Recall that a many-sorted language is a pair $\langle S, L \rangle$ where S is a set of sorts and L is a set of extralogical symbols typed using only the sorts from S. Sorts correspond to the different kinds of values we might want to consider in a logical description, and using sorts to type function and relation symbols tells us which arguments are expected to be of what sort and, in the case of functions, what is the sort of the result of applying the function. Given

---

[†] In fact, at an intuitive level it is clear that in any models of T, T' and T'', N defines a subset of the values in the model corresponding to T', N' defines a subset of the values in the model corresponding to T'', and the translation of N to T'' must define a subset of that defined by N'. The reader may care to think this through, perhaps via some diagrams.

two such languages $\langle S, L \rangle$ and $\langle S', L' \rangle$, and letting $s, a, b, \ldots, c$ be sorts of S and $a', b', \ldots, c'$ be sorts of S', we define an interpretation

$$I: \langle S, L \rangle \rightarrow \langle S', L' \rangle$$

in terms of the following maps:

1. $\varphi: S \rightarrow (S')^+$, mapping each sort of S to a (non-empty) sequence of sorts in S'. Allowing a bit of looseness in notation, we often say that φ maps $s \in S$ to a tuple of sorts $\langle a', b', \ldots, c' \rangle$ of S'. If the sequence of sorts corresponding to $s \in S$ is of length one (i.e. a one-tuple), we identify this sequence with the sort which is its single component.

2. π, mapping function symbols in L to sequences (or tuples) of function symbols over L', respecting the mapping of sorts φ. Thus for f in L of type

$$\langle \langle a, b, \ldots, c \rangle, s \rangle$$

we have

$$\pi(f) = \langle f', g', \ldots, h' \rangle$$

with

f' of type $\langle \varphi(a) \cdot \varphi(b) \cdot \ldots \cdot \varphi(c), a' \rangle$
g' of type $\langle \varphi(a) \cdot \varphi(b) \cdot \ldots \cdot \varphi(c), b' \rangle$
$\vdots$
h' of type $\langle \varphi(a) \cdot \varphi(b) \cdot \ldots \cdot \varphi(c), c' \rangle$

where $\varphi(s) = \langle a', b', \ldots, c' \rangle$. So the typing of arguments of each of the $f', g', \ldots, h'$ is the same and is obtained by simply applying the mapping φ to each of the argument sorts of f in turn[†]. Corresponding to s, the result sort of f, we have a tuple of sorts $\langle a', b', \ldots, c' \rangle$ and each of the $f', g', \ldots, h'$ delivers the value of the corresponding sort $a', b', \ldots, c'$.

3. π mapping a relation symbol of L to one of L' with typing explained as above for function symbols. (Note, we do not need a result for relations and hence we do not need to map one relation symbol to many relation symbols.)

4. $\rho: S \rightarrow L'$ mapping each sort s of S to a relativization predicate N_s with type $\varphi(s)$.

5. v mapping variables of sort s in S to tuples of variables over S'. For $\varphi(s) = \langle a', b', \ldots, c' \rangle$, a variable x of sort s is mapped to the tuple of variables $\langle x'_{a'}, \ldots, x'_{c'} \rangle$. This mapping should be one to one.

[†] Note that composition of sequences is in fact their concatenation, as in $\langle a, b \rangle \cdot \langle c, d \rangle = \langle a, b, c, d \rangle$.

Thus, whereas in PC interpretations mapped single values (terms) to single values, in MPC a single value may be mapped to a tuple of values. (Thus a stack may be represented by an array and a pointer or index into the array, or an integer may be represented by a natural number and a sign.) The definition of π reflects the fact that a function symbol in L, whose target sort is mapped to a tuple of sorts $\langle a', b', \ldots, c' \rangle$, is itself mapped to a tuple of function symbols to take into account the fact that the image must return a number of values. Also notice that in PC the number of arguments of a function or relation symbol was preserved under translation, whereas this is clearly not the case with many-sorted languages. Similarly, we are now forced to take into account what happens to variables under translation. Clearly the constraint on the map v being one to one is meant to prevent the accidental identification of distinct variables by the translation process. Again, whereas we had one relativization predicate in PC, we now need one for each sort in the domain language. Moreover, these predicates need no longer be monadic.

For further discussion of the many-sorted case and for suitable examples, the reader is referred to Section A.7 of the Appendix and Chapter 4, where interpretations play a crucial rôle in explaining what we mean by implementation and refinement.

Chapter 3 Relationships between Specifications and Programs

3.1 Specification languages and programming languages

Programming languages are the most widely used means of expressing solutions to problems intended for computer execution. The reader is no doubt familiar with some programming languages: FORTRAN, Pascal, COBOL, BASIC, Ada, Algol 60, Prolog, Algol 68, LISP, SIMULA, etc.

In Section 2.2 we briefly introduced a specification language Clear. Specification languages are a less widely known (and used) means of expressing problems eventually to be solved by executing a computer program written in a programming language. Specifications are often presented by diagrams, not always strictly formalized, by 'plain prose' requirements, or by a variety of other means, including references to existing software systems ('I want a system like ABC Ltd is using for their payroll, except mine should run on the XYZ computer and print direct bank transfer notes').

Thus, on the surface, it appears that the process of problem solving with computer assistance requires two kinds of languages: one to describe problems (in specification languages), and another to describe solutions (in programming languages). It also appears that the current practice supports a variety of instances of each kind.

Insofar as programming languages are concerned, the existing (and growing) variety is often explained, indeed justified, by claiming that particular languages have specific features which make them exceptionally well suited for particular classes of problems in hand. Almost by definition this applies to problem-oriented languages, designed to ease the task of programming in particular environments, i.e. to describe solutions for problems related to a well understood domain, solutions that consist of combinations of a certain number of predefined routines. Both the routines and the meaningful patterns in which they can be combined are discovered by study of the application domain. Usually, the quality of a problem-oriented language reflects the quality of problem-domain analysis that led to the language design. Occasionally, a problem-oriented language transcends the boundaries of a domain for which it was conceived and assumes a wider role. Such is the case of LISP, a language intended for list processing, and now widely used for almost all programming in the area of artificial intelligence. The example of LISP nicely illustrates a general principle: a problem-oriented language intended for a particular application area gains wider applicability through a combination of two factors. First, it must be a well designed language supported by well engineered implementations; second, the original application area must be capable of being employed as a linguistic level well suited for description of a large variety of structures. Since many artificial intelligence problems can be nicely described in terms of lists and list-processing operations, LISP, in which list processing is easy to write about, became the lingua franca of the artificial intelligence community.

Even with programming languages designed for general use, the survival of quite a few bears witness to perceived advantages each of them possesses. It is beside the point to argue that, say, programming language A is better than programming language B if both these languages are in reasonably common use. The very fact that a population of programmers finds B easier to use (or is more familiar with B, or the computing facilities at their disposal are better controlled by B, or B is more efficiently implemented on the installation they are obliged to patronize) is a sufficient justification for B's continuing use. Apart from a handful of highly technical issues, the programming language is not a goal to be achieved, not an end in itself, but merely a means of description, a medium of expression. The actual choice of such a medium is most often dictated by a great number of trivial factors, very specific to a particular environment; indeed, *ceteris paribus*, by a programmer's predilections that reflect his education and career just as much as his current knowledge.

Thus, unless there are technical differences between programming languages which make an objective expressible in one and inexpressible in another, the choice is (and will remain) largely dependent on matters of taste. This is almost certain to guarantee proliferation of programming languages as new ones are being designed while an ever growing body of professional and casual programmers alike accumulate their individual preferences and objections.

Naturally, even within the class of universal programming languages, there are sufficiently serious technical differences that account for fairly commonly appreciated differences in their scopes of applicability. It is, say, quite awkward to describe character processing in FORTRAN, or express a concurrent bunch of processes in Pascal. This pretty obvious observation points to another general comment, viz. that a programming language, even patently designed to be universal, may lack certain primitives, without which it is unreasonably difficult to describe well understood concepts, operations and processes. Incidentally, it is almost always possible to bypass the lack of a primitive by using some elementary facility of the language. It is possible, for example, to program character processing in FORTRAN by considering integer codes for each representable character and designing appropriate subroutines. No one would consider it elegant or easy, though, even if the resulting package turned out to be efficient and robust. We are inclined to consider such a bypass as an example of programming simultaneously on two distinct levels: that on which characters appear as integer codes and that on which results of suitable subroutines are apparent. A programming language collapses these two levels into one − FORTRAN level − not without ensuing confusion. On the other hand, some primitives cannot be added within a programming language: there is no way to express simultaneous execution of two or more sequences of Pascal statements in Pascal itself, although it may be possible to simulate such a course of events, i.e. describe a calculation which, insofar as an indicated set of criteria is considered, yields the same results as a simultaneously run collection of calculations. In the latter case, as usual with simulation, it is important to notice that meaningful comparisons are possible only for *a priori* indicated observabilia; no attempt to observe any analogies between 'serial' and 'parallel' executions as seen via criteria other than the *a priori* indicated ones can be guaranteed to succeed; indeed, cannot be considered as well designed.

Thus we are led to a dual view of universal programming languages: as a means of description of a wide class of computations and as a somewhat limited means of construction of such descriptive means.

The duality of the programming language rôle is not always noticed. As a consequence, either one or another aspect is considered as the main one, often to the exclusion of the other. Similarly, the activity of programming, especially when conducted entirely within a single programming language, is viewed in an unnecessarily restricted way, viz. as an activity within a fixed set of concepts, or, much less frequently, as an activity that entirely consists in development of concepts. Tradition has it that most industrial programmers, operating within a single programming language, hold the first view, while academic writing tends to present programming in a programming language as a sequence of development steps. The duality of views being unobserved, we readily see here ingredients of a major 'cultural' clash!

Specification languages, as mentioned above, are much less widely used in industrial environments, and those that are used seldom have an appearance even remotely resembling familiar programming languages. (For one thing, the relatively popular specification languages are pictorial rather than verbal.) Thus there is much less scope for any duality of use: in the industrial environment, a specification language is used, if at all, for presentation of requirements, or, more recently, for description of a software component. In more academically minded environments, a specification language is used for design purposes, including development through several steps, but much less frequently, if at all, for actual implementation work. Indeed, the very notion that a specification language could be used as an actual implementation tool appears sufficiently alien not to cause much culture clash.

Following, as we are in this book, the view that the entire process of software design and implementation is a chain of linguistic transformations (see Lehman *et al.*, 1984), one can envisage this process as a sequence of steps, each of which is an implementation of the design posited by a starting representation (described in a current base linguistic system) in another (call it target) linguistic system. The mathematics of such a step is founded on the principles presented in Section 2.3; the technical details are presented in Chapter 4. At the moment we are satisfied with a global view of the design/implementation process, seen as a path from initial conceptual requirements to executable code (microcode), a path consisting of homogeneous links. Thus in every completed design/implementation process quite a few linguistic levels are involved.

The linguistic levels involved in a completed design/implementation process can be *a posteriori* ordered, say by increasing degree of detail (decreasing granularity) of description, or by increasing closeness to the ultimate implementation level. This ordering roughly, but not necessarily exactly, corresponds to the time order in which the design/implementation steps are actually taken. Ideally, a programmer/designer inventing (adopting, choosing) the current target linguistic level for the current transformation step is not only guided by the intention to bring the design/implementation closer to the ultimate level, but also makes no error of judgement in his selection. Should this be the case, the ordering of levels of the completed design would follow the time sequence of levels used. In practice, the design/implementation process is likely to contain loops (backtracking in Lehman *et al.*, 1984) and (partly) misguided steps which, even though never formally backtracked, with hindsight can be considerably straightened, and a sequence of which can be made to look much more purposeful than the actual historic sequence of steps taken.

In fact, the published multistep designs suffer by the authors' (successful) attempts to prettify the design by presenting an idealized sequence of levels. Published designs are seldom, if ever, true protocols of the design as it happened; the idealized versions of 'the design as it should have been developed' are in a sense quite misleading, certainly from the didactic point of view[†]. This is especially true when the author does not

---

[†] In this connection it is, perhaps, instructive to relate a story one of the recognized software engineering experts is fond of telling. Years ago, when as a young graduate student he was admitted into the inner sanctum of one of the better maths departments, he was acutely tempted to study the contents of discarded notes and scribbles of famous mathematicians. Ever since, he recalls, the record of rejected paths of reasoning tells him more about the real nature of the problem than the sanitized *ex post* presentation.

make explicit the principle he is following in preparation of the published version of the design, or when the avowed principle is patently impossible to apply *a priori*, i.e. when faced with a (near) continuum of choices.

In his seminal paper on layered design (of operating systems) Dijkstra (1968) chooses as an ordering criterion the order of magnitude estimates of timings of operations considered as primitives on a particular level. This principle, clear and unambiguous as it is, explains very nicely the layered structure of the completed design; it is quite easy to see why such and such a primitive belongs to this and this level, or, conversely, given two levels, to establish their mutual positions. It would be, however, virtually impossible to apply this criterion as a guide in choosing the target level of a current design/implementation step: the knowledge that the target level primitives are to correspond to operations consuming less time to execute than the operations that correspond to the current base level primitives does not amount to much. It should be added that Dijkstra (1968) makes no claim to propose a principle for step-by-step design; the paper concentrates on hierarchical structure of the completed software product and the duration-of-execution principle is meant to be the one that explains layering of the final product. To conclude the analysis of this example, one is entitled, perhaps, to observe that the hierarchical layering of a finished software product need not correspond with levels of design, sanitized or actual. On the other hand, a tempting hypothesis, stating that a step-by-step design/implementation, executed as a design of linguistic transformations, will certainly be reflected in hierarchical layering of the complete product, is − at the moment − not yet sufficiently investigated. As a corollary, one could venture to say that it is exactly the tendency to present the design sequence of levels as hierarchical layers of the ultimate product which is responsible for the grossest deviation of published 'design protocols' from actual 'design histories'.

One way or another, a completed design/implementation of a software product is presented as a sequence of constructs expressed in a number of linguistic levels, the sequence of levels being ordered in some meaningful way. It is natural to expect that the linguistic levels employed to describe early constructs bear a close resemblance to specification languages, whereas linguistic levels employed to describe final constructs are a lot like programming languages. Indeed, this observation is vacuously correct if we take into consideration the very first and the very last linguistic constructs in the chain: we do start from a specification and end up with a program; however they are expressed, the linguistic means used for expressing a specification is a specification language (by definition!) and the linguistic means used for expressing a program are a programming language (ditto).

Thus, contemplating a completed design/implementation as presented by a chain of linguistic transformations, we cannot avoid observing that as the process progressed (actually or in prettified exposition) the linguistic levels employed for recording achieved progress change from specification to programming languages. If we believe in representing (or viewing) the design/implementation process as a succession of a large number of small steps rather than a small number of large steps, the changeover from specification to programming languages can be neither sharply defined nor abrupt. It is much more realistic to expect that as the design/implementation process progresses the linguistic levels assume more and more the familiar programming flavour.

But is it not true that 'programming languages are executable, whereas specification ones aren't'? Well, we would like to object to the quoted sentence, despite its almost visceral acceptance throughout the computing community. A minor objection, call it pedantic, pertains to the fact that no language, not even COBOL, is, strictly speaking, executable. It is *programs* in COBOL that are (hopefully) executable!

A major objection relates to the use of 'executable'. As often is the case, a commonly used word is employed without much attention being paid to its exact meaning in the particular context in which it appears. Surely, nobody will object if we call

> **begin** x, y: **integer**;
> $read(x)$;
> $y := x + 1$;   (3.1)
> $print(y)$
> **end**

an executable program.

If we do so, however, we silently accept some rather important assumptions. We presume that (3.1) is a correct (well formed) program in a programming language. To fix our attention, let us call this language EPROL. (Whether EPROL stands for the name of a well known programming language or designates our favourite new-generation, high-power language is quite irrelevant: in either case a very thorough familiarity with EPROL is subsumed in the statement that announces (3.1) executable. That such familiarity is usually lacking is yet another indication of how flippantly such statements are made and how credulously they are accepted.)

We also presume that the semantics of EPROL is sufficiently well defined to allow at least *some* interpretation of (3.1) in terms of some − also presumed! − elementary 'actions', 'operations' or 'events'. In short, we presume the availability of some domain in which (3.1) can be valuated.

Most importantly, we presume that (3.1), when applied to suitable data, will produce some results. We expect this to happen also for any reasonable interpretation of (3.1). In addition, we trust that application of interpreted (3.1) to suitable objects in the valuation domain will result

in expected phenomena only. (For example, for a not unusual interpretation, in which $read(x)$ is interpreted as the assignment to integer-
valued object named x of a concrete value delivered by an input device,
etc., we would be quite surprised if the interpretation of the := operator
was such as to destroy all input devices in addition to the usual value
assignment.)

Leaving aside all the less important assumptions of executability of
(3.1), let us concentrate on the central one, viz. on the applicability of
(3.1) to data. (In the following we shall also disregard the interpretation
issues.) 'Executability' of (3.1) seems to imply the same as saying

$$output = y \ \& \ y = x + 1 \ \& \ x = input \ \& \ x, y \in \textbf{integer} \tag{3.2}$$

The formula (3.2) can be simplified, e.g. by elimination of variables x, y;
but so could program (3.1), at least in some languages, and since in fact it
was not, its actual form must have been preferred for some reason. For
the same reason we keep the apparently redundant form of (3.2). (It is
almost certain that some readers would have preferred (3.2) to be written
as

$$x, y \in \textbf{integer} \ \& \ x = input \ \& \ y = x + 1 \ \& \ output = y \tag{3.3}$$

OK, we do not mind.)

Not all programs can be converted into formulae similar to (3.2) just
as easily, but some conversion of this sort must be possible if the meaning
of a program is to be expressible in terms other than purely operational
ones, related to a particular executing agent.

Observe that (3.2), or naturally equivalent (3.3), can be viewed in
two ways: it may be recognized as a fairly legal program in a non-
imperative programming language (e.g. it is very much like a PROLOG
program, apart from syntactic details), or it may be considered as a fairly
typical input/output specification expressed in a language based on first-
order logic. As a non-imperative program it is, of course, eminently
executable by suitable machinery, e.g. provided by a compiler of a
PROLOG-like language on a quite conventional computer. Thus, even if
we are inclined to consider (3.2) as a specification, it is an executable
specification.

With some justification it may be argued that the form of (3.1)
implies a different notion of execution than that of (3.3), say. We are
entitled to expect that the execution of an EPROL program will consist in
reading-in a value from an input device, putting this value into a box
identified by x, taking a copy of the value from x-box, inserting its
successor into a similar box identified by y, taking a copy of the value
contained in y-box and outputting it through an output device. But we are
not entitled to make any assumptions with respect to the nature of boxes
and devices, apart from those stated in (3.1), explicitly or implicitly. Thus
it is legitimate to assume that boxes are identifiable, that there are at least

two different boxes capable of storing an integer value each, that once a value is attached to a box, no matter how many copies of that value are made, the value will not change unless we explicitly say so. We also may expect that once $y := x + 1$ is executed, the previous value associated with the y-box is not observable any more. This implies, of course, that the execution of (3.1) respects (partial) order of statements in EPROL programs. But no expectations with respect to actual timing of statement executions can be considered legitimate.

On the other hand, (3.2) patently disregards any ordering between conjuncts. Under the circumstances, can we still consider (3.2) as equivalent to (3.1)? Yes, if we identify program execution with observable effects in a space of named objects. No, if we identify program execution with unnamed processes that take place during the execution. A form like (3.3) is very poorly suited for specification of a process. But the form (3.1) is not a good process description either. There are better languages than EPROL in which to describe (or prescribe) processes.

The hair-splitting argument about the sense in which (3.1) and (3.2) can be considered equivalent is relevant to our present concerns only in so far as the objections to the claimed executability of (3.2) can be based on dissatisfaction with respect to the way in which (3.2) could be executed. Incidentally, when we say that (3.2) is as much *executable* as (3.1) we do not claim that (3.2) is *executed* in the same way as (3.1); thus, in principle, we could avoid all such objections. If we followed the argument at some length, it was in order to illustrate once more the scope of possible misunderstandings that arise from flippant use of ill-considered terms. As an added bonus we were able to show how smooth could be the transition between a 'program' and a 'specification': (3.2) could be considered as both, and it would be extremely difficult to set up an unbiased criterion to decide in favour of one or other classification.

The above discussion makes one wonder if the notion of executability should not be defined more carefully. (It certainly should, if it is to be used in a technical argument, rather than just in a shouting match.)

For example, one could observe that the process of drawing conclusions from a formula (or a set of formulae) is a possible candidate for a universally applicable process of execution. Of course the kind of conclusions one draws depends on the actual formula, but also on the linguistic system in which the formula is expressed. Thus, while such a notion of execution is universal, in practical terms it refers to different 'things' when linguistic systems differ.

As the linguistic level ('language') in which a formula is written always subsumes a linguistic system, a correctly formed formula will always have an appropriate, particular context in which the particular meaning of execution could be realized.

For example, one could envisage the notion of execution, appropriate for EPROL, according to which application of program (3.1) to input value 3 results in output value 4, with values of integer variables x and y being, respectively, 3 and 4. In other words, execution of (3.1) in a state satisfying *input* = 3 results in a state satisfying *output* = 4 & x = 3 & y = 4.

Similarly, execution of (3.2) in an environment where *input* = 3 & *output* = 5 will result in *false*, whereas in an environment where *input* = 3 & x = 3 & y = 4 & *output* = 4 it will yield as a consequence *true* (for the sake of simplicity, we disregard the type information).

More interestingly, we could say that executing (3.1) establishes the truth of (3.2), while executing (3.2) differentiates between states that satisfy (3.2) and those that do not.

We shall not pursue this point any further here, nor shall we be bothered by the criticism that the design/implementation chain cannot be viewed as consisting of homogeneous steps as it progresses from 'non-executable' specifications to 'executable' programs. We hope the reader is convinced that this criticism carries no more weight than saying that along the chain the particular notion of executability changes, being strictly related to the linguistic systems employed.

On the other hand, it would be foolish not to recognize the pragmatic differences between the languages employed in early steps of the design/implementation chain ('specification' languages) and those that are used in the final steps ('programming' languages). The differences are related to the sort of consequences of the formulae one wishes to draw and investigate, and therefore reflect the guiding principles of linguistic levels. In sections 3.4 and 3.5 we shall consider how objects built on early levels (specifications) can be interpreted as 'programs' and objects built on the final levels (programs) as 'specifications'.

3.2 Permissiveness and its limitations

In Section 2.1 we indicated two major distinct flavours of incompleteness (understood as non-deducibility of some sentences or their negations from axioms of a theory). They were, let us recall, related to insufficiency of factual information contained in the axioms and to a terminological mismatch. The latter cause could have been considered purely technical, were it not for the case in which it is precisely the absence of suitable term-defining axioms that leads to the terminological incompleteness. In this case, even though incompleteness of the theory appears purely terminological, and as such is perhaps easier to detect when a sample sentence is exhibited, one would be equally justified in attributing this instance of incompleteness to insufficiency of information contained in the axioms. Thus, in the present section we shall discuss the completeness issue primarily from the point of view of having sufficient axioms to characterize that in which we are interested.

Early on in this book, we pointed out that certain technical terms, despite their technical status, carry emotional loads, and that when discussing matters identified by such terms one is subconsciously biased by an instinctive dislike of the state of affairs labelled by a term that carries a negative emotional charge. Surely the term 'incomplete' is one that is tainted by negative emotions. In Maibaum and Turski (1984), we have therefore introduced the term 'permissive' to describe a linguistic level that allows some sentences to be neither theorems nor antitheorems ('theorem' being a sentence deducible from a set of axioms, 'antitheorem' a sentence whose negation is so deducible). Naturally, we do recognize that 'permissive' (and 'permissiveness') itself is an emotionally loaded term; indeed, perhaps even more so than 'incomplete'. The advantage of using the term 'permissive' rests in that, while it certainly is not emotionally neutral, its perception is not universal. To some people 'permissive' is rather good, to others, quite bad. Hence the reader, being most likely aware of the ambivalent emotional valuation of the term, is apt to attach more significance to its technical content than to the familiar and uncontested intuitions ('permissive' − what the heck do they mean by *that*?, rather than: 'incomplete' − oh, yeah, I know).

What activity are we actually engaged in when we try to build a specification or linguistic level? It is often termed 'abstraction from detail' or just 'abstraction'. But what is this process of abstraction and what can we say about the nature of the product of the process of abstraction − i.e. specifications or linguistic levels? Let us look first at analogies with other related subject areas.

In mathematics, the most common use of the term is in the context of generalization − the 'abstract' in abstract algebra. So mathematicians ignore the details of real numbers, complex numbers, rationals, etc., and study fields; ignore the details of permutations, invertible matrices, etc., and study groups. Two important aspects of this process should be noted. Firstly, the extralogical language used in the axiomatization of the abstract theory is not really a product of the abstraction process − it is fixed beforehand, although the abstract syntax may not be. Secondly, the details which are ignored are the model-based details − reals, permutation groups, . . .

In science, one is generally in the business of trying to model some aspect of the world mathematically. This often involves defining a 'theory' in the sense of a logical theory. Such mathematical modelling also involves ignoring detail but often in a very different sense from that noted in mathematics. 'Ignoring of detail' here might be better called 'idealization', e.g. in ignoring friction or associating mass with points in space. This is quite different from generalization and its 'ignoring of detail'.

Creating a specification of a program or system involves the creation of an axiomatic theory $\langle L, G \rangle$ in some logic. There are three important and interrelated choices to be made in the process: the choice of the logic, the choice of the extralogical symbols L, and the choice of the axiomatic theory G. As noted above, in mathematics generalization involves a choice of the presentation and sometimes the logic. However, the rôle of the presentation is less central — it is the theory generated which is important. For most mathematicians, the choice of logic is automatic — the subject area's traditions suggest it. New extralogical languages are invented infrequently, only when a new branch of mathematics is being developed. The role of a theory presentation in mathematics is to provide a framework for detailed analysis of the theory defined, for comparison of theory presentations, and for studying the relationships between theories. Theories, if at all validated, are validated against existing models or, sometimes, theories.

Scientists invent theories for a different reason. They are trying to model observable phenomena in the world and hence their criteria of acceptability are quite different from those of mathematics. For the latter, it is judgements of intellectual interest and challenge which are relevant. For the former, it is the descriptive and predictive power of the theory which is important. Moreover, scientific theories can only be invalidated by failing to conform to observation. Mathematical theories, on the other hand, can at best be interesting or uninteresting. Scientists hardly ever invent new logics and the extralogical languages they use do not change much as they are fixed by the part of the world being modelled. They do engage in a lot of theory validation, refinement and modification.

Specification building is a lot like theory construction in science. A theory is put forward to describe the system under consideration, the theory is analysed to see if it matches expectation (testing), and the theory is used to make predictions which can then be put to the test by experiment ('can the predicted property be proved from the specification'). The analogy with science is important because a specification (especially the original design or formal requirements specification) can never be proved correct. It can only provide more and more confidence as it passes more and more tests until it fails some test or makes an unacceptable prediction. The specification must then be tinkered with until it is improved. In extreme cases, a completely new theory must be proposed.

Specification building differs from the scientific paradigm in a very important sense. There is generally no part of the world being modelled. The specification describes an imagined artefact whose realization will become part of the world. This compounds the difficulty of scientific hypothesizing in at least two ways. Firstly, the 'knowledge' of the imagined artefact is much less precisely delineated — no 'world' to act as a check. The very act of realizing the artefact may profoundly change the world. Secondly, of the three degrees of freedom identified in theory building — logic, extralogical language and axioms — none is fixed in specification construction.

As to the nature of the theories (i.e. specifications or linguistic levels) produced by such a process, we can say that it should reflect with precision what we definitely know about the world (in science) or artefact (in programming) and leave open those things which we know or are able to ascertain less precisely. In terms of formal properties, this can only mean rejecting positively the notion of logical completeness of theories in favour of a more permissive approach. This probably complicates the process of validating a specification. There are now three possible outcomes to a query about the specification: 'yes', 'no' and 'I don't know'. However, it should in some respects make it easier to build specifications. For example, if we do not know how to deal with popping the empty stack, we are not forced to make some arbitrary decision in favour of 'error' or anything else. That is, we can work with underdetermined or underdefined concepts.

Pragmatically speaking, there are two reasons why one may *want* the specification to be permissive in some respects: either one does not wish to decide on an issue (too early or not at all), or one genuinely does not know how to decide. It is not very realistic to assume that the question will arise directly with respect to an extralogical axiom: after all, when one writes down an extralogical axiom, it is precisely because one wants to fix a certain aspect of the design. Thus the sentences whose theoremhood cannot be decided within a given linguistic level (and the collection of which constitutes the extent of a specification's permissiveness!) are most likely the correctly formed sentences which cannot be derived from the axioms by application of the rules of reasoning subsumed in the level (i.e. those of the linguistic system in which the level is formulated).

An example of such a sentence, in an easily imaginable linguistic level of natural number arithmetics, is

$$(\mathbf{E}x, y, z, n \geqslant 3)(x^n + y^n = z^n)$$

At the time of writing, the authors genuinely do not know whether this sentence is to be considered as a theorem or as an antitheorem!

A major source of 'unexpected permissiveness' is the difference between the set of correctly formed sentences and that of sentences deducible from axioms by application of rules of reasoning. Actually, we are almost tempted to state that since the theory is — by definition! — the closed set of consequences deducible from axioms, no other sentence is possibly a theorem and therefore must be false. The apparent strictness of such an attitude can be captured by saying: 'I have specified what I wanted, and I do not want anything else' or 'I reject everything that does not follow from my specification'. Unfortunately, the proved undecidability of many mathematical theories (indeed, of all mathematical theories of any interest) tells us that such an approach could be futile because there will always be sentences about which we will not be able to decide if they are in the theory. Declaring all such sentences as antitheorems (and thus accepting their negations as theorems!) is obviously unacceptable, as it extends *a posteriori* the rules of reasoning. Indeed, assume S is a sentence whose theoremhood cannot be decided. Declaring it an antitheorem makes $\neg S$ a theorem (at least in linguistic systems that accept the logical axiom of the excluded middle). Naturally, $\neg S$ cannot be deduced in the linguistic level in question, as had it been the case the question of the theoremhood of S could have been decided. Hence, the only reason by which $\neg S$ is accepted as a theorem is the fiat by which S was declared an antitheorem. It follows, therefore, that the specification, obviously incomplete, can be consistently extended by $\neg S$ as an axiom, independent of the remaining extralogical axioms. Just as easily, however, and just as consistently, we could extend the set of extralogical axioms by S itself. Thus a net effect of discovering an independent (i.e. neither provable nor disprovable) sentence S in the linguistic system of a theory T is that we can form *two* consistent theories $T \cup \{S\}$ and $T \cup \{\neg S\}$ and the choice cannot be based on any reasoning within T and its linguistic system.

If an independent sentence S is discovered, we may treat it as a curiosity and so do nothing about it, provided S is not important. (By this phrase we wish to express the fact that neither S nor $\neg S$ is a candidate for a useful lemma, i.e. that we do not envisage any derivations (proofs) dependent on S (or $\neg S$).) For example, there are not many non-trivial would-be theorems dependent on Fermat's last theorem. The knowledge of the domain of natural numbers depends on the 'truth' or 'falsity' of this theorem to a very slight extent only; it looks like the theorem describes an isolated fact, there are no further interesting (potential) properties that could be established if we knew whether it is 'true' or 'false'. (Actually, we do not even know if this theorem is, properly speaking, independent of axioms of natural numbers; most likely it is not.)

Should S turn out to be important in the above-mentioned sense, we could not avoid making a choice. If there is no solid intelligence on which to base this decision, a prudent course to take is to consider both theories side by side, $T \cup \{S\}$ and $T \cup \{\neg S\}$, perhaps as alternative specifications.

On the other hand, we may choose to eliminate the potential for independent sentences. Obviously, if we set forth to achieve this goal, we cannot afford to ignore the interplay between rules of syntax, axiom sets and rules of reasoning. Indeed, if we do not want to be surprised by a sentence S — a well executed exercise in syntactic derivation — which can neither be proved nor disproved by rules of reasoning taking a given set of axioms for the base, we should make certain that constructible (in the sense of well formedness) and deducible (in the sense of provability from a given set of axioms) are very closely related, if not simply identical, notions.

The controlling element in establishing the desired kinship between constructibility and deducibility is the choice of syntax. We may restrict the rules of well formedness so much that theorems shall be the only admissible sentences. It may be too difficult to apply such constraints in full generality, particularly so when the underlying linguistic system is employed for many different theories (as we expect to be the case in practice). Indeed, what it would have amounted to would be the requirement for a linguistic level in which all admissible (syntactically correct) sentences are theorems (a language in which no false statement could be made). Let us assume that we have such a level, and that S is a sentence, and thus a theorem, in it. Then $\neg S$ must not be an admissible sentence, as its admission to sentencehood would entail its theoremhood, and therefore the inconsistency of the level. If $\neg S$ is to be denied the sentencehood which S enjoys, we must either exclude the negation from the class of admissible functors, or explicitly mix semantic and syntactic rules, e.g. by saying 'negation cannot be applied to a sentence'. Neither of these is a viable proposition.

Even if the attack on permissiveness via an interplay between syntax and semantics is not a panacea, it can be successfully applied in a limited sense. We may select a syntax such that it would be possible to answer the question: Are the given axioms sufficient to ensure that all sentences *of a given kind* are decidably theorems or antitheorems?

When we ask this question, we are requiring considerably less than completeness of the linguistic level in hand, even if the level's completeness guarantees the positive answer. We start with a choice of a particular kind ('shape') of sentences and then ask merely that the sentences of this kind be decidable. The interplay between syntax and semantics is quite obvious in this statement of the problem: the choice of the kind of sentences is a syntactic decision. We are not concerned with deducibility of *all* sentences anymore; we are willing to settle for less − deducibility of statements of a certain kind.

This approach is not as minimalistic as it may appear at first glance. It is quite likely, for instance, that a specification is written as a theory of a newly introduced type[†]. It is quite legitimate in such a context to be concerned primarily with the question whether the definition of the freshly introduced type is sufficiently complete to allow decoding of each linguistic construct involving new objects and operations, i.e. to allow its reduction to terms already known. Expressions that do not involve a newly introduced type may be left outside our current concern (e.g. because they were already considered before, or at least we assume so).

It is exactly against this background that Guttag and Horning (1978) have introduced their notion of *sufficient completeness* of abstract data

---

[†] By *type* we understand a collection of (possibly structured) objects together with operations that act on these objects and/or create or generate them from other objects. Such collections are very similar to what, in mathematics, is known as algebras.

type specifications. Because of the generality of this notion, we are going to present it (and some of its practical consequences) in some detail[†].

Consider a specification of a type TOI (type of interest) by means of some other types. Let the specification be given in terms of a finite set F of mappings

$$F_{jm}: s_{i1} \times s_{i2} \times \ldots \times s_{in} \to s_k$$

where V is the set of sets of values (each set of values corresponding to a type), $(\mathbf{A}1 \leqslant l \leqslant n)(s_{il} \in V)$ & $(s_k \in V)$ and at least one element of the set $\{s_{i1}, s_{i2}, \ldots, s_{in}, s_k\}$ is TOI. Let us partition the set F into two disjoint sets, S and O, $F = S \cup O$, such that S contains all those mappings F_{jm} whose range is TOI and no other mappings belong to S. Thus all operations that generate elements of TOI belong to S. The set O contains all other mappings from F; mappings that belong to O have ranges outside TOI, thus they do not generate elements of TOI but map tuples containing such elements into values of some other type. The set S may be considered as the collection of operations that generate elements of TOI, the set O as the set of operations that relate TOI to other types. Obviously, in all interesting specifications, both sets, S and O, will not be empty (emptiness of S implies that we cannot generate any elements of TOI, emptiness of O — that we cannot define any properties of constructs containing such elements).

Let $I = V - \text{TOI}$; thus I is the collection of sets of values of 'other types'. Denote by $Cl(I)$ the closure of F over I, i.e. the set of results obtainable by applying any admissible combination of mappings from F to tuples obtainable from I by application of such mappings. Intuitively, $Cl(I)$ is the set of all values that can be obtained from I by application of functions from F. Note that $Cl(I)$ includes TOI.

Consider now a set of axioms A. A is said to be a *sufficiently complete axiomatization* of TOI if for every $F_{jm} \in O$ there exists a theorem, derivable from A, of the form

$$F_{jm}(x_1, x_2, \ldots, x_n) = u \quad \text{where } u \in s_i, s_i \in I$$

Informally speaking, an axiomatization is sufficiently complete if all properties of TOI are derivable from axioms. Indeed an expression $F_{jm}(x_1, x_2, \ldots, x_n)$ with $F_{jm} \in O$ and at least one $x_1, x_2, \ldots, x_n$ belonging to TOI is a property of (a tuple containing an element of) TOI. If, based on A, we can establish the value of this property ($u \in s_i$, $s_i \in I$), then all properties of TOI are explainable in terms of the other types.

Observe that the introduced notion of sufficient completeness calls for derivability of 'meaning-providing' theorems only for *some* formulae

---

[†] The reader is referred to Sections 2.2 and 2.3 for discussions of extension, and definitional extension in particular, to think about connections with the concepts about to be described. There seem to us to be some close — as yet unexplored — relationships.

that can be constructed within the syntax of the TOI definition, viz. for $F_{jm} \in O$.

The axiomatization of a TOI will be given by a finite set of equations of the form

$$(\mathbf{A}x_1, \ldots, x_n)(lhs = rhs)$$

where an admissible form of the left-hand side is $F_{jm}(v_1, \ldots, v_n)$ with $F_{jm} \in F$, and each v_i either a free variable or $v_i = F_{km}(x_1, \ldots, x_m)$ with $F_{km} \in F$ and all x_l being free variables. The admissible form of the right-hand sides is described below. Note that the *lhs* admits no more than one level of nesting of operations from F.

The right-hand sides of axioms are any valid expressions all of whose free variables are free in the respective left-hand side. For convenience the *rhs* expressions may contain the conditionals of the form **if** b **then** y **else** z with obvious interpretation (**if** b **then** y **else** $z = y$ if b is true, z if b is false, undefined otherwise).

In order to ensure that all functions of F are total, one may include in all axiomatizations an implicit axiom

$$(\mathbf{A}F_{jm})(x_1, \ldots, x_n \text{ not in domain of } F_{jm} \Rightarrow F_{jm}(x_1, \ldots, x_n) = error)$$

where *error* is a distinguished 'error element', usually taken to be outside of the domain of all F_{jm}. (If *error* indeed is outside the domains of all F_{jm}, any operation applied to a tuple containing an *error* yields *error*.)

The above axiomatization schema is quite powerful. It can be proved that any type (in the earlier given sense of the word), constituent sets of whose I are recursively enumerable and all operations of whose F are partial computable functions, is contained in a linguistic level axiomatizable according to the presented schema. (The proof of this and following results on sufficient completeness is to be found in Guttag and Horning (1978).)

Thus the schema is powerful enough to axiomatize any type of practical interest. Unfortunately, it can also be proved that the sufficient completeness of such axiomatizations is an undecidable problem, i.e. that in general there exists no finite procedure to determine if a concrete axiomatization is sufficiently complete. Following Guttag and Horning, we concentrate in these circumstances on *sufficient* conditions for sufficient completeness. This means that we want to investigate what conditions to impose on the axiomatization so as to be certain of its sufficient completeness. Note that sufficient conditions may turn out to be too restrictive: while ensuring sufficient completeness of the axiomatization, they may not be necessary, viz. there may exist sufficiently complete axiomatizations that defy these conditions.

An important property of conditions that ensure sufficient completeness is that they also ensure that all operations contained in O are total. This means that if the linguistic level, constructed in the described fashion, is guaranteed to be sufficiently complete, all functions from the set O, i.e. all property-determining functions in our specification, are well defined for any combination of arguments (even if they yield the value *error* for some combinations of input values).

Guttag and Horning found a way to solve the problem of sufficient conditions for axiomatizations of a type in a purely syntactic way. They have formulated a number of conditions which when imposed on the structure of equations and on their *lhs* and *rhs* parts ensure sufficient completeness of the axiomatization. The exact statement of conditions is a bit tedious and will not be reproduced here; their main points in a somewhat simplified form are:

1. For all $o \in O$ and $s \in S$ there should be an axiom of the form $o(s(x, y^*), w^*) = z$ where y^* and w^* are tuples (possibly empty) of operands from I and x is a TOI operand.

2. Depth of nesting of operations from $S \cup O$ is greater in the *lhs* of the axiom than in its *rhs*.

(The technical complications leading to the above-mentioned tediousness of exact formulation of the conditions result from admitting the **if** b **then** $z1$ **else** $z2$ form of z. The simple notion of depth of nesting of operations becomes blurred for z of such a form, as one is forced to consider simultaneously two axioms $o(s(x, y^*), w^*) = z1$ and $o(s(x, y^*), w^*) = z2$, each of which should meet the depth of nesting condition and also the relative depths of operation nesting in b and in the *lhs* of the axiom. While this is tedious, the main idea of the depth-of-nesting condition should be quite clear.)

Given an axiomatization of the presented form it is possible to check algorithmically if (exact counterparts) of conditions (1) and (2) are satisfied. The positive result implies the sufficient completeness of the axiom-atization, the negative, strictly speaking, tells us nothing because we were looking for sufficient conditions of sufficient completeness. It is, however, eminently possible to draw heuristic conclusions from such a negative result of the check, and suitably repair the axiomatization. It appears that the extent of permissiveness of a specification is limited on one side by logical completeness — probably impossible to achieve (and undesirable anyway) in practically interesting cases — and some form of sufficient completeness on the other. Various principles according to which a notion of completeness can be introduced and its implementation ensured for viable specification techniques have been discussed by Würges (1981), who considers four approaches to the problem:

1. abandon the notion of specification completeness,
2. weaken it,
3. restrict the set of admissible specifications so that a version of completeness can be established more easily,

4. develop informal guidelines for constructing specifications so that the result (a specification-theory) will be accepted as complete.

The Guttag-Horning approach is a combination of (2) and (3), although it could be argued that it also contains elements of (4). Approach (1) does not appear to be attractive, considering that without somehow identifying the problem, we would not be able to discuss how fully our specification describes what we intended to specify. Approach (4) without (2) and/or (3) does not seem too secure, reducing as it were the problem of specification completeness to mere verbal arguments. Perhaps at very early stages of theory formation, a set of completeness guidelines may be applied to facilitate the choice between alternative axiomatizations. In later stages, however, it must be supplemented, if not altogether superseded, by a more calculable principle.

3.3   Programs that satisfy specifications

In a beautiful lecture, Peter Naur (1985) argues that human intuition is an indispensable contributor to scientific progress in general and to programming activity in particular. It would be foolish to take the opposite view, viz. to maintain that programming activity does not and need not depend in any degree whatsoever on human intuition. The trouble is, however, that 'intuition' − dictionary definitions notwithstanding − is a notion that can be communicated only intuitively. Since there is no formal definition of 'intuition' − yours or mine − there cannot be a calculable argument whether your notion of intuition and my notion of intuition coincide. We hope that they do so, at least in a sense. The whole point of formality (which in this book we tend to equate with any means that allow arguments to be represented in an unambiguous calculable way) is to let intuition do its share of work in mental processes (about which we claim no expertise and which we most emphatically do not equate with, nor even approximate by, formal reasoning!) while making the protocols of this activity, the externally presented arguments, subject to rigorous (calculable) manipulations.

We hope that the readers have an intuitive understanding of what a 'specification' is, and what a 'program' is, and how a program (may) 'satisfy' a specification. Let us assure readers that we too have an intuition and an intuitive grasp of these notions. Our intuition, however, to a considerable extent fortified by teaching and consulting experience, tells us that it is not inconceivable that the intuitions about 'specifications', 'programs' and 'satisfaction' are not perfectly matched.

The goal of this section is two-fold: first we want to explore the intuitive notions, thus, hopefully, bringing to the surface the important issues that contribute to them and influence their eventual extents; then, we aim at exhibiting a formalism that captures (a good part of) intuition and freezes the notions for subsequent use in our discussions. We adopted this plan and announce it quite openly so that the reader may be fully aware of what we are about to do: we start from no preconceived definition although we aim for one. We shall consider various aspects and then select an extent of terms. After this, the terms will cease to mean anything else but what is explicitly said in the definition: it would then be too late to have reservations or to say, 'yes, but *I* understand that specification is...'.

In the natural course of events there is a chronological sequence: from problem through its analysis to its solution. The solution we seek is a program. Problems arise in multitudinous domains where automatic processing of information is (or is about to be) applied. Except for important but relatively few cases, the application domains are very different, in any conceivable sense, from computer programs and their executions. In most practically important situations the dissimilarity between the application domain and the domain of computer programs is so significant that it is virtually impossible to treat them in the same language.

The last statement could be opposed on the following grounds: after all, whenever we treat of anything, we do so in our 'natural' language. Thus this natural (ethnic) language can be used as a vehicle for conversation about both domains. However plausible this argument may seem, it is not quite correct. In fact, it is either very naïve or demagogic. Experts in any field of human endeavour have developed a particular language with a specific 'in' terminology, in which not only terms unknown outside the field are employed, but also apparently common terms assume specific meanings and connotations. As one learns one's trade or profession, the special language of one's occupation is slowly superimposed on the ethnic language. True enough, a person usually has no difficulty in switching between the base ethnic language used for communication outside his field and the specialized language used within. A significant exception to this rule is the situation in which one tries to describe to laymen a problem from one's field of expertise: it takes a great communicator to avoid lapsing into the specialized language. And good communicators do not come along very often!

In the preceding paragraphs we have concentrated upon the most obvious linguistic (terminological) aspect. The difficulty goes much deeper: much of the domain-specific expertise is absorbed so well by people active in the domain that it becomes 'subconscious'. Much of it never gets verbalized: it is subsumed without the expert being aware of the assumptions. (How many mechanical engineers are consciously aware that a fundamental assumption about the design of a wrench is that it can be used only in a gravity field: on board a satellite, or in free fall, the wrench is quite useless — rather than turning a nut, the user will rotate himself around a screw!)

Thus it is unavoidable that between a problem and a program there must be an intervening linguistic level − a language with no hidden (or inherited) 'understanding' of terms. This language is employed to express the problem statement in terms that are as free as possible of any non-explicit semantic content. Such a statement may conveniently be called a problem specification.

On the other hand, the same statement, although now seen in an entirely different rôle, is the program specification. As the problem specification, the statement is (hopefully) an unambiguous description; as the program specification, it is (also hopefully) an unambiguous prescription.

We could have started from a program: the specification would then be a description of the program, free of many program intuitions and preconceived, hidden meanings. It could then be considered as a pre-scription for problems that the program solves. This symmetry of inter-pretations, satisfying and intriguing on a methodological ground, is probably quite irrelevant for any practical purpose.

The necessity of having an intermediary level of description/prescription arises also from the fact that programs are necessarily formal objects, while problems in most cases are not. The switch between informality and formality must occur somewhere. It cannot be a smooth, gradual transition − strict formality is either there or not. 'Semi-formal language' is a nice didactic notion, may be a useful stepping stone towards, say, a formal description, but 'semi-formal' is not formal, and, let us say it once more, programs are formal objects.

It is very tempting to say that the level at which the description becomes formal is the level of specification.

Can we safely assume that these two arguments for an intermediary level lead to the same language? No, if we take the word 'language' literally: certainly there may be more than one language in which quite formal specifications could be expressed. Yes, if we consider the process of programming: whichever path we take from problem to program, there is a level at which expression of our thoughts becomes formal for the first time; at the very same level we no longer rely on any implicit under-standing. Thus, while certainly not unique, the specification level emerges as a unification of two pragmatically necessary stages of programming: introduction of formality of expression and parting with implicit semantics. (It should be observed that the unification may happen − as a pathological limiting case − at the program level: after all, programs are specifications of a sort − see Section 3.4).

From the preceding discussion (which may be considered as a review of Sections 1.1−1.2 although in a slightly different vein) it follows that specification has several important properties:

1. As an expression, a specification is formal.

2. There is no hidden meaning attached to the specification or to any of its parts (all that a specification 'says' is said explicitly).

3. A specification is an accepted description of the problem.

4. A specification is taken as a prescription for the program that solves the problem.

Since the eventual program is also a formal expression, we can meaningfully require that there be a fully calculable relationship (or a class of relationships) between specifications and programs. The relationship we aim at is that of correctness. We want a program to be correct with respect to its specification.

Naturally, we must eventually attach a concrete, precise meaning to 'correctness'. Before doing so, however, let us discuss what it is that is expected to be captured by our rigorously defined 'correctness'.

Assume that our specification is a set of formulae G. It is reasonable to expect that G expresses, in the chosen linguistic system, certain properties which are considered fundamental in both senses of this word: i.e. most important and suitable for deriving consequences from. In other words, it is natural to expect that G is a theory presentation. G being a formal structure it is natural to expect G to have exactly those properties that formal theories have (as described in the Appendix). Because we are realists, and also for the reasons investigated in Section 3.2, we assume that G is a permissive specification, i.e. it generates a theory that is not necessarily complete.

It is a question of choice as to what is the main emphasis of specification: it may be mainly property-oriented (e.g. when it specifies a data type) or relation-oriented (e.g. when it specifies desired reactions to envisaged events). While the differences between the two kinds may seem large and could be exaggerated by the choice of different formalisms for recording G, the principal methodological aspect is the same: one way or another, G is the base for reasoning about all objects that conform to G. (The reader may wish to observe now that we are given to a slight tendency to use circular arguments: with equal justification we could have said that objects that conform to G are those about which we could reason using G as the base. Touché. But if we agree that, in programming, G is formulated before any program-objects conforming to G are ever constructed, the circularity of the argument is not as bad as it could be otherwise.)

A correct program P_r is one of the objects that conform to G. Thus G may be used as the base for reasoning about P_r. It follows that we must select such an interpretation of the notion 'correct' which would ensure that reasoning about P_r, based on G, is meaningful.

Roughly speaking, the just formulated requirement amounts to the following. Assume that within the linguistic system of G we can establish a proposition A using G and, possibly, some auxiliary (logical) axioms of the linguistic system. (In formulae, our assumption may be expressed as $G \vdash A$.)

Then, in the linguistic system appropriate for P_r, there should be an identifiable proposition B, valid on the strength of P_r, $P_r \vdash B$, which we could accept as saying the same thing as A does.

Of course, if the requirement is to approximate the notion of correctness, the above described requirement should be for any A. Thus we have approached the following metastatement:

To any A such that $G \vdash A$, there corresponds a B such that $P_r \vdash B$

$$(3.4)$$

as our requirement for P_r being a program correctly conforming with specification G. (We call (3.4) a metastatement because it refers to two linguistic systems — the two instances of the relation $\vdash$ generally being different — and itself is expressed in yet another linguistic system.)

One could ask if (3.4) is enough, if the correspondence it refers to could not be perverse, in the sense of assigning to As 'wrong' Bs. The answer is no — the correspondence referred to in (3.4) cannot pervert whatever meaning is calculably attributed to G. (The emphasis is on 'calculably'; if a meaning is attached to G by belief, intuition, tradition or any other non-calculable association, the answer may be painfully different.) Fundamental in establishing the non-perversity of the correspondence (3.4) is the observation that if G is strong enough to establish existence, equivalence, non-equivalence, equality, non-equality, etc., of 'abstract' objects, it must do so by means of theorems derivable from G. The requirement (3.4) ensures that corresponding theorems must also be establishable by P_r-based reasoning.

Thus, for example, if we can establish from G that there exist at least two different widgets, then (3.4) ensures that from P_r we can establish the existence of not less than two distinct whatisits, under the added restrictions that

- to the properties of relation 'different' (defined on widget $\times$ widget) there correspond properties of relation 'distinct' (defined on whatisit $\times$ whatisit),

- relation 'at least' corresponds to 'not less than', . . .

On the other hand, if a property does not follow from G, i.e. if it cannot be established in the form of a theorem derivable from G, there need not correspond to it any property based on P_r, or there could even be a counter-property among the consequences of P_r.

In the Appendix the reader may find formulae by which statements of programming languages are converted into axioms (or axiom schemata) amenable to a calculable derivation of consequences. The linguistic

system in which we express programs is assumed to contain such formulae. In general, they are of the following form:

$$A \Rightarrow [\alpha] B \tag{3.5}$$

where α is a programming language construct and A, B are formulae of
the linguistic system.

The most obvious way of interpreting formulae like (3.5) is related to
an operational understanding of a programming language and its constructs. If we wish to think about a program as of a prescription for
actions of some executing agent, then (3.5) could be interpreted as
follows: if the agent undertakes execution of α under circumstances
where A holds, then, upon termination, the obtained circumstances are
such that B holds. Or, somewhat simpler, the execution of α, if it
terminates, is guaranteed to transform a state in which A holds into a
state in which B holds.

There is nothing in (3.5) itself which would point to, let alone necessitate the use of, such operational thinking. It is our view of what the
programming language *really* is that comes through in such an interpretation. As E.W. Dijkstra often points out, there is a fundamental
distinction between the view that programs (and hence programming
languages) are meant to control (direct) calculating machines, and the
view that calculating machines are devices that implement programs.
It appears that the inability to grasp this distinction (and follow its
methodological consequences) is a major contributor to quarrels between
proponents of 'assignment' and 'assignment-free' languages.

Formulae like (3.5) can be used for presentation of semantics of
many different kinds of programming languages (including applicative
and 'logic programming' ones). We shall try to avoid giving any preference
to any particular kind, although greater familiarity with assignment
languages (which familiarity we think we share with the readers) makes
our examples naturally biased towards this particular kind.

Semantics − the meaning − of a program is derived from the semantics
of its constituent statements by means of composition rules that prescribe
how formulae of the (3.5) variety, representing the meaning of constituents, combine into formulae − of the same kind! − representing the
meaning of composite programs. Thus, for example, we had in the
Appendix, Section A.5

$$[\alpha; \beta] A \Leftrightarrow [\alpha][\beta] A \tag{3.6}$$

as a rule which defines the 'meaning transformation' associated with
the semicolon used (in many but not all programming languages) as a
sequential composition operator.

A slightly more detailed way of presenting the essence of the composition rule, as applicable to most programming languages, reads

$$A \Rightarrow [\alpha] B$$
$$\frac{B \Rightarrow [\beta] C}{A \Rightarrow [\alpha; \beta] C} \tag{3.7}$$

Observe that the conclusion of rule (3.7) is exactly in the form of (3.5) with $[\alpha; \beta]$ playing the rôle of the programming construct whose meaning is being defined.

The α in (3.5) may be a concrete, detailed programming language statement (construct) or a form from which such detailed cases can be derived by means of programming language grammar. Thus, for example, one can expect the statement *skip* to be defined by

$$A \Rightarrow [skip] A \quad \text{for any formula } A \tag{3.8}$$

and the assignment statement to be defined by

$$A \Rightarrow [x := E] B \tag{3.9}$$

where x stands for any identifier, E for any expression whose type is compatible with the type of x (identifier, expression, type and type compatibility are technical terms related to the programming language grammar!) and $A = B(x/E)$, i.e. formula A differs from B only by E being substituted for the (free) occurrences of x (whatever B says about x, A says about E).

Observe that while (3.8) defines the semantics of a single, concrete (although not very powerful) statement *skip*, (3.9) defines the semantics of infinitely many concrete assignment statements. The formula (3.9) is a schema in two senses: one can substitute a variety of concrete assignment statements, conforming to the form $x := E$, and one can invent a large variety of formulae B (and, therefore, A).

Incidentally, formulae of the form (3.5) may also be considered as 'equations' to be solved for an unknown transformation $[\alpha]$, given a pair A, B. In this way we may consider

$$A \Rightarrow [\alpha] B$$
$$A = B(x/E) \tag{3.10}$$

as equations, and call their solution, i.e. a transformation which makes the first line of (3.10) hold, an *assignment statement*, denoted by $x := E$. If we follow this path, there are no traces left of operational considerations.

Naturally, if we want to consider formulae similar to (3.5) as equations for α, corresponding A and B must be defined. When A and B are fully defined, we get a unique 'point' transformation; when only a relation between A and B is defined, as in the second line of (3.10), we get a transformation $\alpha: A \mapsto B$ for which the domain and range are classes of formulae.

Since we obviously have

$$\text{if } P \Rightarrow A \text{ and } A \Rightarrow [\alpha]B$$
$$\text{then } P \Rightarrow [\alpha]B \tag{3.11}$$

and also

$$\text{if } B \Rightarrow Q \text{ and } A \Rightarrow [\alpha]B$$
$$\text{then } A \Rightarrow [\alpha]Q \tag{3.12}$$

equation (3.5), with given α and B (respectively A), does not admit unique solutions for A (respectively B). Indeed, let us be given (3.5) with fixed α and B, then if A is a solution so is any P that satisfies (3.11). We may, however, be interested in the *weakest* solution of (3.5), i.e. in finding such W that not only $W \Rightarrow [\alpha]B$, but also for any A satisfying (3.5) we have $A \Rightarrow W$. Similarly, we may define the *strongest* solution of (3.5) with α, A given[†].

It may be helpful to visualize the weakest solution of (3.5) as a description of conditions that are necessary for a transformation to achieve circumstances described by B.

Formulae like (3.5), which define the meaning of programming language statements and constructs, are the extralogical axioms of the linguistic level in which programs are written. With suitable composition rules included in these axioms, we can derive a similar formula, or more precisely a formula of similar structure,

$$P \Rightarrow [\pi]Q \tag{3.13}$$

for any syntactically correct program π. Formula (3.13) determines the meaning of program π from meanings of its constituent constructs; formally, (3.13) is a consequence of the semantic axioms of the language, its derivation guided by the particular program π (more precisely, by the particular syntax of π).

Naturally, we can obtain (3.13) when a syntactically correct program is given. On the other hand, given P and Q one can ask for a program π that would make formula (3.13) hold. The problem of finding a program is the most general expression of the programmer's task: P and Q constitute the so-called *input/output specification* of the program to be composed out of the available programming language constructs.

In the preceding discussion we have glossed over several important points. One of them is the question of program termination; another, that of its determinism.

Observe that we may state problem (3.13) in a very special case as

---

[†] The terminology 'weakest' and 'strongest' is traditional and becomes quite clear when we recall that proposition A in formula (3.5) is often referred to as a 'precondition' and B as a 'postcondition'; thus, given a postcondition and a transformation, it makes sense to consider the weakest (possible) precondition, and, given a precondition and a transformation, the strongest postcondition.

$TRUE \Rightarrow [\pi] \, TRUE$

where *TRUE* is a predicate that holds in all circumstances; or, since

$(\neg TRUE | [\pi] \, TRUE) \equiv [\pi] \, TRUE$

as

$$[\pi] \, TRUE \tag{3.14}$$

This is an input/output specification for a program that 'yields' an arbitrary result. We choose to emphasize not so much a particular condition (conditions) satisfied by the range of the transformation, as the fact that there always is an image of any element of the domain. The formula (3.14) is taken as a requirement for π's termination.

Similarly

$$P \Rightarrow [\pi] \, TRUE \tag{3.15}$$

is the specification for a program that terminates for any inputs which satisfy P (although we do not particularly care what results are delivered at the termination).

If the termination/non-termination terminology seems too operational, we can always avoid it by talking about transformations being defined or undefined for all (or some) circumstances described by the antecedent of the implication (3.5). Thus, for example, (3.15) is the specification for program π that is a transformation defined for any circumstances satisfying P.

Consider now two problems:

$$X \Rightarrow [\pi] P \tag{3.16}$$

and

$$Y \Rightarrow [\pi](\neg P) \tag{3.17}$$

both with fixed π and P.

Problem (3.16) is that of finding precondition X for transformation (program) π elements of whose range make P hold; problem (3.16) is that of finding a precondition for the same transformation establishing $\neg P$. If π is deterministic, there cannot be circumstances for which X and Y would both hold. But it is not necessarily true that $Y \equiv \neg X$, as there may be circumstances for which π is not defined (e.g. program π does not terminate for some inputs). If π is a total transformation (i.e. is defined in all circumstances) and π is deterministic, then, naturally, $Y \equiv \neg X$ (assuming the law of excluded middle holds in the linguistic system).

Consider a slight variation of (3.16)

$$X \Rightarrow ([\pi] P | \pi \text{ is undefined}) \tag{3.16'}$$

The solution of (3.16') is a precondition that guarantees the following: in circumstances that satisfy X either the transformation π is undefined, or the obtained image satisfies P. This solution is traditionally referred to as the *liberal precondition* for program π to establish P; it can be interpreted − very operationally! − as follows. The program π initiated in a state that satisfies X shall either fail to terminate, or will yield results satisfying P. Observe that when we consider the liberal precondition problem, the transformation may be 'slightly' non-deterministic. If this kind of non-determinism is subsumed in interpretation of specification formulae, (3.16') may be written exactly as (3.16).

Solving (3.5) for a precondition, i.e. making the assumption that both the postcondition and program are given and it is only the precondition that needs to be determined, is not the most typical of practical programming problems. The issues of termination and determinism reappear, however, even if the most frequently solved problem is considered. Rewriting (3.5) in a form which clearly indicates what the unknown is:

$$P \Rightarrow [\xi] Q \qquad\qquad (3.5')$$

we should always state which of the possible cases we wish to consider:

1. we accept only such transformations ξ whose proper domains, i.e. domains where ξ is defined, include all circumstances in which P holds;

2. we accept transformations ξ which may be undefined in some circumstances in which P holds;

3. we accept transformations ξ which, if defined, make Q hold;

4. we accept only such transformations ξ which are always defined whenever P holds and which make Q hold.

Of course, when transformation ξ is defined (and the notion of transformation definedness excludes pathological cases, e.g. operationally equivalent to non-terminating programs), formula (3.5') does not leave any room for doubt.

As an example illustrating our discussion, consider three programs

$\pi 0$: *skip*

$\pi 1$: **do** *true* → *skip* **od**

$\pi 2$: **if** *true* → *skip*
    [] *true* → $\pi 1$
    fi

(All these programs are borrowed from Jacobs and Gries (1985); the same source should be consulted for a rigorous discussion of topics raised above.)

The transformation $\pi 0$ leaves any initial state intact, $A \Rightarrow [\pi 0] A$ (see (3.8)); the transformation $\pi 1$ is undefined if pathological extensions of definedness are excluded (program $\pi 1$ never terminates); the transformation $\pi 2$ is non-deterministic: if the first line is chosen[†] the transformation $\pi 2$ has the same effect as $\pi 0$; in case the second line is chosen, $\pi 2$ is equivalent (if we are allowed to use this expression!) to $\pi 1$.

Taking a liberal attitude to definitions of program semantics (3), we may consider $\pi 2$ as equivalent to $\pi 0$. (If programs $\pi 0$ and $\pi 2$ terminate, their results are identical.) This attitude is sometimes referred to as *partial correctness*.

Taking a strict attitude (1), we may consider $\pi 1$ and $\pi 2$ as equivalent in the sense that all transformations which may be undefined for some elements of their domains are equivalent (all possibly non-terminating programs are equivalent). This attitude is sometimes referred to as *total correctness*.

Since neither the liberal nor the strict approach differentiates between all three obviously different programs $\pi 0$, $\pi 1$, $\pi 2$, there seems to be room for yet another approach; see, for example, Barringer *et al.* (1984), Jacobs and Gries (1985). We shall not pursue this topic further[‡].

In subsequent discussion we shall assume that programming language semantics is defined by axioms of the form (3.5) and that respective antecedents of implications include conjuncts that ensure definedness of transformations.

Let us now return to the question of programs that satisfy specifications. We shall consider this question in a somewhat artificial setting; that is, we shall assume that we are given a specification and a program, and we try to establish the precise content of the statement 'program π satisfies specification G'. The artificiality of this set-up is caused by the assumption of the program being given. Usually, one builds a program to satisfy a given specification, and does it so that upon completion of the construction process the program satisfies the specification by virtue of the construction. This sound methodological principle presupposes, however, that we already know a calculable criterion (or criteria) of satisfaction. Thus, while excellent in practice, for theoretical considerations the principle is quite useless, as its application would unavoidably lead to circularity of considerations (*idem per idem*).

Let us briefly recall what the accepted set-up implies in terms of formal considerations.

We are given two linguistic systems, that of specification, Σ^0, and that

---

[†] We assume the reader is familiar with the traditional semantics of Dijkstra's (1976) guarded commands.

[‡] With the possible exception of operating systems and similar continuous, round the clock activities, there is not much interest in non-terminating programs. Whether non-determinism is an aspect of the specifiable system behaviour, or merely an implementation technique, is (at least to us) a debatable issue, on which we do not wish to take a stand in this book.

of programming, Λ^0. The specification language provides a set of extra-logical axioms in Σ^0 (whose syntax may need to be suitably extended), thus creating a linguistic level Σ^1. Similarly, the programming language, by its grammar and semantic axioms in (possibly extended) Λ^0, provides a linguistic level Λ^1. On the specification side we now take a set of consistent statements in Σ^1, G. The statements of G are the description of the problem for which we seek a satisfactory program. We shall disregard here the question of whether G contains only mutually independent statements, or whether some of its constituents could be derived from others. (For purely theoretical purposes it does not matter very much; for practical ones, either case has its peculiar advantages: 'axiomatized', kernel-like, specification is more succinct; inclusion of some derivable statements may make the specification more readable or 'more informative' to human readers.)

On the program side we now take a (syntactically) correctly composed set of programming language statements (and other constructs if available and useful, such as declarations), π. According to the semantic rules of Λ^1 we can establish

$$R \Rightarrow [\pi]Q \tag{3.18}$$

which holds by virtue of the particular selection of statements in π and of the particular way in which they are put together.

We say that π satisfies G iff whenever $G \vdash A$, we can identify a formula B such that $(R \Rightarrow [\pi]Q) \vdash B$.

This definition broadly follows (3.4), arrived at as a result of exploring the intuitive notions of correctness. However, we now make explicit the base for reasoning about consequences that follow from a program. Note also that this definition, as much as (3.4), is in agreement with the understanding of 'meaning' we arrived at in Chapter 1: the meaning of a statement (formula, sentence, etc.) is the set of consequences we can derive from it. Now we can say that a program that satisfies a specification preserves its meaning. (It is not, however, true that a specification and a program that satisfies it have the same meaning, as there may be consequences of a program for which we cannot identify corresponding consequences derived from the specification. In this sense a program may be viewed as being 'richer' in contents than its specification.)

It may appear that (3.18) is a very meagre base for reasoning. In fact, it should be borne in mind that in practice both R and Q which appear in (3.18) may be quite long formulae: R describes the domain of transformation π, i.e. the domain of program applicability; Q does the same for the range of π, i.e. describes the properties of program results. Moreover, it is quite possible that (3.18) is a set of similarly structured formulae, which may be more convenient for actual reasoning about program consequences.

Note that in our definition of satisfaction, A and B are formulae in (possibly) quite different linguistic levels, which may entail considerable technical difficulties in identifying and writing down, say, B when A is given. The mathematical background for this technically tedious procedure is given in Section 2.3.

As an example[†], consider a proof that the following program

$$K: \textbf{while } b - a > \varepsilon \textbf{ do begin } x := \frac{a+b}{2};$$
$$\textbf{if } f(x) * f(a) < 0 \textbf{ then } b := x$$
$$\textbf{else } a := x \textbf{ fi}$$
$$\textbf{end}$$
$$\textbf{od}$$

satisfies the specification 'find an approximate root of $f(x) = 0$ within interval (a, b)'.

First we must make the specification a little more precise. We shall assume that $f(x)$ is continuous in (a, b) and that $f(a) * f(b) < 0$. This guarantees that there is a root of $f(x) = 0$ within (a, b). As an approximation we shall accept an interval (a', b'), embedded in (a, b) such that $f(a') * f(b') < 0$ and $b' - a' < \varepsilon$, where $\varepsilon > 0$ is an arbitrarily small number (given *a priori*). Program K solves the specified problem by the (probably oldest known) technique of bisection.

With the specification rewritten in formulae, the proof obligation is to establish

$$(f(a) * f(b) < 0 \,\&\, b - a > \varepsilon > 0) \Rightarrow$$
$$[K](f(a) * f(b) < 0 \,\&\, 0 < b - a < \varepsilon)$$

or, more succinctly, $P \Rightarrow [K]Q$, with

$$P: f(a) * f(b) < 0 \,\&\, b - a > \varepsilon > 0$$
$$Q: f(a) * f(b) < 0 \,\&\, 0 < b - a < \varepsilon$$

Lemma 1
Let

$$P': f(a) * f(b) < 0 \,\&\, b - a = k \,\&\, k > 0$$
$$Q': f(a) * f(b) < 0 \,\&\, b - a = \frac{k}{2} \,\&\, \frac{k}{2} > 0$$

Then

$$P' \Rightarrow [\textbf{begin } x := \frac{a+b}{2};$$
$$\textbf{if } f(x) * f(a) < 0 \textbf{ then } b := x$$
$$\textbf{else } a := x \textbf{ fi}$$
$$\textbf{end}] Q'$$

[†]This example and the idea for the proof has been suggested to us by Professor A. Salwicki.

Proof

Let us observe:

1. $b - a = k \Rightarrow \left(\dfrac{a+b}{2} - a = \dfrac{k}{2} \right) \& \left(b - \dfrac{a+b}{2} = \dfrac{k}{2} \right)$

2. for all real numbers d:

$$f(a) * f(b) < 0 \Rightarrow (d * f(a) < 0 \,|\, (d * f(a) \geq 0 \,\&\, d * f(b) < 0))$$

Let

$$d = f\left(\frac{a+b}{2} \right)$$

Then, by easy calculations, we have

$$P' \Rightarrow \left(f\left(\frac{a+b}{2} \right) * f(a) < 0 \,\&\, \left(\frac{a+b}{2} - a = \frac{k}{2} \right) \right)$$

$$\left| \left(f\left(\frac{a+b}{2} \right) * f(a) \geq 0 \,\&\, f\left(\frac{a+b}{2} \right) * f(b) < 0 \,\&\, \left(b - \frac{a+b}{2} = \frac{k}{2} \right) \right) \right.$$

By the assignment statement axiom (3.9) we can rewrite this implication as

$$P' \Rightarrow \left[x := \frac{a+b}{2} \right] \left(f(x) * f(a) < 0 \,\&\, x - a = \frac{k}{2} \right)$$

$$\left| \left[x := \frac{a+b}{2} \right] \left(f(x) * f(a) \geq 0 \,\&\, f(x) * f(b) < 0 \,\&\, b - x = \frac{k}{2} \right) \right.$$

The rules of reasoning in the program linguistic level will usually include (c.f. Section A.5.2 of the Appendix)

$$[\pi](R\,|\,S) \Leftrightarrow [\pi]R\,|\,[\pi]S$$

Applying such a rule we get

$$P' \Rightarrow \left[x := \frac{a+b}{2} \right] \left(f(x) * f(a) < 0 \,\&\, x - a = \frac{k}{2} \right)$$

$$\left| \left(f(x) * f(a) \geq 0 \,\&\, f(x) * f(b) < 0 \,\&\, b - x = \frac{k}{2} \right) \right.$$

Observing that

$$Q'(b/x) = f(a) * f(x) < 0 \,\&\, x - a = \frac{k}{2}$$

$$Q'(a/x) = f(x) * f(b) < 0 \,\&\, b - x = \frac{k}{2}$$

we can write

$$P' \Rightarrow \left[x := \frac{a+b}{2} \right] (Q'\,(b/x) \,|\, (f(x) * f(a) \geq 0 \,\&\, Q'\,(a/x)))$$

Another rule of reasoning in the program linguistic level we need is

[if B then π else ρ fi]$R \Leftrightarrow ((B \,\&\, [\pi]R)|(-B \,\&\, [\rho]R))$

by which, observing that $Q'(b/x) \Leftrightarrow (f(x) * f(a) < 0 \,\&\, Q'(b/x))$, we get

$$P' \Rightarrow \left[x := \frac{a + b}{2} \right][\text{if } f(x) * f(a) < 0 \text{ then } b := x$$
$$\text{else } a := x \text{ fi}]\,Q'$$

i.e. using the (sequential composition) axiom (3.6),

$$P' \Rightarrow [\textbf{begin } x := \frac{a + b}{2};$$
$$\text{if } f(x) * f(a) < 0 \text{ then } b := x \text{ else } a := x \text{ fi}$$
$$\textbf{end}]\,Q'$$

which completes the proof.

The proof of Lemma 1 illustrated the main points about proving that a program satisfies the specification. We shall present the remaining steps of the 'big' proof in much less detail.

Lemma 2
For all natural numbers i:

$$(f(a) * f(b) < 0 \,\&\, b - a = k) \Rightarrow [\textbf{begin } x := \frac{a + b}{2};$$
$$\text{if } f(x) * f(a) < 0 \text{ then } b := x$$
$$\text{else } a := x \text{ fi}$$
$$\textbf{end}]^i \left(f(a) * f(b) < 0 \,\&\, b - a = \frac{k}{2^i} \right)$$

Note: $[\pi]^i$ stands for $[\pi][\pi]\ldots[\pi]$ (i times), or, equivalently, for $[\pi; \pi; \ldots; \pi$ (i times)].

Proof
Lemma 2 is a quite straightforward extension (by induction on i) of Lemma 1.

Lemma 3
There exists a natural number n such that

$$(f(a) * f(b) < 0 \,\&\, b - a > 0) \Rightarrow [\textbf{begin } x := \frac{a + b}{2};$$
$$\text{if } f(x) * f(a) < 0 \text{ then } b := x$$
$$\text{else } a := x \text{ fi}$$
$$\textbf{end}]^n (f(a) * f(b) < 0 \,\&\, 0 < b - a < \varepsilon)$$

Proof
Lemma 3 is a simple application of Lemma 2.

From Lemma 3 and from the discussion about characterization of **while** constructs in the Appendix (Section A.5.2) it follows that $P \Rightarrow [K]\, TRUE$ (initiated in circumstances that make P hold, program K always terminates).

We shall need yet another rule of reasoning in the linguistic level of a program, viz.:

$$\frac{R \Rightarrow [M]R,\ [\textbf{while } B \textbf{ do } M \textbf{ od}]\, TRUE}{R \Rightarrow [\textbf{while } B \textbf{ do } M \textbf{ od}]\,(R \ \& \ \neg B)}$$

It is sufficient now to take

$$R : f(a) * f(b) < 0 \ \& \ b - a > 0$$
$$B : b - a \geq \varepsilon$$
$$M : K$$

in order to observe

$$(f(a) * f(b) < 0 \ \& \ b - a > 0) \Rightarrow$$
$$[K](f(a) * f(b) < 0 \ \& \ b - a > 0 \ \& \ b - a < \varepsilon)$$

that is,

$$P \Rightarrow [K]Q \qquad\qquad\qquad\qquad \text{QED}$$

Thus we have proved that program K satisfies the specification. It is worth noticing that the linguistic level in which we reasoned about programs was a conservative extension of the linguistic level in which we stated our specification; in this way we avoided many tedious technicalities involved in translation between significantly different linguistic levels (theories). This is a bonus not to be ignored; it can always be had when programming language semantics is defined as an extension to the language (logic) employed for reasoning about specifications.

As many examples of program correctness (satisfaction of specification) proofs are quite readily accessible in the literature — e.g. Gries (1981) — we shall not pursue this subject any further.

3.4 Programs as specifications

There is one obvious way in which programs can — and, indeed, are — considered as specifications. When we write a program in, say, FORTRAN or LISP, we are specifying another program, in assembler or machine code, which is eventually applied to a computer so that actual calculations could be performed. We can extend the chain further down: the assembler code program may be viewed as the specification for a machine code version which, in turn, may be regarded as the specification for microcode sequences on a microprogrammed computer, etc. Thus, in a quite obvious way, a program in a very pedestrian programming language is a specification for more detailed (more concrete, lower level) programs.

Usually the design/implementation process ends with a program written in a language that may be processed directly by an available computer or accepted by a compiler that will complement the design by automatically executing the next step (or steps). In the latter case we can observe a curious phenomenon: the program to be compiled is clearly a specification for a major design/implementation effort. (To size the magnitude of this effort, imagine that there are no compilers available, and estimate the number of man-months needed to produce, verify and implement a machine-code program specified by a single, five page long Pascal program.) Yet, such a program is almost certainly regarded as a finished, completed product of the software process. The availability of compilers and their, by and large, acceptable quality determine a demarcation line between what is and what is not considered development activity. It is instructive to observe that this line is entirely artificial and in fact merely represents the commonly accepted limit of strict calculability of linguistic levels. Indeed, if the semantics of common programming languages was not strictly calculable, neither the automatic compilation of programs written in these languages, nor, more significantly, a general reliance on their correctness would have been possible.

Another trivial way of treating programs as specifications arises from the regrettably frequent habit of not documenting software development. If a piece of software is presented in a *deus ex machina* fashion as a program in whatever programming language, there is no other way to understand it but to take it literally as its own specification. This way of program 'interpretation' is, unfortunately, propagated by many textbooks, where one finds exercises constructed along the lines of a program text followed by a number of questions, asking, for example, what output would be printed if the input was such and such. To produce the correct answer the reader is forced to follow the program text in a machine-like fashion. If he does the exercise several times, with different input values, he may infer (guess) the meaning of the program. An intelligent reader will then posit his guess as a hypothetical specification for the given program and try to verify his hypothesis. Poor textbooks seldom encourage such an extension of the exercise. (Good textbooks do not contain this sort of 'guess what it means' exercise at all.)

But there is an entirely different way in which programs can be regarded as specifications. A program in a programming language, apart from being capable of compilation into a machine code (or interpreted in it, as the case may be), could be used as a *bona fide* specification for further development steps, to be rendered in another programming language, the rendition being performed not necessarily by an automatic compiler, even though the latter is not all that uncommon (as, for example, when a 'preprocessor' converts a program written in an extended version of a language into one coded in its basic form, or when a 'precompiler' takes a FORTRAN text and produces one in Pascal, or vice versa − not that the latter is always possible!). Since the conversion, automatic or not, between programming languages of the same ilk is not much different from compilation, at least in principle, we shall not pay further attention to this process. An altogether different story happens when the programming languages in question are of different kinds, as would happen, for example, if a program written in Prolog was being converted into one written in Pascal. An automatic conversion (a compilation) is not necessarily immediately available. It may require several intermediary steps. In this case the Prolog program may indeed be viewed as a specification that is developed by a design process into a Pascal program.

It is interesting to consider a symmetric problem: given a Pascal program, can we consider it as a specification for a Prolog program? Most programmers conversant with both languages would probably reject this notion. Why? It is very doubtful that a formal argument could be constructed to resolve this issue, primarily because we do not view 'specification' and 'program' as absolute notions. These two terms are much more closely related to the rôles played by their designations in the process of software construction than to any specific attribute of the terms themselves. This being so, the formula we start the process from is the specification, and the one we eventually arrive at is the program, which suggests symmetry, contrary to the outcome of our imaginary quiz. In fact the symmetry is not there. When we recall the intuitive introduction (see Chapter 1) and precise description of what is meant by translation in this book (see Section 2.3) we readily ascertain that the development of specifications into programs is a process during which various details can be added. Everything that follows from a specification must follow from a program that satisfies the specification (even if 'follows' denotes somewhat different relations in each instance), but not necessarily vice versa. As long as programs satisfy a specification they are its acceptable implementations, but this relationship, being obviously one-to-many, is not bound to be reversible; thus nobody really expects to be able to reconstruct *the* specification from a program that satisfies it.

Now, if we have two similar languages, say Pascal and Algol 60, it is possible to conceive of an Algol 60 program A being considered as a specification for a Pascal program P, and for P to be considered as a specification for an Algol 60 program A'. However, since there may be many different Pascal programs P_1, P_2, ..., each of which is a correct implementation of A, and for each of which there may be many different Algol 60 programs A'_1, A'_2..., there is not much chance of finding any meaningful relationship between A and A'_i. Why then are we prepared to admit either one of A and P as a specification? The answer is quite simple: the amount and kind of detail added in translation $A \rightarrow P$ is about the same as in translation $P \rightarrow A'$. On the other hand, when we have two languages of very different kinds, Pascal and Prolog, the sort of detail added in Prolog $\rightarrow$ Pascal translations very definitely differs from the sort of detail added in Pascal $\rightarrow$ Prolog translation. (Many programmers would be inclined to say that while in the Prolog $\rightarrow$ Pascal translation one indeed adds detail, in the reverse process, Pascal $\rightarrow$ Prolog, one actually loses detail; this is not necessarily so. Consider a Pascal procedure for inverting square matrices; it would require quite a lot of 'detail' being added before this procedure could be implemented in Prolog.)

Most programmers consider the operational structuring of a program to be an implementation detail added during the development of the program from its specification. Since Prolog programs are notoriously short on this kind of information, to most programmers they look more like a specification than a program. Nevertheless, Prolog programs are executable in every sense of the word.

In their excellent book on algorithmic language and program development, Bauer and Wössner (1982) illustrate both the notion of executability and the use of programs as specifications by considering a series of various 'abstract machines' with their corresponding 'programming languages'.

Consider three abstract machines:

M1 search machine: a machine capable of executing an exhaustive search through elements of a finite set and evaluating a computable predicate for each element;

M2 Herbrand−Kleene machine: a substitution machine that evaluates a recursive computable function by unfolding (i.e. by textual replacement of all calls by the body of the called routine with formal parameters replaced by actual ones);

M3 Algol machine: a substitution machine that evaluates a recursive computable function by substituting the body of the leftmost call not containing further calls in the actual parameter (call by value, leftmost-innermost principle);

and a 'real machine':

M4 that obeys principles of 'standard' sequential programming.

The problem of finding the greatest common divisor of two natural numbers, a and b, may be programmed for these machines as follows:

P1: **funct** $gcd = ($**nat** $a,$ **nat** $b: a \neq b \,|\, b \neq 0)$ **nat**:
　　　　ι **nat** $x: x$ **div** a & x **div** b &
　　　　$(\mathbf{A}$ **nat** $y)(y$ **div** a & y **div** $b \Rightarrow y$ **div** $x)$

(where ι stands for 'that ...', r **div** q denotes 'r divides q').

$P2$: **funct** gcd = (**nat** a, **nat** b) **nat**:
                if b = 0 **then** a
                ▯ $b > 0$ & $a < b$ **then** $gcd(b,a)$
                ▯ $b > 0$ & $a \geq b$ **then** $gcd(a - b,b)$ **fi**

(where ▯ is Dijkstra's bar).

$P3$: **funct** gcd = (**nat** a, **nat** b) **nat**:
                if b = 0 **then** a
                         else $gcd(b,mod(a,b))$ **fi**
       funct mod = (**nat** a, **nat** b) **nat**:
                if $a < b$ **then** a
                         else $mod(a - b,b)$ **fi**

$P4$: **funct** gcd = (**nat** a, **nat** b) **nat**:
                begin var nat x; **var nat** y; **var nat** z;
                   $x := a$; $y := b$;
                   while $y \neq 0$ **do** $z := x$;
                             while $z \geq y$ **do** $z := z - y$ **od**;
                             $x := y$;
                             $y := z$
                         od;
                  return x
        end

Each of the programs Pi, i = 1, 2, 3, may be considered as the 'specification' for program $P(i + 1)$, each of Pj, j = 2, 3, 4, as an 'implementation' of $P(j - 1)$. The transition from Pi to $P(i + 1)$ adds no detail about greatest common divisors for i = 2, 3, the transition from $P1$ to $P2$ relies upon

$$a \geq b \Rightarrow gcd(a, b) = gcd(a - b, b)$$

and

$$gcd(a, b) = gcd(b, a)$$

both of which are quite easy to derive from $P1$ considered as the definition of function gcd. Thus even the transition $P1 \rightarrow P2$ does not require any added knowledge about gcd, other than that which is contained in $P1$.

Of course, for the linguistic levels identified with machines $M1$, $M3$ and $M4$, and for $P1$, $P2$ and $P3$ considered as specifications for $P2$, $P3$ and $P4$, respectively, the actual write-up of $P2$, $P3$ and $P4$ is not uniquely determined. Indeed, considerations of efficiency, etc., may guide the programmer to conceive of structures other than those displayed above.

For example, relying again on some easy-to-establish properties of gcd, fully derivable from $P1$, and using obvious extensions of the $M2$-level notation, we can have a considerably more efficient program.

$P2'$: **funct** $gcd = ($**nat** $a,$ **nat** $b)$ **nat**:
     if $b = 0 \mid a = b$ **then** a
     $[] \; b \neq 0$ & $a \neq b$ **then if even** a & **even** b **then**

$$dupl\left(gcd\left(\frac{a}{2}, \frac{b}{2}\right)\right)$$

         $[]$ **even** a & **odd** b **then**

$$gcd\left(\frac{a}{2}, b\right)$$

         $[]$ **odd** a & **even** b **then**

$$gcd\left(a, \frac{b}{2}\right)$$

         $[]$ **odd** a & **odd** b **then**
           if $a < b$ **then** $gcd(b, a)$
           $[] \; a > b$ **then** $gcd(b, a - b)$
           fi
         fi

     fi

Observe that both programs $P2$ and $P2'$ may justifiably be considered as implementations of $P1$ (in the linguistic level of the Herbrand–Kleene machine $M2$). It is also quite appropriate to consider $P3$ as an implementation of $P2$. Perhaps less obvious is the relationship between $P2'$ and $P3$. In a purely formal sense it can be proved that in terms of listed variables both $P2'$ and $P3$ define the same function: given a pair of natural numbers a and b, gcd delivers the same natural number, whether computed by $P2'$ or by $P3$. In a less formal treatment, however, we are not likely to consider $P3$ as an appropriate implementation of $P2'$: the concern with efficiency of calculations, evident from reading $P2'$, is absent from $P3$. Thus, if we take $P2'$ – a program! – as the specification, neither $P3$ nor $P4$ would be acceptable as implementations on their respective linguistic levels.

This observation leads to an important property of programs considered as specifications: in addition to specifying an input/output relation, (source) programs may indicate a specific method of establishing this relation. If a programming language (or, more precisely, its semantic definition) makes available the mechanisms absent in the semantics of the implementation language (itself, of course, a programming language, although perhaps of a 'lower level') then the implementation must either disregard the how-to-achieve-the-desired-result hints contained in the specification or simulate them in a (usually) quite laborious way.

The first solution is adopted in $P4$ considered as an implementation of $P3$. The auxiliary function mod of $P3$ is totally disregarded; not only does its name not appear in $P4$ but there is no part of $P4$ that could be easily identified with mod of $P3$. (Incidentally, this may lead to raising a question whether $P4$ could be considered a proper implementation of $P3$ at all. If $P3$ is taken as the definition of the problem, that is if the steps $P1 \rightarrow P2 \rightarrow P3$ are disregarded or absent, then the problem clearly calls for a sequential implementation of two functions *gcd* and *mod*, and *P4* cannot be accepted. On the other hand, if *P1* is accepted as the problem statement, function *mod* in *P3* is but an auxiliary implement that can be discarded in passing to a purely sequential machine level. A justification for such a move can be easily found in the analysis of *P1* and *P2*, neither of which has terms corresponding to the *mod* function.)

Assume now that we have at our disposal a truly parallel machine, *M4'*, capable of evaluating two or more expressions independently of each other. (In Bauer and Wössner (1982) such a machine is given the name Babbage−Zuse machine and is defined as an abstract machine capable of collateral execution of programs.) In a programming language suitable for *M4'* the greatest common divisor problem can be solved by:

P4': **funct** $gcd = ($**nat** $a,$ **nat** $b)$ **nat**:
$\quad$ **begin** (**var nat** $x,$ **var nat** y) := (a,b);
$\quad\quad$ **while** $y \neq 0$ **do**
$\quad\quad\quad$ $(x,y) := (y,$ **begin var nat** $z := x$;
$\quad\quad\quad\quad\quad\quad\quad\quad\quad$ **while** $z \geq y$ **do** $z := z - y$ **od**;
$\quad\quad\quad\quad\quad\quad\quad\quad\quad$ **return** z
$\quad\quad\quad\quad\quad\quad\quad\quad$ **end**)
$\quad\quad$ **od**;
$\quad\quad$ **return** z
$\quad$ **end**

P4' exploits the collateralism of *M4'*; unfortunately, in this example there is not much to be gained by parallel execution, but this remark is neither here nor there as far as principles are concerned. Thus *P4'* specifies a 'parallel computation' solution of the problem. It can be proved[†] that *P4* is a correct implementation of *P4'* on a sequential machine in a sense similar to that in which *P4* is an implementation of *P3*.

The fact that both *P4* and *P4'* can be considered as equally admissible implementations of *P2* (we disregard, temporarily, the step *P2* → *P3* in order not to confuse the issue with *mod*) obtains from several silent assumptions:

- that we accept an implementation as correct (although, perhaps, not the most desirable) if all relationships that can be established by virtue of the specification can also be established by virtue of the implementation considered (under suitable interpretation, which in the case of our examples is identity of program free variables or formal parameters);

[†] We are omitting the proofs in this section because we are now primarily concerned with analysing *how* programs are (or could be) used as specifications. For detailed treatment of the *gcd* examples see Bauer and Wössner (1982) from where all the programs are borrowed, with minor notational differences.

- that in passing the judgement of correctness (or otherwise) of an implementation, we agree to disregard any properties specific to the implementation but expressed as relationships in which there occur notions not interpretable in terms of the notions of the specification;

- that proper semantics of collateralism (the particular form of parallelism employed in *P4'*) amounts to ensuring that, as far as global program variables are concerned, results of collateral execution of indicated program parts are identical to the combined results of executing these parts in an arbitrary order, including any 'serialization'. ('Global' in this context refers to any variable visible at more than one of the collaterally executed program parts.)

Observe that these assumptions are somewhat heterogeneous: while the first two refer to what could be conveniently abstracted as permissiveness of specification (or non-contradictive nature of implementation[†]), the third one, far from being so general, imposes a restriction on semantics of the language in which the program specification is written. If the semantics of the language does not enjoy this property, i.e. if it is not true that parts that could be 'executed' in parallel could also be executed in any other order without changing the overall effect, then, of course, a sequential implementation may be inadmissible, as it would, for example, introduce a bias that would contradict some fairness property of the specification.

Quite naturally, a specification written in a programming language can itself be biased towards a particular implementation. In general terms, a specification bias occurs when a specification is prematurely restrictive, i.e. some of the permissiveness of the problem statement is lost at too early a stage. Specification bias is not restricted to cases where programming languages are used as linguistic levels on which specifications are expressed (see Jones (1980), Chapter 15), but, because of the frequently operational nature of programming language semantics, and even more the operational meaning attached to individual programs, the bias is much more likely to creep in when such means are used for specification purposes.

In full generality, the problem of a specification being without bias, or 'sufficiently abstract' in Jones's terminology, is one that requires a specific context for its resolution. If a specification is considered separately, as an expression on a linguistic level, without a history (the specification for which the current one is an implementation or 'program') and without future (programs that satisfy the current specification) the problem is not

---

[†] An implementation may possess any property as long as it does not contradict whatever the specification explicitly says. While permissiveness of specification allows us to extend its properties in an implementation, the requirement of non-contradictiveness of the latter sets the limit as to how far it can be extended.

very meaningful. Indeed, an attempt to solve it by saying that 'a specification is sufficiently abstract if it contains only the essential information' leads nowhere, as it only shifts the onus to 'essential'. (Essential for what? Or, in a Hegelian mode, if it is given in the specification, the information is essential *eo ipso*.) Similarly, another approach, exemplified by saying that 'a specification is unbiased if for all reasonable implementations one can retrieve all its properties from any implementation', although attempting to get rid of concern with specific implementations, in fact begs the issue by the use of 'reasonable'. (In fact this approach is a thinly disguised vicious circle, also known as *idem per idem*.)

In practice, the specification bias may occur in any circumstances. When an application domain is being specified, for example, it is not inconceivable that the specification will contain a particular implementation-oriented definition of a function or relation. Many problems in payroll, insurance, etc., are specified by an explicit listing of various tables, such as taxation percentages, risk-by-category, etc. Nearly always such tables are not random collections of figures (which, had it been the case, could not be specified in any other way), but represent a particular implementation of a relation or even function. Should one consider these specifications as biased? Should one consider an implementation by a program, written for a fast computer with limited storage, in which in lieu of the tables an interpolation formula is used, as an 'unreasonable' one? (Observe that if a table is indeed implemented by an interpolation formula, no matter how exact for entries listed in the table, some structural properties of the table cannot be retrieved − e.g. the 'exact' limit starting from which a surtax is applied.)

Such problems largely disappear when the software design/implementation process is considered as a chain of specification/implementation steps, and each successive specification, itself being an implementation of its predecessor, is known to be an outcome of the implementation step executed to satisfy a permissive specification. By the very nature of such a step some information in the current specification is known to be more or less freely added to the 'core' information, carried over from the past history of the design/implementation steps[†].

The added information contained in the particular implementation represents the decisions taken in order to best exploit 'facilities' available in the linguistic level chosen for implementation. Is it possible to separate

---

[†] This, of course, does not apply to the very first specification in the chain. While it may be philosophically interesting to ponder the significance of this 'special' specification, from a practical point of view it is rather insignificant: if the chain consists of many links, the nature of a repetitive link is technologically much more important than the possibly different nature of a unique initial link. Moreover, the evolutionary nature of software problems and solutions in practical applications dispels quite a lot of the first link mystique; very often what was temporarily considered as the first link would turn out to be modified many times, and thus pushed down the chain.

this information from the core information that carries nothing but the 'original' problem statement?

Statically, i.e. analysing a particular specification alone, it is an impossible task. It is also totally unnecessary. The added information, indeed the accumulated added information, represents the design: it is there because the programmer saw a way to solve the original problem in this particular way. If we want to *change* his solution, we shall have to undo his design and replace it with some other. This, however, is not going to be an implementation of the specification he has arrived at.

Hence, if we consider a program in a programming language as a specification, we must realize that the choice of the language necessitates or otherwise influences some aspects of the specification (perhaps making it biased!) but this choice itself represents a (hopefully!) conscious design decision. Thus, for example, when we take $P4'$ as the specification, we accept (and should respect) the designer's decision to specify the *gcd* problem in collateral fashion − pointing towards an implementation on a parallel computer (which under a particular semantics of collateralism may be simulated by a sequential one, if necessary).

Incidentally, the above discussion may be regarded as a contribution to the growing controversy surrounding the use of parallelism in computing. In most cases, parallelism arises as a means, as a possible way to solve a problem. As soon as the problem is specified in a linguistic level (or, even, system) that admits parallelism, the latter becomes a part of the specification (current problem statement) and thus an obligation for the implementors, who have either to use parallel machinery or to ensure results consistent with those that would be expected with its use. Even when the original problem statement relies on the explicit parallelism, there may be a higher abstraction of the problem where no parallelism would be noticed.

Similarly, the controversies about declarative *vs* imperative, functional *vs* procedural, etc., programming being better for specification purposes do not admit unequivocal resolution in strictly technical terms. In Chapter 2 we introduced the mathematical notion of computability independent of the efficiency with which a computation may be executed. (The efficiency always depends on the particular means at one's disposal, computability does not.) Program $P1$ above − given in a purely descriptive way (not unlike Prolog, apart from syntax) − specifies the same computable function *gcd* as program $P4$ − given in a purely imperative way (not unlike Pascal, apart from syntax). While it may be argued that $P1$ and $P4$ describe (or imply) different computations in different machines (and small wonder they do so if the machines are so totally different as $M1$ and $M4$), the meaning of both programs in abstract terms is the same: they define the greatest common divisor for two natural numbers. In the preceding sentence we have relied upon English rendering of an abstract mathematical concept to express the commonality of $P1$ and $P4$ meaning.

This considerably shortens the technical (but utterly boring) argument that would establish the mutual interpretability of *P1* and *P4* in corresponding linguistic levels of *M1* and *M4*.

So which program is 'better' as the specification of the greatest common divisor?

P1 is not biased towards any implementation. All programs, *P2−P4*, including the two primed versions, may be proved to be implementations of *P1*. From the listed collection, *P1* is undoubtedly the most abstract one. It is also the least useful one as far as specifying computations in any machine but *M1*.

On the other hand, *P1* (or some equivalent) can be easily extracted from any other program of the collection as its input/output relation. It is not very difficult to imagine application areas in which relations and functions are defined by procedures (not necessarily computational ones: 'On receipt of a blue slip its top portion is filed under the client's name and two copies of the bottom portion are made. One, on pink card, is despatched to the client's home address; another, on a white self-adhesive label, is attached to the box of candy'). A program may then be written as a specification in an abstract procedural language quite easily, even though the extraction of a descriptive, relational program may be somewhat more difficult. As discussed above, a specification by means of a procedural program is likely to be biased towards a particular class of implementations.

Finally, some brief observations on programming languages as specification vehicles:

1. Many newer programming languages (Ada, Modula, CLU to list but a few) separate heading definitions from body definitions for meaningful building blocks of the language. The headings are sometimes referred to as specification parts of the declarations. Of course, the usage of 'specification' in this context has very little in common with the sense in which the term is used in this book. Headings define the parameters, their types and the type of the construct; they contain − more or less − the same information as that which can be obtained from the first lines of *P1−P4*.

2. It is conceivable to design a programming language in which many different styles of specification would be expressible. Such a language would permit the software development process to be carried out within a single programming language. An obvious advantage of this approach rests in the use of a single support system that can service such a process. This is the main idea of the *wide spectrum language* and project (Bauer and Wössner, 1982; CIP Language Group, 1985).

3. Some programming languages (e.g. Simula) permit the specification of types and relations in a gradual way. This is achieved by the twin devices of prefixing and virtualization. Subject to certain context

restrictions, any Simula class, A, can be used as a prefix in definition
of another class, B. Class B inherits all properties of class A except
those that follow from those constituents of the class A definition that
are marked as virtual in the definition of class A. In addition to
properties inherited from A, class B has its own properties, defined in
the definition of class B which may also introduce a particular set of
definition constituents for those marked virtual in the definition of
class A. The prefixing and virtualization − largely under-recognized
features of Simula and similar languages − are a very powerful
specification building tool, especially in the environment where the
knowledge about the specified domain accumulates gradually. In fact,
it appears that prefixing and virtualization as used, for example, in
Utopist, a Soviet programming language for incremental knowledge
processing (Tyugu, 1984) offer a much more efficient alternative to
heuristic IKBS designs.

3.5 Specifications as programs

Discussing programs as specifications in the preceding section we did not
feel obliged to demonstrate the appropriateness of the heading too
strongly: after all, there are not too many readers of this book who would
intuitively disagree with the claim that programs are specifications (of a
sort, at the very least). Thus we could concentrate on specific features,
idiosyncrasies, of programs viewed as specifications. In this section we are
facing a somewhat different task: we expect that the view of specifications
as programs may take some convincing. Here we go.

To fix our attention, let us assume that the specification is given by
means of a number of theorems on the linguistic level of some constructive logic with some extralogical axioms that bring in the information
about an application domain. We also assume that the extralogical axioms
are constructive, expressed in the form:

$$(\mathbf{A}x)(P(x) \Rightarrow (\mathbf{E}y)Q(x, y)) \tag{3.19}$$

where P does not contain another existential quantifier, P and Q are
predicates over a suitable element-space, and x and y are variables
ranging over 'coordinates' (or groups thereof) of this space. The con-
structiveness requirement can be restated explicity as the requirement
that for each axiom of the form (3.19) there exists a recursive function f,
such that

$$P(x) \Rightarrow (f \text{ is defined}) \& Q(x, f(x))$$

It is also assumed that predicates P and Q are computable.

Of course, some axioms may have simpler forms; for example, when
there is no precondition, $(\mathbf{A}x) Px = true$, (3.19) reduces to $(\mathbf{A}x\mathbf{E}y) Q(x, y)$,
which amounts to saying that the equation $Q(x, y) = true$ can always be

solved for y. In an even simpler case, (3.19) reduces to an assertion about an individual y, $(Ey)Q(y)$, which introduces a constant.

Thus, to all axioms there correspond well defined computations: in the simplest case, a declaration of a constant; in less restricted ones, a procedure for solving an equation; in the most general case, a procedure for solving a set of recursive equations (guaranteed to have a computable solution). We shall henceforth assume that suitable computational procedures for each axiom are known.

Consider now a theorem T from our specification and its derivation from axioms. The formal derivation of T is a finite sequence of steps

$$\left(\frac{P_{i1}, P_{i2}, \ldots, P_{ik_i}, r_i}{Q_i}\right) \quad i = 1, 2, \ldots, n$$

where $Q_n = T$, $P_{11}, P_{12}, \ldots, P_{1k_1}$ are axioms; each P_{ij}, $j=1,2,\ldots, k_i$ is either an axiom or Q_l, $l < i$; the r_i component of the ith step is that one of the inference rules of our constructive logic which on application to $P_{i1}, P_{i2}, \ldots, P_{ik_i}$ yields Q_i.

For example, if A and B are axioms, a derivation may contain a step

$$\left(\frac{A, B}{A \, \& \, B}, \text{definition of conjunction}\right)$$

or a step

$$\left(\frac{A}{(Ex)A(x)}, \text{principle of instantiation}\right)$$

In each step the premises $P_{i1}, P_{i2}, \ldots, P_{ik_i}$ are previously established theorems (or axioms of the specification) and the conclusion Q_i is the newly established theorem (lemma in the derivation).

To each formally derived theorem there corresponds a computational procedure which can be constructed directly from the procedures corresponding to axioms and from the actual derivation steps which establish the theorem.

Indeed, let $p1, p2, \ldots, pm$ be the names of procedures corresponding to axioms of the linguistic level. To each of the logical connectives (&, |, $\Rightarrow$, etc.) there corresponds a well defined program construct. For instance, if pA and pB are procedures corresponding to axioms A and B respectively, to $C \equiv A \Rightarrow B$ there corresponds $pc = \textbf{proc}(pA) \, pB$, i.e. exactly the same procedure as that which corresponds to B, 'guarded' by the restriction on its arguments being compatible with the type of results delivered by pA. Similarly, to $C \equiv A \,|\, B$ there corresponds $pC = \textbf{union}(pA, pB)$, etc. In this notation we are relying on an Algol 68 kind of context type handling; similar expressions can, of course, be formed in any other strongly typed programming language.

In this way we can build program correspondents of expressions com-

posed of expressions that already have program correspondents and from
logical connectives.

Quite similarly we can provide schemata to build program correspondents of rules of inference if program correspondents of constituent
expressions are available. Thus, for example, for *modus ponens*

$$\frac{A, A \Rightarrow B}{B}$$

the program correspondent is $pB = pC(pA)$, where pB is the name of
the newly introduced program construct, pA is the name of a program
construct that corresponds to expression A and pC is the name of the
program construct that corresponds to $A \Rightarrow B$. (For other schemata and a
more detailed exposition, see Tyugu (1984).)

In this way, going step by step along its derivation sequence, we get a
program construct that corresponds to any theorem in our linguistic
system. Thus we can establish a program construct for the specification.

Observe that if we construct the derivation tree (see Figure 3.1(a))
and apply the natural (in the circumstances) composition of procedures
corresponding to each node, the resulting program structure is very much
like an applicative (or functional) program. On the other hand, if we
name the results of each derivation step, we may get a program structure
similar to that of an imperative programming language (see Figure 3.1(d)).
Observe that pA is evaluated once only in the sequential program and
three times in the applicative form. On the other hand, the applicative
form exhibits a certain degree of local independence between subexpres-
sions (see applications of $\alpha(\dots)$ and $\beta(\dots)$ in the final formula) which
lends itself quite naturally to parallel execution. Of course, neither the
saving of pA evaluations in Figure 3.1(d), nor parallelism present in
Figure 3.1(c) makes a lot of difference in this example. What they do
indicate, however, is quite typical for the two styles of programs which
can be obtained as correspondents of the formal derivation of a theorem.

Observe also that not only can we obtain, in a very natural way,
program correspondents of a specification, but, quite similarly, we may
get programs for any consequences of the specification, as long as these
consequences are formally derived. Surely, this supports the statement
about executability of formal specifications *and* points to the way in which
such specifications may be used for exploration of 'what do they mean?'
problems.

The whole construction of program correspondents, as presented
above, is founded on the assumption of the specification being given as a
constructive theory, i.e. by axioms in the form of (3.9). In this connection
it is worthwhile to recall our discussion of computability from Section 2.1.

In the remainder of this section we shall describe a system intended
for writing specifications and their program implementations. In a sense,

(a)

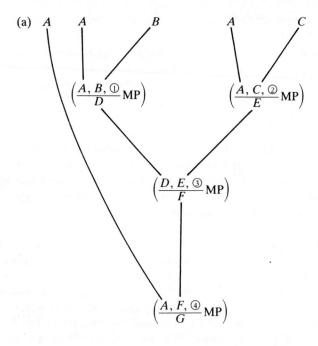

(b) A $pA(x)$
     B $pB(x)$
     C $pC(x)$
     ① $A \& B \Rightarrow D$ $\alpha(x1, x2)$
     ② $A \& C \Rightarrow E$ $\beta(x1, x2)$
     ③ $D \& E \Rightarrow F$ $\gamma(x1, x2)$
     ④ $A \& F \Rightarrow G$ $\delta(x1, x2)$

(c) $\alpha\,(pA(x), pB(x))$ $\beta\,(pA(x), pc(x))$
     $\gamma\,(\alpha(pA(x), pB(x)), \beta\,(pA(x), pC(x)))$
     $\delta\,(pA(x), \gamma\,(\,\alpha\,(pA(x), pB(x)), \beta\,(pA(x), pC(x))))$
     $y = \delta\,(pA(x), \gamma\,(\,\alpha\,(pA(x), pB(x)), \beta\,(pA(x), pC(x))))$

(d) $r1 := pA(x)$
     $r2 := pB(x)$
     $r3 := pC(x)$
     $r4 := \alpha\,(r1, r2)$
     $r5 := \beta\,(r1, r3)$
     $r6 := \gamma\,(r4, r5)$
     $y := \delta\,(r1, r6)$

Figure 3.1 Derivation of a theorem and corresponding programs.
(a) Derivation tree; MP stands for *modus ponens*, encircled figures stand for
axioms thus labelled in (b). (b) Axioms used in the derivation of theorem G and
corresponding program structures. (c) Applicative programs obtained directly
from the derivation tree; the bottom line presents the application of the program
correspondent of theorem G to input x yielding output y. (d) A sequential
program with assignments.

such a system may be regarded as a wide spectrum language mentioned in the preceding section. In another, it is a specification language with a facility to directly specify executable programs. The illustrative material is based on Nakajima *et al.* (1980), a description of the ι system, developed and implemented in Kyoto University.

Specification of a complex domain (rich in types and relations) is greatly simplified by its modularization. It is immaterial to go into prolonged digressions on this subject (see Section 3.1 of Turski (1978)). For our present needs, suffice it to say that a module is a syntactic unit, recognizable as such, which defines a data or procedural abstraction. In ι there are three kinds of module: t-modules, s-modules and p-modules. The first two kinds of module define sorts, the third one procedures. Sorts are divided into types and sypes (hence the t and s designation of modules). The difference between types and sypes consists in the fact that the induction rule on types is included in the inference rules of ι whereas for sypes this is not the case. (In Clear, considered in Section 2.2, the induction rule was never implied; a special operation on theories, **induce**, was introduced to indicate explicitly when this rule was to be applied.)

A module has several parts; two of them, **interface** and **specification**, clearly correspond to the syntactic and axiomatic (semantic) part of familiar abstract data type definitions. The following is an example of a t-module defining the type of natural numbers.

interface type *NN*
  fn *ZERO*: $\rightarrow £$ **as** 0
     SUC: $£ \rightarrow £$
     LESS: $(£, £) \rightarrow BOOL$ **as** $£ \leq £$
     EQUAL: $(£, £) \rightarrow BOOL$ **as** $£ = £$
  end interface

specification type *NN*
  var $X,Y,Z,U,V: £$
  axiom 1: $SUC(X) = SUC(Y) \Rightarrow X = Y$
       2: $\neg(SUC(X) \leq X)$
       3: $X \leq Y \Rightarrow SUC(X) \leq SUC(Y)$
       4: $X \leq Y \mid Y \leq X$
       5: $X \leq Y \& Y \leq X \Rightarrow X = Y$
       6: $X \leq Y \& Y \leq Z \Rightarrow X \leq Z$
end specification

Notes on notation: In ι, $£$ denotes the type being defined. Thus in the above example $£$ stands for *NN*; **as** introduces a more convenient notational variant – thus $LESS(X, Y)$ may be written as $X \leq Y$; all free variables in the **specification** part are universally quantified.

Notes on substance: The axioms in the **specification** part are not in the form (3.19), the type *NN* as defined above is not constructive. In the sequel we shall see how the system introduces program correspondents for the specified types. The axioms would be simpler, and their number smaller, if *LESS* was stated to be antisymmetric, transitive and reflexive. In fact, the axioms of *NN* define more than just natural numbers; they also define the notation of ordering relation *LESS* on *NN*. Finally, since we have here a t-module, the induction rule applies; thus if *A* is any formula,

$$\frac{A(x/0),\ A \Rightarrow A(x/SUC(x))}{A}$$

is a rule of inference, where x is a variable of type *NN* (and $A(x/t)$ is the formula *A* with t (of type *NN*) substituted for each occurrence of x).

Note on terminology: The choice of **specification** as the identifier for the second part of a module (the one in which all the axioms are listed) is most unfortunate; we kept it from the original ι syntax to facilitate reading of ι programs appearing in the literature.

To develop a sizable example, we shall need two more types, *INTPOLY* and *INTARRAY*, polynomials with integer coefficients and integer arrays, respectively.

> **interface type** *INTPOLY*
>   **fn** *ZERO*:   → £ **as** 0
>   *TERM*: *NN*   → £
>   *CM*:   (*INT*, £) → £ **as** *INT* × £
>   *ADD*: (£, £)   → £ **as** £ + £
>   *COEF*: (£, *NN*) → *INT*
>   *DEG*: £   → *NN*
> **end interface**

> **specification type** *INTPOLY*
>   **var** *X,Y,Z*: £; *M, N*: *NN*; *I*: *INT*
>   **axiom**   1: $COEF(0, N) = 0$
>   2: $DEG(0) = 0$
>   3: $COEF(TERM(N), N) = 1$
>   4: $M \neq N \Rightarrow COEF(TERM(N), M) = 0$
>   5: $DEG(TERM(N)) = N$
>   6: $X \neq 0 \Rightarrow COEF(X, DEG(X)) \neq 0$
>   7: $DEG(X) < N \Rightarrow COEF(X, N) = 0$
>   8: $(\mathbf{A}N)(COEF(X, N) = COEF(Y, N)) \Rightarrow X = Y$
>   9: $COEF(\mathbf{I} \times \mathbf{X}, N) = I \times COEF(X, N)$
>   10: $COEF(X + Y, N) = COEF(X, N) + COEF(Y, N)$
> **end specification**

Notes on substance: In the two parts of the *INTPOLY* definition, as in all subsequent modules, equality and its axioms (symmetry, transitivity, reflexivity) are implicitly assumed. Type *INT* of integers is assumed to be defined, including the basic operations on *INT* type objects, such as 0, 1, +, ×, ≤, etc. Relations < and ≠ on *NN* type, assumed available by

axioms of *INTPOLY*, could be added by a suitable p-module extension of
the *NN* definition (see below). When the same function name is introduced for two or more types, in contexts where some confusion could
arise, they may be distinguished by prefixing the function name with that
of the type. Thus we could (and where a confusion would otherwise arise,
should) write *INTPOLY#ADD* and *INT#ADD* to denote two functions
from two different modules.

    interface type *INTARRAY*
      fn *CREATE*: $(NN, INT) \rightarrow £$
         HIGH: £ $\rightarrow NN$
         FETCH: $(£, NN)$ $\rightarrow INT$ **as** $£[NN]$
      op *STORE*: $(£ : NN, INT)$ **as** $£[NN] := INT$
         SHRINK: $(£)$
         STRETCH: $(£ : INT)$
    end interface

    specification type *INTARRAY*
      var X, Y: £; M, N: *NN*; I: *INT*
      axiom 1: $HIGH(CREATE(N, I)) = N$
             2: $N \leq HIGH(X) \Rightarrow HIGH(STORE(X, N, I)) = HIGH(X)$
             3: $HIGH(STRETCH(X, I)) = SUC(HIGH(X))$
             4: $1 \leq HIGH(X) \Rightarrow SUC(HIGH(SHRINK(X)))$
               $= HIGH(X)$
             5: $N \leq M \Rightarrow FETCH(CREATE(M, I), N) = I$
             6: $N \leq HIGH(X) \Rightarrow FETCH(STORE(X, N, I), N) = I$
             7: $N \leq HIGH(X) \& M \leq HIGH(X) \& M \neq N$
               $\Rightarrow FETCH(STORE(X, N, I), M) = FETCH(X, M)$
             8: $SUC(N) \leq HIGH(X) \Rightarrow FETCH(SHRINK(X), M)$
               $= FETCH(X, M)$
             9: $FETCH(STRETCH(X, I), SUC(HIGH(X))) = I$
          10: $N \leq HIGH(X) \Rightarrow FETCH(STRETCH(X, I), N)$
               $= FETCH(X, N)$
          11: $(HIGH(X) = HIGH(Y) \& (AN)(N \leq HIGH(X)$
               $\Rightarrow FETCH(X, N) = FETCH(Y, N))) \Rightarrow X = Y$
    end specification

    Notes on substance: In the t-module *INTARRAY*, of which two parts
(**interface** and **specification**) are exhibited above, a shorthand notation is
introduced for *operations* which are quite similar to procedures in many
programming languages. Names of operations are introduced after the
special marker **op**; to the right of the colon that follows an operation
name one can find the type information on parameters. Parameters that
precede the colon in the list are 'call-by-variable' ones, those to the right
are 'call-by-value'. If no colon appears in the parameter list, all parameters are of 'call-by-variable' variety. Since only the type information

about the parameters is given in the **interface** part, should there arise a need to refer to a parameter in the **specification** part, the variable parameters may be named by $n, where n is the ordinal number of their occurrence. Thus $STORE(X:m, i)$, equivalent to $X[m]:=i$ in the familiar style of programming languages, refers to a single variable parameter and in axiom 2 we could have written $STORE\$1$ instead of $STORE$. The use of operations can be avoided by introduction of simultaneous assignment, thus $P(X, Y:S, T)$ is equivalent to $(X, Y:= P\$1(X, Y, S, T), P\$2(X, Y, S, T))$, where $P\$1$ and $P\$2$ are names of auxiliary functions that would have to be added in the **interface** part and constrained by suitable axioms in the **specification** part.

The role of p-modules can be illustrated by:

interface procedure *INTSEARCH*
    fn *SORTED*: *INTARRAY*   → *BOOL*
        LOCATE: $(INTARRAY, INT) \rightarrow (BOOL, NN)$
end interface

specification procedure *INTSEARCH*
    var $X:INTARRAY; M, N:NN; I:INT$
    axiom 1: $SORTED(X) \Leftrightarrow (AM\ AN)\ (0 \le M\ \&\ M < N$
                            $\&\ N \le HIGH(X)$
                            $\Rightarrow X[M] < X[N])$
        2: $SORTED(X) \Rightarrow (LOCATE\$1(X, I)$
                         $\Rightarrow (0 \le LOCATE\$2(X, I)$
                         $\&\ LOCATE\$2(X, I)$
                         $\le HIGH(X)$
                         $\&\ X[LOCATE\$2(X, I)]$
                         $= I))$
        3: $SORTED(X) \Rightarrow (-LOCATE\$1(X, I)$
                         $\Rightarrow (AM)(0 \le M$
                         $\&\ M \le HIGH(X)$
                              $\Rightarrow X[M] \ne I))$
end specification

A p-module adds new functions to a type defined by a t-module. Observe that the £ symbol is conspicuously absent from a p-module as it refers to the type being defined and no type is being defined in a p-module.

A module may be implemented by a **realization** part as in the following example.

realization type *INTPOLY*
    rep = *INTARRAY*
    fn ↓ $COEF(X:\mathbf{rep}; N:NN)$ **return** $(I:INT)$
        if $N \le HIGH(X)$ **then** $I:= X[N]$ **else** $I:= 0$ **fi**
    end fn

fn $\downarrow$ *ZERO* **return** (*X*:**rep**)
    $X := CREATE(0, 0)$
end fn
fn $\downarrow$ *TERM* (*N*:*NN*) **return** (*X*:**rep**)
    $X := CREATE(N, 0)$;
    $X[N] := 1$
end fn
fn $\downarrow$ *CM(I:INT; X*:**rep**) **return** (*Y*:**rep**)
    var *K*:*NN*;
      if $I = 0$ **then** $Y := \downarrow ZERO$
             else $Y := CREATE(HIGH(X),0)$;
             for *K* **from** 0 **to** $HIGH(X)$ **do** $Y[K] := I{\times}X[K]$ **rof**
      fi
end fn
fn $\downarrow$ *ADD(X, Y*:**rep**) **return** (*Z*:**rep**)
    var *N, K*:*NN*;
      if $HIGH(X) \le HIGH(Y)$ **then** $N := HIGH(Y)$
        else $N := HIGH(X)$ **fi**;
      $Z := CREATE(N, 0)$;
      for *K* **from** 0 **to** *N* **do** $Z[K] := \downarrow COEF(X, K)$
        $+ \downarrow COEF(Y, K)$ **rof**;
      while $N \ne 0$ & $Z[N] = 0$ **do** $SHRINK(Z)$;
        $N := HIGH(Z)$ **od**
end fn
fn $\downarrow$ *DEG(X*:**rep**) **return** (*N*:*NN*)
    $N := HIGH(X)$
end fn
fn $\downarrow$ *EQUAL(X, Y*:**rep**) **return** (*B*:*BOOL*)
    var *K*:*NN*;
      if $HIGH(X) \ne HIGH(Y)$ **then** $B :=$ **false**
             else $K := 0$; $B :=$ **true**;
             while $K \le HIGH(X)$ & *B* **do**
             if $X[K] \ne Y[K]$ **then**
               $B :=$ **false fi**;
               $K := SUC(K)$
             od
  end fn
end realization

A **realization** part describes an implementation of a type (*INTPOLY* in this case) by means of other types (in this case, *INTARRAY*). Each function *F* of the abstract type is implemented by a concrete function $\downarrow F$. (For example, *COEF*: (*INTPOLY, NN*) $\to$ *INT* is implemented by $\downarrow COEFF$: (**rep**, *NN*) $\to$ *INT*.) In addition to functions which implement abstract ones, a realization part may contain functions of local significance, i.e. used only in the realization. Such functions need not have abstractions in the sense that e.g. *COEF* is an abstraction of ↓ *COEF*.

Some functions introduced in p-modules are intended only as convenient abbreviations for otherwise clumsy expressions. One such is function *SORTED* in *INTSEARCH*. In the realization part of a p-module no concrete functions need be defined for such abstract functions introduced for convenience only. Thus we shall have

> **realization procedure** *INTSEARCH*
> **fn** ↓ *LOCATE*(X:*INTARRAY*; I:*INT*) **return** (B:*BOOL*; L:*NN*)
>   **var** M,N: *NN*
> $M := 0; N := HIGH(X)$
>   . . .
>
> **end fn**
> **end realization**

with obvious code replaced for brevity with an ellipsis.

In any hierarchical modularization we are faced with transitive dependencies between modules, as discussed in Section 4.1.1 of Turski (1978). Thus a module q depends directly on all modules used in its **realization** part, and transitively on all modules which support[†] any module p on which q depends. In proving the representation correct (for details applicable to ι see Nakajima *et al.* (1980) and Honda *et al.* (1983)) one relies not only on the union of theories presented by supporting modules but also on the **realization** part which introduces concrete functions with their bodies playing the rôle of axioms (defining the semantics of each concrete function).

Naturally, the process of specification and realization in the style suggested by ι could go on indefinitely, always implementing the required types by more and more primitive ones. For such a design procedure to terminate, one needs a collection of elementary types, whose implementation (**realization** parts) are 'hidden' and provided by the underlying system core. In ι the collection of elementary types contains the usual *NN, BOOL, INT* types.

Commenting on the example of t-module *NN*, we have remarked that it defines not only the usual natural numbers but also the properties of the ordering relation. Of course, the notion of order is common to many types. To define such shared notions, which differ from types primarily by absence of elements, an ι programmer may use an s-module, introducing a suitable sype. For instance, the notion of order may be defined by

---

[†] If q depends on p we say that p supports q. When we say 'depends' we mean 'depends directly or transitively'.

interface sype *ORDER*
  fn *LESS*: $(£, £) \rightarrow BOOL$ **as** $£ \leq £$
      EQUAL: $(£, £) \rightarrow BOOL$ **as** $£ = £$
end interface

specification sype *ORDER*
  var X, Y, Z: $£$
  axiom 1: $X \leq Y \mid Y \leq X$
         2: $X \leq Y \ \& \ Y \leq Z \Rightarrow X \leq Z$
         3: $X \leq Y \ \& \ Y \leq X \Rightarrow X = Y$
end specification

Sypes may be employed to impart a notion they capture to type definitions; hence, for example, one can define *NN* simply by

interface type *NN*
  is *ORDER*
  fn *ZERO*: $\rightarrow £$ **as** 0
     SUC: $£ \rightarrow £$
end interface

specification type *NN*
  var X, Y: $£$
  axiom 1: $SUC(X) = SUC(Y) \Rightarrow X = Y$
         2: $\neg(SUC(X) \leq X)$
         3: $X \leq Y \Rightarrow SUC(X) \leq SUC(Y)$
end specification

where **is** *ORDER* in the **interface** part causes the axioms of sype *ORDER* to be imported into the **specification** part of *NN*, thanks to which *ORDER#LESS*, *ORDER#EQUAL*, converted to *NN#LESS* and *NN#EQUAL*, may be treated as if they appeared in the **interface** part. Observe that the symbol $£$ in an s-module does not refer to the type being defined (as no such thing is meant when an s-module is written) but to that type in whose defining t-module the sype is referred to. If a sype is used to impart the same property to several types (occurs after **is** in several different t-modules), the symbol $£$ refers each time to a different type.

     A sype may be considered as a class of types that enjoy a certain property, like being ordered or forming a ring structure. The latter may be defined by:

interface sype *RING*
  fn *ZERO*: $\rightarrow £$ **as** 0
     ONE: $\rightarrow £$ **as** 1
     ADD: $(£, £) \rightarrow £$ **as** $£ + £$
     MULT: $(£, £) \rightarrow £$ **as** $£ \times £$
     REV: $£$ $\rightarrow £$ **as** $-£$
end interface

specification sype *RING*
  var $X, Y, Z: £$
  axiom 1: $X + 0 = X$
        2: $X + Y = Y + X$
        3: $(X + Y) + Z = X + (Y + Z)$
        4: $X \times Y = Y \times X$
        5: $(X \times Y) \times Z = X \times (Y \times Z)$
        6: $X \times (Y + Z) = X \times Y + X \times Z$
        7: $1 \times X = X$
        8: $X + (-X) = 0$
end specification

Polynomials with coefficients from a ring may then be defined by

interface type *POLY(P:RING)*
  fn *ZERO*: $\to £$ **as** 0
    TERM: *NN* $\to £$
    CM: $(P, £)$ $\to £$ **as** $P \times £$
    ADD: $(£, £)$ $\to £$ **as** $£ + £$
    COEF: $(£, NN) \to P$
    DEG: $£$ $\to NN$
end interface

specification type *POLY(P: RING)*
  var $X, Y: £; M, N: NN; I: P$
  axiom 1: $COEF(N, 0) = 0$
        2: $DEG(0) = 0$
        3: $COEF(TERM(N), N) = 1$
        . . .
end specification

In this way one can define a parameterized type. If now we have a type T of the class determined by sype *RING*, we can use $POLY(T)\#COEF$, which is a function $(POLY(T), NN) \to T$ obeying axioms of $POLY(P:RING)$. (Note that if a type is defined by a t-module with an **is** construct in its **interface** part, its membership in a sype class can be detected by purely syntactic means.) The ι system allows separate compilation of parameterized modules, even though actual parameters can themselves be parameterized, e.g. $POLY(POLY(T))$.

We shall not describe here the proof techniques associated with the ι system, beyond saying that the system has a highly developed set of automatic and semi-automatic tools. We should like, however, to point out that quite apart from these tools ι is a powerful and fully implemented linguistic system in which a large class of linguistic levels may be defined. The mechanisms provided by ι are very similar to mechanisms of a modern programming language: hierarchical modularization of definitions, parameterization, extensibility, neat and highly readable syntax, etc.

A special mention should be made of the significance of the **realization** parts of t-modules. First, let us emphasize that this part is a first-class citizen of a definition[†], i.e. it is as much required as the remaining two parts. Even though one is inclined to consider the **specification** part as the only part that defines a type meaning, the bodies of concrete functions from the **realization** part contribute sufficiently important semantic information to earn the **realization** part an equally semantic standing. Roughly speaking, it is through this part of a t-module that the meaning of a type being defined (and its associated abstract functions) is related to types that are already accessible (known).

The **realization** parts are clearly program-like in their appearance. Indeed, they are programs that implement a type in terms of what is already available. It is, however, worthwhile to note that although a **realization** part is a program (or a collection of programs), it makes no reference to the implementation details of supporting modules. The concrete functions of the module being defined rely on *abstract* functions of the supporting modules. It would be therefore quite improper to consider the ι style of specification as implementation biased, merely because implementation is a constituent of definition.

We have illustrated in this section two important ways in which specifications can be viewed as programs: on the one hand, from a constructive specification a program correspondent can be obtained by mechanical transcription, while on the other, a programming-like system, exemplified here by ι (but also by Clear, although with fewer system facilities), may be constructed to allow specification writing in a style which not only admits compilation and (almost) mechanical verification of implementation correctness, but also explicitly contains programs.

[†] Because of the choice of 'specification' as an identifier for the axiom part of a type definition we try to avoid confusion that would probably have ensued if we used expressions like the **specification** part of type specifications.

Chapter 4   **Program Design and Implementation**

4.1 The step-by-step approach

Having established in the previous chapters the context in which we wish to discuss program development, we now wish to proceed to outline our ideas concerning the development of computer programs from specifications using a step-by-step approach. After all, the phrase 'step-by-step approach' has now an almost religious aspect. The incantation of this or related phrases (such as stepwise refinement, stepwise development) at appropriate points in a text is meant to bestow the blessing of rationality to a program development method without which it might no longer be considered respectable[†].

But what exactly underlies this blessing of rationality induced by phrases such as the above? It is the basic contention of this book that the ultimate meaning which can be attributed to such statements is that all the 'steps' are in some deep sense a repetition of the same step and that such steps are easily and mechanically composable. Thus the (mega-)step relating a specification to a running system is actually a composition of many (micro-)steps.

Before getting on with the business at hand, we should answer a number of queries which we assume that the above remarks will arouse. Firstly, what do we mean by the 'deep sense' in which steps are thought to be the 'same'? An analogy might be helpful here. Consider the concept(s) of proof as described in the Appendix. A proof (in the predicate calculus) consists of a sequence of formulae, where each formula in the sequence is (an instance of) the conclusion of a rule of inference whose premises (more precisely instances thereof) occur earlier in the sequence (or the formula in question is an axiom or an assumption). If one now thinks of constructing such a proof, the (idealized) process is one in which each step in the construction consists of adding some appropriate formula to the already constructed sequence. Clearly, we do not expect each proof

---

[†] These phrases encapsulate ideas which are clearly related to Polya's work on problem solving by decomposition, but we will not dwell on the relationship here. See, for example, Veloso (1982). There is also a relationship with the concepts of tactics and tacticals in theorem proving systems such as LCF (see Gordon *et al.*, 1979).

to consist of the same formulae in the same sequences. This is *not* the sense in which all proofs and steps in proofs are thought to be the same.

What relates steps in different proofs is that they are all instances of a single, precise (i.e. mathematical), and, moreover, calculable relationship. (At least this is true of proofs in a fixed deductive system. The nature of the relationship might be quite different in distinct deductive systems.) Thus, our contention is that the development of programs in a step-by-step fashion can be explained by considering a sequence of objects (the nature of which is yet to be defined, but which play a rôle analogous to formulae in proofs), where each object is related to the previous object in the sequence by the same single, precise (i.e. mathematical), and calculable relation[†]. We postpone discussion of the technical aspects of this relationship to later sections.

The second question which may have arisen in the mind of the reader is what might be meant by 'easily and mechanically composable' steps. The analogy with proofs turns out to be useful again (although, as we will have occasion to observe, not completely exact). Suppose that by some (inference) step we manage to construct the sequence of formulae Pf (as part of a proof of some formula B). The next step in constructing the proof (of B) comes up with the formula A as the appropriate candidate for developing the proof. The fact that it is suitable (as opposed to being helpful) can easily be checked by applying the usual criterion: is there a rule of inference, an instance of whose conclusion A is, such that instances of the premises of this rule occur already in the sequence Pf? Composing the previous steps with the present step consists in the easy and mechanical process of concatenating the formula A onto the sequence of formulae Pf.

Reiterating, note that all the creativity involved in doing the next step in a proof is directed towards determining which formula to use next. Making the formula a part of a proof is basically a book-keeping exercise. Although with proofs it is also a straightforward process to show that the putative candidate for the next step in the proof is a legitimate candidate, with the development of programs such legitimization steps will be somewhat more involved[‡].

[†] The careful reader will note that, as with all analogies, there is already a subtle difference between the relationship governing the occurrence of formulae in proofs and the relationship between the objects of step-by-step development: a formula is related to others (often more than one) which may occur anywhere in the previous sequence, whereas an object considered in program development may be related only to the object occurring immediately before it in the sequence. At least, we will claim that this is the case.

[‡] Generally, there is another difference between developing proofs and developing programs. With proofs, the end of the process is fixed, but the beginning is not. That is, we know the formula with which the sequence must end, but with what formula shall we start? With programs, the opposite is the case — we know the specification with which we start (but see Chapter 1) and do not know with which reformulation of it as programs we will end up.

Some remarks concerning what it is that one can calculate in such steps are also in order. Knowing that formula A is a suitable next step in a proof involves a judgement which deals with a lot more than can be calculated. There may be many more formulae $A1$, $A2$, ..., An, all of which are technically (i.e. as far as calculation can tell us) suitable. But which of them is the most appropriate to use at this point? This aspect of the judgement is not generally subject to simple mechanization and involves the use of creativity on the part of the agent carrying out the proof. Similarly, in program development, the phrase about steps being 'easily and mechanically composable' is not at all meant to deny the use of and need for creativity. So, once we have made a decision about which next step is appropriate and constructed it, we do not want to waste what little creativity we have left re-doing some previous creative work!

4.1.1   The evidence for the step-by-step approach

By doing a little bit of archaeology, we can demonstrate the legitimacy of our statement concerning the sameness of steps, as well as gain some understanding of how one might characterize mathematically the relationship of which any step is an instance. It is generally accepted that the seminal work in this area is due to the endeavours of Dijkstra and Wirth, as exemplified by Dahl *et al*. (1972) and Wirth (1971). In the latter, it is stated (page 221) that '...program is developed in a sequence of *refinement steps*' (author's italics).

Furthermore, 'in each step, one or several instructions of the given program are decomposed into more detailed instructions'. So stepwise refinement has something to do with expressing instructions appearing in a given program in terms of more detailed ones — representing an operation (instruction) in terms of more detailed ones. We understand that, in this context, the meaning of 'more detailed' is often expressed as 'more concrete' or 'more primitive'. That is, the motivation for stepwise refinement is to use instructions (operations) which are seen to be closer to those available in a programming language or computer.

It will be important for us to understand exactly what is meant by 'decomposing instructions into more detailed ones'. We will not, however, be concerned with the more creative, design aspects of this process. Thus, again from Wirth (1971), we have: 'A guideline in the process of stepwise refinement should be the principle to decompose decisions as much as possible, to untangle aspects which are only seemingly interdependent, and to defer those decisions which concern details of representation as long as possible'. Such recommendations are contingent — their use can only be taught and learned through example (one of the points which Wirth attempts to illustrate) and are pertinent, in particular, to possibly ill-defined situations. Essentially, they are guidelines which are to be used to decide which refinement step to apply at any given moment, and in what order to put such steps together to achieve the desired effect. This is the essence of design or development *methods*.

Let us now return to Wirth (1971) and proceed with teasing out the nature of the basic steps: 'This successive decomposition or refinement of specifications terminates when all instructions are expressed in terms of an underlying computer or programming language, and must therefore be guided by the facilities available in that computer or language. The result of the execution of a program is expressed in terms of data, and it may be necessary to introduce further data for communication between the obtained subtasks or instructions. As tasks are refined, so the data may have to be refined, decomposed or structured, and it is natural to *refine program and data specifications in parallel*' (author's emphasis). Note firstly that the object with which we start each refinement step and the object which we construct by means of the step are both *specifications* – 'This successive decomposition or refinement of specifications...'. Thus the objects with which we are concerned in the stepwise refinement process are all instances of the same generic object – a specification. It clearly makes no sense to distinguish the resulting object as being a program (somehow different from a specification) as we could then not apply a further refinement step to it, at least without some further transformation.

Secondly, a very important aspect of refinement is the decomposition or structuring of data: 'As tasks are refined, so the data may have to be refined...'. Moreover, it is natural to think of decomposition steps as 'refining program and data specifications in parallel'. So, it seems that each refinement step is somehow a subtle interplay between how operations (instructions) may be decomposed and related to corresponding refinement or decompositions of data representations.

The early work on stepwise refinement dealt with programs which would normally be regarded as 'small'. That is, the result of development is a handful of procedures which, properly organized, constitute the desired implementation. Attempts were then made to extend the ideas to what might be called system specification. Exemplars of this trend were Jackson (1975), Myers (1975), Yourdon and Constantine (1978) and de Marco (1978). We will take a brief look at the way in which stepwise development is described by de Marco (1978).

'Structured analysis is the use of these tools:

- *Data Flow Diagrams*
- *Data Dictionary*
- *Structured English*
- *Decision Tables*
- *Decision Trees*

to build a new kind of Target Document, the Structured Specification.'

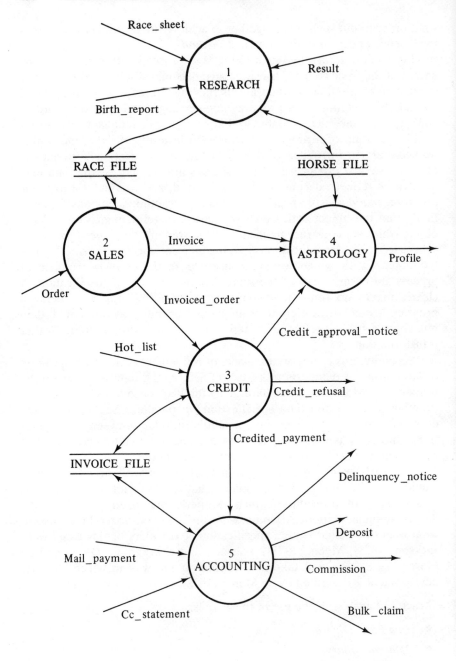

Figure 4.1   Top level data flow diagram for Astro-Pony Toutshops operations
(after de Marco, 1978).

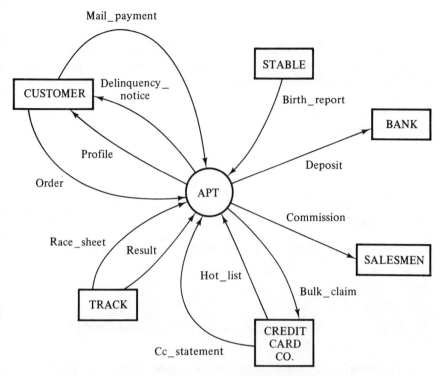

Figure 4.2   Context diagram for Astro-Pony Toutshops (APT) operations
(after de Marco, 1978).

A *data flow diagram* is a graph with directed, labelled edges and
labelled nodes, the latter being divisible into a number of disjoint subsets.
The diagram is meant to show the flow of data through a system. The
labelled edges indicate what kind of data flow from some origin to some
destination with the label indicating what data values may be thought of
as flowing along the edge. The nodes may represent (component) transformations of (incoming to outgoing) data values, in which case they are
called processes, or files and databases which the system needs to access,
or sources and sinks which represent objects outside the system (like
people!). An example of a dataflow diagram is illustrated in Figure 4.1.
The nodes labelled 1: RESEARCH, 2: SALES, 3: CREDIT, 4: AST-
ROLOGY, 5: ACCOUNTING denote processes, while the nodes
labelled RACE FILE, HORSE FILE and INVOICE FILE denote files
or databases. The edges without origins correspond to edges which originate
in or go to nodes outside the system. Thus, in Figure 4.2 we see a data
flow diagram (called a context diagram) in which the square boxes correspond to components of the environment and where only those edges
which originate at or go to one of these components are shown. All other

nodes and edges have been subsumed by the new node labelled APT, the intended system.

A *data dictionary* is a set of definitions of the data to which labels or edges correspond. There must be a definition for each label on an edge, and the definitions must be given in terms of a small number of constructs — tupling (records), repetition (sequences) with possible upper and lower bounds on admissible length of repetition, alternation, and indication of provisional components. For example,

Credited_payment = [Check|Credit_card_voucher] + Invoice_copy

means that a value of type 'Credited_payment' is a tuple with two components, the first of which is, alternatively, a value of type 'Check' or a value of type 'Credit_card_voucher', and the second of which is a value of type 'Invoice_copy'. Again,

Race_file = {Track_name + Race_number + Horse_name}

defines 'Race_file' as a sequence of records (each record consisting of three components) with no lower or upper limits on the length of the sequence.

Order = Customer_name_and_address + Time_and_date_of_birth + (Race_specifier) + (Payment)

defines 'Order' as a tuple with at least two components and at most four components.

The rôle of refinement in structured analysis is to define processes which do not have a short enough description (in structured English, decision trees and decision tables) in terms of more concrete data flow diagrams. For example, the node labelled 5: ACCOUNTING in Figure 4.1 may be decomposed into the diagram of Figure 4.3. The labelling '5.X...' on the process nodes is meant to indicate that these process nodes are being used to decompose node 5 on a previous diagram (Dewey strikes again!). The edges which have no origin or destination in this figure correspond exactly to the edges of Figure 4.1 which have the node labelled 5: ACCOUNTING as either their destination or origin, respectively. Thus the net data flow into and out of a refinement of a node must be exactly the same as that into and out of the corresponding node being refined. (Note also how the bidirectional arrow from node labelled 5: ACCOUNTING to INVOICE FILE is decomposed in Figure 4.3.)

This refinement (decomposition) has illustrated the process decomposition, without introducing any data refinement. Some data flows which are purely internal to the refinement were introduced (Payment and Commission_note), but Cc_statement, Credited_payment, ...were not refined. The next step in decomposing 5.2: ACCEPT FUNDS does introduce such a refinement. This is illustrated in Figure 4.4, where the edge labelled Payment in Figure 4.3 no longer appears and two new edges

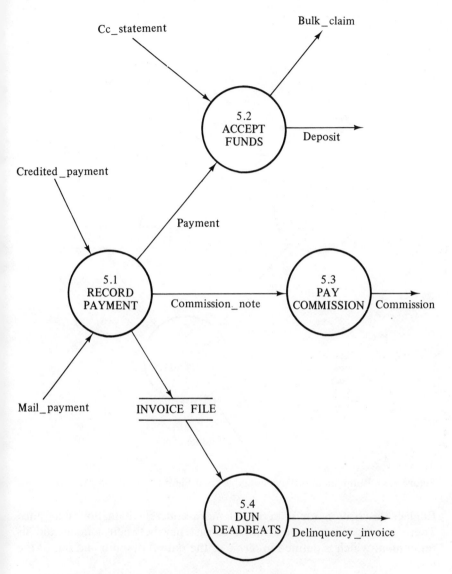

Figure 4.3   Refinement of 5: ACCOUNTING of Figure 4.1
(after de Marco, 1978).

have seemingly descended from nowhere − Voucher and Check. It turns
out that there are two kinds of 'Payment' which are alternatives. Thus
the data dictionary should contain a definition of this data refinement
(Payment = [Voucher|Check]) which until this point was not relevant
for the definition of the system.

    To reiterate, processes (whose meanings are supposed to be self-
evident from their names) are defined either in terms of 'short', structured

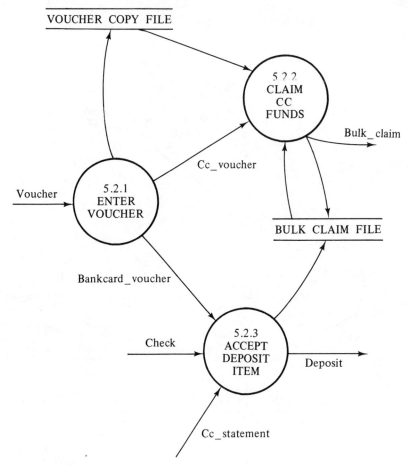

Figure 4.4   Refinement of Payment edge from Figure 4.3 (after de Marco, 1978).

English descriptions or in terms of more concrete data flow diagrams. There is a specific relationship of consistency between a node and its refinement which is defined in terms of the data flows into and out of the node.

So in both the early work on programs and the later work on systems we find that the concept of refinement or decomposition consists of two interrelated parts. Firstly, there is the representation (definition) of an operation, instruction, or process appearing at the more abstract level in terms of (more primitive) operations, instructions or processes at the more concrete level. Secondly, there is a corresponding representation of data types (structures) appearing at the more abstract level in terms of data types at a more concrete level. Furthermore, there is supposed to be a certain relation holding between two adjacent levels of representation or refinement which makes the step correct (if not necessarily helpful or appropriate). In Section 4.2 we proceed to characterize what this step is.

4.1.2 Formal development and stepwise refinement

Both the above considered approaches to stepwise refinement are examples of an informal view of the step-by-step development of programs. We are interested in a formal basis for step-by-step development and so we use an example from the literature which very early on illustrated many of the ideas we advocate in this book. The example was meant by its author to illustrate the ideas of developing programs to be correct by construction. However, from our perspective it also illustrates a formal step-by-step development, although the formal underpinnings of the step-by-step approach are missing from the paper.

The example we now present is our reconstruction of the development of a program to implement the Fisher–Galler Algorithm for recording equivalences as presented in Correll (1978). Given a finite set S of elements numbered $1, \ldots, N$ and a set E of recorded equivalences, we would now like to be able to

1. record further equivalences by adding them to E, and
2. query if a pair of elements, represented by the corresponding pair of numbers (i, j), is equivalent.

The answers to queries are determined by examining if the pair (i, j) is in E explicitly or, failing this, if the equivalence follows from the contents of E by the properties of equivalence[†]. Thus, for example, if E contains the pairs $(1, 2)$ and $(2, 7)$, and *equiv* is the equivalence relation which E is meant to record, then:

equiv$(2, 1)$	holds	(by symmetry)
equiv$(1, 7)$	holds	(by transitivity)
equiv$(1, 2)$	holds	(as it is in E)
equiv$(2, 7)$	holds	(as it is in E)

To formalize these ideas, we use the following functions and relations:

INIT:	$\rightarrow \mathbf{E}$
ENTER: $\mathbf{E} \times \mathbf{S} \times \mathbf{S} \rightarrow \mathbf{E}$	
EQUIV: $\mathbf{E} \times \mathbf{S} \times \mathbf{S} \rightarrow \{$*true, false*$\}$	

Note that we have used $\mathbf{E}$ and $\mathbf{S}$ as the names of sorts corresponding to the E and S referred to above. Clearly *ENTER* will be used to update the set of equivalent pairs, and *EQUIV* is a query function which can be used to ask if a pair of values is equivalent (either because it is explicitly

---

[†] Recall that an equivalence relation *equiv* on a set S is a binary relation which has the following properties:
1. reflexivity – for each a in S, *equiv*(a, a);
2. symmetry – for each a, b in S, *equiv*$(a, b) \Leftrightarrow equiv(b, a)$;
3. transitivity – for each a, b, c in S, $(equiv(a, b) \ \& \ equiv(b, c)) \Rightarrow equiv(a, c)$

recorded in a given value of **E** or because the equivalence follows from the information recorded in E).

Letting i, j, k, l be variables over **S** and e a variable over **E**, we postulate two axioms:

$$\vdash EQUIV(INIT, i, j) \Leftrightarrow (i = j) \tag{4.1}$$
$$\vdash EQUIV(ENTER(e, i, j), k, l)$$
$$\Leftrightarrow (EQUIV(e, k, l)$$
$$|(EQUIV(e, i, k) \ \& \ EQUIV(e, j, l))$$
$$|(EQUIV(e, i, l) \ \& \ EQUIV(e, j, k))) \tag{4.2}$$

where the equality in the first axiom is the equality on the natural numbers (used to represent values). Thus, if there are no recorded equivalences, the values are equivalent only to themselves. If there are recorded equivalences, then two values are equivalent if they are equivalent to the most recent values entered or if it could be established that they were equivalent before the last equivalent pair was recorded.

Refinement now proceeds by providing more concrete data representations and/or algorithmic details for the above functions and relations. The first step is to provide representatives for whole classes of equivalences by using a single representative for each equivalence class[†].

The idea is that initially each value in S represents itself, but when a pair (i, j) is entered, the representative for the set to which i belongs becomes the representative for the set formed by joining the set to which i belongs to the set to which j belongs.

The language for this representation consists of *INIT* and *ENTER* as before and

$$REP: \mathbf{E} \times \mathbf{S} \rightarrow \mathbf{S}$$

with axioms:

$$\vdash REP(INIT, i) = i$$
$$\vdash REP(ENTER(e, i, j), k) \tag{4.3}$$
$$= \textbf{if } REP(e, j) = REP(e, k) \textbf{ then } REP(e, i)$$
$$\textbf{else } REP(e, k) \tag{4.4}$$

where the second axiom is shorthand for

$$\vdash (REP(e, j) = REP(e, k) \Rightarrow (REP(ENTER(e, i, j), k) = REP(e, i)))$$
$$\& \ (\neg (REP(e, j) = REP(e, k)) \Rightarrow$$
$$(REP(ENTER(e, i, j), k) = REP(e, k))) \tag{4.5}$$

The *EQUIV* predicate is no longer directly available and so we must

---

[†] Recall that an equivalence relation *equiv* on a set S partitions it into a set of pairwise disjoint subsets which together exhaust S. Each such subset consists of different equivalent values and no values taken from different subsets are equivalent.

'recover' it by demonstrating how we can define this predicate in terms of the functions which are available:

$$\vdash EQUIV(e, i, j) \Leftrightarrow (REP(e, i) = REP(e, j)) \tag{4.6}$$

(Note that this occurrence of *EQUIV* is not really the same symbol as introduced previously. Strictly speaking, it is an altogether different symbol which we are introducing by definition (see Section 2.3). However, in the original presentation (Correll, 1978) this distinction is not made; it is one of the already mentioned problematic aspects which we hope to correct in subsequent sections. For the purposes of this example we will stick to the original notation.)

To justify this step it is necessary to show that (4.1) and (4.2) follow from (4.3) and (4.4). As for the first, we have

$$EQUIV(INIT, i, j) \Leftrightarrow (REP(INIT, i) = REP(INIT, j)) \Leftrightarrow i = j$$

by using (4.5) and the definition of *EQUIV*, (4.6). The reader may care to demonstrate (4.2) − it is a somewhat lengthier and more tedious analysis by cases.

At the next level of refinement, data and algorithmic detail are added. Equivalences are represented via a forest structure. The latter is manipulated by using the following:

$$
\begin{array}{lll}
LINK: & \mathbf{E} \times \mathbf{S} \times \mathbf{S} \rightarrow \mathbf{E} \\
FATHER: & \mathbf{E} \times \mathbf{S} & \rightarrow \mathbf{S} \\
ROOT: & \mathbf{E} \times \mathbf{S} & \rightarrow \{true, false\} \\
INIT: & & \rightarrow \mathbf{E}
\end{array}
$$

LINK is used to construct the forest from the initial tree *INIT* (again not the same as the *INIT* used before, but never mind!). *FATHER* is a function which returns the direct ancestor of a given node in the forest and *ROOT* is a predicate which defines the roots.

The postulated axioms are:

$$\vdash ROOT(INIT, i) \tag{4.7}$$
$$\vdash \neg ROOT(LINK(e, i, j), j) \tag{4.8}$$
$$\vdash (ROOT(LINK(e, i, j), k) \,\&\, \neg (j = k)) \Rightarrow ROOT(e, k) \tag{4.9}$$
$$\vdash FATHER(LINK(e, i, j), k) =$$
$$(\textbf{if } j = k \textbf{ then } i \textbf{ else } FATHER(e, k)) \tag{4.10}$$

The first axiom defines each value to be a root of the initial forest. The next two define root in the obvious way, while the last gives a partial definition of *FATHER*.[†]

[†] Thus *FATHER* is meant to be a total function with some 'don't care' conditions about some values in its domain. This is an illustration of the permissiveness of specifications which we advocate.

We can now define *REP* and *ENTER* as follows:

$\vdash REP(e, i) = \{t:= i;$
$\qquad\qquad$ **while** $\neg ROOT(e, t)$
$\qquad\qquad\qquad$ **do** $t:= FATHER(e, t)$ **od**;
$\qquad\qquad$ **result** $t\}$ (4.11)
$\vdash ENTER(e, i, j) = $ **if** $REP(e, i) = REP(e, j)$
$\qquad\qquad\qquad\qquad$ **then** e **else** $LINK(e, REP(e, i), REP(e, j))$ (4.12)

The first assertion takes us out of the realm of first-order logic (MPC). Thus in order to prove the correctness of this refinement with respect to the previous one, we require the use of a programming language logic and an interface between it and MPC. In Correll (1978) this was done on an *ad hoc* basis and we will not repeat the reasoning here. Note that the definition of *EQUIV*, (4.6), needed to relate the first refinement to the original specification, can be carried forward to relate the original specification to this new level of refinement, via the definitions (4.11) and (4.12). (Why this should be so is again not explained but is assumed to be reasonable.)

There is one final step, which we will not illustrate, presenting forests in terms of a one-dimensional array indexed by values in *S*, where the entry at index *i* is the value representing the father of *i* in the forest. If the father does not exist, a default value is used. The reader may find this step a useful exercise to go through.

4.2   The canonical step

System development is supposed to take place by means of small steps of development or decomposition, each of which is intended to take us closer to the final running system − whatever that may be. But what is the nature of these steps? Clearly, one of the aims of development is to add more detail, to make our specifications less permissive. This is the opposite of the injunction we follow when trying to specify software: ignore unnecessary detail, just state essentials in a language which is natural for describing the problem or system. The purpose of adding the detail is to introduce those refinements which give us specifications or programs which are runnable on the machines we have available (and, often, more efficiently runnable). For example, in specifying sorting of sets into sequences, we might use:

$$sort(k) = l \Leftrightarrow ordered(l) \ \& \ same(k, l) \qquad (4.13)$$

which states that *l* is the sorted sequence obtained from the set *k* if and only if *l* is ordered and the set *k* and sequence *l* have the same components. Even if such a definition were 'executable', it would be hopelessly inefficient. (In Prolog, the equivalent program *sort*(*k*, *l*) **if** *ordered*(*l*) & *same*(*k*, *l*)

would generate ordered sequences and then test to see if such a generated sequence was a permutation of elements in *k*.) We want an implementation whose behaviour is reasonable. In this case, the addition of algorithmic detail would allow us to achieve our aims.

There is another aspect of this process which makes it more complicated than just the activity of adding more detail. This is hinted at in the phrase 'a language which is natural for describing the problem or system'. Thus the language used for specification is unlikely to be directly realizable in a programming language. So the adding of detail must be accomplished, at least in part, by the process of translation − realizing the description stated in the 'natural' language by means of another description in another language (perhaps a programming language).

Now, in logic we already have a simple concept corresponding to the notion of adding more detail − extension. Non-conservative extension consists, at least in part, in the attributing of additional properties to the extralogical symbols of the language chosen for the description of some application (see Section 2.3 for more details).

However, we have here an added dimension to be considered in the process of 'adding detail'. Additional properties are acquired not only explicitly but also implicitly, through the process of representing one description (specification) in terms of another description (specification). For example, we might represent the function *sort* of (4.13) by a procedure *SORT* in Pascal. This procedure *SORT* would have to satisfy at least the same properties as *sort*. Furthermore, it would be expected to have extra properties over and above those attributed to *sort*.

For example, *SORT* might produce the sorted sequence by using a merge-sort algorithm. The properties of such a specific sort algorithm would clearly be more extensive and detailed than the general properties of an arbitrary sort function satisfying (4.13). A merge-sort is quite different from an insertion sort or quicksort!

The point of the above considerations is that the explicit representation of one linguistic level in terms of another linguistic level implicitly introduces extra properties due to the availability of new properties at the 'lower' linguistic level. How this comes about will become clearer as we make precise our ideas and discuss some examples at length.

4.2.1 Definition of canonical step

Let us now try to make precise what we have just loosely described. Let $Sp = \langle L, G \rangle$ be a specification (i.e. a theory) over language L (in some fixed linguistic system). An *implementation* of Sp in $Sp1 = \langle L1, G1 \rangle$ is a pair $\langle I1, e1 \rangle$ where

$e1: Sp1 \le Sp1'$

is a conservative extension of *Sp1* to *Sp1'* and

$$I1: Sp \rightarrow Sp1'$$

is an interpretation between theories. In diagrammatic form, we have:

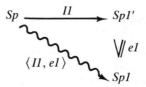

We have used the wavy arrow to indicate the implementation relationship $\langle I1, e1 \rangle$ between the two specifications.

The motivation for this definition is as follows: We have often heard statements of the form 'represent (or implement) X in terms of Y'. X is usually some (formal or informal) specification and so is Y. (Sometimes Y is a programming language, e.g. specified by its axiomatic semantics.) The process of implementation then conventionally consists of two parts:

1. representing the data objects of X in terms of those of Y, and

2. defining operations and tests corresponding to those defined in X in terms of the operations and tests of Y.

If Y happens to be a programming language, then (1) corresponds to making various type declarations (in languages such as Pascal) and assigning values of such types to the abstract objects of X, while (2) corresponds to procedure definitions, one for each operation or test in X.

In the above definition of implementation, the representation of data ((1) above) is defined by the interpretation $I1$. Firstly, which objects of Y count as representations of objects in X is delineated by the relativization predicates associated with the definition of $I1$. Secondly, the correspondence between objects of X and those of Y is set up in terms of the translation between terms defined using the language of X and terms defined using the language of Y. This is because our notion of object or value is intimately bound up with names of objects or values, i.e. terms.

The definition of corresponding operations is accomplished by constructing the extension $e1$. It is via this extension that corresponding symbols are introduced and characterized in terms of their relationship to the language of Y. It is also here that extra details are introduced, as these definitions may ascribe more properties to the corresponding symbols (i.e. those being defined by the extension) than are actually required by the characterization of X.

As an example, consider the specification INT $= \langle L_{int}, G_{int} \rangle$ of integers (Figure 4.5). (We have used a so-called *syntax diagram* to present the (extralogical) language of the specification. Labelled nodes cor-

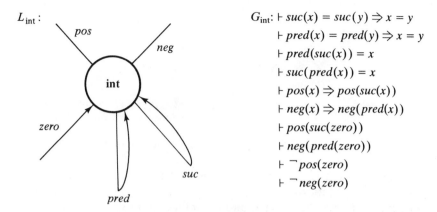

L_{int}:

G_{int}:
$\vdash suc(x) = suc(y) \Rightarrow x = y$
$\vdash pred(x) = pred(y) \Rightarrow x = y$
$\vdash pred(suc(x)) = x$
$\vdash suc(pred(x)) = x$
$\vdash pos(x) \Rightarrow pos(suc(x))$
$\vdash neg(x) \Rightarrow neg(pred(x))$
$\vdash pos(suc(zero))$
$\vdash neg(pred(zero))$
$\vdash \neg pos(zero)$
$\vdash \neg neg(zero)$

Figure 4.5 Specification of integers.

respond to sorts − in this case we have only one, **int**. A constant is represented by a directed edge with no origin, labelled by the name of the constant; hence the representation of *zero*. A function is represented by a directed multi-edge with one origin each at the node corresponding to each argument sort and the common target node representing the result sort of the function; hence, for instance, the representation of *insert* in Figure 4.7 and, in Figure 4.5, the multi-edge reduced to a single edge for *suc*. Relation symbols are represented by undirected multi-edges with one edge corresponding to each argument sort of the relation symbol; hence the representation of *same* in Figure 4.7 and, in Figure 4.5, the multi-edge reduced to a single edge for *neg*.)

We have the usual operations of successor and predecessor and monadic relations used to determine whether a value is positive or negative. It is well known that we can represent integers as signed natural numbers. We would now like to make this precise by implementing integers in terms of natural numbers and signs. We take the specification of natural numbers NAT $= \langle L_{\text{nat}}, G_{\text{nat}} \rangle$ (Figure 4.6) to which we want to add 'signs'. This can be done easily by adding the sort **sign** and constants *plus, minus* of sort **sign** to the specification of NAT. We also need to add the axiom $\vdash \neg(plus = minus)$. We then have NAT + SIGN $= \langle L_{\text{nat}} \cup L_{\text{sign}}, \ G_{\text{nat}} \cup G_{\text{sign}} \rangle = \langle L_{\text{NS}}, \ G_{\text{NS}} \rangle$ and we would like to define an implementation *Impl*: INT $\rightsquigarrow$ NAT + SIGN. According to our definition of implementation, we must construct a conservative extension e: NAT + SIGN $\leq$ X and an interpretation I: INT $\rightarrow$ X. This is where design rears its head, as there is a strong interplay between the constructions of suitable e and I. In fact, in general there are many possible combinations of extension and interpretation which could define a technically correct implementation. The art of design is to choose the pair which is not only technically correct but also methodologically correct.

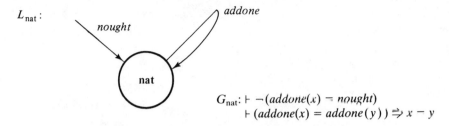

G_{nat}: $\vdash \neg(addone(x) \doteq nought)$
$\vdash (addone(x) = addone(y)) \Rightarrow x \doteq y$

Figure 4.6   Specification of natural numbers.

Our intention is, of course, to represent the integer n (an abbreviation for n applications of *suc* to *zero*) by n applications of *addone* to *nought* of **nat** and *plus* of **sign**, and the integer $-n$ (an abbreviation for n applications of *pred* to *zero*) by n applications of *addone* to *nought* of **nat** and *minus* of **sign**. *zero* of **int** can be represented in two ways (as *nought* and *plus* or as *nought* and *minus*).

There is some leeway in implementing the function symbols of L_{int}. Each one can be implemented either as a single function that returns a pair of values (one from **nat** and one from **sign**), or as a pair of functions each returning one value (one function having result **nat** and the other, result **sign**). We choose the latter option here, but in general choose whichever option seems more appropriate for a given context.

To represent a term t of $Term(L_{\text{int}})$ we will use two components $t_N{}^I$ and $t_S{}^I$, both of $Term(L_{\text{NS}})$, where the subscripts N and S provide us with sort information, **nat** and **sign** respectively. Thus our interpretation I consists in the following:

1. We associate with the sort **int** the pair of sorts **nat** and **sign**.

2. We associate with **int** a relativization predicate *is-int* of type $\langle$**sign, nat**$\rangle$ which we add to L_{NS} and which is defined by the following axiom:

$$\vdash \textit{is-int}(x_S, x_N) \tag{4.14}$$

   This axiom states that any pair of sign and natural number values represents some integer. (In general, we will not be so lucky with interpretations. Usually, only some values in the target of an interpretation will represent values in the source.)

3. We associate with each function symbol (including the constants) of L_{int} a pair of function symbols which are added to L_{NS} and whose typing respects the mapping of sorts defined in (1). So we associate with *zero* of **int** the *nought* of **nat** and *plus* of **sign**. (Thus we choose one of the two possibilities mentioned earlier. The other, the pair *nought* and *minus* will be made equivalent to the pair *nought* and *plus*.) With *suc* (*pred*) of L_{int} we associate *sucrepN* (*predrepN*) of type $\langle\langle$**sign, nat**$\rangle$, **nat**$\rangle$ and *sucrepS* (*predrepS*) of type $\langle\langle$**sign, nat**$\rangle$, **sign**$\rangle$.

4. We associate with each predicate symbol of L_{int} a predicate symbol which we add to L_{NS} and whose typing respects the mapping defined in (1). Thus with *pos* (*neg*) we associate *posrep* (*negrep*) of type $\langle$**sign, nat**$\rangle$. With $=_{\text{int}}$ we associate $=_{\text{rep}}$ of type $\langle$**sign, sign, nat, nat**$\rangle$. (Note that equality is implemented like any other predicate.)

5. We associate with every variable x of sort **int** a corresponding pair of variables x_{N} and x_{S} of sorts **nat** and **sign**, respectively.

For easy reference, this is summarized in Table 4.1.

We also add to G_{NS} axioms defining the new symbols added in steps (3) and (4). (*is-int*, added in step (2), was also defined there via a new axiom added to G_{NS}.) Note that $=$, *addone*, *nought*, *plus*, and *minus* are symbols in L_{NS}:

$$\vdash posrep(x_{\text{S}}, x_{\text{N}}) \Leftrightarrow (x_{\text{S}} = plus \ \& \ \neg(x_{\text{N}} = nought)) \tag{4.15}$$
$$\vdash negrep(x_{\text{S}}, x_{\text{N}}) \Leftrightarrow (x_{\text{S}} = minus \ \& \ \neg(x_{\text{N}} = nought)) \tag{4.16}$$
$$\vdash =_{\text{rep}} (x_{\text{S}}, y_{\text{S}}, x_{\text{N}}, y_{\text{N}}) \Leftrightarrow ((x_{\text{N}} = y_{\text{N}} \ \& \ x_{\text{S}} = y_{\text{S}})|(x_{\text{N}} = nought \ \& \ y_{\text{N}} = nought)) \tag{4.17}$$

(Two pairs representing integers are equivalent − represent the same integer − if the pairs are identical or if the natural number element in each pair is *nought*.)

Table 4.1　Translation of L_{int} into L_{NS}.

	L_{int}	L_{NS}
sorts:	**int**	**nat, sign**
relativization:	**int**	*is-int*: **sign** $\times$ **nat** $\rightarrow$ {*true, false*}
functions:	*zero*	*nought*: $\rightarrow$ **nat**, *plus*: $\rightarrow$ **sign**
	suc	*sucrepN*: **sign** $\times$ **nat** $\rightarrow$ **nat** *sucrepS*: **sign** $\times$ **nat** $\rightarrow$ **sign**
	pred	*predrepN*: **sign** $\times$ **nat** $\rightarrow$ **nat** *predrepS*: **sign** $\times$ **nat** $\rightarrow$ **sign**
predicates:	*pos*	*posrep*: **sign** $\times$ **nat** $\rightarrow$ {*true, false*}
	neg	*negrep*: **sign** $\times$ **nat** $\rightarrow$ {*true, false*}
	$=_{\text{int}}$	$=_{\text{rep}}$: **sign** $\times$ **sign** $\times$ **nat** $\times$ **nat** $\rightarrow$ {*true, false*}
variables:	x: **int**	x_{N}: **nat**, x_{S}: **sign**
	y: **int**	y_{N}: **nat**, y_{S}: **sign**
	. . .	. . .
	. . .	. . .
	. . .	. . .

$$\vdash x_S = plus \Rightarrow ((sucrepN(x_S, x_N) = addone(x_N))$$
$$\& \ (sucrepS(x_S, x_N) = plus)) \tag{4.18}$$
$$\vdash (x_S = minus \ \& \ \neg(x_N = nought)) \Rightarrow ((sucrepS(x_S, x_N) = minus)$$
$$\& \ (\mathbf{E}y_N(sucrepN(x_S, x_N) = y_N \ \& \ addone(y_N) = x_N))) \tag{4.19}$$
$$\vdash (x_S = minus \ \& \ x_N = nought) \Rightarrow ((sucrepS(x_S, x_N) = plus)$$
$$\& \ (sucrepN(x_S, x_N) = addone(nought))) \tag{4.20}$$

(These three axioms define *sucrepN* and *sucrepS* by cases. To avoid repetition, similar axioms for *predrepN* and *predrepS*, which must be included in G_{NS}, are not listed here.)

Having added the above symbols and axioms to NAT + SIGN, we get a specification X. $(1-5)$ can be used to define a translation I of terms from INT to X. Thus, for example:

$$(zero)_N{}^I = nought$$
$$(zero)_S{}^I = plus$$
$$(suc(t))_N{}^I = sucrepN(t_S{}^I, t_N{}^I)$$
$$(suc(t))_S{}^I = sucrepS(t_S{}^I, t_N{}^I)$$
etc.

We extend this translation to atomic formulae. Thus, for example:

$$(pos(t))^I = posrep(t_S{}^I, t_N{}^I)$$
$$(neg(t))^I = negrep(t_S{}^I, t_N{}^I)$$
$$(t = u)^I = {}_{rep}(t_S{}^I, u_S{}^I, t_N{}^I, u_N{}^I)$$

Extending this to formulae gives us, for example:

$$((\mathbf{A}x\mathbf{A}y)(suc(x) = suc(y) \Rightarrow x = y))^I$$
$$= (\mathbf{A}x_S\mathbf{A}x_N\mathbf{A}y_S\mathbf{A}y_N)((is\text{-}int(x_S, x_N) \ \& \ is\text{-}int(y_S, y_N))$$
$$\Rightarrow (=_{rep}(sucrepS(x_S, x_N), sucrepS(y_S, y_N), sucrepN(x_S, x_N),$$
$$sucrepN(y_S, y_N)) \Rightarrow =_{rep}(x_S, y_S, x_N, y_N))) \tag{4.21}$$

To assure ourselves that the translation I is faithful in the sense of preserving the properties of integers as we have defined them, it is sufficient to show that, firstly, the axioms G_{int} translate under I to theorems of X and, secondly, that the closure axioms for I can be deduced from X. (See Section 2.3 on Translations.)

Dealing with the second matter first, we must show that

$$X \vdash (\mathbf{E}x_S\mathbf{E}x_N)is\text{-}int(x_S, x_N) \tag{4.22}$$

We know that

$$X \vdash is\text{-}int(x_S, x_N) \tag{4.23}$$

since $\vdash is\text{-}int(x_S, x_N)$ is part of the theory $X = \langle L_X, G_X \rangle$ by assertion. Then, clearly,

$$X \vdash is\text{-}int(plus, nought) \tag{4.24}$$

and so

$$X \vdash (\mathbf{Ex}_S \mathbf{Ex}_N) \textit{is-int}(x_S, x_N)$$

We now deal with the constants and functions. We must show that the translation of *zero* (the only constant of INT) satisfies the corresponding relativization predicate − *is-int*. So we must show

$$X \vdash \textit{is-int}(\textit{plus, nought}) \tag{4.25}$$

which clearly, as with (4.24), follows from (4.23).

For *suc*, we must check

$$X \vdash (\mathbf{Ax}_S \mathbf{Ax}_N)(\textit{is-int}(x_S, x_N) \Rightarrow$$
$$\textit{is-int}(\textit{sucrepS}(x_S, x_N), \textit{sucrepN}(x_S, x_N))) \tag{4.26}$$

to show that the domain satisfying the relativization predicate *is-int* is closed under the operations representing *suc*. This reduces, by the use of *modus ponens* with $X \vdash \textit{is-int}(x_S, x_N)$, to showing that

$$X \vdash (\mathbf{Ax}_S \mathbf{Ax}_N)(\textit{is-int}(\textit{sucrepS}(x_S, x_N), \textit{sucrepN}(x_S, x_N))) \tag{4.27}$$

This again follows trivially from (4.14).

Similarly, we can show:

$$X \vdash (\mathbf{Ax}_S \mathbf{Ax}_N)(\textit{is-int}(x_S, x_N) \Rightarrow$$
$$\textit{is-int}(\textit{predrepS}(x_S, x_N), \textit{predrepN}(x_S, x_N))) \tag{4.28}$$

We must now show that for each A in G_{int}

$$X \vdash (A)^{\text{I}}$$

For example, the first axiom for integers is translated in (4.21) which is easily shown to be equivalent to

$$X \vdash (\mathbf{Ax}_S, y_S \mathbf{Ax}_N, y_N)(=_{\text{rep}}(\textit{sucrepS}(x_S, x_N), \textit{sucrepS}(y_S, y_N),$$
$$\textit{sucrepN}(x_S, x_N), \textit{sucrepN}(y_S, y_N))$$
$$\Leftrightarrow ((\textit{sucrepN}(x_S, x_N) = \textit{sucrepN}(y_S, y_N)$$
$$\& \textit{sucrepS}(x_S, x_N) = \textit{sucrepS}(y_S, y_N)) | (\textit{sucrepN}(x_S, x_N) = \textit{nought}$$
$$\& \textit{sucrepN}(y_S, y_N) = \textit{nought}))) \tag{4.29}$$

Again, we have

$$(\neg(\textit{pos}(\textit{zero})))^{\text{I}} = \neg(\textit{posrep}(\textit{plus, nought}))$$

and from (4.15)

$$\textit{posrep}(x_S, x_N) \Leftrightarrow ((x_S = \textit{plus}) \& \neg(x_N = \textit{nought}))$$

we can obtain that

$$((x_S = \textit{plus}) \& (x_N = \textit{nought})) \Rightarrow \neg(\textit{posrep}(\textit{plus, nought}))$$

The reader is welcome to try some of the other axioms of INT and demonstrate that in each case the translated axiom is a consequence of

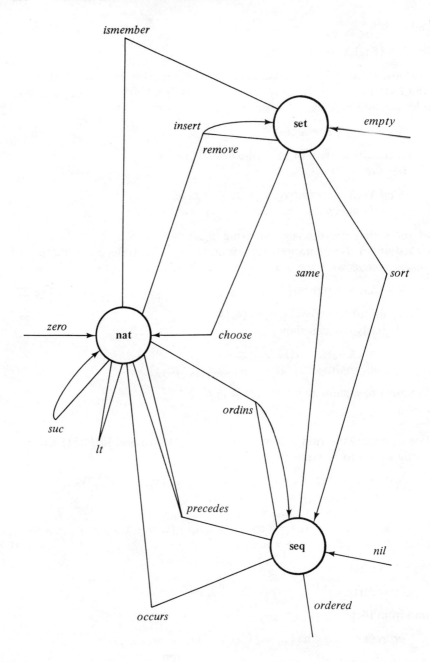

Figure 4.7(a)   Specification of SORT_NAT: the language L_{SN}.

$$\vdash \neg(zero = suc(n)) \tag{1}$$

$$\vdash (suc(m) = suc(n)) \Rightarrow m = n \tag{2}$$

$$\vdash lt(suc(m), suc(n)) \Leftrightarrow lt(m, n) \tag{3}$$

$$\vdash lt(zero, suc(n)) \tag{4}$$

$$\vdash \neg lt(zero, zero) \tag{5}$$

$$\vdash \neg lt(suc(n), zero) \tag{6}$$

$$\vdash (\mathbf{A}n(ismember(n, s) \Leftrightarrow ismember(n, t))) \Rightarrow s =_{set} t \tag{7}$$

$$\vdash \neg ismember(n, empty) \tag{8}$$

$$\vdash ismember(m, insert(n, s)) \Leftrightarrow ((m = n)|ismember(m, s)) \tag{9}$$

$$\vdash ismember(m, remove(n, s)) \Leftrightarrow (\neg(m = n) \,\&\, ismember(m, s)) \tag{10}$$

$$\vdash \neg(s = empty) \Rightarrow ismember(choose(s), s) \tag{11}$$

$$\vdash \neg occurs(n, nil) \tag{12}$$

$$\vdash ordered(q) \Rightarrow ordered(ordins(n, q)) \tag{13}$$

$$\vdash occurs(m, ordins(n, q)) \Leftrightarrow ((m = n) \mid occurs(m, q)) \tag{14}$$

$$\vdash (sort(t) = q) \Leftrightarrow (ordered(q) \,\&\, same(q, t)) \tag{15}$$

$$\vdash same(q, t) \Leftrightarrow \mathbf{A}n(occurs(n, q) \Leftrightarrow ismember(n, t)) \tag{16}$$

$$\vdash ordered(q) \Leftrightarrow \mathbf{A}m\mathbf{A}n(occurs(m, q) \,\&\, occurs(n, q)) \,\&\, lt(m, n) \Rightarrow$$
$$precedes(m, n, q)) \tag{17}$$

$$\vdash occurs(m, q) \,\&\, occurs(n, q) \Rightarrow (precedes(m, n, q) \mid precedes(n, m, q)) \tag{18}$$

$$\vdash \neg(precedes(m, n, q) \,\&\, precedes(n, m, q)) \tag{19}$$

$$\vdash precedes(m, n, q) \,\&\, precedes(l, m, q) \Rightarrow precedes(l, n, q) \tag{20}$$

Figure 4.7(b)   Specification of SORT_NAT: the axioms.

G_X. When such a proof is carried out for each axiom A in G_X, we are done and have demonstrated that the translation I is an interpretation between theories. Given that e: NAT + SIGN $\leq$ X, i.e. X is a conservative extension of NAT + SIGN, we have also demonstrated that $Impl = \langle I, e \rangle$: INT $\rightsquigarrow$ NAT + SIGN is at least a technically correct implementation.

4.2.2   Another example

We would now like to present an example which illustrates how programs are introduced during stepwise development. The example also illustrates the case of interpretation between two theories in different linguistic systems. Because we have not formalized such interpretations, the presentation will be at an intuitive level. We repeat in Figure 4.7 the specification of SORT_NAT from the Appendix, Section A.6. Our intention is to implement the operation *sort* in a programming language like Pascal. What in effect we actually do is define a procedure in a theory which will be constructed from the linguistic system of the Appendix Section A.5.

This linguistic system characterizes (a fragment of) the Pascal programming language. Operation and predicate names of SORT_NAT will be mapped to procedure names of Pascal. The names will be characterized by procedure definitions in the programming language.

To simplify matters (and illustrate a principle of good design), we will implement only *sort*, leaving the refinement of the operations and predicates of the set and sequence data types to a later stage of development.

Now *sort* will be mapped to the symbol (procedure name) *SORT* which will be characterized as follows:

> **function** *SORT*(*t0*: *set*): *seq*;
> **var** *t*: *set*; *q*: *seq*; *n*: *nat*;
> **begin**
> *t*:= *t0*; *q*:= *NIL*;
> **while** $\neg (t = EMPTY)$ **do**   (4.30)
>   *n*:= *CHOOSE*(*t*);
>   *q*:= *ORDINS*(*n*, *q*);
>   *t*:= *REMOVE*(*n*, *t*)
>   **od**;
> *SORT*:= *q*
> **end**

The sorts **nat**, **seq** and **set** will be mapped to the types *nat, seq* and *set* respectively, declared in the programming language.

The operations *nil, ordins, ..., empty, choose, remove, ...* will be mapped to the procedure names *NIL, ORDINS, ..., EMPTY, CHOOSE, REMOVE, ...* The definitions of these procedure names will be provided via input/output specifications of the form

$$A \Rightarrow [\alpha]B$$

where 'α' is a procedure declaration and *A, B* are formulae derived from the axioms defining the corresponding symbol in SORT_NAT.

Now, from the characterization of *sort*, we can determine that the interpretation is correct if we can show that:

$$[SORT(t0)](ordered(SORT) \,\&\, same(SORT, t0)) \qquad (4.31)$$

so after the program *SORT*, with input *t0*, terminates the result (the value of *SORT*) will be ordered and will have the same constituent values as the input set *t0*. Note that this program has a trivial precondition (*t0* = *t0*).

That formula (4.31) is satisfied by the program (4.30) can now be easily demonstrated. An annotated version of the body of the *SORT* function is given by (4.30′) where the predicate *is-trans*, forming part of the loop invariant, is defined by:

$$\vdash is\text{-}trans(t0, t, q)$$
$$\Leftrightarrow (\mathbf{A}n)(ismember(n, t0) \Leftrightarrow (ismember(n, t)|occurs(n, q))) \quad (4.32)$$

The intuition is that after each loop iteration every value in the input set *t0* will either be in the current value of set *t* or a component of the present value of the sequence *q*. The loop invariant asserts further that the present value of *q* is ordered.

```
var t: set; q: seq; n: nat;
begin
t:= t0; q:= NIL;
while ¬(t = EMPTY) do
{ordered(q) & is-trans(t0, t, q)}
   n:= CHOOSE (t);
   q:= ORDINS(n, q);                                    (4.30′)
   t:=REMOVE(n, t)
  od;
SORT:= q
end
{sort(t0) = SORT}
```

The partial correctness of the sorting program can be demonstrated by deriving verification conditions from the text of the annotated program and then showing that these verification conditions are consequences of the properties we can attribute to the operations and types appearing in it. The verification conditions for the program (4.30′) are:

$$(t = t0 \ \& \ q = nil) \Rightarrow (ordered(q) \ \& \ is\text{-}trans(t0, t, q)) \qquad (4.33)$$

$$(\neg(t = empty) \ \& \ ordered(q) \ \& \ is\text{-}trans(t0, t, q))$$
$$\Rightarrow (n = choose(t) \Rightarrow (ordered(ordins(n, q)))$$
$$\& \ is\text{-}trans(t0, remove(n, t), ordins(n, q)))) \qquad (4.34)$$

$$(t = empty \ \& \ ordered(q) \ \& \ is\text{-}trans(t0, t, q)) \Rightarrow sort(t0) = q \qquad (4.35)$$

Note that we have used the languages defined in Figure 4.7 for the statement of the above invariants rather than the language employed in (4.30′) (*NIL, EMPTY, CHOOSE,...*), to make it easier for the reader to try to prove the formulae (4.33)−(4.35) directly from the axiomatization of Figure 4.7 rather than from the incomplete description of how the language of (4.30′) is actually characterized. (This is a bit of a cheat and we admit it! However, the points we want to make are that such proofs can be carried out, together with the flavour of such proofs, and both of these are well enough illustrated. See also an example of a more detailed proof in Section 3.3.)

As an example of proving verification conditions, consider (4.33). Clearly,

$$q = nil \Rightarrow ordered(q)$$

follows from (17) of Figure 4.7(b) (since in the formula

$$(AmAn)((occurs(m, q) \ \& \ occurs(n, q) \ \& \ lt(m, n)) \Rightarrow$$
$$precedes(m, n, q))$$

occurs(m, q) and *occurs(n, q)* both fail to hold (*q = nil!*) forcing the whole formula to be vacuously true). Similarly, we must show that

$$(t = t0 \mathrel{\&} q = nil) \Rightarrow is\text{-}trans(t0, t, q)$$

which is equivalent to showing that

$$\mathbf{A}n(ismember(n, t0) \Leftrightarrow (ismember(n, t0)\,|\,occurs(n, nil)))$$

This reduces to showing ($occurs(n, nil)$ being false) that

$$\mathbf{A}n(ismember(n, t0) \Leftrightarrow ismember(n, t0))$$

which is a tautology.

4.2.3 Summary

The objective of this section is two-fold: to give a technical definition of the step which constitutes the 'atomic' component of stepwise refinement methods and to illustrate the definition via some examples. The definition takes to heart the well founded, if somewhat informal, expression of what it means to refine an abstract specification in terms of some concrete specification (with 'abstract' and 'concrete' being relative terms applicable contingently at a particular point in the process of development). The concrete specification must be extended in two ways: a data representation must be defined (indicating how combinations of concrete values are used to represent abstract values) and operations of the abstract specification must be implemented or defined in terms of the operations made available in the concrete specification (presumably making some use of how the data representation is defined). A notion of translation is introduced because of the technical requirement that we need to make explicit the correspondence between abstract and concrete versions of values and operations.

The examples illustrate how steps concentrating on data refinement and steps introducing programs both fit neatly into the same paradigm. The reader may now like to go back to Section 4.1 and reformulate the first step in the refinement process for the Fisher−Galler Algorithm (and the others, if he feels energetic!) as a proper implementation step, as technically defined in this section.

4.3 Chain of specification/program links

It is very likely that having constructed the implementation $\langle II, e1 \rangle$: $Sp \rightsquigarrow Sp1$, whose diagram is given by:

where *Sp1* is not yet a programming language (logic), nor *e1* a set of procedure definitions, we will continue stepwise refinement implementing *Sp1* in terms of some *Sp2*. Thus, on another application of a canonical step, we would get

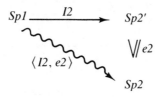

How are these two steps related?

If the activity of implementation was properly modularized, one expects that the work involved in the construction of ⟨ *I1, e1* ⟩ (at least the creative part of it) need not be redone. However, the extension *e1* must somehow be 'carried forward' so as to make sense of the definitions introduced to extend *Sp1* in terms of the latter's implementation.

Thus, given ⟨ *I1, e1* ⟩ (implementing *Sp* in terms of *Sp1*) and ⟨ *I2, e2* ⟩ (implementing *Sp1* in terms of *Sp2*) we want to automatically (i.e. purely algorithmically, without relying on any creativity) construct an ⟨ *I12, e12* ⟩ implementing *Sp* in terms of *Sp2*. Diagrammatically, we want

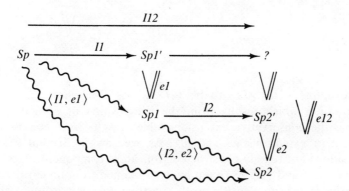

with the mystery object '?' filled in. In fact, we can take a fragment of the above diagram, namely

$$Sp1'$$
$$\bigvee e1$$
$$Sp1 \xrightarrow{ I2 } Sp2'$$

and show that we can construct a specification $Sp2''$ such that:

$$
\begin{array}{ccc}
Sp1' & \xrightarrow{\;\;I2'\;\;} & Sp2'' \\[2pt]
\Big\Vert e1 & & \Big\Vert e1' \\[2pt]
Sp1 & \xrightarrow{\;\;I2\;\;} & Sp2'
\end{array}
$$

Now $e1'$: $Sp2' \leq Sp2''$ is a conservative extension which is nothing but the extension $e1$ under translation by $I2$. Similarly, $I2'$: $Sp1' \rightarrow Sp2''$ is an interpretation which, restricted to $Sp1$, is identical to $I2$ but more or less identically translates the symbols introduced by $e1$. An explanation of this construction will be given below.

So, having obtained the above 'box', we now have

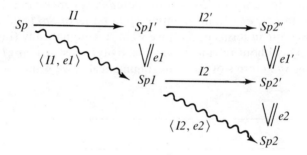

and we define $\langle I12,\ e12 \rangle$ to be $\langle I1 \cdot I2',\ e2 \cdot e1' \rangle$ where $I1 \cdot I2'$ is the interpretation which results from the composition of $I1$ and $I2'$, and $e2 \cdot e1'$ is the conservative extensions which results from composing the conservative extensions $e2$ and $e1'$. As we saw in Section 2.3, such compositions are readily constructed from their component parts. Thus, given $\langle I1,\ e1 \rangle$ and $\langle I2,\ e2 \rangle$ (and having obtained from them $e1'$ and $I2'$, as described), we can algorithmically construct the composition of the two implementation steps.

As an aside, let us consider a situation which is quite common and requires the same technical result as above to make it manageable. Consider a specification Sp. Let us assume that Sp has already been implemented by $\langle I1,\ e1 \rangle$: $Sp \rightsquigarrow Sp1$ (see the first diagram in this section).

Our client now asks us to add some bells and whistles to the existing system. If we want the specification of the additions not to interfere with the properties we have assumed for the existing system, we would specify these additions as a conservative extension of Sp. What we now have is:

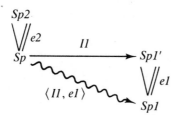

What we would like is a guarantee that our non-interfering additions to *Sp* are carried forward by the implementation $\langle I1, e1 \rangle$ and can be used to extend the theory *Sp1'* conservatively. We are thus led to the same question as before: Can we complete the rectangle

$$
\begin{array}{ccc}
Sp2 & \xrightarrow{\quad I1' \quad} & ? \\[2pt]
\Big\Vert e2 & & \Big\Vert e2' \\[2pt]
Sp & \xrightarrow{\quad I1 \quad} & Sp1'
\end{array}
$$

mechanically?[†]

The result we require is related to the Extended Robinson Consistency Theorem of Section A.4 in the Appendix. There we have three specifications *Sp*, *Sp1*, *Sp2*, with *Sp1* and *Sp2* both being extensions of *Sp*, at least one of which is conservative. Diagrammatically, using $\subseteq$ to denote (non-conservative) extension, we had

$$
\begin{array}{c}
Sp2 \\[2pt]
\Vert \\[2pt]
Sp \subseteq Sp1
\end{array}
$$

and the theorem stated (implicitly) that we could complete the rectangle in the following way:

$$
\begin{array}{c}
Sp2 \subseteq Sp' \\[2pt]
\Vert \quad \Vert \\[2pt]
Sp \subseteq Sp1
\end{array}
$$

Our interest is to extend this result by replacing the extension $Sp \subseteq Sp1$ by an interpretation between theories $I1 : Sp \to Sp1$.

[†] The completion of the above rectangle also turns out to be a requirement to make sense of the notion of parameterized specification and the interaction of parameter instantiation and refinement/implementation steps (see Maibaum and Turski (1984), Maibaum *et al.* (1985)).

4.3.1 The Modularization Theorem

Suppose that *Sp*, *Sp1* and *Sp2* are specifications, and suppose that

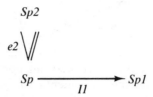

There exists a specification *Sp'*, an interpretation between theories *II'* and a conservative extension *e2'* such that

$$Sp2 \xrightarrow{\quad II' \quad} Sp'$$

$$e2 \Vert \qquad\qquad \Vert e2'$$

$$Sp \xrightarrow{\quad II \quad} Sp1$$

We outline the construction which demonstrates the existence of the requisite *Sp'*, *II'*, and *e2'*. For each new sort or symbol introduced in extending *Sp* to *Sp2*, we introduce a corresponding (e.g. primed) version of the symbol as an extension to the language of *Sp1*. The translation *II* is now extended to deal with symbols and sorts introduced via *e2* by mapping these to the corresponding symbols introduced to extend the language of *Sp1*. (For new sorts in the extension *e2*, in extending *II* to *II'* we must also create corresponding relativization predicates.) We can now translate terms and formulae of *Sp2* using the extended translation *II'*, and we use this to complete the extension *e2'* by adding — as axioms defining this extension — the translations of the axioms used in the extension *e2*. (For new relativization predicates introduced to cope with new sorts introduced in *e2*, we have to add the trivial axioms asserting that the predicate is always true.) What remains to be checked is that *Sp'* is consistent and that *e2'*: *Sp1* → *Sp'* is a conservative extension. (This can be done by recourse to the Craig Interpolation Lemma, see Section A.4 of the Appendix.)

The conservativeness of the extension *e2* is essential for the Modularization Theorem to hold. If the extension *e2* from *Sp* to *Sp2* is not conservative (introduces new properties for the symbols in the language of *Sp*), then, in general, *Sp'* and *II'* need not exist. Indeed, suppose that the language of Sp includes a monadic predicate p and a constant a with $p(a)$ being a well formed formula.

Suppose further that neither

$Sp \vdash p(a)$

nor

$Sp \vdash \neg p(a)$

Now, assume that

$Sp2 \vdash p(a)$

This is clearly possible, since the extension is not conservative. Also, let $I1: Sp \rightarrow Sp1$ be such that p is mapped to p', a to a' and we have

$Sp1 \vdash \neg p'(a')$

The purported extension of $I1$ would clearly have to map p and a of $Sp2$ to p' and a' of Sp'. Moreover, such an interpretation would require the property

$Sp' \vdash p'(a')$

This clearly makes Sp' inconsistent!

We called the result just presented the Modularization Theorem to indicate its fundamental role in allowing stepwise refinement to take place without having to redo non-mechanical (creative) activities. Similarly, this theorem plays a crucial role in allowing us to build on top of existing systems by extending their specifications. It then guarantees that an implementation of the extension will be consistent with an implementation of the existing system[†].

4.3.2   Composing implementations

We shall now briefly illustrate the composition of implementations by implementing NAT + SIGN in NAT (associating *plus* with *addone(nought)* and *minus* with *nought*) and composing this with the implementation *Impl*: INT $\rightsquigarrow$ NAT + SIGN, thus obtaining an implementation of integers in terms of natural numbers alone. Let us add to NAT the following symbols:

is-sign: **nat** $\rightarrow \{true, false\}$
plus': $\rightarrow$ **nat**

[†] Furthermore, the theorem imposes a requirement on theories of specifications. If we want modularization of specification and development activity, we must have such a theorem in our linguistic system. It seems that the crucial requirement to establish the result is that the Craig Interpolation Lemma holds in the linguistic system.

$$='_{\text{sign}}: \quad \textbf{nat} \times \textbf{nat} \to \{\textit{true, false}\}$$
$$\textit{is-nat}: \quad \textbf{nat} \quad\quad\quad \to \{\textit{true, false}\}$$

and the axioms:

$$\vdash \textit{is-sign}(x) \Leftrightarrow (x = \textit{nought} \,|\, x = \textit{plus}') \tag{4.36}$$
$$\vdash \textit{plus}' = \textit{addone}(\textit{nought}) \tag{4.37}$$
$$\vdash x ='_{\text{sign}} y \Leftrightarrow ((x = \textit{nought} \;\&\; y = \textit{nought}) \,|\, (x = \textit{plus}' \;\&\; y = \textit{plus}')) \tag{4.38}$$
$$\vdash \textit{is-nat}(x) \tag{4.39}$$

Clearly, since we will map natural numbers to natural numbers identically, axiom (4.39) asserts the trivial fact that all natural numbers are used to represent natural numbers. The axiom (4.37) just introduces a new name *plus'* for the term *addone(nought)*. The fact that only two values in NAT are used to represent signs is characterized by axiom (4.36), and (4.38) provides the obvious definition of what it means for two sign representatives to be equal. We now map the sorts **nat** and **sign** both to **nat**. We associate with **nat** and **sign** the relativization predicates *is-nat* and *is-sign* respectively. Then association of symbols is defined by mapping *minus* to *nought, plus to plus'*, $=_{\text{sign}}$ to $='_{\text{sign}}$ and all other symbols of NAT + SIGN to themselves. Let us denote this extension of NAT by ENAT. (We leave it to the reader to demonstrate that the thus defined $Im1 = \langle I1,\ e1 \rangle$ really is an implementation.)

Thus we have the following:

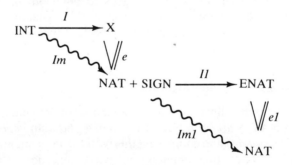

The next stage is the completion of the rectangle:

Now, the extension e: NAT + SIGN $\leq$ X adds no new sorts and introduces the symbols and axioms used in representing integers as a sign and a natural number (e.g. symbols *is-int, posrep*, $=_{rep}$, *sucrepN, predrepN*, ..., and axioms like (4.14)−(4.20) of the previous section). The application of the translation *I1′* (the extension of *I1*) is straightforward.

For example,

$(x_S = plus$
$\quad \Rightarrow ((sucrepN(x_S,x_N) = addone(x_N)) \ \& \ (sucrepS(x_S,x_N) = plus)))^{I1′}$
$= is\text{-}sign(n_S) \ \& \ is\text{-}nat(n_N) \Rightarrow (x_S = plus)^{I1′}$
$\quad \Rightarrow ((sucrepN(x_S,x_N) = addone(x_N))^{I1′} \ \& \ (sucrepS(x_S,x_N) = plus)^{I1′}))$
$= is\text{-}sign(n_S) \ \& \ is\text{-}nat(n_N) \Rightarrow ((n_S = plus')$
$\quad \Rightarrow ((sucrepN'(n_S,n_N) = addone(n_N)) \ \& \ (sucrepS'(n_S,n_N) = plus')))$

where we have assumed $(x_S)^{I1′} = n_S$ and $(x_N)^{I1′} = n_N$.

4.3.3 Problem description

Having developed the main technical ideas on specification/implementation steps, we would like to illustrate the ideas in a (simple) intuitive example (rather than the simple technical examples used so far). Academic readers may find the example hauntingly familiar.

The Very Important Funding Agency (VIFA) is responsible for funding academic research in science and technology. The work is done by various secretariats responsible for particular areas of research. One of these secretariats is the Secretariat for Information Technology (SIT). SIT itself has four Committees which have responsibilities in the following areas: Software Engineering (SE); Intelligent Knowledge Based Systems (IKBS); Very Large Scale Integration (VLSI); and Man−Machine Interface (MMI). All applications for research funding must be considered by one of these committees. The administrative head of the Secretariat is the Secretary. It is his responsibility to ensure the smooth and proper functioning of the Secretariat.

The Secretary has decided that in order to ensure this smooth and proper functioning of SIT in this age of rapid growth for IT, the Secretariat requires an automated system to aid in the processing of applications for research funding. After consultation with colleagues, he issues the following requirements specification.

4.3.4 Requirements for application processing in SIT

1. Details of applications are entered into the system as they arrive at the Secretariat.
2. Applications are validated (see Validity of Applications, Document

No VIFA/SIT/VA1983). Non-valid documents are returned to applicants with notes indicating reasons why the application has failed to pass the validity test.

3. Valid applications are classified by the Secretary into one of the four designated areas (SE, IKBS, VLSI, MMI) as per Classification of Applications, Document No VIFA/SIT/CA1984.

4. Each of the four designated Committees then produces a ranking for each of the applications for which it is responsible. The rankings are 'reject', 'postpone' (to be reconsidered on reapplication or after further investigation by the Committee), α (approved with a high degree of merit), and β (approved but with a lower degree of merit). See Ranking of Applications, Document No VIFA/SIT/RA1981.

5. Each of the four Committees then ranks its approved applications in order of merit.

6. The Secretariat's Advisory Board then produces a single merit ordering for all applications approved by the four Committees.

7. Funds are allocated strictly according to the order of merit resulting from (6) above as far as funds will allow.

8. All applicants are notified of the success or otherwise of their application.

4.3.5 Formal specification

Given the above description, a consultant proceeded in the following manner to produce a design specification for the required system. We reproduce here the fragment which we will find useful to illustrate our ideas on specification and system development.

The consultant initially decided to use two basic data structures on which to build his specification: sets and sequences. This is because he felt that applications (1 above), valid applications and non-valid applications (2, 3 above), SE applications (3 above), etc., are best thought of as collections or sets, while orders of merit (5, 6 above) are best represented as (ordered) sequences.

We first describe the specification of the data type SET (of applications) (Figure 4.8). We want to be able to build sets by inserting new applications into the set − (1), (2), (3) above − and removing particular applications from the set − (2), (3) above. We also want to be able to choose an arbitrary element of a set for further consideration − (2), (3), (4), (5) above. As our specification proceeds, we may find other operations and predicates (relations) on sets to be useful. One which will certainly be useful is the relation of equality between sets.

Note that we will specify very little about the sort **appl** from Figure 4.8. This is because we will have little use for subject matter information relating to contents of applications. For illustrative purposes, we will

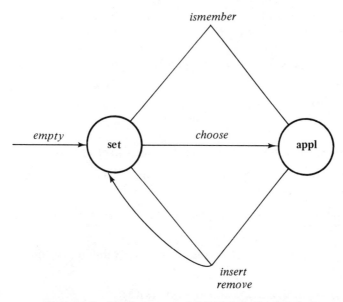

Figure 4.8   The language of SET (of applications).

mention a few functions and predicates over this sort, indicating how they could represent relevant facts. Some of these are:

postmark: **appl** → **integer**

(the date the application was posted)

signed: **appl** → {*true, false*}

(Was the application signed by all applicants?)

signed-by-HoD: **appl** → {*true, false*}

(Was the application signed by the Head of the Department where the applicants work?)

no-of-pages-of-case-for-support: **appl** → **integer**

(the number of pages contained in the case for support)

correct-no-copies: **appl** → {*true, false*}

(Did the applicants send the correct number of copies?)

Another important point about the above presented language of sets and applications is that we have not explicitly included equality predicates for the two sorts:

$=_{set}$: **set** × **set**   → {*true, false*}
$=_{appl}$: **appl** × **appl** → {*true, false*}

We will always assume such equality predicates to be present and will not state them explicitly.

We are now ready to characterize sets defined in terms of the above functions and predicates. We use the linguistic system MPC (see the Appendix). The extralogical axioms we write are fairly straightforward and can be understood after a moment's thought. Let a, b be variables of sort **appl**, and s, t of sort **set**.

$$\vdash \neg ismember(a, empty) \tag{4.40}$$

(i.e. no value is in the empty set).

$$\vdash ismember(a, insert(b, s)) \Leftrightarrow ((a =_{appl} b) | ismember(a, s))) \tag{4.41}$$

(i.e. a is in the set $insert(b, s)$ if a is b — and b has just been added to the set — or, recursively, a is in s).

$$\vdash ismember(a, remove(b, s)) \Leftrightarrow (\neg(a =_{appl} b) \ \& \ ismember(a, s)) \tag{4.42}$$

(i.e. a is in the set $remove(b, s)$ if a is not the value b just removed but a is in the set s).

$$\vdash \neg(s = empty) \Rightarrow ismember(choose(s), s) \tag{4.43}$$

Thus *choose* selects some member of the set it is given as an argument. It is intended that this chosen member is not removed from the set. Observe that the axiom tells us nothing about what happens if s is the empty set. Nor does it tell us which particular element is selected. (Our specification is quite permissive.)

$$\vdash (Aa(ismember(a, s) \Leftrightarrow ismember(a,t))) \Rightarrow s =_{set} t \tag{4.44}$$

(i.e. if sets s and t have exactly the same members, they are the same set).

We have not included any axioms for the predicate $=_{set}$. Such 'equality axioms' will not be given explicitly as they are assumed to be present in the same way that the equality symbol itself is implicitly present in all specifications. The implicit axioms we require are those that make $=_{set}$ into a congruence:

1. reflexivity:

   $$s =_{set} s$$

2. symmetry:

   $$s =_{set} t \Rightarrow t =_{set} s$$

3. transitivity:
   $$(s =_{set} t \ \& \ t =_{set} u) \Rightarrow s =_{set} u$$
   (u is of sort **set**)

4. substitutivity:
   for each function and for each argument of that function of sort **set**, there is an axiom of the form

   $$s =_{set} t \Rightarrow f(x_1, \ldots, x_{i-1}, s, x_{i+1}, \ldots, x_n) =_m$$
   $$f(x_1, \ldots, x_{i-1}, t, x_{i+1}, \ldots, x_n)$$

where m is the sort of the result of f.

Thus for the specification of sets we have

$$s =_{set} t \Rightarrow insert(a, s) =_{set} insert(a, t)$$
$$s =_{set} t \Rightarrow remove(a, s) =_{set} remove(a, t)$$
$$s =_{set} t \Rightarrow choose(s) =_{appl} choose(t)$$

The last of these, together with axiom (4.43), implies that *choose* is not a non-deterministic function, i.e. one which could deliver one of a possible number of different results, it is just an underdetermined function. (There is a limit to our permissiveness!)

Let t be the set $insert(a, insert(b, empty))$ which denotes the set containing two applications a and b. From the axioms (4.40)–(4.44) (and those for equality), using MPC, one can deduce (i.e. prove) the following:

1. $ismember(b, t)$
2. $\neg(t = empty)$
3. $t = insert(b, insert(a, empty))$
4. $remove(b, t) = insert(a, empty)$

(Note we have dropped the subscript from $=_{set}$ when the context makes clear which equality is meant. We will follow this practice with the various equality symbols we may have occasion to use.)

We can of course deduce

$$ismember(choose(t), t)$$

since t is not the empty set. We can also deduce

$$choose(t) = a \,|\, choose(t) = b$$

but we cannot deduce either

$$choose(t) = a$$

or

$$choose(t) = b$$

This is an example of permissiveness and of what we meant by underdeterminedness. It would be premature at such a level of specification to describe exactly which particular element is to be picked. This should be left to a later stage when the consequences of such a decision can be better evaluated.

Now, let us consider the sequences that we have mentioned above. We start with the usual version of sequences with a function to add an object to the front of a sequence (*cons*), a function to yield the object at the front of a non-empty sequence (*head*), and a function to deliver the sequence obtained by removing the object at the front of a non-empty sequence (*tail*). The empty sequence will be called *nil*.

In order to cope with the ranking of approved applications (requirement (5) above), we use the idea of creating a sequence of applications from the set of approved applications. We do this by putting a given application in its 'correct' position in the sequence with items near the front of the sequence representing the better applications. The 'correct' position is determined by a resurrected Delphic oracle, the Committee! The operation will be called *put-in-position*,

$$put\text{-}in\text{-}position\colon \textbf{appl} \times \textbf{seq} \rightarrow \textbf{seq}$$

For the sort **nat** with variables m, n we postulate the axioms:

$$\vdash \neg(suc(n) =_{nat} zero) \tag{4.45}$$
$$\vdash suc(m) =_{nat} suc(n) \Rightarrow m =_{nat} n \tag{4.46}$$
$$\vdash zero \leq n \tag{4.47}$$
$$\vdash suc(m) \leq suc(n) \Leftrightarrow m \leq n \tag{4.48}$$

Axioms (4.45) and (4.46) ensure that we will not have trivial models of the natural numbers. (Thus, for example, 'adding one' by applying the successor operation, *suc*, really does yield a different natural number.) Axioms (4.47) and (4.48) define the predicate $\leq$ to be a total order on the natural numbers. Note that we use infix notation for $\leq$ just as we have for equality.

Below are listed the axioms for sequences, with k, l variables of sort **seq** and m, n variables of sort **nat**:

$$\vdash (cons(m, k) =_{seq} cons(n, l)) \Leftrightarrow (m =_{nat} n \,\&\, k =_{seq} l) \tag{4.49}$$

(Two sequences are equal if and only if their respective constituents are the same.)

$$\vdash head(cons(m, l)) =_{nat} m \tag{4.50}$$
$$\vdash tail(cons(m, l)) =_{seq} l \tag{4.51}$$

(The above are the usual axioms about *head* and *tail*.)

$$\vdash tail(nil) =_{seq} nil \tag{4.52}$$

(We arbitrarily choose the *tail* of the empty sequence to be the empty sequence.)

$$\vdash length(nil) =_{nat} zero \tag{4.53}$$
$$\vdash length(cons(a, l)) =_{nat} suc(length(l)) \tag{4.54}$$

(The above give the usual recursive definition of the length of a list.)

$$\vdash put\text{-}in\text{-}position(b, zero, l) =_{seq} cons(b, l) \tag{4.55}$$

(Putting b in position *zero* in l is asking for it to be put at the front of l.)

$$\vdash (suc(n) \leq length(l)) \Rightarrow$$
$$(put\text{-}in\text{-}position(b, suc(n), l) =_{seq} cons(head(l),$$
$$put\text{-}in\text{-}position(b, n, tail(l)))) \tag{4.56}$$

(If the position, $suc(n)$, after which we are trying to position b in l is less than or equal to the length of l, then we recursively put the $head(l)$ at the front of the sequence obtained by putting b in position n (one less than before) in l. Nothing is said about the situation where $suc(n)$ is greater than $length(l)$. This is another example of permissiveness of specification.)

Consider now the requirements for our system. A very good method for informally analysing the flow of information and the nature of the actions in a proposed system is to use the so-called data flow analysis (see Section 4.1). This determines the way data flows into, out of and between components of the system, and the nature of that data. Actions on the data are represented as transformations. After some simple analysis of the requirements, we arrive at the data flow diagram presented in Figure 4.9.

The nodes in the diagram represent transformations as prescribed in the requirements. For example, requirement (2) indicates that all applications are validated according to some preset criteria. The top node (bubble) labelled 'Validate applications' is meant to reflect the transformation which divides the set of all applications into those that are valid and those which are not. Thus we also have bubbles to represent the transformations of classifying valid applications (requirement (3)), ranking applications (requirements (4), (5)), merging applications (requirement (6)), allocating funds (requirement (7)), and notifying successful and unsuccessful applicants (requirement (8)).

The arcs in the diagram of Figure 4.9 represent flows of data into, out of and through parts of the proposed system. Thus the arc at the top represents the flow of the set of applications into the system. (We are ignoring the requirement that the applications are entered into the system as they arrive. This is assumed to be already taken care of in the make-up of the set of applications.) The labels in our diagram are variables of one sort or another, the nature of which will become clear below.

In order to characterize the Validate Applications transformation we need an auxilliary monadic predicate

$$valid: \textbf{appl} \rightarrow \{true, false\}$$

which will be used to determine whether a particular application is valid or not. It might be defined by an axiom of the following kind.

$$\vdash ((postmark(a) \leq closing\text{-}date) \ \& \ signed(a) \ \& \ signed\text{-}by\text{-}HoD(a)$$
$$\& \ (no\text{-}of\text{-}pages\text{-}of\text{-}case\text{-}for\text{-}support(a) \leq 6)$$
$$\& \ correct\text{-}no\text{-}copies(a) \ \& \ \ldots)$$
$$\Rightarrow valid(a) \tag{4.57}$$

The conditions under which the application a is valid are determined from the appropriate document (as set out in requirement (2)). A function

$$validate: \textbf{set} \rightarrow \textbf{set}$$

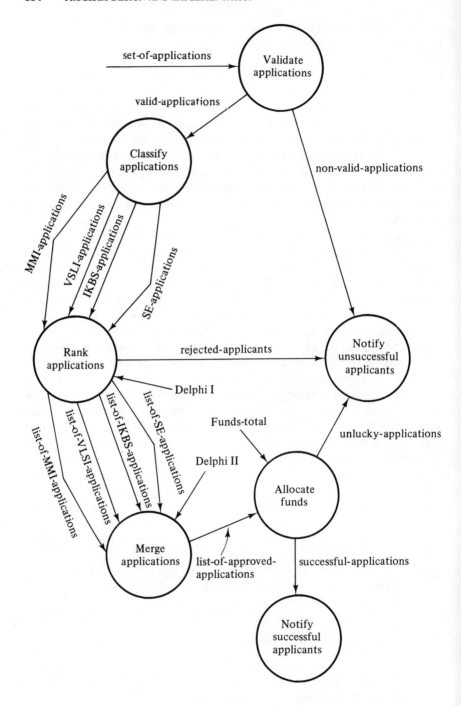

Figure 4.9   Dataflow analysis of VIFA.

will be used to obtain from the set of all applicants that subset which has all the valid applications in it. Thus we can characterize it by:

$\vdash (validate(set\text{-}of\text{-}applications) = valid\text{-}applications)$
$\quad \Leftrightarrow Aa((ismember(a,set\text{-}of\text{-}applications)\ \&\ valid(a))$
$\quad\quad \Leftrightarrow ismember(a,valid\text{-}applications))$ (4.58)

That is, *validate* produces a set, called *valid-applications*, which contains an application *a* from the original set if and only if *a* is valid. (Clearly, the set of *non-valid-applications* is obtained by removing all valid applications from the original set. We will not formally define this set here.)

Consider now the Classify Applications transformation. There are four possibilities, as named in the requirements, and thus we need a sort, say **class**, with four constants:

$MMI: \rightarrow$ **class**
$IKBS: \rightarrow$ **class**
$VLSI: \rightarrow$ **class**
$SE: \quad \rightarrow$ **class**

We also need an auxilliary function

$classification\text{-}of:$ **appl** $\rightarrow$ **class**

with axioms of the form

$\vdash$ 'conditions for being an X application'
$\quad \Rightarrow classification\text{-}of(a) =_{class} X$ (4.59)

for each of the four categories ($X = MMI, IKBS, VLSI, SE$).

The transformation associated with the classification procedure can be characterized in terms of functions of the form:

$classify\text{-}X:$ **set** $\rightarrow$ **set**

with

$\vdash (classify\text{-}X(valid\text{-}applications) =_{set} X\text{-}applications)$
$\quad \Leftrightarrow (Aa(ismember(a, X\text{-}applications)$
$\quad\quad \Leftrightarrow (ismember(a, valid\text{-}applications)$
$\quad\quad\quad \&\ classification\text{-}of(a) =_{class} X)))$ (4.60)

We now come to requirement (4) which involves the constants α, β, *postpone* and *reject* of sort **rank**. The only axiom we can state characterizing the function

$ranking:$ **appl** $\rightarrow$ **rank**

is that

$\vdash (ranking(a) =_{rank} \alpha)|(ranking(a) =_{rank} \beta)|\ldots$ (4.61)

because the ranking of applications is the Delphic right (or is it rite?) of each of the Committees, and the criteria used are not so easily classified as to be prescribed by rules, such as those for requirements (2) and (3). (As we will see, this permissive aspect of the specification will not be completely eliminated because no automatic decision making process will be available. The Delphic intervention will always be required.)

Each Committee has to produce an order of merit for the approved applications. This again requires Delphic intervention and so all we can state about the function

$$rank: \textbf{set} \rightarrow \textbf{seq}$$

mapping the approved applications to an order of merit, reflected by the ordering in the resulting sequence, is

$$\vdash ((rank(approved\text{-}X\text{-}applications) =_{seq} order\text{-}of\text{-}merit\text{-}for\text{-}X)$$
$$\& \; isin(a, order\text{-}of\text{-}merit\text{-}for\text{-}X)$$
$$\& \; isin(b, order\text{-}of\text{-}merit\text{-}for\text{-}X)$$
$$\& \; (classification\text{-}of(a) = \alpha)$$
$$\& \; (classification\text{-}of(b) = \beta))$$
$$\Rightarrow precedes(a, b, order\text{-}of\text{-}merit\text{-}for\text{-}X) \tag{4.62}$$

and

$$\vdash \text{A}a(ismember(a, set\text{-}of\text{-}applications)$$
$$\Leftrightarrow isin(a, rank(set\text{-}of\text{-}applications)))) \tag{4.63}$$

Both the above axioms impose consistency conditions on *rank*. The first bars orders of merit in which applications with an β rating appear before any application with an α rating, while the second imposes the condition that the order of merit must not omit any approved applications.

We have used some auxilliary predicates on sequences:

$$isin: \textbf{appl} \times \textbf{seq} \qquad\qquad \rightarrow \{true, false\}$$
$$precedes: \textbf{appl} \times \textbf{appl} \times \textbf{seq} \rightarrow \{true, false\}$$

The following axioms will serve to define them:

$$\vdash isin(a, l) \Leftrightarrow (\neg(l = nil) \; \& \; (head(l) = a \, | \, isin(a, tail(l)))) \tag{4.64}$$

(For a to occur in l, l must be non-empty. If it is non-empty, then a must occur either at the front of l or somewhere in the rest of l.)

$$\vdash precedes(a, b, l)$$
$$\Leftrightarrow (\neg(l = nil) \; \& \; ((head(l) = a \; \& \; isin(b, tail(l)))$$
$$| precedes(a, b, tail(l)))) \tag{4.65}$$

(Again, l must be non-empty and then either a is the front of l and b occurs in the rest of l or a precedes b in the rest of l.)

We have not added any new properties of sequences (or of applications) which were not already consequences of axioms (4.49)–(4.56), thus the introduction of the symbols *isin* and *precedes*, together with the axioms (4.64) and (4.65), defines a conservative extension of the theory of sequences. Therefore, if someone had gone off and correctly implemented sequences as specified by the theory (4.49)−(4.56), no alterations would have to be made in light of the introduction of the above predicates which can be implemented by add-on code. More on this later.

The final step that we want to consider is merging of orders of merit (requirement (6)). Here we would use a function

merge: **seq** $\times$ **seq** $\rightarrow$ **seq**

which we can characterize only by stating consistency conditions similar to (4.62) and (4.63) above. The intervention of an oracle (this time embodied in the Secretariat's Advisory Board) would again be required.

We have not attempted a complete characterization of the required system, as this might not be more instructive than what we have outlined so far and, anyway, we certainly have no room for it! Nor have we tried to explain fully how we arrived at the functions, predicates and axioms we have written. We wish to concentrate more on how such a specification is turned into a running system.

Finally, note that our (partial) characterization of some transformations from the data flow diagram defines a conservative extension of the specifications of sets and sequences of applications.

4.3.6   Canonical implementation steps

Having obtained (in some manner) the specification of a system, we would like eventually to produce a running system corresponding to this specification. We now concentrate on illustrating how the steps, out of which such a process of implementation is constructed, can be contemplated in a paradigmatic manner. That is, we claim that the process of implementing a specification by a running (executable) system is accomplished by repeating (what we call) the *canonical* implementation step a sufficient number of times.

We illustrate the canonical step via a simple example. If we are to implement the above presented specification, we will have to implement the data type *set of applications* which we will now call SET. This specification consists of the language L_{SET} introduced in Figure 4.8 and the axioms (4.40)−(4.44) which we will call G_{SET}.

When an experienced software engineer is asked to implement sets, he might very well reply that he can do so by representing sets as sequences and realizing set operations in terms of the operations provided to manipulate sequences. What sense can we make of this?

Well, first of all, we have a candidate specification of sequences. This is given by the language L_{SEQ} and axioms (4.49)−(4.56) which we call G_{SEQ}. Thus sequences are specified by SEQ = $\langle L_{SEQ}, G_{SEQ} \rangle$. Let us consider separately the two parts of the description of how a software engineer proceeds.

Firstly, what exactly do we mean by representing sets as sequences? In our example system, sets and sequences both have the same kind of components; namely, applications. So if we have a set s and a sequence l we might consider that l represents s if l and s had the 'same' components. Another way of putting it is that any sequence represents a set, viz. the set consisting of those objects which are components of the sequence. To state this formally we require a monadic predicate

$$set\text{-}rep1\colon \mathbf{seq} \to \{true, false\}$$

which we can use to characterize those sequences that represent sets. Based on the above, the axiomatization of *set-rep1* would be

$$\vdash \mathbf{A}l(set\text{-}rep1(l))$$

It could be claimed that this might not turn out to be a very efficient representation of sets, as sequences with repeated components contain redundant information. Thus the sequence with a given application '*cons*'ed five times onto the empty sequence represents the same set as the sequence with the single '*cons*' of our application onto the empty sequence.

A better representation might be to use sequences with non-repeated components. (This will have the unfortunate consequence of leaving us with some sequences which do not represent sets.) Let us use the predicate

$$set\text{-}rep\colon \mathbf{seq} \to \{true, false\}$$

and the axiom

$$\vdash set\text{-}rep(l) \Leftrightarrow (\mathbf{A}a(isin(a, l) \Rightarrow once(a, l))) \tag{4.66}$$

where l represents some set in case every application which occurs in l occurs only once. Here we have

$$once\colon \mathbf{appl} \times \mathbf{seq} \to \{true, false\}$$

with

$$
\begin{aligned}
\vdash once(a, l) \Leftrightarrow{} & \neg(l = nil) \\
& \&\,((head(l) = a\ \&\ \neg isin(a, tail(l))) \\
& \,|(\neg(head(l) = a)\ \&\ once(a, tail(l)))))
\end{aligned} \tag{4.67}
$$

So a occurs once in l if l is not empty and if either a is at the front of l and does not occur in the remainder of l, or a is not the head of l but occurs once in the remainder of l. (*isin* was defined by axiom (4.64) and *set-rep* is the relativization predicate referred to in Section 4.2; see also Section A.7 of the Appendix and Section 2.3.)

Now, let us turn to the second part of our description of a software engineer's intentions and attempt to ascertain what is meant by 'representing operations on sets by using those on sequences'. The software engineer would mean that he had available procedures for manipulating

sequences and he expected to write procedures for each of the set operations (which would make use of the sequence procedures). Thus, for each
of the symbols in L_{SET}, we will have to add to SEQ a corresponding
'procedure name' and definition. At this point we have no programming
language yet and we must work by analogy. Firstly, the 'procedure
names':

$$
\begin{aligned}
&empty' : \textbf{seq} &&\rightarrow \{true, false\} \\
&insert' : \textbf{appl} \times \textbf{seq} &&\rightarrow \textbf{seq} \\
&remove' : \textbf{appl} \times \textbf{seq} &&\rightarrow \textbf{seq} \\
&choose' : \textbf{seq} &&\rightarrow \textbf{appl} \\
&ismember' : \textbf{appl} \times \textbf{seq} \rightarrow \{true, false\} \\
&='_{set} : \textbf{seq} \times \textbf{seq} \rightarrow \{true, false\}
\end{aligned}
$$

These are essentially the syntax definitions of Figure 4.8 but with **set**
replaced by **seq**, as we should expect, since we are using (some) sequences
to represent sets. We can now provide the 'procedure definitions' with all
occurrences of equality without subscripts being either $=_{seq}$ or $=_{appl}$:

$$\vdash empty' = nil \tag{4.68}$$

(The constant *nil*, the empty sequence, is equivalent to the constant
representing the empty set.)

$$
\begin{aligned}
&\vdash (insert'(a, k) = l) \\
&\quad \Leftrightarrow ((isin(a, k) \,\&\, k = l)|(\neg isin(a, k) \,\&\, l = cons(a,k)))
\end{aligned}
\tag{4.69}
$$

(The 'procedure' for inserting a into the set represented by the sequence
k defines the result as k itself, if a already occurs in k, or is $cons(a, k)$
otherwise.)

$$
\begin{aligned}
&\vdash (remove'(a, k) = l) \\
&\quad \Leftrightarrow ((\neg isin(a, k) \,\&\, k = l) \\
&\quad |(isin(a, k) \,\&\, ((a = head(k) \,\&\, l = tail(k)) \\
&\quad |(\neg(a = head(k)) \,\&\, l = cons(head(k), remove'(a, tail(k))))))))
\end{aligned}
\tag{4.70}
$$

(If a does not occur in k, removing a from k has no effect on k. If a
occurs in k, then either a is at the front of k and the result is the rest of k,
or a is not at the front of k and removing a from k results in the sequence
with the front of k at the front and the rest of the sequence obtained by
removing a from the remainder of k.)

$$\vdash (choose'(k) = a) \Leftrightarrow isin(a, k) \tag{4.71}$$

(This is just a consistency condition on *choose'*; it still makes no commit-
ment about how the arbitrary element is chosen.)

$$\vdash ismember'(a, l) \Leftrightarrow isin(a,l) \tag{4.72}$$

(Representation of set membership is the predicate *isin* defined previously for sequences.)

$$\vdash (k ='_{set} l) \Leftrightarrow \mathbf{A}a(isin(a, k) \Leftrightarrow isin(a, l)) \tag{4.73}$$

(Two sequences represent the same set if and only if they have exactly the same constituents.)

Note that the definitions above assume implicitly the representations of sets defined by *set-rep* and not those defined by *set-rep1*. For example, the definition of *remove'* would not work for *set-rep1* since a sequence with multiple copies of an application would only have the first of them removed. Thus, combined with the definition of *ismember'*, we would get an unexpected answer for set membership. The following would have to be used to replace (4.70):

$$\vdash (remove1'(a, k) = l)$$
$$\Leftrightarrow ((\neg isin(a, k) \ \& \ k = l)$$
$$| (isin(a, k) \ \& \ (a = head(k) \ \& \ l = remove1'(a, tail(k)))))$$
$$| (\neg (a = head(k))$$
$$\& \ l = cons(head(k), remove1'(a, tail(k)))))) \tag{4.70'}$$

Our implementation would now work again with *set-rep1* and axiom (4.70'). The redundant check for occurrence in the definition of *insert'* (axiom 4.69) does not cause logical problems but clearly introduces an unnecessary restriction on further implementations. That is, it is less permissive than it might be.

Let $SEQ1 = \langle L_{SEQ1}, G_{SEQ1} \rangle$, where L_{SEQ1} is L_{SEQ} together with the symbols {*set-rep, isin, once, empty', insert', remove', choose', ismember',* $='_{set}$}. G_{SEQ1} is G_{SEQ} together with axioms (4.64) and (4.66)–(4.73). SEQ1 is a conservative extension of SEQ. The additions (defining the extension) are essentially data representation invariants and operation (i.e. function and relation) definitions. The purpose of this extension was to facilitate a definition of what we meant by 'implementing sets in terms of sequences'. At this point we have two specifications which our intuition tells us are related — SET and SEQ1. But what is the relationship? Clearly, the primed symbols in SEQ1 (such as *empty', insert',...*) are meant to correspond to the respective symbols in SET. Moreover, the phrase 'implementing set operations in terms of sequence operations' is meant to ascribe to the primed symbols the properties which are similar to those of the corresponding symbols in SET.

To formally establish this correspondence between symbols (a translation) and pin down what we mean by similar properties, we use an interpretation between theories.

Let SET_to_SEQ1: $L_{SET} \to L_{SEQ1}$ be an interpretation defined by:

1. ϕ : **set** $\mapsto$ **seq**
   appl $\mapsto$ **appl**

2. π : Symbols associated with **appl** are mapped to themselves. Otherwise:

$$empty \quad \mapsto empty$$
$$insert \quad \mapsto insert'$$
$$remove \quad \mapsto remove'$$
$$choose \quad \mapsto choose'$$
$$ismember \mapsto ismember'$$
$$=_{set} \quad\quad \mapsto ='_{set}$$

3. ρ : **set** $\mapsto$ *set-rep*
   appl $\mapsto$ *is-appl*

We shall not make explicit the translations of variables.

The symbol *is-appl* is not in L_{SEQ1}. Its meaning could be defined by

$$\vdash is\text{-}appl(a) \tag{4.74}$$

That is, all applications are still applications!

To prove that we have a proper interpretation, we must demonstrate property preservation. As indicated in the Appendix, Section A.7, this can be done by:

1. showing that the axioms of SET, when translated, are theorems (consequences) of SEQ1;

2. showing that the domain of values defined by the relativization predicate is non-empty and closed under the operations to which the set operations are translated.

For example, take the axiom

$$\vdash ismember(a, remove(b, s))$$
$$\Leftrightarrow (\neg (a =_{appl} b) \& ismember(a, s)) \tag{4.42}$$

This is translated to:

$$(set\text{-}rep(l) \& is\text{-}appl(a) \& is\text{-}appl(b))$$
$$\Rightarrow (ismember'(a, remove'(b, l))$$
$$\Leftrightarrow ((\neg a ='_{appl} b) \& ismember'(a, l))) \tag{4.75}$$

where s is mapped to l and a,b to a,b respectively.

Another example is axiom

$$\vdash \neg (s =_{set} empty) \Rightarrow ismember(choose(s), s) \tag{4.43}$$

which translates to

$$set\text{-}rep(l) \Rightarrow (\neg (l ='_{set} empty') \Rightarrow ismember'(choose'(s), s)) \tag{4.76}$$

Note that amongst the axioms of sets whose translations must follow from our extended theory of sequences there are the axioms concerning set equality. Thus, for example, we must show that the translation of

$$(s =_{set} t) \Rightarrow (insert(a, s) =_{set} insert(a, t))$$

(which states the substitutivity property of $=_{set}$ with respect to *insert*), i.e. the theorem

$$(set\text{-}rep(l) \ \& \ set\text{-}rep(k) \ \& \ is\text{-}appl(a))$$
$$\Rightarrow ((l ='_{set} k) \Rightarrow (insert'(a, l) ='_{set} insert'(a, k)))$$

must follow from SEQ1.

To show that the domain of the relativization predicates is non-empty, we have to show that $\mathbf{E}l(set\text{-}rep(l))$ and $\mathbf{E}a(is\text{-}appl(a))$ hold.

From the definition of *set-rep* we clearly have that *set-rep(nil)* holds. Indeed from axiom (4.66) we get

$$set\text{-}rep(nil) \Leftrightarrow (\mathbf{A}a(isin(a, nil) \Rightarrow once(a, nil)))$$

Now, *isin(a, nil)* is false for any *a* since the definition (4.64) requires the second argument of *isin(a, l)* be non-*nil*. This then makes

$$isin(a, nil) \Rightarrow once(a, nil)$$

true for any *a*; hence we have

$$\mathbf{A}a(isin(a, nil) \Rightarrow once(a, nil))$$

Thus $G_{SEQ1} \vdash set\text{-}rep(nil)$.

The sentence $\mathbf{E}a(is\text{-}appl(a))$ is trivially true (as long as the original set of applications was non-empty!).

To show that the domain defined by the relativization predicates is closed under the translated set operations, we must show that for each operation which returns a set object, if the arguments satisfy the appropriate relativization predicate, then so does the result. Thus, for example, we must demonstrate that

$$\mathbf{A}l \ \mathbf{A}a((set\text{-}rep(l) \ \& \ is\text{-}appl(a)) \Rightarrow set\text{-}rep(insert'(a, l)))$$

To gain a firm grasp of the concepts discussed in this section, the reader may care to do all the proofs and translations.

4.4   Preservation of main properties

Many contributors working on program development have claimed that a main rôle of abstraction − often embodied in the form of a specification − and implementation (or reification) is to modularize a difficult and highly detailed process by use of the ubiquitous 'separation of concerns'. To fully understand this rôle, we must understand the notions of detail and change involved; these issues are discussed in the two subsequent sections.

The title of this section focuses our attention on two important questions:

What do we mean by properties?

and

> What is it that is preserved, and how is it preserved (by the process of implementation)?

To deal with the first question first, we must initially decide what we mean by 'properties'. Since a specification is an (axiomatic) presentation of a theory (linguistic level) in some logic (linguistic system), it is clear that, in the context of a given specification, 'properties' must mean formulae which belong to the theory generated by the specification. So 'what is a property' is intimately related to that which is derivable in the theory.

As to our second question, we ask two subsidiary questions: what do we mean by 'preservation' and what is the relationship between 'properties' that are preserved and the properties discussed above? The discussion of our first question would seem to indicate that the properties in which we are interested at least include *all* those which we posited in the specification (including those provable from the specification) we have assumed as our starting point.

However, the concept of 'implementation' seemingly throws a spanner into the works because an implementation step is mediated by a translation, and we are thus unable even to state (directly) the properties in which we may be interested. As an illustration, consider the property expressed by the axiom (4.40)

$$\vdash \neg\, ismember(a, empty)$$

(defining the non-membership of any application in the empty set of applications). Given the implementation of sets by sequences discussed in Section 4.3, the symbols *ismember* and *empty* are not in the language over which the implementation is defined. In what sense, then, can we say that the property (4.40) (and all other properties of sets) are preserved? Now, the notion of translation sets up a correspondence between the two languages and, consequently, between terms and formulae over these languages. As explained in Sections 2.3 and 4.2, it is properties *as mediated by the translations* which are actually preserved.

4.4.1 Abstraction and main properties

The building of a specification is a little bit like building a scientific theory. A specification is built to provide an unambiguous prescription for some system or system component, a prescription which can then be subject to analysis. Whether the specification is required as a first step in building the system or required to support the next implementation step (i.e. as the putative target of a translation) is irrelevant from this perspective. In analogy with scientific theories, specifications cannot be proved to be correct, they can only be invalidated on the basis of experiments. Either some property implied by the specification is not a desired property of the system being prescribed or some desired property of the required system is not predicted from (a consequence of) the specification. Thus experiments in this context are comparisons of desired properties of the required system with the 'deductions' based on the specification. One way in which scientific theories differ from specifications is that the former are rooted in more or less real phenomena (we do not want to open that can of worms) while the latter pertain to non-existent artefacts (i.e. desires).

One of the most important processes contributing to activity of specification building is that of *abstraction*. This is a hard concept to define; in the context of Computing Science, the most common usage relates to elimination of unnecessary detail. The obvious question which arises is: unnecessary for what? Specifications (as the initial stage of system definition) are supposedly more to do with the 'what' of the system rather than the 'how'. Actual algorithms for sorting, or finding square roots, are not as relevant to system specification as the attribution of the appropriate properties to function (and predicate) symbols which are meant to embody the functions (or relations) computed by such algorithms.

Abstraction and specification are modularization principles which are meant to be applied to the process of building a system. The 'module' with which a system specification is then concerned is the definition of the essential properties of the system. (Unfortunately, one person's essential is another's irrelevant! This is another (smelly) kettle of fish with which we do not want to deal in this book.) Thus, at least initially, before we have done any development, a main property is one which is included in the original specification — either explicitly, as an axiom, or implicitly, as a consequence of the axioms — because it was thought to be essential for the 'scientific theory' being defined.

Considering the specification of VIFA's activities, there is clearly a plethora of decisions to be made when turning the original requirements into a proper specification. These decisions range from the choice of non-logical symbols in terms of which to frame the specification, to the more difficult problems of deciding what exactly the main properties are. Certainly, the fact that the ranking of applications defines an α (approved with a high degree of merit) to be better than a β (approved with a lower degree of merit) is inescapable and must somehow be dealt with in the specification. The *how* of such a representation is certainly contingent — we have chosen to use the implicit structural property of 'coming before' in a sequence (see axiom (4.62)). Thus all α-rated applications must precede any β-rated applications in orders of merit. We could just as easily have chosen another implicit formulation or some explicit formulation of this property.

Sometimes we can express fairly precisely what we have in mind, as is the case with sets and sequences in the VIFA example. This happens because we are familiar with the object we want to characterize. For example, we have constructed specifications of sets and sequences before and so thought about their essential properties and in terms of what language to state them. Sometimes, what we want to describe exists already in the real world and we have a standard of comparison which might not tell us what is essential but at least gives us a fixed object against which to compare our efforts. Such is the case for the various committees and classifications of the SIT in VIFA.

Often, we do not know very precisely what it is that we are trying to characterize. We may not be able to say very much about it, and it is thus difficult to decide what is essential and what can be left out. For example, although we are able to say a little about functions such as *rank* ((4.62), (4.63)) and *merge*, we are certainly unable to give the kind of 'complete' characterization we provided for sets and sequences. But, as with most things, being a main property is a relative concept. Thus with program development. From the point of view of someone using the result of the first implementation step, $SEQ1 = \langle L_{SEQ1}, G_{SEQ1} \rangle$ of our VIFA specification, as defined by (4.64), (4.66)−(4.73) and by the interpretation between theories SET_to_SEQ1: SET → SEQ1, the main properties (for sets and sequences) are those implied by SEQ1.

The specification of the other aspects of SIT/VIFA are provided in terms of conservative extensions of sets and sequences (of applications) and are automatically carried forward by a unique extension of the interpretation SET_to_SEQ1. (This is an instance of the 'rectangle' property used in the composition of implementation steps. See Section 4.3.)

Part of the benefit of modularizing our activities in specifying and implementing a system should be that the execution of a given step need only assume the results of a previous step (if any) and definitely not the history of the manner in which this was achieved − yet another instance of the 'what' *vs* 'how' demarcation. The implementor now has at hand more explicit (i.e. more algorithmic) versions of the *insert* and *remove* operations on sets (*insert'* and *remove'*, respectively; see (4.69), (4.70)). He knows such details as 'the last element inserted into the set, if it was not already a member of the set, is now at the front of the sequence representing that set' (although to determine this he needs to apply sequence operations).

Hence, the earlier in the development process a property is introduced, the more 'main' it is, with properties of the original specification being the most important, and those introduced at the end of the development process being the most contingent. As we will see later on (Section 4.6), this is not just a matter of playing with words but has some correlation with the amount of work involved in revising an implementation by changing some required properties. Generally, the more 'main' the property, the more work is involved in following through the consequences of a change. The less 'main' a property, the easier it is to make requisite changes in program development.

4.4.2 Modularity and main properties

Is modularity of specification itself a 'main' property? We have found it useful (and we would maintain it is an absolute necessity) to modularize our specifications by using the notion of conservative extension. Thus sets of natural numbers and sequences of natural numbers are specified by means of conservative extensions of the specification of natural numbers; sorting of sets into sequences is specified in terms of a conservative extension of sets and sequences; SEQ1, required to support an implementation of sets in terms of sequences, is built as a conservative extension of SEQ, so as to protect (and validate for use in this context) any existing implementation of SEQ.

Clearly, modularity of specifications (as opposed to modularity of the development process itself, as discussed in the previous subsection) is very important both for the process of building a particular specification − writing large, unmodularized specifications is no more fun than writing massive unstructured programs − and for developing programs from specifications by using teams working on separate parts. But is the modularity built into a specification sacrosanct? Is it a 'main' property?

For the simple reason that it may lead to a lot of redundancy, we do not believe that it is sacrosanct. If we assumed that modularization was rigid, we could get the kinds of relationships between specifications in a given development illustrated in Figure 4.10.

S is the specification with which we start; it is implemented in terms of specifications *S0, S1* and *S2*; *S0* is itself implemented in terms of specifications *S00* and *S01*, etc. The appropriate relationships are represented by trees. What happens if two nodes of a tree are the same? For example, consider the implementation of integers in terms of NAT and SIGN. Figure 4.11 illustrates the relationships involved, and we see implementations of NAT appearing twice as a leaf.

Clearly, we do not want to force two separate implementations of NAT but would often like to use the same one to support both instances[†]. The same phenomenon occurs with implementing sets in terms of sequences for the VIFA example.

The actual modularity within a Specification is not a 'main' property. The question of when to 'demodularize' is a difficult problem for managers of software development. It assumes a large degree of control of, and global knowledge about, a modularized development process to make sure that redundancy in work is eliminated. Forcing certain development paths to bring forward the opportunity to 'demodularize' with effort-saving consequences is even more sophisticated. This becomes more important as the re-use of components becomes feasible.

There is a subsidiary notion of 'main' property which is also relevant

---

[†] Of course, we sometimes do want separate implementations of the same specification, e.g. when different efficiency criteria so dictate.

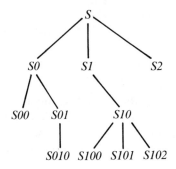

Figure 4.10   Dependency relationships between specifications in an
implementation.

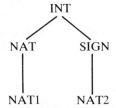

Figure 4.11   Dependency relationships in implementing integers in terms of
naturals.

for the modularization of specifications. It has to do with the use of so-called *parameterized specifications*. Without wishing to go into too many details, we want to make a few remarks about the relationship of this concept to our notion of 'main' property.

We have seen in previous sections how the concept of set and sequence have been applied to natural numbers and applications. They may also be applied to any other kind of objects (including sets and sequences themselves as, for example, in sets of sequences, sets of sets, etc.). Similarly, sorting may be applied not just to natural numbers, but also to integers or any other kind of object with a total order defined on it. We would like, in each such case, to define a template for extending specifications of the parameter objects (i.e. specifications) involved.

Without getting too technical, let us explore this idea through an example. Consider the parameterized specification SET_of_X; the set part is specified by axioms of the same form as axioms (4.40)−(4.44) but with variables *a, b* now replaced by *x, y* ranging[†] over the *formal parameter* sort **X**.

[†] Clearly the typing of the symbols involved will also have to change to reflect the replacement of the sort **appl** by the formal parameter sort **X**.

$$\vdash \neg ismember(x, empty) \tag{4.77}$$
$$\vdash ismember(x, insert(y, s)) \Leftrightarrow ((x =_X y) | ismember(x, s)) \tag{4.78}$$
$$\vdash ismember(x, remove(y, s)) \Leftrightarrow (\neg(x =_X y) \ \& \ ismember(x, s)) \tag{4.79}$$
$$\vdash \neg(s = empty) \Rightarrow ismember(choose(s), s) \tag{4.80}$$
$$\vdash (\mathbf{A}x(ismember(x, s) \Leftrightarrow ismember(x, t))) \Rightarrow s =_{set} t \tag{4.81}$$

We can now *instantiate* the formal parameter X in SET_of_X by the actual parameter *natural number* (NAT) by associating the sort **nat** of NAT with the formal parameter sort **X**. This should give us a specification equivalent to the original. We could also replace **X** by **appl** to get sets of applications.

The situation is generally not quite so straightforward. Usually, our template constrains the kind of actual parameters we are willing to accept. Suppose that we want to use sets as part of a specification of sorting but we want to develop a parameterized version of sorting. We can achieve this by means of axioms ascribing some properties to the formal parameter sort. Take axioms (4.77)–(4.81) and add to them the following axioms defining the totally and strictly ordered SET_of_X:

$$\vdash \neg LT(x, x) \tag{4.82}$$
$$\vdash LT(x, y) \Rightarrow \neg LT(y, x) \tag{4.83}$$
$$\vdash (LT(x, y) \ \& \ LT(y, z)) \Rightarrow LT(x, z) \tag{4.84}$$
$$\vdash \mathbf{A}x\mathbf{A}y(LT(x, y) | LT(y, x) | x =_X y) \tag{4.85}$$

where *x, y, z* are variables of sort **X**.

This defines an order called *LT* on objects of sort **X**. The parameter X can no longer be instantiated by sort **appl** because the latter has no total order defined on it. However, if we take the specification of natural number with the relation *lt* as defined by axioms (A.1)–(A.6) of the Appendix, Section A.6, we can instantiate the formal parameter by associating with **X** the sort **nat**, and with the symbol *LT* of X the symbol *lt* of the natural number specification[†].

Note that the situation is potentially quite complicated because the axioms employed to define *LT* are quite different from those that we used to define *lt*. (The latter relation is fully constructive, whereas the former is not.) To make sure that the instantiation is correct, we must demonstrate that the properties required by the formal parameter are implied by the specification of the actual parameter (with appropriate replacement of symbols). The reader may care to show that the definition of *lt* in the Appendix, Section A.6, does imply the axioms (4.82)–(4.85).

[†] We will not deal here with the actual mechanics of this association, except to say that it is accomplished via (non-conservative) extension of X using a formula of the form

$$lt(x, y) \Rightarrow LT(x, y)$$

which indicates that the relation defined by LT is subsumed in the relation defined by lt.

Note also that if instead of *lt* we specified an order called, for example, *divides*, which defines the relation 'natural number *n* divides evenly into natural number *m'*, and tried to associate *divides* with *LT*, we would get an inconsistency because *divides* should not satisfy axiom (4.85) defining *LT* to be a total order. (See also Section 2.3 and the discussion of extensions.)

It is in this sense that constraints on formal parameters in parameterized specifications are a 'main' property. We have no choice but to obey the constraints when instantiating parameters, or we get an inconsistent, therefore nonsensical, specification.

4.4.3   Plus ça change, plus c'est la même chose

Having dealt at length with what we mean by 'main' property, we now want to discuss in what sense main properties are preserved. Properties are relative to a language, as already hinted at in this section. Thus the concept of conservative extension makes sense only in the context of preserving properties directly relevant to (i.e. statable using only) some fixed underlying extralogical symbols. Although this point is not generally emphasized, it is a very important aspect of dealing with theories and specifications.

Clearly, then, main properties are preserved if we do nothing! However, we generally want to do something – define an implementation step. Such a step is mediated by an interpretation between theories, which itself is a translation between two languages with an added ingredient. This additional requirement is that of property preservation (see Section 2.3 and the Appendix, Section A.7). But surely we are using 'property preservation' in a very loose way here! What sense does it make to say that a property (main or not) is preserved, when we now have two languages involved?

Recall that an interpretation between (many-sorted) languages

$$I: \langle S, L \rangle \rightarrow \langle S', L' \rangle$$

allows us to translate terms and formulae of $\langle S, L \rangle$ to terms and formulae, respectively, of $\langle S', L' \rangle$.

If

$$I: \langle \langle S, L \rangle, G \rangle \rightarrow \langle \langle S', L' \rangle, G' \rangle$$

is an interpretation between theories, the added ingredient is that for any formula A over $\langle S, L \rangle$

if $G \vdash A$, then $G' \vdash A^I$

Hence we are able to represent a property defined over one language, A *over* $\langle S, L \rangle$, by using a corresponding formula over another language, A^I over $\langle S', L' \rangle$. The sense of the correspondence is very important. The fact that I is an interpretation between theories $\langle \langle S, L \rangle, G \rangle$ and $\langle \langle S', L' \rangle,$ $G' \rangle$ demonstrates that we can *simulate* the former via the latter. Anything we can say about the former − construction of terms, formulae, proofs,... − we can simulate via the latter by using corresponding terms, formulae, proofs,... .

Perhaps, then, 'preservation of main properties' is best rephrased as 'simulation of main properties'[†]. It is in fact a very particular kind of simulation as what we really want to be able to simulate is the ability to derive consequences of G. Thus any proof involving a derivation of some consequence of G can now be simulated by a proof using a derivation of the corresponding property from G'. In the example of the sorting program presented in Section 4.2, the proof of partial correctness of the program (4.30) can be simulated in terms of some implementation of sequences, preserving the partial correctness of the program over the implementation step. It should be clear that if we are unable to construct this proof from the given one, and, moreover, in an automatic way, we are going to have to redo previous work. We would have to redo some of the partial correctness proof which we had already worked hard to get. The point of introducing development steps was to introduce modularity into the process of program construction. This had the beneficial result of allowing us to split into manageable parts the work we had to do in constructing the program. Consequently, there is not much point to a modularization principle which does not properly separate concerns!

Another important ingredient in the property preservation game is the use of many steps in the development process, and the necessity to preserve at the next step *all* the properties which are consequences of the previous step. Thus the real requirement is that simulations compose to form simulations. Moreover, the order in which simulations are composed should also be irrelevant (associativity of composition). The concepts of interpretations between theories and conservative extensions both meet these requirements and, together with our result on composing implementations (the Modularization Theorem), we have the desired properties of simulation (implementation).

At this point, it is worth pointing out that, contrary to what we have illustrated in this book, not all approaches to specification and implementation provide such guarantees about implementation and the composition of implementations (Ehrich, 1982; Ehrig *et al.*, 1982).

[†] As with all simulations, the simulator has properties other than those strictly required by the simulatee. Hence, if X simulates Y, it is not necessarily the case that Y simulates X. We do not generally have the relationship of *bisimulation* − a good candidate for defining *equivalence* between specifications. See also the next section.

4.5 Addition of detail

4.5.1 Interpretations and the introduction of detail

In the previous section we looked at how the process of development preserves certain desired aspects of specifications. However, if the process of abstraction used in building specifications is meant to ignore unnecessary detail, 'unimportant' details of the 'real world', then the process of development (reification) is meant to put (some of) such details back in, like how the system is implemented by means of a particular programming language on some particular machine. So in this section we want to look at how the flip side of the coin of property preservation works.

Let us begin with an example – the decision to implement *choose*, the underdetermined choice operator which delivers some element of a non-empty set. Take axioms 1−11 of Figure 4.7(b) (see also the similarly numbered axioms of the Appendix, Section A.6) which characterize sets of natural numbers (the latter totally ordered by the relation *lt*). We can implement this in sequences of natural numbers by means of the interpretation ι defined in the Appendix, Section A.7.

Note that the axiom

$$\vdash (choose'(k) = m) \Rightarrow isin(m,k)$$

does not really tell us any more about how *choose* (or its translation *choose'*) works than we knew before. We do have the implementation knowledge that *choose* is implemented by selecting some arbitrary component of the sequence which represents the set, but no more. This only tells us that sequence operations may somehow be used but does not actually tell us how.

Suppose that we now decide to fix the meaning of *choose* by always picking the least element of a set. This can be accomplished by means of a very small implementation step ι' which maps EXTSEQ = $\langle \langle S_{\text{extseq}}, L_{\text{extseq}} \rangle, G_{\text{extseq}} \rangle$ to EXT1SEQ = $\langle \langle S_{\text{ext1seq}}, L_{\text{ext1seq}} \rangle, G_{\text{ext1seq}} \rangle$ in which all the symbols and variables of L_{extseq}, but *choose'*, are mapped to themselves. *choose'* is then mapped to *choose''* which is characterized as follows:

$$\vdash choose''(l) = m \Leftrightarrow (\neg(l = nil) \,\&\, isin(m, l) \\ \&\, (\text{A}n(isin(n, l) \Rightarrow ((m = n)|lt(m, n)))))$$ (4.86)

(There are still the definitions of relativization predicates to deal with, but these are just the trivial ones, as expected:

$$m =_{nat} m$$

for naturals and

$$l =_{seq} l$$

for sequences.

Note that we are using the more general notion of relativization introduced in Section 2.3. Then, in any formula translated by ι, the relativization predicates disappear by means of a simple reduction.)

We now clearly have an additional property of sets:

$$\vdash choose(s) = m$$
$$\Leftrightarrow (\neg(m = empty) \ \& \ ismember(m, s)$$
$$\& \ (\mathbf{A}n(ismember(n, s) \Rightarrow ((m = n)|lt(m, n)))))) \qquad (4.87)$$

This cannot be proved from the previous characterization of sets, but clearly translates under $\iota \cdot \iota'$ (the composition of the interpretations ι and ι') into a formula which is a consequence of (4.86). This is an example of what we mean by the 'addition of detail' — provision of algorithmic information, the 'how' as opposed to 'what', which makes a specification less underdetermined.

An implementation step usually adds another kind of detail which we have illustrated already — data structure representation and the addition of algorithmic detail in terms of this representation. This kind of step may or may not add any abstract properties for the objects being implemented. (Does the implementation of sets in sequences (via ι) add any properties of sets?)

We have to be very careful about how such details or additional properties are added. Some intuitively obvious choices may cause problems — like being unable to prove that a translation is an interpretation between theories. If we asked readers before they read this section how they would implement *choose* in terms of sequence operations, we would almost certainly get the response: choose the head of the sequence which represents the set:

$$\vdash choose1(cons(m, l)) = m \qquad (4.88)$$

The mapping ι'' could then be defined exactly as for ι but mapping *choose'* to *choose1*; it certainly is a translation, but is it an interpretation between theories?

Consider

$$\vdash m =_{nat} m \qquad (4.89)$$

the reflexive property of (abstract) natural number equality and its translation under ι and ι''. After a few trivial reductions, we obtain (4.89) again as a consequence of our concrete theory.

Consider the substitution property as applied to *choose*:

$$\vdash s =_{set} s' \Rightarrow (choose(s) =_{nat} choose(s')) \qquad (4.90)$$

This translates under ι and ι'' (after a few reductions) to

$$(set\text{-}rep(l) \ \& \ set\text{-}rep(l'))$$
$$\Rightarrow (l =_{set} l' \Rightarrow choose1(l) =_{nat} choose1(l')) \qquad (4.91)$$

Consider now the substitution defined by

$$l = cons(zero, cons(suc(zero), nil)) \qquad (4.92)$$

and

$$l' = cons(suc(zero), cons(zero, nil)) \qquad (4.93)$$

The reader should easily convince himself that if G_{badseq} is the set of axioms defining the target of ι'', then we have

$$G_{badseq} \vdash set\text{-}rep(l) \qquad (4.94)$$
$$G_{badseq} \vdash set\text{-}rep(l') \qquad (4.95)$$
$$G_{badseq} \vdash l =_{set} l' \qquad (4.96)$$

Thus from (4.91) and (4.94) − (4.96) we get (by applying *modus ponens* several times) that

$$G_{badseq} \vdash choose1(l) =_{nat} choose1(l')$$

i.e.

$$G_{badseq} \vdash choose1(cons(zero, cons(suc(zero), nil))) =_{nat}$$
$$choose1(cons(suc(zero), cons(zero, nil)))$$

i.e. by (4.88)

$$G_{badseq} \vdash zero =_{nat} suc(zero) \qquad (4.97)$$

The attentive reader should by now be suspicious because we clearly supposed that 0 is not 1. In fact the relevant axiom (see axiom (1) in Figure 4.7(b)) is

$$G_{badseq} \vdash \neg(suc(m) = zero)$$

which, with *zero* substituted for m, gives us

$$G_{badseq} \vdash \neg(suc(zero) = zero) \qquad (4.98)$$

So (4.97) and (4.98) yield a contradiction. Note that this contradiction arose because we assumed that ι'', as defined by (4.88), defined an interpretation between theories. This assumption is clearly false in the light of the contradiction just derived and so something must be wrong. The only possibility in this case would seem to be the definition (4.88) as everything else is the identity mapping.

What exactly has gone wrong with such an intuitively obvious idea? This is not easy to rationalize − there are a number of contributing factors, none of which on its own would always cause problems. Somehow, the representation knowledge is being used illegitimately. We cannot bar use of representation knowledge in general, as this is exactly the mechanism being used to reify our designs. In this example, the use seems to be illegitimate because we are abandoning guidance from the abstract domain and using only representation information. Thus in the case of *choose1*, we forget problems of multiple representatives for abstract objects, and think of all lists standing for the same set as being equally well represented by a given list. This may be legitimate in some cases but certainly not in general. The situations where this attitude is admissible certainly include cases in which each abstract object is represented by exactly one concrete object, and a generalization of this situation, when we can define canonical forms for concrete representatives.

Thus if we had defined the relativization predicate for *i* to be

$$set\text{-}rep2(l) \Leftrightarrow (set\text{-}rep(l) \ \& \ ordered(l)) \tag{4.99}$$

with *ordered* having the meaning that the head of *l* is the least element in *l*, the second component of *l* is the second smallest component of *l*, etc., then each abstract set would have had a unique concrete representative, and using (4.88) would have been right — equivalent set representatives would have had the same value at the head of the sequences. Similarly, we could have obtained the same effect by using a canonical form, obtained by applying the function *canonical* to a sequence satisfying *set-rep*. The former may be defined simply by

$$\vdash canonical(nil) = nil \tag{4.100}$$
$$\vdash set\text{-}rep(l)$$
$$\Rightarrow (canonical(cons(m, l)) = ordins \ (m, canonical(l))) \tag{4.101}$$

with *ordins* being ordered insertion (see the Appendix, Section A.6). Then we modify (4.88) to:

$$\vdash canonical(cons(m, l)) \Rightarrow (choose1(cons(m, l)) = m) \tag{4.88'}$$

and we would again be all right.

Thus there is a very strong interplay between how concrete objects are used to represent abstract objects and how we introduce algorithmic (and other) details. This interaction is hard to characterize and involves the use of creativity to choose the 'best' combination of choices. What is 'best' clearly depends on many factors such as experience, global knowledge about the overall direction being taken for the particular development of which the 'local' decision forms a part, some feeling for what is mathematically right and/or mathematically tractable, etc.

Another important aspect of addition of detail is 'how much detail?'. How much should be done at each step in the development process? Just as we have pragmatic guidelines about how to modularize programs by defining the maximum size of program units (procedures, functions), for which 50 lines or a page (screenful) of Pascal text is often suggested, it should be just as important to modularize the development process itself. Taking a specification consisting of thousands of axioms and defining an implementation step which deals with all aspects of this specification (i.e. adds detail to all parts of the specification) at once does not seem to be a safe or profitable approach to take.

Here, the use of modularized specifications, by means of conservative extensions, allows us to concentrate efforts on a small part of our specification. This is where the Modularization Theorem pays its way. It guarantees that doing implementations of some parts will not affect other parts.

SORT_NAT is a conservative extension of SET (of natural numbers) by adding sequences and sorting. Thus we have

and, given the implementation of SET in terms of sequences,

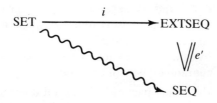

we get

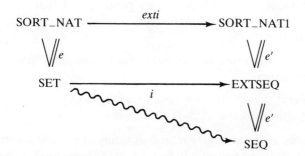

SORT_NAT1 is the extension obtained from EXTSEQ by adding the symbols introduced by e to get SORT_NAT from SET, while *exti* is the

---

† It should be noted that, technically, the symbols for sequences added to SET by e are distinguished by *exti* so that SORT_NAT1 actually has two copies of the SEQ specification. The extra copy can clearly be eliminated by a trivial interpretation which identifies the two copies. So, although the Modularization Theorem guarantees the soundness of what we want to do, it need not give us a non-redundant version of what we require.

extension of i which maps these new symbols to themselves[†] (see the Modularization Theorem and its proof, Section 4.3).

4.5.2 Another notion of refinement

Suppose that we have some specification SPEC = $\langle\langle S, L\rangle, G\rangle$ which we have been using (either as the initial linguistic level forming the starting point for development, or as the linguistic level supporting some development step). We suddenly decide that SPEC is not altogether suitable for its envisaged use because we have left something out. Two situations can arise:

1. We have left out a whole 'component' of what we now recognize is required, and we can add it as a conservative extension of SPEC. If SPEC is our initial specification, the Modularization Theorem guarantees that we can carry this addition through all development steps involving SPEC (and its descendants): we have to implement the component added by the conservative extension itself. It may, of course, happen that there is a better implementation of the extended SPEC, obtained by starting over again from the beginning, but at least there is one guaranteed way of preserving our previous work.

2. We have decided that some part of SPEC itself does not have enough detail. For example, when specifying sets we knew we wanted a function (*choose*) to deliver an arbitrary element of the set, but we did not care about any other details of this function. Later on in development, we decide for some good reason that what we really wanted was not an arbitrary element of the set, but the maximum value in the set.

Situation (2) is not a case of a conservative extension of SPEC, as adding the relevant axiom

$$\vdash choose(s) = m \Leftrightarrow (\neg(s = empty) \,\&\, ismember(m, s)$$
$$\&\, (\mathbf{A}n(ismember(n, s) \Rightarrow ((m = n)\,|\,lt(n, m)))))) \qquad (4.102)$$

certainly adds a new property stated in terms of the old language which could not be deduced before. (In fact, (4.102) can be used to deduce

$$\neg(s = empty) \Rightarrow ismember(choose(s), s)$$

but this formula cannot be used to deduce (4.102).) On the other hand, as long as what we add is consistent with SPEC, as (4.102) certainly is, there would seem to be no problem in adding such detail to our initial linguistic level later in the development process.

Let us analyse the situation carefully. We have an extension e: SPEC $\subseteq$ SPEC1 which is non-conservative. If SPEC is implemented via interpretation *int* into SPEC2, then we have

SPEC1

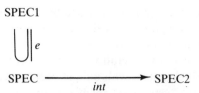

$$\text{SPEC} \xrightarrow[int]{} \text{SPEC2}$$

This is similar to the initial conditions for the Modularization Theorem and so we might expect that we can complete the diagram in the same way. However, as we have shown in Section 4.3, this is not in general possible if e is not conservative. In fact, suppose SPEC2 is EXT1SEQ and int is $i \cdot i'$. Then we have (4.86)

$$G_{\text{ext1seq}} \vdash (choose''(l) = m) \Leftrightarrow (\neg\, (l = nil)\ \&\ isin(m,\, l)$$
$$\&\ (\textbf{A}n(isin(n,\, l) \Rightarrow (m =\ n\,|\,lt(m,n)))))\tag{4.103}$$

whereas applying $i \cdot i'$ to (4.102) and doing a bit of reduction we get

$$set\text{-}rep(l) \Rightarrow ((choose''(l) = m) \Leftrightarrow (\neg\, (l = nil)\ \&\ isin(m,\, l)$$
$$\&\ (\textbf{A}n(isin(n,\, l) \Rightarrow ((m = n)\,|\,lt(n,\, m)))))) \tag{4.104}$$

This is inconsistent as, for example, for

$$l = cons(zero,\, cons(suc(zero),\, nil))$$

(4.104) requires $choose''(l) = zero$ and (4.103) requires $choose''(l) = suc(zero)$, which would yield

$$zero = suc(zero)$$

It is thus very important to sort out our specifications properly before we start using them. Otherwise, design decisions may make the addition of further detail to the original specification rather costly.

In general, an *ex post* non-conservative addition of detail is also problematic because the consistency of the added detail with the original specification is not necessarily easy to determine, whereas for conservative extensions we have at least some criteria which are sufficient to guarantee consistency (see Sections 2.2 and 2.3).

4.6 Notions of change

Development implies change. The obvious kind of change implied is of course the aforementioned addition of detail. But there is a less obvious kind of change, which comes to the fore when one leaves the world of theory and speculation and actually tries to put these ideas into practice. This change is caused by the need to backtrack in the development process in order to redesign a specification used in a previous step, or a previous implementation step itself. Such situations arise because it is not always very easy to foresee the consequences of one's decisions.

Thus a decision to represent a set by any sequence, as long as it contains the same components as the set (i.e. satisfies *set-rep1* of Section 4.2), may turn out to be bad if a lot of use is made of tests of set membership and deletion operations. On the other hand, a representation using ordered sequences with unique occurrences of components may be very efficient for tests of set membership and deletion, but is not as efficient for insertion as the one satisfying *set-rep1* or *set-rep* (of Section 4.2) would be. A good designer may anticipate such problems and make better design decisions, but this is not always possible — especially when less familiar territory is being explored.

What happens when such problems are detected? Well, the short answer is that the redesign has to take place by backtracking through previous development steps and identifying the root problem necessitating the redesign. Having made the alteration to this identified root cause (and more on this later), the consequences of the change have to be followed through the existing subsequent development steps. At the extremes, this may mean abandoning everything that came after the identified root step or having to change nothing.

The former tends to happen when the basis for some development step is completely changed. If we abandoned the idea of using sequences to represent sets and decided to use something else instead (e.g. arrays), we would have to redevelop the subsequent implementation anew. On the other hand, if it turned out that there was no need to make any changes at all to subsequent development steps, it would certainly be because any subsequent development decisions we made were independent of the consequences of the change we wanted to introduce. For example, the original implementation of sets by sequences would not have to be changed if we just wanted to refine the set specification with the axiom defining *choose* as a selection of the least element in the set. As noted previously, this is because our implementation was neutral with respect to which component was being selected; the axiom

$$(choose'(b) = m) \Rightarrow isin(m,l)$$

is still not imposing any constraints on exactly which element is to be selected[†]. However, the justification of this (and subsequent) development step(s) would still have to be modified to take account of the fact that a new property had to be properly simulated. So even seemingly unobtrusive changes to earlier development steps can cause non-trivial checking of subsequent ones.

Generally, most backtrackings for redesign do not give rise to either extreme situation. There thus remains the problem of 'limiting the damage' — trying to determine exactly which parts of subsequent steps

---

[†] Note, however, that if the next implementation step defines *choose''* by means of the axiom (4.102), the neutrality of implementation is lost and redesign becomes unavoidable.

must be altered to cope with the change just introduced. In most cases, this is a very difficult problem indeed.

Consider a situation where from a given specification $S1$ we develop an implementation via a number of steps:

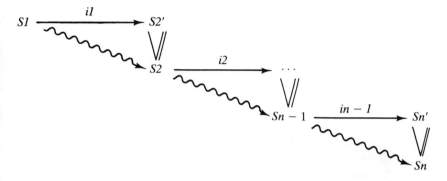

Let $Si = \langle\,\langle\,S_{Si}, L_{Si}\,\rangle, G_{Si}\,\rangle$.

Suppose that $A \in Form(L_{S1})$. If $G_{S1} \vdash \neg A$ and we want to introduce A as a new property into $S1$, we have an inconsistency which might or might not easily be overcome.

If $\neg A \in G_{S1}$ and G_{S1} is irreducible (i.e. no B in G_{S1} follows from $G_{S1} - \{B\}$), then $\neg A$ may be replaced by A without problems[†]. However, to regain correctness of implementation, the subsequent development steps may all then have to be changed. How large a change is induced depends on how crucial the fact $\neg A$ had become in subsequent development. A property becomes crucial to the extent that it becomes necessary for guaranteeing the required properties. Roughly, if $G_{S2} \vdash (\neg A)^{i1}$ was essential in establishing many required properties, such as

$$G_{S1} \vdash B \text{ implies } G_{S2} \vdash B^{i1}$$

then we have a lot of problems. This observation has a pragmatic consequence. Conducting a systematic development process, we are well advised to keep track of all uses made of the axioms constituting the extralogical component of specifications (for instance, by a continually updated index or concordance, listing each occurrence of each particular axiom in all proofs). Then, whenever there is a wish to change or delete a particular axiom, we can immediately see the 'volume' of proofs that will be affected. While the mere volume of proofs affected by the proposed change is not a definite measure of the cost to implement this change (primarily because changes seldom happen singly and the cost of imp-

---

[†] The concept of irreducibility is yet another modularization principle of some merit. It also allows us to isolate contributions to properties. And, again, it is obtained at the expense of other requirements on specification such as comprehensibility, ease of proof, etc.

lementing a cluster of related changes need not be a linear function of the implementation costs of the constituents), it can be used as a first-order approximation.

More subtle problems arise if we have

neither $G_{SI} \vdash A$ nor $G_{SI} \vdash \neg A$

but we do have

$$G_{Sn} \vdash (\ldots(((\neg A)^{i1})^{i2})\ldots)^{in-1}$$

Which decisions along the development path contributed to the introduction of (the translation of) $\neg A$ into Sn? It certainly is not, in general, a single obvious decision, but a whole series of small ones which probably made (the translation of) $\neg A$ to hold. How to disentangle these contributions and consequent changes is a difficult problem which is unlikely to admit a simple solution.

The little guidance we do have in this area is rather heavy handed in nature and depends on the applicability of the Modularization Theorem and Robinson's Consistency Theorem (and its variations). For example, we know that if S_of_X is a parameterized specification whose parameter will be instantiated by specification SI and we implement S_of_X and SI independently into S'_of_X and SI', respectively, then instantiating S'_of_X by SI' yields the same result as combining the two implementations and applying it to S_of_X instantiated by SI. If we now had to change either (the non-parameter part of) S_of_X or SI (or both), we could correspondingly attribute the consequent changes in development to that of the appropriate component. This result is guaranteed by the Modularization Theorem[†].

Dealing with a specification S and (the extension part of) a conservative extension $e: S \leq SI$ independently is also a modularization tactic which guarantees the kind of independence in decision making which we seek. To see this, note that the relationship between the base specification (S in e) and its extension (SI in e) is like that between a formal parameter X and the parameterized data type which uses it — conservative extension. So the Modularization Theorem, which guarantees that things will come out well if we proceed to implement a parameterized specification and an actual parameter independently, will also guarantee a good result if we separate a specification (S in e) and its extension ($(SI - S)\_of\_$ *something* in e) and deal with them independently. As noted previously in a footnote, this may actually interfere with possible optimization steps in the development process which work against this kind of independence.

[†] Note, however, that the maintenance of this independence may be at the cost of having to abandon the use of 'remodularization' development steps. These, like the exhibited implementations of both natural numbers and signs by naturals, destroy exactly the independence we might value when backtracking for redesign.

It is a talented designer indeed who can play off against each other these contradictory requirements in a productive way.

Once again we see an interplay between modularity of (within) specifications and modularity of the specification and implementation process itself. The right amount of granularity of modules within a specification can play an important role in limiting the damage when change and backtracking becomes necessary. In some sense, this is a generalization of Myers' (1975) idea of loose coupling between program components. As long as you can present the same face to the world, it does not really matter what goes on inside, i.e. a module can maintain its independence.

This brings us back to another aspect of modularity in the development process (mentioned in the previous section) — the use of small development steps. The more that changes in a given step, the more difficult it becomes to trace through consequences of change to an earlier part of the development. This is really the same observation we made in the previous section in another guise. We want each development step to introduce a simple detail or two so that the construction of the single step in question and its justification (settling of accounts with respect to proof obligations) does not burden us with too many minutiae. When steps in development are small and easily comprehended, so should be the consequences of change.

4.7 The nature of useful tools

Now that we have considered in some detail the canonical step of the software development/implementation process and investigated the logical underpinnings of various goal-directed activities that may be performed by taking a number of such steps, we should like to discuss the nature of tools that may assist a programmer in the execution of his job. First, however, let us for a moment consider the notion of a tool, as applicable to the software development/implementation process.

The use of tools in the course of performing a task is a very old trick with human beings, although not their exclusive property. (Some animals also use tools.) On the other hand, *manufacturing* of tools is almost certainly restricted to human beings. The manufactured tool — an artefact conceived and produced to be applied in the course of executing a task — is a material witness of an analytic design activity on the part of the task's performer. (Of course, the 'performer' in the last sentence may be a collective noun, denoting, for example, a group engaged in a task, a group in which individuals may assume — or be assigned — partial rôles: some will be tool-makers, others tool-users. Similarly the 'analytic design activity' may be a collective undertaking: a part of this activity, tool design, may even achieve a degree of independence.) Before a tool may be manufactured, two things must happen: an aspect of the task to be performed must be identified as amenable and worthwhile for a tool application, and characteristics of a corresponding tool must become sufficiently apparent. In other words, we must realize that there exists a potential for a tool application, and we must arrive at a rough idea as to the salient points of the tool's design.

The degree of universality of a tool is in a sense proportional to the degree of abstraction of the task aspect to which the tool is to be eventually applied. A hammer, its deceiving simplicity notwithstanding, is a pretty universal tool because performance of many different tasks involves an activity abstractly described as an instantaneous application of a localized and strongly directed pressure (delivering a blow in a given direction at a given point). As soon as we add more detail to the description of tool-assisted activity, thus making it less abstract, the corresponding tool becomes less universal. Indeed, in addition to a universal hammer, there are scores of specialized hammers, well suited for a particular job, but often less useful for another job than a universal hammer would be.

Do we need any tools in a software specification/design/implementation activity (that is, apart from the proverbial pencil and back of a suitably large envelope)? Or, in a milder form: would any tools be useful in this activity? The answer is unequivocal: yes.

Throughout the body of this book we have insisted that there is no viable alternative to a formal presentation of specifications. As far as possible we have avoided committing ourselves to any particular formalism because, by and large, most well conceived formalisms are pragmatically equivalent, in the sense that whatever can be expressed in one can also be expressed in another. (This is not necessarily a very precise statement: a formalism which embodies a kind of temporal logic, see the Appendix, Section A.5, may be employed to express notions inexpressible in classical, first-order-logic-based formalisms.) To a very large extent the choice of a particular formalism is therefore dictated by the programmer's taste and loyalty, themselves often conditioned by ergonomic considerations (what the programmer finds it easy to work with). The availability and quality of tools is an important ingredient in the programmer's assessment of a formalism's ergonomy.

Thus the toolbox associated with a particular formalism plays a similar role as, say, diagnostic tools associated with a compiler. The analogy can be extended: certain qualities of a programming language are germane for good diagnostics (e.g. absence of default options in the language greatly enhances the typing control diagnostics); similarly, certain qualities of a formalism make it easier to construct desirable tools. Or even further: a programming language can be used without any diagnostic tools, indeed without a compiler! – but it is not a very practical proposition to ask the programmers to hand-code a program presented in a high-level language. Similarly, it is possible to use a specification formalism without any accompanying tools, but it would not be a very practical proposition. And for the very same reasons: the volume of required formal transformations is staggering! True enough, all the necessary transformations are trivial; after all, there are no sophisticated transformations in a formal system. But human beings are notoriously bad performers of large volumes of trivial transformations!

It is just the sheer volume and exceedingly monotonous nature of formal transformations which are the prime reason for our unequivocally stated request for tools that assist formal manipulations.

What kind of tools? The current practice somewhat diverges on this issue. There are two possible extreme approaches: an attempt to create tools as universal as possible, or an attempt to create as complete as possible a set of dedicated (specialized) tools. These two tendencies can be observed in nearly all branches of computing: universal software (tools or applications) *vs* sets of dedicated software, with the concept of integrated software system emerging as an (almost) unifying notion.

It should be observed that an integrated software system is not the same as a universal software tool, even if its applicability is not as restricted as that of a simple sum of its components. Integration of a system usually means only that its components are made so that they can cooperate: for instance, that outputs generated by a component can be directly input to another one, or that two or more components share data files. The use of an integrated system of software tools is certainly more pleasant and efficient than the use of individual tools, even if the available collection includes all the tools constituting the system. Tools from an 'unintegrated' collection may be difficult to apply in certain combinations; they may require extensive copying and even reformatting of data passed from one tool to another. Thus a proper integration of a collection of tools is certainly a step forward.

On the other hand, the universality of a tool implies its applicability across the whole range of tasks that fit the tool's abstract specification, without having to construct tools for any individual tasks from this range, indeed without having to identify any specific tasks at all.

Consider a simple example. For programming in a multi-language environment we may distinguish three levels of tools:

1. *An 'unintegrated' collection of tools*: a set of compilers, one for each language used in the environment. Given a program in any of these languages, it can be compiled into object code. It does not necessarily follow that we can combine object codes generated by two different compilers from the collection; thus if we wish to execute a program written partly in language *L1* and partly in *L2*, we may face serious practical difficulties.

2. *An integrated compiling system*: a set of compilers which operate on

common principles with respect to object code generation. The strategy employed is probably that of separate compilation, which allows each syntactic module of source language code to be compiled separately from any other module, generating an object code module prepared to interface with any other similarly generated module. Thus, given a program consisting of syntactic modules written in different languages of the considered environment, the integrated compiling system generates a set of object code modules that can be run together. Note that to obtain an integrated compiling system one probably needs not only to adhere to a common strategy in generating object code modules, but also to introduce a run-time system common for all (compiled) languages.

3. *A universal compiling system*: a metacompiler plus a suitable run-time system. A metacompiler would accept a programming language definition, probably presented by a sort of annotated grammar, and generate a compiler for whatever language was thus presented. Since all compilers are generated by the same metacompiler, they can easily adhere to a common strategy in generating object code. There is only one run-time system so no heterogeneity could arise here. We retain all the advantages of level 2 and, in addition, we avoided specifying individual programming languages; any − even an *ad hoc* − programming language can be used, as long as it can be described by a grammar of the chosen type (accepted by the metacompiler). Thus while there is a restriction on a kind of language, no individual language is singled out and we have a considerable latitude in choice of a concrete programming language.

It is to be expected that specialized tools for individual tasks, like level 1 single-language compilers in our example, can be made very efficient by taking advantage of any known idiosyncrasy of a particular task. This advantage rapidly disappears when the task changes, sometimes in an otherwise insignificant way. This happens because the tool designer is usually preoccupied with exploring the concrete attributes of the task rather than with its abstract properties. In his analysis he usually makes no distinction between an inherent attribute of the task (an attribute which is there because it is an essential feature of a class of tasks) and a spurious attribute (which just happens to be there). An example will illustrate this point.

A database designer found out that in a particular application all record fields were short enough to be packed into two bytes each. The machine on which he was implementing the database had a special addressing arrangement for quick retrieval of two-byte units. He used this happy coincidence quite extensively in the design, obtaining a very efficient implementation. Unfortunately, with no major change in the application that the database supported, some numeric data, essential for the user, started taking on values which could not be packed into two bytes without loss of the required precision. The tool − the implemented database storage̓ manager − lost not only its efficiency, but also its validity, and when hastily repaired to cope with larger fields, was found hopelessly inefficient.

One can, of course, argue that this example is quite silly. Unfortunately, nearly all errors of design, in hindsight, are quite silly.

The lesson we would like to draw from the observation about the instability of advantages of highly specific tools is that one should always try to build as general tools as possible. (Even integrated tools suffer from the instability.)

In the context of the software specification/development/implementation process, the notion of tool generality assumes two, possibly distinct, interpretations. One relates to the spectrum of formalisms that may be used in the process, another to various activities that constitute the process. We may call the first interpretation *generality across the process*, the second, *generality along the process*.

The generality across the process is very similar to the generality of a metacompiler. Adhering to the oft-repeated principle of not giving preferences to particular formalisms, we would like to admit in the process many different formalisms (within reason, of course!). Thus it would be counterproductive to build specific tools assisting in the performance of whatever tasks there are to be performed within a chosen formalism. It is much more advantageous to decide on a syntax-directed tool generator, a meta-tool capable of generating specific tools for specific formalisms.

As far as generality along the process is concerned, it is just here that the method we advocate brings its greatest rewards. As we have shown, the software development process can be presented as a series of homogeneous steps. There is no distinction of kind between 'early' and 'late' steps: regardless of the actual pragmatic content of a step (why this particular step is taken), the formal nature of each step is the same: a step is a transformation between two linguistic levels, a combination of an extension and an interpretation, involving two or three formal systems (two, if no extension of the current target system is necessary; three, if the current target is conservatively extended). Thus we can concentrate on tools that assist such transformations, disregarding the pragmatic objectives achieved by any particular step.

The advantage we achieve becomes quite apparent when one contrasts this approach with that underlying the software-development-by-named-steps methods. If we are told that software development progresses from structural specification to functional specification, to module interface specification, to module functional specification, to..., we are tempted to consider specific tools for each named transformation and for each named level. Thus we may wish to have special tools that assist in the description (or recording) of functional specifications, and tools that facilitate linking together structural and functional specifications, etc. While design and implementation of such tools would perhaps be possible, the resulting collection of tools would require a lot of foresight and/or hard work to pass for an integrated system of tools. Even so, it would certainly suffer from the instability of a specific tool system.

Hence, there emerges the general pattern for the type of tools that would be consistent with the proposed view of the software specification/ development process. We need tools that assist in meaning-preserving transformations and conservative extensions between linguistic levels, and which themselves can be generated by a syntax-directed meta-tool.

Within this general pattern there are three particular kinds of tool that may be considered (the notion of 'kind' refers now to a particular aspect of canonical step execution activity).

First, there is a place for a tool which would facilitate description of various constructs within a linguistic level. Such a tool is in fact very similar to a syntax-directed editor. A number of such tools are now in existence (see Henderson, 1984; Barringer *et al.*, 1984).

Second, once we have established a linguistic level and can write in it (perhaps assisted by a suitable editor), we wish to establish some consequences of what has been written, for instance by proving that a certain syntactically correct formula is a theorem in the linguistic level considered. Formal proofs involve a lot of manipulations with symbols; even though one can eventually derive any theorem from axioms quite formally, a proof is usually much shorter if the derivation is guided by human ingenuity. Thus while fully automatic theorem provers are available, we do not think that they would play a significant role in the practice of software development for quite some time yet. On the other hand, interactive theorem provers and other clerical aids to proof formation already in existence (see Gordon *et al.*, 1979; Erickson and Musser, 1980; Shostak *et al.*, 1982), as well as their incorporation into systems designed to provide assistance to program specification and development (see Nakajima *et al.*, 1980; Honda *et al.*, 1983; Guttag *et al.*, 1985) justify the belief that tools of this kind are realistically to be expected.

Finally, one may hope that, combining the available knowledge about program transformations with that about metacompilers, suitable transformation tools, i.e. systems capable of executing a transformation of a given program (specification) into another language (or another level of the same wide-spectrum language, see Section 3.4) while preserving the meaning of the source program ('preserving correctness' in the terminology of research on program transformation), will become available. For a fairly recent survey of this field see Partsch and Steinbruggen (1983).

So far we have considered only the subject-matter tools, i.e. tools that assist a programmer in executing his primary task of software specification/ development/implementation. It is only natural to expect this process to progress through many tentative steps, including ones that have to be discarded upon discovering their futility, thus leading to the phenomena of backtracking (see Lehman *et al.*, 1984). It is also natural to expect that the volume of relevant documentation will be quite considerable. This raises the issue of entirely different sorts of tools, clerical in nature, viz. tools that assist and, as far as possible, automate collection, structuring and coherent retrieval of pertinent design/development documentation. We speak here of a well structured repository of step protocols which should allow the reconstruction of the *status quo ante* of the software process (for any specified step of this process). Such a repository will be relied upon, when backtracking becomes necessary, to recreate the situation at an indicated point in the design/development process, free of any traces of subsequent changes and additions. It will also come in useful in preparation of the sanitized version of the process to be presented as the clean derivation of the final form of a given piece of software (see Sections 3.1 and 4.6).

Lastly, a host of managerial tools, including, but not restricted to, accounting, version control, progress report generator and scheduling may be envisaged.

Important as they are, the last two sorts of tools are clearly outside the scope of this book.

Appendix

A.1 Introduction

The main concern of logic as applied to computing is the analysis and formalization of the patterns of thought that are used in reasoning about the behaviour of computers, the algorithms they process, and the development of algorithms to meet particular requirements. It is the last of these activities which concerns us in this book. In this appendix, we will not in general be concerned with analysis of 'patterns of thought' used in this activity as this is the subject matter of the bulk of the book. Our concern will be formalization and the embodiment of this formalization — formal systems/logics/linguistic systems. We will use these three phrases interchangeably, although we will try to stick to the last.

We will not deal with the motivation for formalization here as this has already been dealt with in the body of the book. Rather, we wish to illustrate how the requirements of the subject being investigated may be met by adapting/developing appropriate linguistic systems. Most logic books read by computer scientists will introduce the subject matter by presenting the classical logician's approach to the so-called first-order predicate calculus (PC). This is probably not the most useful way to introduce logic to computer scientists. Moreover, it is not really good enough to say that we can 'encode' or 'express' the other logics/linguistic systems we wish to study in PC. That is a bit like saying that we could do all our programming using Turing machines. We know that this formalism is powerful enough to express all computable functions, but would we want to give up writing our programs in Pascal, Prolog, Hope or even FORTRAN in favour of it?

We now want to look at the elements (component parts) of linguistic systems at an intuitive level before embarking on formal details. As indicated above, we are interested in the 'formalization of patterns of thought' in the program development process. Formalization is generally thought to involve the invention of a system of notation which can be used to stand for the 'objects of thought' and the development of rules of reasoning to express what is meant by 'patterns of thought'.

The 'objects of thought' referred to above depend on the subject matter being formalized but generally involve at least the following:

1. the ability to denote or refer to data and how this data may be built or constructed from 'simpler' kinds of data, and

2. means of ascribing basic or primitive properties to data and the means for developing compound properties based on these.

These factors are said to determine the *expressibility* of the linguistic system in the same sense that different programming languages are said to be more or less expressive. The objects being described by programs are computable functions and we say that Pascal is more expressive than assembler because Pascal programs are shorter than corresponding assembly language programs, Pascal is more readable (more human-oriented) than assembler, and Pascal uses data descriptions (sets, arrays, files, records, etc.) which are more application- or human-oriented than assembler (which has only integers or bytes). One reason why PC may not be as universally useful as some people would like to maintain is exactly because of this expressibility requirement.

The rules of reasoning mentioned above are meant to be formal counterparts of our intuitions about 'what follows from what'. Since we are interested in reasoning within our linguistic system, these rules of reasoning must be such that premises and conclusions for these rules depend solely on examining patterns of symbols in the language being used for description.

Thus they are more or less complicated systems of rewrite (symbol manipulation) rules which depend solely on forms and *not* on our intuitive reading of these forms. Whether these rules (or the language used for description/expression) match our intuitions is a question of adequacy and, of course, very important. More on this subject later. Note also that different rules of reasoning may be needed in different situations. Again, more on this later.

Given a linguistic system (an adequately expressive language and rules of reasoning), we wish to describe particular applications within the system. This leads us to the concept of a theory. A theory is meant to characterize a particular application and thus consists of two parts:

1. a particular set of symbols used in describing the particular application and chosen from the symbols made available in the linguistic system being used; and

2. all properties attributable to the application and statable in terms of the chosen set of symbols.

Almost all interesting applications will have an infinite set of 'different properties' and hence we generally want to describe theories axiomatically. That is, we want to find some subset of the properties from which all other properties in the theory are then deducible (by the rules of reasoning available in the linguistic system). We might want the axiomatization to be finite (whatever that might mean), decidable (i.e. there should be an effective, purely mechanical way of deciding whether we have an instance of an axiom or not) or have some other desirable property. This is particularly important in our context as axiomatizations of theories (i.e. specifications!) are the objects of study in this book.

As we emphasized above, linguistic systems (language and rules of reasoning) are purely syntactic in nature. How do these activities relate to our 'patterns of thought'? Or, to paraphrase a famous quotation, 'What does it all mean?' When we invent our linguistic systems we have in mind some systems or applications which we would like to characterize or formalize with (and within) the linguistic system. We would like to relate descriptions back to the intuitive descriptions we might have of such systems or applications. But the problem is again in the word 'mind'; our relating back is not worth a lot because of the usual inadequacies of informal descriptions. So what we generally try to do is define valuation systems which allow us to give explicit descriptions of the system or application in terms of well understood and intuitively appealing objects such as sets, functions, relations, etc., organized into mathematical structures called models. We can then ask questions such as: What models within a valuation system are 'described' by a given theory? Is there just one such? If there is more than one, why? Within a valuation system, is there a match between linguistic levels and corresponding models in the sense that when some property P is deducible from some set of facts S in the linguistic system, then whenever S is true in some model, so is P? (i.e. deductions in the linguistic system adequately reflect relationships between properties in models). Of course, it would be a pretty poor state of affairs if the corresponding linguistic system and valuation system did not have this adequacy property!

We do not always have to provide valuation systems corresponding to a linguistic system as no adequate definition for the former may be obvious. The reasonableness of the linguistic system may be demonstrated in some other way. However, the linguistic systems that we shall study have associated valuation systems. (A notable linguistic system which did not for a long time have a corresponding valuation system – but now does – is the lambda calculus. Much important work was done before the valuation system was developed.)

We propose to present below just enough information about linguistic systems, theories and valuation systems to make the book intelligible. So, many deep results are ignored or just mentioned in passing but enough references are given so that the interested reader may pursue a particular topic if he wishes. We warn readers that our presentation is in many ways non-standard but we also feel that the usual presentations of logic would be unhelpful for computer scientists.

It is also important to realize that, unlike most mathematicians or most other user communities for logic(s), computer scientists must acquire the facility for reasoning in a number of different linguistic systems and, as far as the research community is concerned, actually adapt existing linguistic systems or invent new ones to cope with the formalization process for this young subject.

A.2 Linguistic systems

A.2.1 Languages

The language associated with a linguistic system is like a programming language in the sense that it determines what are the correctly formed or admissible statements in the linguistic system. Like with programming languages, we will generally have descriptions of a number of categories of statements and formation rules for putting elements of these categories together to make further well formed statements.

> **Example: SC**
> Our first example will be classical propositional, or sentential, logic. We may want this as a first attempt at understanding boolean valued expressions in languages such as Pascal. We must define two things: categories of statements or linguistic objects and formation rules for putting them together. With SC we have three categories of objects: propositional variables, propositional operators and propositional statements or formulae.
>
> Propositional variables are used to stand for atomic or basic statements whose truth or falsity are 'immediately obvious'. (The purpose of SC is then to study the truth or falsity of combinations of such statements.) We will call this category (of propositional variables) P and have
>
> $$P = \{p, q, r, p1, p2, \ldots\}$$
>
> The propositional operators form a category of objects O whose use will be as connectives to form compound statements from constituent ones. For SC we have:
>
> $$O = \{\neg, |, \&, \Rightarrow, \Leftrightarrow\}$$
>
> The category of formulae F then is defined by the formation rules:
>
> 1. $P \subseteq F$ (i.e. every propositional variable is also a formula);
> 2. Let $s1$ and $s2$ be any formulae. Then the following are also formulae:
>
> $(\neg s1)$
> $(s1|s2)$

$$(s1 \; \& \; s2)$$
$$(s1 \Rightarrow s2)$$
$$(s1 \Leftrightarrow s2)$$

3. Nothing else is a formula.

Note that *s1* and *s2* are *metavariables* in the sense that *s1* and *s2* are not in any category of SC. Similarly, each of the formation rules in (2) is a metastatement in the sense that if we replace *s1* and *s2* by any pair of objects from the category *F*, we get another object in *F*. As they stand, the statements in (2) are not in *F*! Note also the use of punctuation (bracketing). This is another category of symbols not explicitly mentioned.

Another way of describing the language of SC is by using the familiar BNF notation.

Thus:

$$F ::= P \,|\, (-F) \,|\, (F|F) \,|\, (F \; \& \; F) \,|\, (F \Rightarrow F) \,|\, (F \Leftrightarrow F)$$

We then need to supply a rule or rules to define *P*. We will not do this here. Rule (3) above is reflected in the usual interpretation of BNF rules as generating the least set of objects satisfying the rules. We will generally adopt BNF (or simple extensions) to describe the 'syntax' of linguistic systems.

Example: S_4

Our second example is concerned with a linguistic system introduced to study the concepts of possibility and necessity (a so-called modal logic; see Sections A.2.2 and A.2.5).

Let *P* be as above and define *MF* as

$$MF ::= P \,|\, (-MF) \,|\, (MF|MF) \,|\, (MF \; \& \; MF)$$
$$|\, (MF \Rightarrow MF) \,|\, (MF \Leftrightarrow MF) \,|\, (\Box MF)$$

Basically, we have introduced a new operation $\Box$ over and above those of SC. The intended reading of $\Box A$ is: it is necessarily the case that *A* is true, where *A* is in *MF* (i.e. *A* is a formula). If this seems strange, think of invariant assertions!

The above examples illustrate a very important idea − languages may be related in the sense that one is contained in another. We say that a language *L'* is an *extension* of a language *L*, denoted $L \subseteq L'$, exactly in the case that the set of categories of *L* is contained in those of *L'* and each object of each category in *L* is in the corresponding category of *L'*. Another way of putting the second condition is that the formation rules of *L* are contained in those of *L'*. Thus the language of S_4, $L(S_4)$, is an extension of the language of SC, $L(\text{SC})$. Another, rather trivial, extension of $L(\mathrm{SC})$ could have been obtained by replacing the definition of P by:

$P^1 = \{u, v, w, u1, u2, \ldots\} \cup P$

A.2.2 Rules of reasoning

We have looked at one aspect of expressibility in linguistic systems. We now want to look at the relationships between properties and how these may be determined by rules of reasoning. We begin by defining a binary relation

$\vdash \subseteq \mathbf{P}(\mathrm{Form}) \times \mathrm{Form}$

on the formulae Form of some linguistic system where $\mathbf{P}$ is the usual powerset operation on sets[†]. The symbol $\vdash$ is the name of the *derivability* relation and is meant to reflect in a linguistic system some notion of deducibility. Clearly we expect this relation itself to have certain properties. We do not normally expect anything to follow from anything!

For example, for SC, we would expect at least the following properties for

$\vdash_{SC} \subseteq \mathbf{P}(F) \times F$

(We usually write $\vdash$ in infix position and we do so below.)

Let G, G' be sets of formulae, i.e. G, $G' \subseteq F$, and A, B be formulae, i.e. $A, B \in F$. Then:

1. If $A \in G$, then $G \vdash_{SC} A$; i.e. if A is in G, then we expect to be able to deduce it from G.

2. If $G \subseteq G'$ and $G \vdash_{SC} A$, then $G' \vdash_{SC} A$; i.e. if we can deduce A from G, then if we start with more, we do not expect to get less!

3. If $G \vdash_{SC} A$ and $G' \cup \{A\} \vdash_{SC} B$, then $G \cup G' \vdash_{SC} B$; i.e. if we can deduce A from G and by adding A to G' we can deduce B, then we can deduce B directly from G and G' (for instance, by deducing A from G and then using G' to get B).

4. If $G \vdash_{SC} A$, then $G' \vdash_{SC} A$ for some finite subset G' of G; i.e. we expect each of our deductions to depend on only a finite number of facts.

There is a final property for which we need a definition. This definition and property relate to the idea of consistent replacement. The definition tells us what we mean by consistent renaming (of propositional variables)

[†] If S is a set, then $\mathbf{P}(S)$ is the set of all subsets of S; i.e. $\mathbf{P}(S) = \{S' : S' \subseteq S\}$.

and the property tells us that deductions should be independent of the names we use for basic (or atomic) facts.

A *substitution*, then, is a map $a: P \rightarrow P$.

So a substitution tells us 'which propositional variables are replaced by which'. We can extend this map a to

$$a^*: F \rightarrow F$$

by the following:

$$a^*(\neg s1) = \neg a^*(s1)$$
$$a^*(s1 \,|\, s2) = a^*(s1) \,|\, a^*(s2)$$
etc.

and

$$a^*(prop) = a(prop) \text{ for any propositional variable } prop \in P.$$

We can also extend a to

$$a^*: \mathbf{P}(F) \rightarrow \mathbf{P}(F)$$

by $a^*(G) = \{a^*(s1): s1 \in G\}$. So we then have:

5. If $G \vdash_{SC} A$ and a is a substitution, then $a^*(G) \vdash_{SC} a^*(A)$; i.e. if we can deduce A from G, then consistently renaming propositional variables in A and G will not change deducibility.

The derivability relation $\vdash$ is usually infinite in the sense that there is an infinite set of pairs G and A which satisfy the relation $\vdash$. We thus would like to find some finite way of representing this infinite object. One way to do this is *axiomatically* as follows.

First, we assert that some formulae are *axioms*, i.e. we postulate that they hold. As they obviously require no premises, instead of writing $\emptyset \vdash_{SC} A$, where $\emptyset$ is the empty set, we will write $\vdash_{SC} A$ in such cases.

Let A, B, C be in F. Then

$$\vdash_{SC} A \Rightarrow (B \Rightarrow A) \tag{AX1}$$
$$\vdash_{SC} (A \Rightarrow (B \Rightarrow C)) \Rightarrow ((A \Rightarrow B) \Rightarrow (A \Rightarrow C)) \tag{AX2}$$
$$\vdash_{SC} (\neg B \Rightarrow \neg A) \Rightarrow ((\neg B \Rightarrow A) \Rightarrow B) \tag{AX3}$$

These are called *axiom schemata* in the sense that we get an axiom by consistently replacing the A, B, C in one of them by actual formulae. Such consistent replacement is called *instantiation* and the result is an *instance* of the axiom schema. For example, from the second schema we get the axiom

$$\vdash_{SC} (p \Rightarrow ((p1 \,\&\, p2) \Rightarrow (\neg q))) \Rightarrow ((p \Rightarrow (p1 \,\&\, p2)) \Rightarrow (p \Rightarrow (\neg q)))$$

by the replacement of A by p, B by $(p1 \,\&\, p2)$, and C by $(\neg q)$, respectively.

Note that the above axiom schemata do not say anything about &, |

and $\Leftrightarrow$. This is because we can reduce these to $\neg$ and $\Rightarrow$ by using the following definitions:

$(A \& B)$ for $\neg(A \Rightarrow \neg B)$ (D1)
$(A \,|\, B)$ for $(\neg A) \Rightarrow B$ (D2)
$(A \Leftrightarrow B)$ for $(A \Rightarrow B) \& (B \Rightarrow A)$ (D3)

The meaning of (D1), for example, is that for any $A, B \in F$, $(A \& B)$ is an abbreviation for $\neg(A \Rightarrow \neg B)$.

We also need some way of generating other elements of the relation $\vdash_{SC}$ from existing ones. This is accomplished via the definition of rules of inference/reasoning whose use is encapsulated in the definition of a derivation. SC has only one rule, called *modus ponens* (MP):

$$\frac{A, \; A \Rightarrow B}{B}$$

The rule indicates that formula B follows from the formula A and the formula $A \Rightarrow B$. A and $A \Rightarrow B$ are called the *premises* and B the *conclusion* of the rule.

Definition: A *derivation* or *proof* of a formula A from a set of formulae[†] G is a finite, linearly ordered sequence of formulae, ending in A, each of which is either:

1. a member of G,
2. an instance of one of the axiom schemata, or
3. an instance of the conclusion of the rule (*modus ponens*) where the corresponding instances of the two premises occur earlier in the sequence.

Then $G \vdash_{SC} A$ if and only if there is a derivation of A from G. In order to check that this definition of $\vdash_{SC}$ really does give a derivability relation, we would have to check that the properties of the derivability relation posited above really are satisfied by the above definition. This is left to the interested reader. We now exhibit an example of a proof (derivation).

Example
We will show that $p \Rightarrow p$ is a *tautology*[‡], i.e. $\vdash_{SC} p \Rightarrow p$. We do this by exhibiting a derivation. Each step (i.e. each formula in the linear

---

[†] Set G is intended to contain premises other than those postulated in axioms of the logic, i.e. extralogical information (see Section A.4.3).

[‡] A *tautology* is a formula which follows from the logical axioms alone, hence from the empty set of extralogical premises (see Section A.4.3).

sequence) is numbered consecutively and we indicate for each step the justification in terms of axioms or rules for that step.

1. $(p \Rightarrow ((p \Rightarrow p) \Rightarrow p)) \Rightarrow ((p \Rightarrow (p \Rightarrow p)) \Rightarrow (p \Rightarrow p))$ (AX2)

   where we have instantiated the A, B, C of the schema (AX2) by p, $(p \Rightarrow p)$, and p, respectively.

2. $p \Rightarrow ((p \Rightarrow p) \Rightarrow p)$ (AX1)

   with the same instantiation of A and B of schema (AX1) as above for (AX2).

3. $(p \Rightarrow (p \Rightarrow p)) \Rightarrow (p \Rightarrow p)$ (1, 2, MP)

   because (1) and (2) are instances of the premises of MP and (3) is the corresponding instance of the conclusion of MP.

4. $p \Rightarrow (p \Rightarrow p)$ (AX1)

   where we have instantiated the A, B of schema (AX1) by p and p, respectively.

5. $p \Rightarrow p$ (3, 4, MP)

   because (3) and (4) are instances of the premises of MP and (5) is the corresponding instance of the conclusion of MP.

We could actually describe many similar derivations by exhibiting derivation schemata or *metaderivations*. Thus, for instance, we can derive the metatautology $A \Rightarrow A$:

1. $(A \Rightarrow ((A \Rightarrow A) \Rightarrow A)) \Rightarrow ((A \Rightarrow (A \Rightarrow A)) \Rightarrow (A \Rightarrow A))$ (AX2)
2. $A \Rightarrow ((A \Rightarrow A) \Rightarrow A)$ (AX1)
3. $(A \Rightarrow (A \Rightarrow A)) \Rightarrow (A \Rightarrow A)$ (1, 2, MP)
4. $A \Rightarrow (A \Rightarrow A)$ (AX1)
5. $A \Rightarrow A$ (3, 4, MP)

We get an actual tautology by uniformly substituting any formula for A in the metatautology. Thus, by substituting p for A, we obtain the tautology $(p \Rightarrow p)$ we derived before.

Just as we defined what we meant by one language being an extension of another, we can define what it means for one derivability relation, $\vdash'$, to be an extension of another, $\vdash$. The definition is quite simple: every instance of the relation $\vdash$ is also an istance of $\vdash'$. Another way of putting this is that the relation $\vdash$ is contained in the relation $\vdash'$.

Thus we can define $\vdash_{S_4}$, the derivability relation for our simple modal system (see Section A.5) as consisting of the axiom schemata (AX1), (AX2), (AX3) together with:

$\vdash_{S_4} (A \Rightarrow B) \Rightarrow (\Box A \Rightarrow \Box B)$ (M1)

$\vdash_{S_4} \Box A \Rightarrow A$ (M2)

$\vdash_{S_4} \Box A \Rightarrow \Box\Box A$ (M3)

and the rule MP together with the *necessitation* rule (N):

$$\frac{A}{\Box A}$$

A derivation is defined exactly as before and for $G \subseteq MF$, A in MF we have

$$G \vdash_{S_4} A$$

exactly in the case that A can be derived from G. That $\vdash_{S_4}$ is an extension of $\vdash_{sc}$ is based on the observation that every derivation in SC also qualifies as a derivation in S_4 (since it uses only some of the axioms and rules of the latter).

A.2.3   Theories

So far, we have discussed just the linguistic systems consisting of symbols, formation rules and the derivability relation (perhaps generated by rules of reasoning from formulae assumed to be true). Thus a linguistic system LS is a pair $\langle L_{LS}, \vdash_{LS} \rangle$ where L_{LS} is the symbols and formation rules and $\vdash_{LS}$ is the derivability relation. We now wish to study what we mean by the statement of 'application dependent' properties of some symbols in such a linguistic system.

> **Definition:** A *theory* T in a linguistic system $LS = \langle L_{LS}, \vdash_{LS} \rangle$ is a set of formulae of L_{LS} which is closed under $\vdash_{LS}$.

That is, T consists of all formulae of L_{LS} which are derivable from some formula already in T. A theory T uses, in general, only some of the symbols available in L_{LS} and we call this set of symbols, L_T, the *language* of T. We will often refer to the 'formulae of T' to mean the 'formulae of L_{LS} using only symbols from L_T'. Intuitively, T is saying something about the properties of − characterizing − the symbols in L_T (and does not purport to say anything about those symbols available in L_{LS} but not in L_T). Hence the application dependency − the symbols in L_T have been chosen presumably because they are useful in describing such an application. A useful analogy to linguistic systems and theories might be programming languages and programs written within this language.

Again, as with the derivability relation $\vdash_{LS}$ itself, we want to present the generally infinite set of formulae T in terms of some more easily described subset A_T, called the *axiomatization* (*presentation*) of T, from which all formulae of T can be derived by means of the derivability relation $\vdash_{LS}$. The formulae in A_T are called the *axioms* of T. The usual meaning ascribed to 'more easily described' in most logics is 'effectively decidable'. This means that we have an algorithm which, given any formula of L_{LS}, determines if it is an axiom (i.e. is in A_T) or not. We will stick to this meaning most of the time but will loosen it on occasion when we feel this is appropriate.

> **Definition:** A theory T is *consistent* if and only if it is not the case that there is a formula A of L_T such that $T \vdash_{LS} A$ and $T \vdash_{LS} (\neg A)$.

If the latter situation could occur, we must have done something wrong! Consistency, i.e. the absence of contradictory information, is a hard property to determine and plays an especially crucial role in specification. More on this subject in the main body of the book and in the later sections of the appendix.

> **Definition:** A theory T is *(negation) complete* (sometimes, confusingly, called *decidable*) if and only if for every formula A of L_T, either $T \vdash_{LS} A$ or $T \vdash_{LS} (\neg A)$.

That is, for every statement we can make in the language L_T, either it or its contradiction (negation) is true in the theory T. Thus T gives a complete (in the colloquial or dictionary meaning of the word) description of 'the application'. There are no loose ends or indeterminable properties. It is, in general, very difficult to obtain and usually undesirable to work with complete theories in the particular context of this book.

Just as with languages and the derivability relation, we can define a notion of extension for theories. This becomes a basic tool in the world of specification. A linguistic system $LS1 = \langle L_{LS1}, \vdash_{LS1} \rangle$ is an *extension* of $LS = \langle L_{LS}, \vdash_{LS} \rangle$ if and only if $L_{LS} \subseteq L_{LS1}$ and $\vdash_{LS} \subseteq \vdash_{LS1}$. Again we write $LS \subseteq LS1$ and say LS is a *restriction* of $LS1$. Now, a theory T is characterized for our purposes by the pair $\langle LS_T, A_T \rangle$ – the linguistic system LS_T of T and the axiomatic description/presentation A_T of T. In case $LS \subseteq LS1$ and we have $\vdash_{LS} \subseteq \vdash_{LS1}$ just because $L_{LS} \subseteq L_{LS1}$ (i.e. we have not added any axioms or rules of reasoning to $\vdash_{LS}$ to get $\vdash_{LS1}$ but only extended the set of formulae) we write $T = \langle L_T, A_T \rangle$ and $T1 = \langle L_{T1}, A_{T1} \rangle$ and leave $LS = \langle L_{LS}, \vdash_{LS} \rangle$ implicit. Another way of putting this is that if we have two theories within the same linguistic system, we characterize the theories by their respective languages and axiomatic descriptions, leaving the underlying linguistic system implicit.

> **Definition:** A theory $T1 = \langle L_{LS1}, A_{T1} \rangle$ is an *extension* of another theory $T = \langle L_{LS}, A_T \rangle$ if and only if $L_{LS} \subseteq L_{LS1}$ (i.e. the linguistic system of the former extends that of the latter) and for all A in A_T, $A_{T1} \vdash_{LS1} A$ (i.e. every property derivable from A_T using LS is derivable from A_{T1} using $LS1$).

Thus $T1$ is an extension of T, written $T \subseteq T1$, if and only if the properties defined by T for the symbols of L_T are still there in $T1$, but perhaps we are able to prove some new properties. We call T a *restriction* of $T1$.

> **Definition:** We say that an extension $T = \langle L_{LS}, A_T \rangle \subseteq T1 = \langle L_{LS1}, A_{T1} \rangle$ is *conservative*, written $T \leqslant T1$, if and only if for all formulae A of L_T, if $A_{T1} \vdash_{LS1} A$ then $A_T \vdash_{LS} A$.

To understand this, note that if $T \subseteq T1$, then $L_T \subseteq L_{T1}$, i.e. the language of T is included in the language of $T1$. Thus every formula A of L_T is a formula of L_{T1} as well. The above definition then says that $T \leqslant T1$ exactly when $T1$ says no more (cannot be used to derive more properties than) T as far as L_T is concerned. Of course $T1$ may say new things about the symbols in L_{T1} but not in L_T, or even about properties of combinations of symbols in L_T and L_{T1}, but that is not the point.

More about extensions of theories and conservativeness, as well as some examples, can be found in Section 2.3 and also in later sections of this appendix.

A.3 Valuation systems

We now wish to consider how we relate our linguistic systems and theories within them to 'what we want to describe' with them. Sometimes, we are satisfied that a linguistic system is internally coherent without a need to connect it formally with another formalization of things (whose properties) we want to describe. This may be because we have somehow convinced ourselves, perhaps through use, that our 'thought patterns' are reasonably represented.

If, however, we do want to connect, in a mathematical sense, what we do with a linguistic system and theories to the 'real world', we have another problem to solve, as indicated above by the phrase 'another formalization of things'. Formal connections can only be made between objects which themselves are mathematically characterized. Our view of the real world, the 'things...we want to describe', is usually highly inexact. It involves an uncheckable process (from 'real world' to this different formalization) before we can make our connection. This formal connection between two mathematical systems both at one remove (and an uncheckable one at that) from the systems we are trying to describe is not always enlightening, but often it is, so we will consider it here. Another motivation is that this area of study is an important part of what is normally meant by logic/formal system.

This second way of formalizing applications is called a *valuation system*. These systems are intimately connected with the linguistic systems for which they are valuation systems. There is no Esperanto of valuation systems which will do for all different linguistic systems.

Let us consider the sentential logic, SC, and a structure

$$W = \langle M, D, f, g_1, g_2, g_3, g_4 \rangle$$

where:

1. M is a set with at least two elements,
2. D is a proper subset of M with at least one element,
3. $f\colon M \quad \rightarrow M$
   $g_1\colon M \times M \rightarrow M$
   $g_2\colon M \times M \rightarrow M$
   $g_3\colon M \times M \rightarrow M$
   $g_4\colon M \times M \rightarrow M$

Definition: A *valuation system* V for SC is the structure W together with an association of propositional operators of SC with functions of W: $\neg$ with f, $|$ with g_1, & with g_2, $\Rightarrow$ with g_3, and $\Leftrightarrow$ with g_4.

The propositional operators, $\neg$, $|$, ..., $\Leftrightarrow$ are called *logical* symbols and their interpretation is fixed within a given valuation system. What is left open within such a valuation system is what we mean by (what meaning is assigned to) the propositional variables P.

Definition: An (SC-) assignment for V is a function mapping P (the set of propositional variables) to M.

Thus an assignment attributes a (possibly different) value in M to each propositional variable in SC.

Definition: Each assignment $a\colon P \rightarrow M$ induces a *valuation* $v_a\colon F \rightarrow M$ defined inductively by

1. $v_a(p) = a(p)$ for p in P,
2. $v_a(\neg A) = f(v_a(A))$
3. $v_a(A|B) = g_1(v_a(A), v_a(B))$
4. $v_a(A \& B) = g_2(v_a(A), v_a(B))$
5. $v_a(A \Rightarrow B) = g_3(v_a(A), v_a(B))$
6. $v_a(A \Leftrightarrow B) = g_4(v_a(A), v_a(B))$

This basically means that once we decide on what values propositional variables take in M, we can (mechanically) evaluate any formula of SC and get a value in M as the result.

Definition: We say that formula A is *entailed* in v by a set of formulae G, written

$$G \vDash_v A$$

if and only if for every assignment a such that $v_a(B) \in D$ for all B in G, we have $v_a(A) \in D$.

That is, if for every assignment a which simultaneously evaluates every B in G to some value in D, we also have that A evaluates to some value in D, then A is entailed by G. Perhaps an example will help.

Consider $V_{\text{CLASS}} = \langle \{T, F\}, \{T\}, \text{NOT, OR, AND, IMPLIES, IFF} \rangle$ with:

A	NOT (A)
T	F
F	T

A	B	OR(A, B)
T	T	T
T	F	T
F	T	T
F	F	F

A	B	AND(A, B)
T	T	T
T	F	F
F	T	F
F	F	F

A	B	IMPLIES(A, B)
T	T	T
T	F	F
F	T	T
F	F	T

A	B	IFF(A, B)
T	T	T
T	F	F
F	T	F
F	F	T

read in the obvious way. Clearly, we intend T to be read as *true* and F as *false* with NOT, OR, etc., having their usual meanings. Thus the role of D is to pick out the values which indicate that statements (i.e. formulae) are significant or true. So, in this setting entailment of A by G means that whenever all formulae in G are *true*, we must also have that A is *true*.

Another valuation system for SC is given by

$$V1 = \langle \{TT, TF, FT, FF\}, \{TT\}, \text{NOT1, OR1}, \ldots \rangle$$

with:

A	NOT1 (A)
TT	FF
TF	FT
FT	TF
FF	TT

A	B	OR1(A, B)
TT	TT	TT
TT	TF	TT
TT	FT	TT
TT	FF	TT
TF	TT	TT
TF	TF	TF
TF	FT	TT
TF	FF	TF
FT	TT	TT
FT	TF	TT
FT	FT	FT
FT	FF	FT
FF	TT	TT
FF	TF	TF
FF	FT	FT
FF	FF	FF

and so on.

As for the system S_4, a valuation system is given in terms of any quasi-ordered set $(S, \leq)$.

> **Definition:** A *quasi-ordering* $\leq$ on a set S is a reflexive and transitive relation on S. (A relation $\leq$ is reflexive if for every x we have $x \leq x$ and transitive if $x \leq y$ and $y \leq z$ implies $x \leq z$.) A quasi-ordering is a partial ordering if it is also antisymmetric (i.e. $x \leq y$ and $y \leq x$ implies $y = x$).

> **Definition:** A *valuation system* V for S_4 is a valuation system $\langle M, D,$ NOT, OR, AND, IMPLIES, IFF$\rangle$ for the underlying linguistic system SC in which the following additional conditions are satisfied:
> 1. D is a singleton set (a set with a single element), and this single element is a set S with a quasi-ordering with order relation $\leq$.
> 2. M is the power set $\mathbf{P}(S)$ of S, i.e. M is the set of all subsets of S.
> 3. NOT is the complement operation on the set S, OR is union, AND is intersection, IMPLIES is the subset relation (i.e. IMPLIES $(S1, S2)$ with $S1$, $S2$ in M exactly when $S1$ is a subset of $S2$), IFF is the equality relation on sets.
> 4. $v_a(\Box A)$ for any assignment a and formula A is defined as: x in $v_a(\Box A)$ if and only if for all $y \leq x$, we have y in $v_a(A)$.

To make sense of this, we use the so-called 'possible worlds' interpretation of $(S, \leq)$. The idea is that each assignment $a: P \to \mathbf{P}(S)$ from propositional variables to subsets of S assigns to some p in P a subset $S1$ of S. The intention is that S is a possible set of worlds (states) and a

assigns to p the subset of S in which p is supposed to be *true*. The complement of $S1$, $S - S1$, is then the set of worlds in which p is to be *false*. The use of complement, union, etc., for $\neg$, $|$, etc., respectively, should now be clear. What about $v_a(\Box A)$? The quasi-ordering $\leq$ on S can be thought of as an *accessibility* (or *reachability*) relation, telling us which worlds (states) can be reached from which other ones. Then, for $x \in S$, we can interpret the definition of $v_a(\Box A)$ as: a formula A is necessarily true at world x (in state x) if and only if for every world (state) y from which x can be reached (accessed), y makes A true.

Before we say more about linguistic systems, derivability, theories and valuation systems, let us look at a more substantial example.

A.4　First-order predicate calculus – PC

A.4.1　The language

The (first-order) predicate calculus is certainly the best known and most extensively studied formal system in logic. A first order language L_{PC} has the following categories of symbols (where we indicate in parentheses the name we will use for the category):

- **Variables** *(Var)* $x, y, z, x1, y1, \ldots$
- **Logical symbols** $\neg, \&, |, \Rightarrow, \Leftrightarrow, \mathbf{E}, \mathbf{A}$,
- **Punctuation symbols** $(,)$, ',' (i.e. comma)
- **Predicate symbols** *(Pr)* $p, q, r, p1, q1, r1, \ldots$
- **Function symbols** *(Fn)* $f, g, h, f1, g1, h1, \ldots$
- **Constant symbols** *(C)* $c, d, c1, d1, \ldots$

We assume that *Var, Pr, Fn, C* are defined by appropriate BNF equations. Each function or predicate symbol has associated with it a fixed rank (or degree). The idea is, of course, that in valuation systems we will associate functions and relations with function symbols and predicate symbols, respectively. Constant symbols will have fixed values associated with them in any given valuation system. Punctuation symbols are used purely for readability. Logical symbols are the symbols in PC whose meaning is always fixed in a valuation system. Predicate, function and constant symbols will not have fixed interpretations and it is their properties we are interested in defining via theories when we describe a system or application in PC. Variables will range over terms – expressions built up from constants, variables and function symbols. Some further categories in which we will be interested are:

$$Name ::= C \mid F\_of\_1(Name)$$
$$\mid F\_of\_2(Name, Name)$$

$$| F\_of\_3(Name\ \{,Name\}^2)$$
$$\vdots$$
$$| F\_of\_n(Name\ \{,Name\}^{n-1})$$
$$\vdots$$

(not exactly BNF!) where F_of_n is the category of function symbols of degree n. Thus a name is (an expression which is) a constant or a function symbol followed by a left parenthesis, followed by some expression,... followed by a right parenthesis. The number of expressions matches the degree (rank), k, of the function symbol.

$$Term ::= C \mid Var \mid F\_of\_1(Term)$$
$$| F\_of\_2(Term,\ Term)$$
$$| F\_of\_3(Term\ \{,Term\}^2)$$
$$\vdots$$
$$| F\_of\_n(Term\ \{,Term\}^{n-1})$$
$$\vdots$$

Thus terms are similar to names but treat variables like constants. Names are variable free terms.

$$Atomic ::= Pr\_of\_1(Term) \mid Pr\_of\_2(Term\ \{,Term\}^1)$$
$$\vdots$$
$$| Pr\_of\_n(Term\ \{,Term\}^{n-1})$$
$$\vdots$$

Atomic formulae state basic or primitive properties of objects. Since objects are in some sense represented by terms, the atomic properties are those of terms and it is terms that appear as the arguments of the relation symbols of the language. PC will be seen to be an extension of SC in the sense that the propositional variables of the latter are really best thought of as relation symbols of zero rank, i.e. they take no arguments. (Hence no term building mechanism was incorporated in SC.) So one way in which PC extends SC is by allowing relation symbols of rank greater than zero and, since these require objects about which to state properties, means of building names (a new category) for objects.

$$PCF ::= Atomic \mid (\neg PCF) \mid (PCF \mid PCF) \mid (PCF\ \&\ PCF) \mid (PCF \Rightarrow PCF)$$
$$| (PCF \Leftrightarrow PCF) \mid (\mathbf{E}\ Var\ PCF) \mid (\mathbf{A}\ Var\ PCF)$$

Thus formulae of PC are built up from atomic formulae in the same way that formulae of SC are built from propositional variables but we have two further formula 'constructors'. Both $\mathbf{E}$ and $\mathbf{A}$ are known as *quantifiers* and their use together with a variable, say x, and a formula A qualifies the range of application of the property specified by A with respect to the variable x. Thus $\mathbf{E}xA$ indicates that we expect A to be true for at least one instantiation of x by a term. Similarly, we expect A to be true for all possible instantiations of x when we assert $\mathbf{A}xA$. Note that we will often drop the enclosing brackets around formulae when no ambiguity will arise.

We will adopt the following conventions for (meta-) variables ranging over our various categories of symbols:

$a, b, \ldots$: *Var* (variables ranging over variables again!)
$n, m, \ldots$: *Name*
$t, u, v, \ldots$: *Term*
$A, B, C, \ldots$: *PCF*

and

$G, H, \ldots$: **P**(*PCF*)   (i.e. sets of formulae)

Definition: In the formulae $\mathbf{E}aA$, $\mathbf{A}aA$, A is said to be the *scope* of the quantifier, and a is said to be the *bound variable*. A particular occurrence of a variable b in a formula A is said to be *bound* if and only if the occurrence in question immediately follows a quantifier (i.e. we have $\mathbf{A}b$ or $\mathbf{E}b$) or the occurrence in question is within the scope A of a quantifier within B (i.e. B contains $\mathbf{A}bA$ or $\mathbf{E}bA$). Otherwise it is said to be *free*.

Definition: A variable is said to be *free in a formula* if and only if there is at least one free occurrence of the variable in the formula. We use the (conventional) notation $A(x_1, \ldots, x_n)$ to indicate that some of the variables occurring free in A are among $x_1, \ldots, x_n$.

Thus, we intend to indicate by 'free in a formula' that the truth of the formula will depend on the objects we substitute for the (free) variable.

Example

R is a predicate symbol of degree 2 and

$$A = \mathbf{A}x(Rxy \Rightarrow \mathbf{E}yRyx)$$

The first occurrence of y is free.
All further occurrences of y and all occurrences of x are bound.
y is free in the formula A.
x is not free in the formula A.

Definition: A term t is said to be *free for a in A* if and only if no free occurrences of a in A lie within the scope of any quantifier $\mathbf{E}b$, $\mathbf{A}b$ where b is a variable in t.

In other words, we examine the variables occurring in t and then make sure that the variable in which we are interested (a above) does not occur free within the scope of any quantifier involving such variables. Note that the variable a above need not occur in the term t.

Example

With A as in the above example and f a function symbol of rank 1:

> $f(y)$ is free for y in A.
>
> $f(x)$ is not free for y in A.
>
> Both $f(y)$ and $f(x)$ are free for x in A.

Example

R is a predicate symbol of rank 2, f is a function symbol of rank 2, c is a constant, and

$$A = \mathbf{A}y\mathbf{E}xR(z, f(x, z))$$

All occurrences of z in A are free.

The occurrence of y and each occurrence of x are bound.

c is free for z in A.

$f(x, z)$ is not free for z in A.

y is not free for z in A.

Facts:

1. a is not free for a in any formula.
2. Any term t is free for a in A if A does not contain any free occurrences of a.
3. Any name (variable free term) is free for any a in any A.

Definition: We say a formula A is a *sentence* (or *closed*) if no variable occurs free in A.

The concepts of free, bound, free in, free for a in A are going to be used to determine how we can make various substitutions of terms for variables in different circumstances.

Definition: Let t, t' be terms and $A(x)$ a formula (with (at least) variable x occurring free in A). We define the *substitution* of t' for x in t as the textual replacement of each occurrence of x (as a symbol) in (the string of symbols) t by (the string of symbols) t'. We thus get a new term which we denote as

> $t(x/t')$

We extend this to *simultaneous substitution* as follows. If $t'_1, \ldots, t'_n$ are terms and $x_1, \ldots, x_n$ variables, then

> $t(x_1/t'_1, \ldots, x_n/t'_n)$

denotes the term which results from simultaneously replacing each occurrence of x_1, each occurrence of x_2, $\ldots$, each occurrence of x_n in t by

$t'_1, t'_2, \ldots, t'_n$ respectively. Similarly for formula A we denote by

$$A(x/t')$$

the replacement of each free occurrence of x in A by t' with the added proviso that t' is free for x in A. The extension of this to simultaneous substitution is also straightforward.

A.4.2 Derivability in PC

Our first use of some of the above definitions will be in an axiomatic presentation of the derivability relation $\vdash_{PC}$. Note that when $A(a)$ and $A(t)$ are used together, we assume $A(t)$ is the formula obtained from $A(a)$ by replacing every free occurrence of a by t. We also write $\vdash$ for $\vdash_{PC}$ and $G, A \vdash B$ for $G \cup \{A\} \vdash B$.

Axioms:

$$\vdash A \Rightarrow (B \Rightarrow A) \tag{AX1}$$
$$\vdash (A \Rightarrow (B \Rightarrow C)) \Rightarrow ((A \Rightarrow B) \Rightarrow (A \Rightarrow C)) \tag{AX2}$$
$$\vdash (\neg B \Rightarrow \neg A) \Rightarrow ((\neg B \Rightarrow A) \Rightarrow B) \tag{AX3}$$
$$\vdash (Aa(A \Rightarrow B)) \Rightarrow (A \Rightarrow AaB) \quad \text{where } a \text{ is not free in } A \tag{AX4}$$
$$\vdash (AaA(a)) \Rightarrow A(t) \quad \text{where } t \text{ is free for } a \text{ in } A \tag{AX5}$$

(The import of the restriction on (AX5) is that if $A(a)$ is true for all a, we can substitute a term t for a if and only if variables occurring in t do not get accidentally bound by quantifiers still occurring in A.)

Rules:

$$\frac{A, A \Rightarrow B}{B} \tag{MP}$$

$$\frac{A}{AaA} \tag{GEN}$$

The first rule (*modus ponens*) is the same as in SC while the second is known as the *generalization rule*.

Example
R is a predicate symbol of degree 2. Let us prove

$$Ax Ay Rxy \vdash Ay Ax Rxy$$

1. $Ax Ay Rxy$		(Assumption)
2. $Ax Ay Rxy \Rightarrow Ay Rxy$		(AX5)
3. $Ay Rxy$		(1, 2, MP)
4. $Ay Rxy \Rightarrow Rxy$		(AX5)
5. Rxy		(3, 4, MP)
6. $Ax Rxy$		(5, GEN)
7. $Ay Ax Rxy$		(6, GEN)

Step (1) is an axiom or assumption (appears in G in '$G \vdash A$'). Step (2) is an application of (AX5) with a being instantiated by x, A by $\mathbf{A}y\,Rxy$, and t by x. The reader should verify that x is free for x in $\mathbf{A}y\,Rxy$. The remaining steps follow a similar pattern.

In all branches of mathematics we often find ourselves in the situation where we want to prove a statement of the form 'A implies B'. We do this by assuming the truth of A and then proving B. The following is a metaresult (i.e. a result *about* the logic PC, not within it) which is of fundamental importance in justifying such procedures.

The Deduction Theorem
If $G, A \vdash B$ and A is a closed formula (sentence), then

$$G \vdash (A \Rightarrow B)$$

Proof
Suppose $B_1, \ldots, B_n$ ($= B$) is the proof (derivation) of B from G, A. We prove by induction on the length of the proof that $G \vdash A \Rightarrow B_i$ for $1 \leqslant i \leqslant n$ and thus that we have a proof of $G \vdash (A \Rightarrow B)$ (since $B = B_n$).
Case analysis: Each B_i

1. is either an axiom or a member of G in which case $B_i \Rightarrow (A \Rightarrow B_i)$ is an axiom (instance of (AX1)) and so by MP we have $G \vdash A \Rightarrow B_i$;

2. or it is the formula A in which case because $\vdash A \Rightarrow A$, we have $G \vdash A \Rightarrow B_i$;

3. or it follows from B_j and $B_k = B_j \Rightarrow B_i$ by MP for $j < i$, $k < i$. Then, by the inductive hypothesis, we have $G \vdash A \Rightarrow B_j$ and also $G \vdash A \Rightarrow (B_j \Rightarrow B_i)$. But by (AX2) we have $\vdash (A \Rightarrow (B_j \Rightarrow B_i)) \Rightarrow ((A \Rightarrow B_j) \Rightarrow (A \Rightarrow B_i))$ and so by two applications of MP (which the reader is asked to work out) we get $G \vdash A \Rightarrow B_i$;

4. or it is $\mathbf{A}x B_j$, say, with $j < i$ and B_i follows from B_j by GEN. Then, as x is not free in A (because A is closed!), by (AX4) we have

$$\vdash (\mathbf{A}x(A \Rightarrow B_j)) \Rightarrow (A \Rightarrow \mathbf{A}x B_j)$$

So, since $G \vdash A \Rightarrow B_j$ (by our inductive assumption), we have by GEN $G \vdash \mathbf{A}x(A \Rightarrow B_j)$ and the desired result by MP applied to this last formula and the instance of (AX4) displayed above. (Note that $A \Rightarrow \mathbf{A}x B_j \Leftrightarrow A \Rightarrow B_i$.)

Note that the proof is constructive (we construct a proof of $G \vdash A \Rightarrow B$ given a proof of $G, A \vdash B$). Also note that neither (AX3) nor (AX5) was used in the proof (and so a logic without these would still guarantee that the Deduction Theorem was valid).

A.4.3   A valuation system for PC

Definition: A symbol in a linguistic system is a *logical symbol* (*logical constant*) if and only if for each associated valuation system the meaning of the symbol is fixed in all structures of the given valuation system.

If we associate two different valuation systems with a given linguistic system, a logical symbol may have different meanings in the different valuation systems, e.g. the two valuation systems for SC exhibited in (A.3).

For SC the symbols &, |, ¬, ⇒, ⇔ are logical constants and thus we used tables to define their fixed meanings. For PC, the meanings of **E** and **A** are also fixed.

Definition: A symbol in a linguistic system is an *extralogical symbol* (*extralogical constant*) if and only if it is not a logical constant.

Thus, in SC, the propositional variables are extralogical symbols. In PC, the constant, function and predicate symbols are extralogical, as are variables. It is the meaning of these symbols which is open to interpretation.

When we discussed SC, we defined two valuation systems corresponding to this linguistic system. Each valuation system was given in terms of a fixed meaning of the logical symbols (¬, |, & ...) defined by the given tables. Different structures could be built from such a given valuation system by choosing different assignments of values to the propositional variables. We extend this idea to PC, recalling that propositional variables in SC are best thought of as degree zero relation symbols in PC.

We again start defining our valuation system by fixing the meanings of ¬, |, ... just as in the first valuation system for SC. We also fix the meaning of = as identity (two things are equal if and only if they are identical). Before defining the fixed meanings of the quantifiers (as they are also considered to be logical symbols), we generalize the 'assignment' of SC which was used to build different structures within the valuation system.

Definition: An *interpretation* (*valuation*) I for a classical first order language L_{PC} (i.e. the language of PC) consists of:

1. a non-empty set D – the *domain of the interpretation*;
2. a function I from the predicate, function and constant symbols of L_{PC}, such that:

   (a) for a predicate symbol R of degree n, $I(R) \subseteq D^n$ (i.e. $I(R)$ is an n-ary relation on D);

    (b) for a function symbol f of degree n, $I(f): D^n \to D$ (i.e. $I(f)$ is a function of n arguments from D to D);

    (c) for a constant symbol c, $I(c) \in D$ (i.e. a constant names a value in D).

Definition: A *sequence* (or *assignment*) in I, say s, is a function from the variable symbols of L_{PC} to D (i.e. $s: Var \to D$). Such an assignment s can obviously be extended to a function s^* from the set of terms of L_{PC} to D (i.e. $s^*: Term \to D$) by:

    If f is a function symbol of degree n and $t_1, \ldots, t_n$ are terms, then $s^*(f(t_1, \ldots, t_n)) = I(f)(s^*(t_1), \ldots, s^*(t_n))$

When two sequences s and s' agree on all variable symbols except possibly a, we write $s \sim_a s'$. (Thus for all $b \neq a$, $s(b) = s'(b)$.)

Definition: A sequence s *satisfies* a formula A in I in the following cases:

1. If A is an atomic formula, say $R(t_1, \ldots, t_n)$ then s satisfies $R(t_1, \ldots, t_n)$ in I if and only if $\langle s^*(t_1), \ldots, s^*(t_n) \rangle \in I(R)$; that is, the tuple of values obtained by evaluating $\langle t_1, \ldots, t_n \rangle$ with s is in the relation assigned to R by I;

2. s satisfies $\neg A$ in I if and only if s does not satisfy A in I;

3. s satisfies $A \mid B$ in I if and only if s satisfies A in I or s satisfies B in I;

4. s satisfies $A \& B$ in I if and only if s satisfies A in I and s satisfies B in I;

5. s satisfies $A \Rightarrow B$ in I if and only if s does not satisfy A in I or s satisfies B in I;

6. s satisfies $A \Leftrightarrow B$ in I if and only if either (s satisfies A in I and s satisfies B in I) or (s does not satisfy A in I and s does not satisfy B in I);

7. s satisfies $\mathbf{E}aA$ in I if and only if for some s' we have $s \sim_a s'$ and s' satisfies A in I; that is, we can find an assignment which differs at most in its assignment to a and which satisfies A.

8. s satisfies $\mathbf{A}aA$ in I if and only if for all s', if $s \sim_a s'$ then s' satisfies A in I; that is, all assignments differing from s only in their assignment to a must satisfy A. (In such cases, the meaning or truth value of A is in some sense independent of which value in D we assign to a.)

Definition: A formula A is *true* in I if and only if A is satisfied by all assignments in I.

A formula A is true in an interpretation exactly when it does not matter how we assign values to (free) variables appearing in A. Similarly, a formula A is *false* in I if and only if no sequence in I satisfies A in I.

Note that a formula A is false in I if and only if its *negation* $\neg A$ is true in I. Also, closed formulae (sentences) are either true or false in each I, but in general formulae with free variables are neither.

> **Definition:** A formula A (of L_{PC}) is *valid* if and only if it is true in all interpretations. A formula A (of L_{PC}) is *satisfiable* if and only if it is satisfied by some sequence s in some interpretation I. A set of formulae G (of L_{PC}) is *simultaneously satisfiable* if and only if there is an s in some I such that for each A in G, s satisfies A in I. A formula A is a *semantic consequence* of (is *entailed* by) a set of formulae G, denoted $G \vDash A$, if and only if, in every interpretation, any sequence that simultaneously satisfies G also satisfies A. The fact that A is valid is equivalent to $\vDash A$ (shorthand for $\emptyset \vDash A$; A is a semantic consequence of the empty set of formulae $\emptyset$).

Some simple consequences of the above definitions are:

1. AaA is true for a given interpretation I if and only if A is true for I.
2. If A has as free variables $a_1, \ldots, a_n$ and $s(a_i) = s'(a_i)$, for $1 \leq i \leq n$, then s satisfies A in I if and only if s' satisfies A in I. Proof is by induction on the construction of A.
3. If t is free for a in $A(a)$, then s satisfies $A(t)$ if and only if s' satisfies $A(a)$ where $s' \sim_a s$ and $s'(a) = s^*(t)$. Proof is again by induction on the construction of A.
4. The axiom (AX5) for $\vdash_{PC}$, $(AaA(a)) \Rightarrow A(t)$ for t free for a in A, is valid. Proof follows from (3) and the observation that if s satisfies $AaA(a)$, it satisfies $A(t)$.
5. (AX4) for $\vdash_{PC}$, $(Aa(A \Rightarrow B)) \Rightarrow (A \Rightarrow AaB)$ for a not free in A, is valid. Proof is by contradiction: Suppose that the above formula is not true for some interpretation. So there is a sequence s such that s satisfies $Aa(A \Rightarrow B)$ and s does not satisfy $A \Rightarrow AaB$ (by clause (5) in the definition of satisfaction). Thus s satisfies A and does not satisfy AaB. Then for some s', $s' \sim_a s$, s' does not satisfy B. As a is not free in $Aa(A \Rightarrow B)$ and in A, and s satisfies both $Aa(A \Rightarrow B)$ and A, so does s' by (2) above. Hence s' satisfies $A \Rightarrow B$ and A and thus B. This is a contradiction.
6. The deduction theorem for validity ($\vDash$): $G, A \vDash B$ and A closed implies

   $$G \vDash A \Rightarrow B$$

Example 1
Let $\leq$ be an (infix) binary predicate symbol. Let I be given by: D is

the natural numbers (non-negative integers) and $I(\leqslant)$ is the less than or equal to relation on D. Then

$\quad x \leqslant y$ is satisfied by s if and only if $s(x)I(\leqslant)s(y)$

$\quad \mathbf{A}y(x \leqslant y)$ is satisfied by s if and only if $s(x) = 0$

$\quad \mathbf{E}x\mathbf{A}y(x \leqslant y)$ is true in D

That is, there is a smallest natural number.

Example 2
Let D' be the set of integers and $I(\leqslant)$ be the usual less than or equal to relation.

$\quad \mathbf{E}x\mathbf{A}y(x \leqslant y)$ is false in D'.

Example 3
$\quad \vdash \mathbf{A}a(A \mid \neg A)$

This is because for any sequence s in some I, either A or $\neg A$ is satisfied by s (proof is by induction on the construction of A). So s satisfies $A \mid \neg A$ and hence satisfies $\mathbf{A}a(A \mid \neg A)$.

Example 4
$\mathbf{A}x\mathbf{E}y\,Rxy \Rightarrow \mathbf{E}y\mathbf{A}x\,Rxy$ is not valid. We can show this by exhibiting a counter-example. Again take D' as the set of integers and a binary predicate $<$ with $I(<)$ being the usual less than relation on D'. Hence $\mathbf{A}x\mathbf{E}y\,Rxy$ is true but $\mathbf{E}y\mathbf{A}x\,Rxy$ is false! (The latter asserts the existence of a maximum integer.)

A.4.4 Theories in PC

We begin with some examples of theories in PC.

Example 1
The 'theory of partial orders' has as axioms:

$\quad \vdash \mathbf{A}x(x \leqslant x)$
$\quad \vdash \mathbf{A}x\mathbf{A}y((x \leqslant y \;\&\; y \leqslant x) \Rightarrow (x = y))$
$\quad \vdash \mathbf{A}x\mathbf{A}y\mathbf{A}z((x \leqslant y) \;\&\; (y \leqslant z) \Rightarrow (x \leqslant z))$

Example 2
Peano's axioms for the natural numbers (with *zero* a constant symbol and *suc* ('add one') a unary function symbol) defining the theory NAT:

$\quad \mathbf{A}x(\neg(suc(x) = zero))$
$\quad \mathbf{A}x\mathbf{A}y(suc(x) = suc(y) \Rightarrow x = y)$

For any formula $A(a)$ of L_{NAT}:

$\quad A(zero) \Rightarrow ((\mathbf{A}a(A(a) \Rightarrow A(suc(a)))) \Rightarrow \mathbf{A}aA(a))$

The last is the usual induction axiom for the natural numbers: An assertion about the natural numbers can be proved by proving the assertion for *zero* and then showing that the assumption of the property for an arbitrary natural number allows us to prove the property for the successor of that natural number.

> **Definition:** For the definitions of (*syntactically*) *consistent* and *complete*, we refer the reader to Section A.3.3. A set of formulae G is said to be *independent* if and only if it is not the case that for some A in G, $G - \{A\} \vdash A$.

The reader should compare the notion of consistency of a set of formulae T with the idea of the set of formulae T being simultaneously satisfiable and show that, in PC, T inconsistent implies T complete, and T incomplete implies T consistent.

The definitions of extension for languages of a theory, theory, etc., are as before. We now present some important results[†] about PC.

The Robinson Consistency Theorem
If $T = \langle L_T, A_T \rangle$ is a consistent complete theory and $T0 = \langle L_{T0}, A_{T0} \rangle$ and $T1 = \langle L_{T1}, A_{T1} \rangle$ are consistent extensions of T with $L_{T0} \cap L_{T1} = L_T$, then the theory $T0 \cup T1 = \langle L_{T0} \cup L_{T1}, A_{T0} \cup A_{T1} \rangle$ is consistent.

(By $L_{T0} \cap L_{T1}$ is meant the symbols and so formulae that L_{T0} and L_{T1} have in common. Similarly, $L_{T0} \cup L_{T1}$ is just the union of the symbols of L_{T0} and L_{T1} and formulae generated from this expanded collection of symbols.)

Thus if we start with a consistent theory which is also complete, and we extend this theory in two different directions (by using different symbols in the two extensions), then if we have not messed things up by making our extensions inconsistent, we can glue the extensions together safely. This expresses something about the modularity of extensions.

The Craig Interpolation Lemma
If $T \vdash A$, then there is a formula B such that $T \vdash B$ and $B \vdash A$ and such that the only predicate, function and constant symbols appearing in B are those that appear in both T and A (i.e. '$L_B = L_T \cap L_A$').

Extended Robinson's Consistency Theorem
If $T = \langle L_T, A_T \rangle$ is a consistent (not necessarily complete) theory and $T0 = \langle L_{T0}, A_{T0} \rangle$, $T1 = \langle L_{T1}, A_{T1} \rangle$ are consistent extensions of T at

---

[†] These results also hold in some other logics. For discussion and proofs, see Enderton (1972).

least one of which is conservative and $L_T = L_{T0} \cap L_{T1}$, then $T0 \cup T1$ as defined above is consistent.

This is another modularity result for glueing extensions together – one which will be more useful than the original Robinson's Theorem. These results have analogues in the valuation system defined above; the analogies are obtained by replacing ⊢ by ⊧, and 'consistency' by 'simultaneously satisfiable'.

> **Definition:** An interpretation I is said to be a *model* for a set of formulae G if and only if every formula of G is true in I.

A.5   Modal and programming logics

In this section, we present some extensions of propositional and predicate linguistic systems to illustrate a number of important ideas. Chief among these will be refinements of the concept of modality, as already introduced earlier, and a modification of the notion of what is acceptable as an axiom or rule of inference, and hence what is our accepted notion of derivability or proof.

We will proceed by starting from propositional or predicate logic (SC or PC, respectively) and providing various extensions by defining:

1. extensions to the underlying language, i.e. providing new symbols and appropriate formation rules for extending what counts as a formula;
2. extensions to the derivability relation, i.e. a standard semantic interpretation of the new symbols.

Sometimes, we have to characterize the acceptable interpretations in a valuation system. This is in order to avoid a possible mismatch between the logical apparatus we are trying to introduce and intuitive notions of meaning associated with particular functions and constants in the underlying structure of the valuation system.

> **Definition:** A *standardness condition* for a symbol is a constraint on the possible meaning ascribed to that symbol over and above that normally allowed by the valuation system.

For example, the equality symbol is assigned a meaning which is a binary relation. This binary relation must be a congruence (i.e. an equivalence relation which also has the substitutivity property), but we also generally impose the standardness condition that it must actually be the relation of identity. (Note that, in some linguistic systems, equality is regarded as a logical constant and its meaning is thus fixed in that way[†].)

A.5.1 Modal logics

We begin by discussing at greater length the concepts of modal logic, as various versions of modal logic are finding wider and wider use in computer science. We start with SC, the propositional system described in Section A.2.1. The logical system to be described is usually called K and its extensions are called *normal* systems. We extend L_{SC} by the symbols $\square$ ('box') and $\diamond$ ('diamond') and add the formation rule:

If A is a formula, so are $\square A$ and $\diamond A$

We extend the derivability relation $\vdash_{SC}$ by the addition of the axioms and rules:

$$\text{(Distribution axiom)} \quad \vdash_K \square(A \Rightarrow B) \Rightarrow (\square A \Rightarrow \square B) \tag{M1}$$

$$\text{(Rule of necessitation)} \quad \frac{\vdash_K A}{\vdash_K \square A} \tag{N}$$

$$\text{(Definition of } \diamond) \quad \vdash_K \square A \Leftrightarrow \neg \diamond \neg A \tag{M$\diamond$}$$

(Note that A1, A2, A3 and MP automatically become part of the definition of $\vdash_K$ as the latter is defined as an extension of $\vdash_{SC}$.)

(As an exercise, the reader might care to show that M1 and N can be replaced by the single rule

$$\frac{A_1, \ldots, A_n \vdash_K B}{\square A_1, \ldots, \square A_n \vdash_K \square B}$$

and vice versa. If we denote by K1 the extension of SC we get by adding the above rule and M$\diamond$, then for G a set of formulae and A a formula,

$$G \vdash_K A \text{ if and only if } G \vdash_{K1} A)$$

A valuation system for such modal logics can be given in terms of the so-called 'possible worlds' and 'accessibility relation' concepts outlined at the

---

[†] Suppose that f is a function symbol of rank n. $I(f)$ is said to have the *substitutivity* property for some interpretation I and equivalence relation R defined on the domain D of the interpretation I if and only if for all a_i, b_i, $1 \leqslant i \leqslant n$, in the domain D of the interpretation I, if

$$R(a_i, b_i), 1 \leqslant i \leqslant n$$

then

$$R(I(f)(a_1, \ldots, a_n), I(f)(b_1, \ldots, b_n))$$

R has the substitutivity property if and only if all function symbols have interpretations with the substitutivity property with respect to R.

end of Section A.3. The version we present in the following definition is a generalization of our earlier presentation. We will explain the restriction implicit in the earlier definition when we extend K.

Definition: A structure M for L_K (the language of K) is a pair $\langle W, R \rangle$ where:

1. W is a collection of *possible worlds*, each of which is a valuation of the propositional symbols (of SC), and

2. $R \subseteq W \times W$, called the *accessibility relation* (or, sometimes, *reachability relation*).

Clearly, the valuations corresponding to each $w \in W$ can be extended to non-modal formulae (i.e. those of SC) in the obvious inductive way. For formulae including modal symbols ($\Box$ and $\Diamond$), we use the following[†]:

1. $M \vDash_w \Box A$ if and only if for all w' such that $\langle w, w' \rangle \in R$, we have $M \vDash_{w'} A$;

2. $M \vDash_w \Diamond A$ if and only if there is some w' such that $\langle w, w' \rangle \in R$ and $M \vDash_{w'} A$.

Thus $\Box A$ evaluates to true in world w of $M = \langle W, R \rangle$ if and only if for every w' reachable from w, A evaluates to true. $\Diamond A$ evaluates to true at w if and only if there is at least one world reachable from w where A is true.

Definition: We write $M \vDash A$ if and only if $M \vDash_w A$ for all $w \in W$ in $M = \langle W, R \rangle$. We write $\vDash A$ if and only if $M \vDash A$ for all M.

Theorem

If $M = \langle W, R \rangle$ and R is reflexive (i.e. for all w, $\langle w, w \rangle \in R$), then

$$M \vDash \Box A \Rightarrow A$$

Proof

Using the definition of implication, we have $(\neg \Box A) | A$. Then, for any w:

If $M \vDash_w A$, then $M \vDash_w (\neg \Box A) | A$ and so $M \vDash_w \Box A \Rightarrow A$.

If $M \vDash_w \neg A$ then $M \vDash_w \neg \Box A$ as A is not necessarily valid (w is an exception!), and so $M \vDash_w \Box A \Rightarrow A$.

Since for arbitrary w we have $\vDash_w \Box A \Rightarrow A$, we get our result $M \vDash \Box A \Rightarrow A$.

[†] In order to exhibit the context of the structure and the world within the structure in which validity is claimed, we will write $M \vDash_w A$ to indicate validity of formula A in world w of structure M.

We can also prove the following:

Theorem
If $M = \langle W, R \rangle$ and R is transitive (i.e. for all $w1$, $w2$, $w3$, $\langle w1, w2 \rangle$, $\langle w2, w3 \rangle \in R$, implies $\langle w1, w3 \rangle \in R$), then

$$M \vDash \Box A \Rightarrow \Box\Box A$$

If we want to extend the derivability relation $\vdash_K$ further by adding to it axioms (M2) and (M3) of Section A.2.2 (thus obtaining S_4), the two theorems just stated guarantee that reflexivity and transitivity of the reachability relation is sufficient for the validity of these axioms. Observe that, in the definition of valuation systems for S_4 given in Section A.3, the assumption of reflexivity and transitivity of the reachability relation was explicit. In the present, more general, case we take these requirements as standardness conditions on structures.

In general, we have a linguistic system LS which we extend to $LS1$ and when we add axioms to extend the derivability relation $\vdash_{LS} \subseteq \vdash_{LS1}$, we want to restrict the range of allowable structures in a valuation system for LS to ones which correspond to this extension $\vdash_{LS1}$. This is the role of standardness conditions. The interplay between additional axioms and standardness conditions will be amply illustrated by our discussion of programming logics in the next section.

A.5.2 Programming logics

Our interpretation of the formula $\Box A$ is that it is a modally qualified assertion. If we follow our intuitions about possible worlds corresponding in some loose sense to computing notions of state (of a computation, of a database, etc.), then modalities tell us something about relationships between states. In general, we find ourselves unhappy with an (un-structured) relation, such as the accessibility relation R, for reasons analogous to our dissatisfaction with the original definition of the derivability relation $\vdash_{LS}$ as a relation. We want to be able to *generate* this relation, and so we introduce the concept of proof and from it build $\vdash_{LS}$. In computing, we are often much more interested in what caused the relationship between two states than we are in just the existence of this relationship. Thus we want the equivalent of the axioms and rules of inference generating proofs for the relation of accessibility.

We do this by extending our treatment of modalities[†]. We introduce several variants of the $\Box$ symbol, $[\alpha]$ say, for several $\alpha \in Ac$ (where Ac is to be defined), with the interpretation that $[\alpha]A$ tells us in what way the

---

[†] Much of what follows in this section is based on Goldblatt (1982) which should be consulted for proofs and further details.

formula A is modally qualified. It is intended that $\alpha \in Ac$ somehow corresponds to an action (moving something from one state to another) and we will read $[\alpha]A$ as 'after the action named by α, the formula A will be true in that world (state) to which α takes us'.

Example: Databases

$$\neg IN(Jack) \Rightarrow ([add\_Jack]IN(Jack))$$

i.e. if *Jack* is not in the database, then after the action of adding *Jack*, *Jack* will be in the database. A parameterized version to allow for the addition of different people to the database might look as follows:

$$\mathbf{A}x(\neg IN(x) \Rightarrow ([add(x)]IN(x)))$$

Example: Expert systems

$$(A_1 \& \ldots \& A_n \Rightarrow B) \Rightarrow ([add\text{-}A](A_1 \& \ldots \& A_n \& A \Rightarrow B))$$

where the *add_A* action changes the rule $A_1 \& \ldots \& A_n \Rightarrow B$.

Example: Programs

$$n \neq 0 \Rightarrow ([remainder(m, n, r)](Eq((m = q * n + r) \& (r < n))))$$

This expresses an input/output specification for a remainder program which has as parameters the natural numbers represented by the variables m, n, r. The input condition is $n \neq 0$, while the output condition expresses the usual characterization of the relationship between divisor, dividend, quotient and remainder.

We will now again follow the format outlined above to extend SC by extending the language and the derivability relation and by providing the appropriate standardness conditions on models to restrict them to those suitable for interpreting the extended linguistic system.

Let Ac be a collection of action symbols. The fact that Ac may be structured in some way is for the moment irrelevant. We will comment later on the possibility of generating Ac from statements of a conventional (Pascal-like) language. We will use α as a metavariable ranging over Ac.

Now if α is an action and A a formula, then $[\alpha]A$ is a formula.

(Distribution axiom) $\vdash ([\alpha](A \Rightarrow B)) \Rightarrow ([\alpha]A \Rightarrow ([\alpha]B))$ (P1)

(Rule of necessitation) $\dfrac{\vdash A}{\vdash [\alpha]A}$ (NE)

Note the similarity of P1 and NE to the corresponding M1 and N of the modal system K above. Also note that we have ceased naming the extensions we are building and have left the subscripts on $\vdash$ implicit.

A structure M over the above language is a pair $\langle S, \{R_{\alpha \in Ac}\} \rangle$ where

S is a collection of states (worlds) and each $R_\alpha \subseteq S \times S$. Each α is assigned a relation on states and actions are interpreted as moves from state to state. The relationship of this family of relations $\{R_\alpha\}$ to the accessibility relation used above for modal systems should be intuitively clear. We will usually write R_α as $[\![\alpha]\!]$ and use infix notation. We postulate

$$M \vDash_s [\alpha]A \text{ if and only if for all } s' \in S \text{ if } s [\![\alpha]\!] s', \text{ then } M \vDash_{s'} A$$

Thus the modally qualified formula $[\alpha]A$ is true in state s of structure M exactly when A is true in all states reachable from s by the action α.

We can express functionality of actions within this formalism in a straightforward manner. Given $M = \langle S, \{R_\alpha\} \rangle$ (for convenience we drop '$\alpha \in Ac$' as a subscript), the relation $[\![\alpha]\!]$ is a function exactly when $s[\![\alpha]\!]t$ and $s[\![\alpha]\!]u$ implies $t = u$. Then for any formulae A and B, any action α, and any structure M we can prove each of the following:

1. $M \vDash ([\alpha]A \Rightarrow [\alpha]B) \Rightarrow [\alpha](A \Rightarrow B)$
2. $M \vDash [\alpha](A\,|\,B) \Rightarrow ([\alpha]A\,|\,[\alpha]B)$
3. $M \vDash ([\alpha]A)\,|\,([\alpha]\,\neg A)$
4. $M \vDash (\neg[\alpha]A) \Rightarrow ([\alpha]\,\neg A)$

Theorem
The above formulae are equivalent, i.e. each is derivable from any of the others.

Theorem
For fixed M as above, if for a given $\alpha \in Ac$ we have $\vDash ([\alpha]A)\,|\,([\alpha]\,\neg A)$ for all formulae A, then $[\![\alpha]\!]$ is a function.

Thus, the two results above characterize functionality of an action in a structure M via the validity of the formula

$$([\alpha]A)\,|\,([\alpha]\,\neg A) \tag{F}$$

for arbitrary A. In fact, any of the equivalent formulae above will do.

Another important property of a relation $[\![\alpha]\!]$ is totality. $[\![\alpha]\!]$ is total if and only if for every $s \in S$, there exists $t \in S$ such that $s[\![\alpha]\!]t$. In programming, we know this concept as *termination*. The question naturally arises: can we characterize termination (totality) in the same way we have done for functionality above? We now demonstrate that this in fact is the case. Let us denote by *FALSE* any formula which is not satisfied in any state of M. (An obvious candidate for *FALSE* is $A \,\&\, (\neg A)$ for any A.) Then for any $\alpha \in Ac$,

$$[\alpha]FALSE$$

expresses non-termination of $[\![\alpha]\!]$. This is because if for any $s \in S$ we had $s[\![\alpha]\!]t$ for some t, then t would make *FALSE* true (valid)! Thus $\neg([\alpha]FALSE)$ expresses termination of the action α. For any given $\alpha \in Ac$, we might have an axiom of termination

$$\neg([\alpha]FALSE) \tag{T}$$

Now

$$M \vDash_s \neg([\alpha]FALSE)$$

if and only if there is some $s' \in S$ such that $s[\![\alpha]\!]s'$ (and $M \vDash_{s'} \neg FALSE$). Thus

$$M \vDash \neg[\alpha]FALSE$$

if and only if for all $s \in S$, there exists $s' \in S$ such that $s[\![\alpha]\!]s'$. Note that termination and functionality together give

$$\vDash([\alpha]\neg A) \Leftrightarrow (\neg[\alpha]A)$$

which characterizes $[\![\alpha]\!]$ as a total function (from states to states).

We sometimes want to talk about conditional termination and this is expressed by formulae of the form

$$A \Rightarrow \neg([\alpha]FALSE)$$

where we interpret the formula A as a precondition for termination. Our example of the remainder program specification was in fact of the form

$$A \Rightarrow [\alpha]B$$

We might think of A as a precondition and B as the postcondition of the action (program) α. (The reader may note that the A and B of the remainder program example were formulae of PC, not SC. Up to this point, we are building our logic on top of SC so such formulae would not be allowed. This can be overcome with care, although we will not do so here. The reader is referred to Goldblatt (1982).)

We now wish to characterize the nature of actions as defined in some simple programming language. To do this, we introduce basic actions (or commands) and indicate how we may characterize compound actions in terms of the properties of the constituent actions. Compound actions are defined in terms of constructs conventionally called 'control structures'. We begin by defining some of the basic actions (*NULL*, *ABORT*) and then define some of the conventional control structures: sequencing (composition), conditional, iteration (*WHILE* loops). We also mention the less conventional non-deterministic choice operation. Finally, we deal briefly with the problems of characterizing assignment statements (the principal kind of basic action).

Let *NULL* be an action, i.e. *NULL* $\in Ac$. We add the axiom schema

$$\vdash([NULL]A) \Leftrightarrow A \tag{Nu}$$

for any formula A and the standardness condition

　　$s[\![NULL]\!]t$ if and only if $s = t$

restricting structures to those in which the axiom $([NULL]A) \Leftrightarrow A$ will be true. The *NULL* action is meant to mimic the idea of 'no effect' for a program.

　　Let *ABORT* be an action, $ABORT \in Ac$. We add the axiom:

　　$\vdash[ABORT]FALSE$　　　　　　　　　　　　　　　　(Ab)

and the standardness condition

　　$\{t\colon$ there is an s such that $s[\![ABORT]\!]t\} = \varnothing$

Executing ABORT is meant to stop the program's further processing and thus does not allow the program to terminate normally. Hence *ABORT*'s only attributed property is that it does not terminate! The standardness condition requires that the relation $[\![ABORT]\!]$ be the empty relation.

　　Let α, $\beta \in Ac$. Then the *composition* $\alpha; \beta$ of α and β is also an action. Thus ; is an operation on actions (a *combinator*) which creates a new action. We add the axiom

　　$\vdash([\alpha; \beta]A) \Leftrightarrow ([\alpha][\beta]A)$　　　　　　　　　(Seq)

and the standardness condition

　　$s[\![\alpha;\beta]\!]t$ if and only if there exists $u \in S$ such that $s[\![\alpha]\!]u$ and $u[\![\beta]\!]t$.

Thus, doing the composite action $\alpha; \beta$ is exactly the same as first doing α and then doing β. The standardness condition indicates that we can get from state s to state t by performing $\alpha; \beta$ if and only if there is some state u which α takes us to from s and from which we can reach t by performing β. Observe that, as a result of this condition, the relation $[\![\alpha; \beta]\!]$ is fully determined by the relations $[\![\alpha]\!]$ and $[\![\beta]\!]$ (since $[\![\alpha; \beta]\!]$ is the relational composition of $[\![\alpha]\!]$ and $[\![\beta]\!]$).

　　If α, $\beta \in Ac$ and A is a formula of SC, then

　　IF A THEN α ELSE β FI

is an action. We add the axiom

　　$\vdash[IF\ A\ THEN\ \alpha\ ELSE\ \beta\ FI]B$
　　$\Leftrightarrow ((A \Rightarrow ([\alpha]B)) \ \&\ ((-A) \Rightarrow ([\beta]B)))$　　　　(Cond)

and the standardness condition

　　$s[\![IF\ A\ THEN\ \alpha\ ELSE\ \beta\ FI]\!]t$
　　if and only if
　　$(M \vDash_s A$ and $s[\![\alpha]\!]t)$ or $(M \vDash_s -A$ and $s[\![\beta]\!]t)$.

The axiom defines the conditional as having postcondition B if and only if either action α with precondition A makes B true or action β with precondition $\neg A$ makes B true. The standardness condition expresses the idea that the execution of the conditional takes us from state s to state t if and only if either A is true in s and α takes us from s to t, or A is false in s and then β takes us from s to t. Both correspond to our intuition concerning conditionals — we evaluate A; if it is true, we do α; if it is false, we do β.

The analysis of *WHILE* loops requires a little bit of care and provides our first point of departure from classical logic's concept of axiom and proof.

Let $\alpha \in Ac$ and A be a formula of SC. Then

WHILE A DO α OD

is also an action. The intention is, of course, that α is executed repeatedly until A becomes false. If A is false to start with, then α is not executed (so the effect of the while loop is that of *NULL*). Thus the standardness condition for the above should be:

$s[\![WHILE\ A\ DO\ \alpha\ OD]\!]t$ if and only if there exists a sequence $\langle s_0, \ldots, s_n \rangle$ such that

1. $s_0 = s, s_n = t$
2. $s_i[\![\alpha]\!]s_{i+1}, 0 \leq i < n$
3. $M \vDash_{s_n} \neg A$
4. $M \vDash_{s_i} A, i < n$

The *WHILE* loop's execution causes the change from state s to state t (condition (1)) if α takes us from s_i to s_{i+1} for each s_i in the sequence (condition (2)), and for each such step A is true before α is done (condition (4)). To try to capture this idea in the linguistic system, let us start by defining:

$\alpha^0 = NULL$
$\alpha^{k+1} = \alpha; \alpha^k$ for $k \geq 0$

α^k is meant to correspond to executing α k times in succession. The motivation is clearly that of having executed the body of the *WHILE* loop exactly k times for some $k \geq 0$. Then the formula

$[\alpha^k](\neg A \Rightarrow B)$

(or in general, $C \Rightarrow [\alpha^k](\neg A \Rightarrow B)$) means that having executed α exactly k times, if A (the test guarding the loop) is false, then the postcondition B holds. If the *WHILE* loop terminates, it will do so after some finite number of executions of α, say $k \geq 0$. Thus

$$\frac{[\alpha^k](\neg A \Rightarrow B) \text{ for each } k \geq 0}{[WHILE\ A\ DO\ \alpha\ OD]B} \qquad \text{(I)}$$

So what we would like is for the following formula to hold:

$[WHILE\ A\ DO\ \alpha\ OD]B$

$$\Leftrightarrow ((\neg A \Rightarrow B)$$
$$\& (A \Rightarrow [\alpha](\neg A \Rightarrow B))$$
$$\& (A \Rightarrow [\alpha](A \Rightarrow [\alpha](\neg A \Rightarrow B)))$$
$$\& \dots \qquad\qquad\qquad\qquad\qquad) \qquad (II)$$

(I) seems to point to a rule of inference which has an infinite number of formulae as premises: $[\alpha^k](\neg A \Rightarrow B)$ for $k \geqslant 0$. On the other hand, (II) is not a normal formula − it is infinite!

The normal procedure would be to characterize the *WHILE* loop in terms of the so-called fixed-point approach: the relation defined by the *WHILE* loop, *WHILE A DO α OD*,

$[\![WHILE\ A\ DO\ \alpha\ OD]\!] =$
$[\![IF\ A\ THEN\ (\alpha;\ WHILE\ A\ DO\ \alpha\ OD)\ ELSE\ NULL\ FI]\!]$

defines the meaning of a *WHILE* loop in terms of itself. We would then require the axioms:

$\vdash \neg A \Rightarrow \neg[WHILE\ A\ DO\ \alpha\ OD]FALSE$
$\vdash[WHILE\ A\ DO\ \alpha\ OD]B \Rightarrow (A \Rightarrow ([\alpha]([WHILE\ A\ DO\ \alpha\ OD]B)))$

or their equivalent. This has the disadvantage that, whereas we were able to reduce the other control structures to more primitive concepts, we are not able to do the same for *WHILE* loops. Another way of putting this is that to characterize ; and *IF...THEN...ELSE...FI* we need only a single formula without a self-reference. For the *WHILE* loop, we need the infinite set of formulae (letting $\beta = WHILE\ A\ DO\ \alpha\ OD$):

$[\beta]B \Rightarrow (A \Rightarrow ([\alpha]([\beta]B)))$
$[\beta]B \Rightarrow (A \Rightarrow ([\alpha](A \Rightarrow ([\alpha]([\beta]B)))))$
etc.

Whatever approach we take, *WHILE* loops would seem to require a characterization which goes beyond what is normally allowed in the logics we have discussed up to this point.

We will give a characterization of, *WHILE* loops using so-called infinitary rules of inference (requiring an infinite set of premises). We could also introduce infinitary formulae such as (II) above, but we will not do so here. Our notion of what constitutes a proof must now be changed. We must abandon the idea that proofs are finite sequences of formulae with the appropriate properties − the convention we have assumed since the first section. In the present setting, we require proofs which admit the statement of possibly infinite sets of premises for a given step. (The fact that the premises in this infinite set will in general be proved by induction is what saves us!)

Proceeding, we let

$$B_0(A, \alpha) = ((\neg A) \Rightarrow B)$$
$$B_{n+1}(A, \alpha) = (A \Rightarrow [\alpha] B_n(A, \alpha)) \text{ for } n \geqslant 0$$

and we would like

$$[WHILE\ A\ DO\ \alpha\ OD]B \Leftrightarrow (B_0\ \&\ B_1\ \&\ B_2\ \&\dots)$$

One can show the following result:

$$M \vDash_s [WHILE\ A\ DO\ \alpha\ OD]B \text{ if and only if for all } n \geqslant 0, M \vDash_s B_n(A, \alpha)$$

That is, after executing the loop, B is true if and only if the formulae $B_n(A, \alpha)$ are true for all $n \geqslant 0$. In other words, if and only if no matter how many times we execute α, if A becomes false, then B becomes true.

We can generalize this as follows.

Definition: The class of admissible forms, $ADFM$, is defined as follows:

1. $\# \in ADFM$.
2. If $D \in ADFM$ and $\alpha \in Ac$ then $([\alpha] D) \in ADFM$.
3. If $D \in ADFM$ and A is a formula then $A \Rightarrow D \in ADFM$.

For $D \in ADFM$, $D(A)$ is the formula obtained by replacing the occurrence of $\#$ in D by the formula A. (One can think of $\#$ as a prompt for a formula.) The reader may care to show that if $D \in ADFM$, D has exactly one occurrence of $\#$.

Theorem
If $D \in ADFM$, then $M \vDash_s D([WHILE\ A\ DO\ \alpha\ OD]B)$ if and only if for all $n \geqslant 0$ we have $M \vDash_s D(B_n(A, \alpha))$.

Thus admissible forms provide equivalent 'contexts' for the loop construct and the B_ns. To characterize while loops, we add the following infinitary rule:

$$\frac{\vdash D(B_n(A, \alpha)) \text{ for all } n \geqslant 0}{\vdash D([WHILE\ A\ DO\ \alpha\ OD]B)} \tag{W}$$

Finally, let us consider a non-deterministic choice operation: if $\alpha, \beta \in Ac$ then $\alpha\ OR\ \beta \in Ac$.

The intended meaning is that either α or β is done (but not both), and the choice as to which is purely random. We add the axiom:

$$\vdash ([\alpha\ OR\ \beta]A) \Leftrightarrow ([\alpha]A\ \&\ [\beta]A) \tag{ND}$$

and the standardness condition

$$[\![\alpha\ OR\ \beta]\!] \text{ is the set union of } [\![\alpha]\!] \text{ and } [\![\beta]\!]$$

Note that deterministic behaviour is functional behaviour — there is only one result (or at most one) from a given state. So the axiom (F) for functional behaviour serves as well to characterize deterministic behaviour.

The reader might care to compare the above development and notation with the Hoare logics for program verification (see Goldblatt, 1982). Hoare's formula

$$A\,\{\alpha\}\,B$$

is equivalent in the notation of this section to

$$A \Rightarrow [\alpha]\,B$$

However, Hoare logics normally restrict A and B above to non-modal formulae (i.e. no $[\alpha]$s!). Hoare's axioms and rules are simple consequences of those presented above.

Finally, as promised earlier, let us turn briefly to assignment, the main generator of actions in (conventional) programming languages. The standard Hoare assignment rule

$$A\,(x/t)\,\{x:= t\}\,A$$

becomes

$$A\,(x/t) \Rightarrow ([x:= t]A)$$

in our programming logic notation.

So far so good. However, we now encounter problems with what was in first-order logic a rather simple concept — variable substitution. Consider the assertion

$$[x:= y + 1]\,(x = y + 1)$$

which certainly seems intuitively correct. Let us now evaluate the seemingly innocuous substitution

$$([x:= y + 1]\,(x = y + 1))\,(y/x)$$

and we obtain

$$[x:= x + 1]\,(x = x + 1)$$

This clearly cannot be correct.

The assignment

$$x:= x + 1$$

is perfectly reasonable, so the problem must lie with how substitution in the whole formula was carried out.

The direction in which a solution is to be found is to think of an assignment as a variable binding operation analogous to $\mathbf{E}x$ and $\mathbf{A}x$. For example, in

$$[x:= x + 1]\,(x > 1)$$

the first and third occurrences of x are bound, while the second is free. Thus

$$([x:= x + 1](x > 1))(x/0) = [x:= 0 + 1](x > 1)$$

In the previous example,

$$([x:= y + 1](x = y + 1))(y/x)$$

is not a valid substitution because the second occurrence of y (the one in $x = y + 1$) is not free for x as an x appearing in this position would become bound by the assignment to x. The first occurrence of y (the one in $x:= y + 1$) is free for x!

Roughly speaking, the free variables in an expression are those whose function or meaning is not indicated by their syntactic rôle, but which have to be given a particular value before the whole expression can be said to have meaning. This suggests that the free occurrences in a program are those that serve only to denote the value of a variable prior to execution, and which do not alter their denotation as a result of that execution. Thus in

$$(y:= y + 1; x:= y)$$

the second occurrence of y should be free, but the other two bound, and in

$$WHILE\ r > y\ DO\ (r:= r - y)OD$$

both occurrences of y are free, while r has no free occurrence at all!

In summary, we would note that seemingly straightforward and intuitive concepts, such as those of inference rule and proof and even substitution can become problematic in new settings. New intuitions must be brought to bear to decide on appropriate definitions in novel settings.

A.6   Many-sorted theories

Up to this point we have been considering languages in which objects were all of the same kind. For example, the structure corresponding to a language L in PC consisted of a set (of objects) and an association of an object $a \in D$ with a constant c of L, a function from D^n to D with a function symbol f of rank n in L, and a subset of D^n with a relation symbol r of rank n in L. This is what is normally studied by mathematicians, but is not very convenient in computing. For example, we may wish to study a system in which we have lists of natural numbers. This system would have natural numbers and lists as objects, sets which we would not like to mix. For an operation like *cons* which is meant to take as arguments a natural number and a list and produce a list, it is very important that we be able to distinguish which kind of object we have.

We could actually cope in PC, but it would be awkward. It could be done as follows: introduce two new predicate symbols called *is-nat* and *is-list* which will be defined to be true in the appropriate situations. So we would need axioms such as:

is-nat(*zero*)
is-nat(*suc*(*zero*))
¬*is-nat*(*nil*) − the empty list is not a natural number
⋮

Also, when axiomatizing the theory of lists of naturals, we would have to condition axioms as follows:

$(is\text{-}nat(x) \ \& \ is\text{-}list(y)) \Rightarrow hd(cons(x, y)) = x$
$(is\text{-}nat(x) \ \& \ is\text{-}list(y)) \Rightarrow tl(cons(x, y)) = y$
⋮

Readers with some interest in programming language concepts will immediately recognize that 'PC is not strongly typed'. We will now proceed to define a strongly typed version of PC as an example of a many-sorted linguistic system. The phrase 'many-sorted' is highly suggestive of the nature of the system. An alternative adjective to describe such systems is 'heterogeneous'.

A.6.1 Many-sorted predicate calculus − MPC

As for PC, we will define the various syntactic categories we intend to use:

- **Sorts** (St) $s, s_1, s_2, s', \ldots$
- **Variables** $(SVar)$ $x^s, y^s, \ldots,$
  $$x^{s_1}, y^{s_1}, \ldots,$$
  ⋮
  We call $s, s_1, \ldots$ the *sorts* of the variables $x^s, x^{s_1}, \ldots$ and denote by $SVar_s$ the variables of sort s.
- **Logical symbols**, as in PC
- **Punctuation symbols**, as in PC
- **Predicate symbols** (SPr) for each sequence $t = \langle s_1, \ldots, s_n \rangle$ with $n \geq 1$ we have: $p^t, q^t, r^t, \ldots$. We call t the *type* of p^t and denote by SPr_t the set of all predicate symbols of type t.
- **Function symbols** (SFn) for each sequence $t = \langle s_1, \ldots, s_n \rangle$ with $n \geq 1$ and for each $s \in St$ we have: $f^{t, s}, g^{t, s}, h^{t, s}, \ldots$. We call $\langle t, s \rangle$ the type of $f^{t, s}$ and denote by $SFn_{\langle t, s \rangle}$ the set of all function symbols of type $\langle t, s \rangle$.
- **Constant symbols** (SC) for each $s \in St$ we have: $c^s, d^s, c_1^s, \ldots$. We call s the sort of c^s and denote by SC_s the set of all constant symbols of sort s.

The set St is meant to define (be names for) the different kinds of objects with which we might deal in MPC. Variables are *typed* in the sense that these variables will be allowed to assume values only from a particular set of objects. So if *list* is a sort and we have x^{list}, then we cannot substitute *zero* for x^{list} (always assuming *zero* is known to be a constant of sort natural number). Predicate, function and constant symbols are typed as well. If $f^{t,s}$ is a function symbol with $t = \langle s_1, \ldots, s_n \rangle$ then $f^{t,s}$ is expected to have an interpretation in a many-sorted structure (yet to be defined) which respects this typing: its first argument will come from objects of sort s_1, the second from sort s_2, etc. The range of the interpretation of $f^{t,s}$ in this structure is expected to be objects of sort s. Interpretations of predicate and constant symbols in a structure will have similar typing.

Names and terms are again defined in an inductive fashion; however, we now require a mutual recursion to define names and terms of a particular sort. We can think of SC as a family of sets $\{SC_s\}$ indexed by St. Similarly we can think of SFn as a family of sets $\{SFn_{\langle t,s \rangle}\}$ indexed by $St^+ \times S$, i.e. pairs of the form $\langle \langle s_1, \ldots, s_n \rangle, s \rangle$. ($St^+$ is the set of finite, non-empty strings of symbols over the set St.) Let $SName_s$ be the set of names of sort s. Then $SName$ is again a family $\{SName_s\}$ indexed by St which we define mutually recursively by:

$$SName_s ::= C_s \mid SFn_{\langle t_0, s \rangle}(SName_{s(0, 1)}, \ldots, SName_{s(0, n_0)})$$
$$\text{for } t_0 = \langle s(0, 1), \ldots, s(0, n_0) \rangle$$
$$\mid SFn_{\langle t_1, s \rangle}(SName_{s(1, 1)}, \ldots, SName_{s(1, n_1)})$$
$$\text{for } t_1 = \langle s(1, 1), \ldots, s(1, n_1) \rangle$$
$$\mid \ldots$$

where $t_0, t_1, \ldots$ is an enumeration of the set St^+. Thus we are allowed to substitute only names of the appropriate sort as arguments of function symbols of a particular type.

Terms are defined in a mutually recursive fashion as above, but allowing variables of the appropriate sorts along with constants. We let $STerm = \{STerm_s\}$.

The atomic formulae for a many-sorted language are defined as follows:

$$SAtomic ::= SPr_{t_0}(STerm_{s(0, 1)}, \ldots, STerm_{s(0, n_0)})$$
$$\text{for } t_0 = \langle s(0, 1), \ldots, s(0, n_0) \rangle$$
$$\mid SPr_{t_1}(STerm_{s(1, 1)}, \ldots, STerm_{s(1, n_1)})$$
$$\text{for } t_1 = \langle s(1, 1), \ldots, s(1, n_1) \rangle$$
$$\mid \ldots$$

where, again $t_0, t_1, \ldots$ is an enumeration of the set St^+. The set of formulae $SPCF$ is defined exactly as for PCF except for the alternatives involving quantifiers. We now require an alternative of the form

E $SVar_s$ $SPCF$

for each $s \in St$. Similarly for the universal quantifier **A**. Definitions of *bound, free* and *scope* are as before. *Derivability* is also as before with the exception of replacing the inference rule GEN with versions of the rule for each sort $s \in St$:

$$\frac{A}{\mathbf{A}x^s A} \tag{GEN_s}$$

A valuation system for MPC is again a straightforward generalization of that given for PC.

Definition: An interpretation I for a many-sorted first-order language L_{MPC} (i.e. the language of MPC) consists of:

1. a family

   $$\{D_{s \in St}\} = D$$

   of non-empty sets — the *domain of the interpretation*;

2. a function I from the predicate, function and constant symbols of L_{MPC} such that:
   a) for a predicate symbol $r \in SP_t$ with $t = \langle s_1, \ldots, s_n \rangle$,

      $$I(r) \subseteq D_{s_1} \times \ldots \times D_{s_n}$$

      (i.e. $I(r)$ is a subset of the correctly typed cartesian product of sets from D);
   b) for a function symbol $f \in SFn_{\langle t, s \rangle}$ with $t = \langle s_1, \ldots, s_n \rangle$,

      $$I(f):D_{s_1} \times \ldots \times D_{s_n} \rightarrow D_s$$

      (i.e. $I(f)$ is a function with first argument of sort $s_1, \ldots, n$'th argument of sort s_n, and result of sort s);
   c) for a constant symbol $c \in SC_s$, $I(c) \in D_s$ (i.e. a constant of sort s names a value in D_s, the domain of sort s).

A *sequence* or *assignment* in I is a family of functions from the family $\{SVar_s\}$ to the family $\{D_s\}$, mapping variables of sort s to values of sort s. *Satisfaction* is as before, as are *validity, satisfiability, simultaneous satisfiability* and *semantic consequence*.

Theories are also defined as before with a minor notational variant. If T is a theory in MPC, we say that the language of T is the pair $\langle S_T, L_T \rangle$ where L_T is the set of non-logical symbols used in T and S_T is the set of sorts used to type symbols in L_T.

At this point, an example might be helpful. We will describe a theory SORT_NAT (abbreviated as S_N in much of what follows) which would be adequate to discuss a program to sort a (finite) set of natural numbers into an ordered sequence. The theory SORT_NAT is developed to formalize exactly what we might mean by such concepts as set, ordered sequence, natural numbers and sorting.

Let us first consider the language of SORT_NAT, i.e. $L_{S\_N} = \langle S_{S\_N}, L_{S\_N} \rangle$, $S_{S\_N} = \{\mathbf{set}, \mathbf{seq}, \mathbf{nat}\}$.

For L_{S_N} we will use the following notation to indicate typing:

1. For function symbol f of type $\langle\langle s_1, \ldots, s_n\rangle, s\rangle$ we write

   $f: s_1 \times \ldots \times s_n \to s$

2. For relation symbol r of type $\langle s_1, \ldots, s_n\rangle$ we write

   $r: s_1 \times \ldots \times s_n \to \{true, false\}$

3. For constant symbol c of sort s we write

   $c: \to s$

Thus we have for natural numbers:

$zero:$ $\quad\quad\quad\;\to$ **nat**
$suc:$ **nat** $\quad\quad\to$ **nat**
$lt:$ **nat** $\times$ **nat** $\to \{true, false\}$

So we have a constant *zero*, a unary function *suc* ('add one') and the binary relation *lt*.

For sets we have

$empty:$ $\quad\quad\quad\quad\to$ **set**
$insert:$ **nat** $\times$ **set** $\quad\to$ **set**
$remove:$ **nat** $\times$ **set** $\to$ **set**
$choose:$ **set** $\quad\quad\quad\to$ **nat**
$ismember:$ **nat** $\times$ **set** $\to \{true, false\}$

empty will name the empty set, *insert* is to be used to add a value to a set, *remove* takes a particular value out of the set, *choose* is meant to display an arbitrary value from a set (without removing it), and *ismember* is the usual set membership predicate.

For sequence we have:

$nil:$ $\quad\quad\quad\quad\quad\quad\quad\to$ **seq**
$ordins:$ **nat** $\times$ **seq** $\quad\quad\to$ **seq**
$precedes:$ **nat** $\times$ **nat** $\times$ **seq** $\to \{true, false\}$
$occurs:$ **nat** $\times$ **seq** $\quad\quad\to \{true, false\}$

nil will name the empty sequence, *ordins* will be used to insert a value in order in a sequence, *occurs* is a predicate to be used to determine whether a value occurs in a sequence, and *precedes* is a predicate to be used to check whether one value occurs before another in a sequence.

For sorting we have:

$sort:$ **set** $\quad\quad\to$ **seq**
$ordered:$ **seq** $\quad\to \{true, false\}$
$same:$ **seq** $\times$ **set** $\to \{true, false\}$

sort is to be used to map a set to the corresponding ordered sequence, *ordered* is to be used to check whether a sequence is ordered, and *same* is to be used to check whether a sequence contains exactly those values to be found in a set.

We have grouped the symbols of L_{S_N} to aid intuition and we will do the same now with the axioms defining SORT_NAT. Note that we are assuming that equality is a logical concept and there is a typed equality predicate $=_s$ for each sort s. We usually drop the subscript when the sort is clear from the context. We will use the following variables:

m, n: **nat**
s, t : **set**
q : **seq**

For natural numbers we have:

$$\vdash \neg(zero = suc(n)) \tag{A1}$$
$$\vdash suc(m) = suc(n) \Rightarrow m = n \tag{A2}$$
$$\vdash lt(suc(m), suc(n)) \Leftrightarrow lt(m, n) \tag{A3}$$
$$\vdash lt(zero, suc(n)) \tag{A4}$$
$$\vdash \neg lt(zero, zero) \tag{A5}$$
$$\vdash \neg lt(suc(n), zero) \tag{A6}$$

(A1) and (A2) are used to exclude trivial models, i.e. we want to make sure that 'adding one' really does give us a different value. (A3)–(A6) are used to define the *less than* relation on natural numbers.

For sets we have:

$$\vdash (An(ismember(n, s) \Leftrightarrow ismember(n, t)) \Rightarrow s = t \tag{A7}$$
$$\vdash \neg ismember(n, empty) \tag{A8}$$
$$\vdash ismember(m, insert(n, s)) \Leftrightarrow ((m = n) | ismember(m, s)) \tag{A9}$$
$$\vdash ismember(m, remove(n, s)) \Leftrightarrow (\neg(m = n) \& ismember(m, s)) \tag{A10}$$
$$\vdash \neg(s = empty) \Rightarrow ismember(choose(s), s) \tag{A11}$$

(A7) indicates that if sets have the same values in them then they are equal. (A8) tells us that nothing belongs to the empty set. (A9) defines insertion recursively in terms of equality and belonging. (A10) defines *remove* recursively in terms of equality and belonging. (A11) tells us that *choose* does give us a value from a (non-empty) set.

For sequences we have:

$$\vdash \neg occurs(n, nil) \tag{A12}$$
$$\vdash ordered(q) \Rightarrow ordered(ordins(n, q)) \tag{A13}$$
$$\vdash occurs(m, ordins(n, q)) \Leftrightarrow (m = n | occurs(m, q)) \tag{A14}$$

(A12) tells us that no value occurs in the empty sequence. (A13) tells us that *ordins* preserves the orderedness of sequences. (A14) defines *ordins* recursively in terms of equality and *occurs*.

For sorting we have:

$$\vdash (sort(t) = q) \Leftrightarrow (ordered(q) \ \& \ same(q, t)) \tag{A15}$$

$$\vdash same(q, t) \Leftrightarrow \mathbf{A}n(occurs(n, q) \Leftrightarrow ismember(n, t)) \tag{A16}$$

$$\vdash ordered(q) \Leftrightarrow \mathbf{A}m\mathbf{A}n(occurs(m, q) \ \& \ occurs(n, q) \ \& \\ lt(m, n) \Rightarrow precedes(m, n, q)) \tag{A17}$$

$$\vdash occurs(m, q) \ \& \ occurs(n, q) \Rightarrow (precedes(m, n, q)| \\ precedes(n, m, q)) \tag{A18}$$

$$\vdash \neg (precedes(m, n, q) \ \& \ precedes(n, m, q)) \tag{A19}$$

$$\vdash precedes(m, n, q) \ \& \ precedes(l, m, q) \Rightarrow precedes(l, n, q) \tag{A20}$$

(A15)–(A20) define *sort* in terms of *ordered*, *precedes* and *same* which are ascribed their obvious meaning.

To define a model of SORT_NAT we need to give a domain D and interpretation I, as follows:

$$D_{nat} = \{0, 1, 2, \dots\}$$
$$D_{set} = \{S : S \text{ is a finite subset of } D_{nat}\}$$
$$D_{seq} = D_{nat}^*$$

where, for a given set R, R^* is the set of possibly empty finite strings from R. For sequences, i.e. elements of D_{nat}^*, we shall use the notation: λ for the empty sequence, $Q_1.Q_2$ for concatenation of sequences Q_1 and Q_2, and $k.Q$ for the sequence with natural number k at the front and followed by the sequence Q. Clearly then we have:

$I(zero) = 0$
$(I(suc))(k) = k + 1$ for $k \in D_{nat}$
$I(lt) = <$ (the usual less than relation of D_{nat})
$I(empty) = \emptyset$ (the empty set)
$(I(insert))(k,S) = S \cup \{k\}$ for $S \subseteq D_{nat}$
$(I(remove))(k,s) = S - \{k\}$ for $S \subseteq D_{nat}$
$(I(choose))(S) = min(S)$ (the minimum value in S) if $S \neq \emptyset$ and an arbitrary element of D_{nat} otherwise[†]

$I(ismember) = \in$ (the usual set membership)
$I(nil) = \lambda$
$(I(ordins))(k, \lambda) = k$ (the string with only one symbol, the value k)
$(I(ordins))(k,j.Q) = k.j.Q$ if $k < j$, and $(j.(I(ordins))(k,Q))$ otherwise
$\langle k, Q \rangle \in I(occurs)$ if Q is of the form $Q_1.k.Q_2$ for strings Q_1, Q_2

[†] In building a computer implementation, one could for instance select an integer which cannot be handled by standard arithmetic routines. This will ensure that every application of *choose* to an empty set (which should not occur in decent programs) causes a run-time error or interrupt.

$\langle j, k, Q \rangle \in I(precedes)$ if Q is of the form $Q_1.j.Q_2.k.Q_3$ for strings Q_1, Q_2, Q_3

We leave the definitions of $I(sort)$, $I(ordered)$ and $I(same)$ to the reader. To confirm that this structure is a model of SORT_NAT, we have to show that (A1)–(A20) are valid. We again leave this to the reader.

Note that we could have obtained a different model of SORT_NAT by replacing the qualification 'finite' in the definition of D_{set} by 'countable'. What corresponding change would have to be made in the definition of D_{seq}? Yet a different model could be defined by replacing D_{nat} by some non-standard model of the naturals with corresponding changes elsewhere. Neither of these two changes would lead to models which would be useful in computing.

A.7   Interpretations between theories

Finally, we want to consider a very important activity in program development – translation. An automatic form of this activity is compiling. Other examples include the concept of implementation or stepwise refinement as outlined in the main body of the book. Aside from the mere technical details of the definition, the most important property of translations is that they be property preserving. If we prove some properties of a program based on some theory of the abstract data objects used in that program and we then implement these by more primitive/ concrete data objects, we expect that the reasoning we did at the abstract level still holds for the abstract objects as translated to concrete objects. Otherwise we would loose all the work we had done at the abstract level and would presumably have to redo all the work at the more concrete level. This is in general much more difficult because of the extra details used at the concrete level and exactly what we wanted to avoid by the use of abstraction and stepwise refinement.

Since we want to discuss property preserving translations, we can ask whether such translations deal with theories as the objects of interest or whether they deal with (translations between) linguistic systems. Because we are interested in this book in the concept of specification and identify specifications with theories, the former alternative is the one we wish to explore[†].

Several different notions of translation have been proposed in the literature (Enderton, 1972; Veloso and Pequeno, 1978; Goguen et al., 1978). It is not quite clear which one is the most appropriate. In the

---

[†] A largely neglected, but for computer science very important area of concern is the concept of translation between two theories in different linguistic systems. It is not at all clear here what the appropriate notion of translation should be and extensive work is required.

case of PC, an obvious candidate has been developed by logicians: interpretations between theories. Computer scientists have extended this idea to MPC, many-sorted first-order logic, and it is this that we will discuss below. Some efforts have also been made by computer scientists to develop an appropriate notion of translation for equational logics (Ehrig *et al.*, 1982; Ehrich, 1982), although the results are less general and therefore have been less useful than those for PC and MPC.

Now, each linguistic system will have its own technical definition of translation/interpretation between theories depending on the nature of the linguistic system. The common factors relating these concepts can however be identified as including the following:

1. The logical constants (symbols) need no translation as they form the common infrastructure for the two theories under consideration. Thus translations concentrate on realizing the extralogical symbols of one theory in terms of those of another.

2. Translations between theories will induce translations between corresponding models. Some (abstract) objects in a model of the theory being translated may be represented by more than one (concrete) object in the model of the theory which is the target of the translation. In our example below, we will choose to represent a set (of natural numbers) by any list (of natural numbers) with no repetition of values in the list, as long as it contains the 'same' natural numbers as the set.

3. Given the induced translation between models, we may have some concrete objects in the model of the target theory which are not used to represent any objects in the model of the abstract theory. We will need to differentiate between representatives and such non-representatives within models of the target theory in order to make sense of property preservation. The concept of relativization predicate (see below) is introduced to cope with this problem.

4. Translation of formulae involving quantifiers may be tricky in the following sense. Quantifiers usually relate the quantified variable to the range of possible values in structures. Since formulae are used to define properties, when these property definitions are translated, care must be taken to make sure that the translated formulae are restricted in the domain of values to which they might potentially be applied. The concept of relativization is again pertinent.

We now proceed in stages to define for MPC the concept of interpretations between theories. The stages are:

1. interpretations between many sorted languages;

2. interpretations between a many sorted language and a many sorted theory; and

3. interpretations between two many sorted theories.

Definition:

Let $\langle S, L \rangle$ and $\langle S', L' \rangle$ be two languages in MPC. Let s, a, b, ..., c be sorts of S and let a', b', ..., c' be sorts of S'. An *interpretation* ι of $\langle S, L \rangle$ in $\langle S', L' \rangle$ consists of the following maps:

1. $\phi\colon S \to (S')^+$ assigning to each sort $s \in S$ some (non-empty) sequence of sorts $\langle a', b', \ldots, c' \rangle$ over S'. (The intention is that an object of sort s will be represented in general by a tuple of objects of sorts a', b', ..., c' respectively in S'.)

2. $\pi\colon L \to (L')^+$ assigning to each symbol of L some (non-empty) sequence (or tuple) of symbols of L' where:

   a) If $c_s \in L$ is a constant of sort $s \in S$, then

   $$\pi(c_s) = \langle c_{a'}, c_{b'}, \ldots, c_{c'} \rangle$$

   where $\phi(s) = \langle a', b', \ldots, c' \rangle$. Thus a constant of L is assigned a tuple of constants of L' with sorts respecting the assignment defined by ϕ.

   b) If $f \in L$ is a function symbol of type $\langle \langle a, b, \ldots, c \rangle, s \rangle$, then

   $$\pi(f) = \langle f', g', \ldots, h' \rangle$$

   where f', g', ..., h' are functions of L' with

   f' of sort $\langle \phi(a) \cdot \phi(b) \cdot \ldots \cdot \phi(c), a' \rangle$
   g' of sort $\langle \phi(a) \cdot \phi(b) \cdot \ldots \cdot \phi(c), b' \rangle$
   $\vdots$
   h' of sort $\langle \phi(a) \cdot \phi(b) \cdot \ldots \cdot \phi(c), c' \rangle$

   where $\phi(s) = \langle a', b', \ldots, c' \rangle$.

   Thus, to each function of L there corresponds a tuple of function symbols of L'. The number of function symbols of L' used depends on the sort $s \in S$ which defines the target sort of f. Each function symbol of L' in this tuple has the same *arity* (sorting of the arguments). This is again determined by the images under ϕ of the sorts defining the arity of $f \in L$.

   c) If $r \in L$ is a predicate symbol of type $\langle a, b, \ldots, c \rangle$ then

   $$\pi(r) = r'$$

   where $r' \in L'$ has type $\phi(a) \cdot \phi(b) \cdot \ldots \cdot \phi(c)$. Thus to each predicate symbol of L there corresponds a predicate symbol of L' with typing consistent with that of L and the map ϕ.

3. $\rho\colon S \to L'$ assigning to each sort $s \in S$ some predicate symbol $r_s \in L'$ of type $\phi(s) = \langle a', b', \ldots, c' \rangle$.

4. $\upsilon\colon MVar \to (MVar)^+$ assigning to each variable x of sort $s \in S$ some tuple of variables $v(x_s) = \langle x_{a'}, x_{b'}, \ldots, x_{c'} \rangle$ where $\phi(s) = \langle a', b', \ldots, c' \rangle$. This map must be one to one.

We will show how to translate the language of sets of natural numbers (sorts **nat**, **set**; symbols *zero*, *suc*, $=_{\text{nat}}$, *lt*, *empty*, *insert*, *remove*, *choose*, *ismember*, = $_{\text{set}}$) into a language employed to define sequences of naturals together with some extra symbols added to support the representation of sets in terms of sequences. (Why and how these symbols are added is discussed at length in the body of the book.) This language, $\langle S_{\text{extseq}}, L_{\text{extseq}} \rangle$ is defined as follows:

$$S_{\text{extseq}} = \{\textbf{seq, nat}\}$$

Technically, this **nat** is different from the **nat** of sets of naturals; also the symbols *zero, suc,* = $_{\text{nat}}$, *lt* below will differ from the corresponding symbols for naturals in sets of naturals.

zero :	→ **nat**
suc : **nat**	→ **nat**
= $_{\text{nat}}$: **nat** × **nat**	→ {*true, false*}
lt : **nat** × **nat**	→ {*true, false*}
nil :	→ **seq**
head : **seq**	→ **nat**
tail : **seq**	→ **seq**
cons : **nat** × **seq**	→ **seq**
set-rep : **seq**	→ {*true, false*}
isin : **nat** × **seq**	→ {*true, false*}
once : **nat** × **seq**	→ {*true, false*}
is-nat : **nat**	→ {*true, false*}
insert' : **nat** × **seq**	→ **seq**
remove' : **nat** × **seq**	→ **seq**
choose' : **seq**	→ **nat**
= $'_{\text{set}}$: **seq** × **seq**	→ {*true, false*}

The intended meanings of the symbols *nil, head, tail* and *cons* are their conventional ones. *set-rep* will be used as the relativization predicate for the sort **set**; *isin* and *once* will be used to define *set-rep* and have the meanings: 'does *n* occur in the sequence *l*', 'does *n* occur exactly once in the sequence *l*', respectively. *is-nat* will be the relativization predicate for **nat** of sets of naturals. The primed symbols will be used as interpretations of some of the symbols of sets of naturals.

We are now ready to define an interpretation

$$\iota : \langle S_{\text{set}}, L_{\text{set}} \rangle \to \langle S_{\text{extseq}}, L_{\text{extseq}} \rangle$$

ϕ is defined by the assignments[†]:

    set ↦ **seq**
    nat ↦ **nat**

π is defined by the assignments:

    zero ↦ *zero*
    suc ↦ *suc*

[†] where $a \mapsto b$ denotes *assignment* of *b* to *a*.

$$=_{nat} \qquad\qquad \mapsto\ =_{nat}$$
$$lt \qquad\qquad\qquad \mapsto lt$$
$$empty \qquad\quad \mapsto nil$$
$$insert \qquad\quad \mapsto insert'$$
$$remove \qquad \mapsto remove'$$
$$choose \qquad \mapsto choose'$$
$$ismember \mapsto isin$$
$$=_{set} \qquad\qquad \mapsto\ ='_{set}$$

ρ is defined by the assignments:

set $\mapsto$ *set-rep*

nat $\mapsto$ *is-nat*

υ is defined by the assignments (of the form):

$n \mapsto n$ for n of sort **nat**

$t\ \mapsto l$ for t of sort **set** and l of sort **seq**

(Recall that υ must be one to one!)

Given an interpretation $\iota : \langle S, L \rangle \rightarrow \langle S', L' \rangle$, we can give a straight-forward inductive definition for a map which translates terms over $\langle S, L \rangle$ to (tuples of) terms over $\langle S', L' \rangle$. We will, for convenience, also denote this translation by ι and write $(t)^\iota$ to denote the application of this map to term t. (For the sake of simplicity, we will ignore the fact that this new map is really a family of maps ι_s, indexed by S.)

Definition: Given $\iota : \langle S, L \rangle \rightarrow \langle S', L' \rangle$, we define

$()^\iota : Term\ (\langle S, L \rangle) \rightarrow (Term(\langle S', L' \rangle))^+$

inductively as follows:

1. If $t = x$ for variable x, then

   $(x)^\iota = \upsilon(x)$

2. If $t = c$ a constant, then

   $(c)^\iota = \pi(c)$

3. If $t = f(t_1, \ldots, t_m)$, then

   $(t)^\iota = \langle f'_1((t_1)^\iota, \ldots, (t_m)^\iota), \ldots, f'_n((t_1)^\iota, \ldots, (t_m)^\iota) \rangle$

where $\pi(f) = \langle f'_1, \ldots, f'_n \rangle$.

Example

Given the interpretation ι of the previous example, we have the following examples of a translation of terms:

$(remove(choose(t), t))^\iota$

$\qquad\qquad\qquad$ where $t = insert(suc(suc(n)), empty)$

$= \pi(remove)((choose(t))^\iota, (t)^\iota)$

$= remove'(\pi(choose)((t)^\iota), (t)^\iota)$

$= remove'(choose'((t)^\iota), (t)^\iota)$

$$(t)^\iota = (insert(suc(suc(n)), empty))^\iota$$
$$= \pi(insert)((suc(suc(n)))^\iota, (empty)^\iota)$$
$$= insert'(\pi(suc)((suc(n))^\iota), \pi(empty))$$
$$= insert'(suc(\pi(suc)((n)^\iota)), nil)$$
$$= insert'(suc(suc(n)), nil)$$

We may now proceed to translations of formulae.

We first define $tr(\iota)$: $Form(\langle S, L \rangle) \rightarrow Form(\langle S', L' \rangle)$ inductively on the structure of formulae:

1. If A is atomic and of the form

   $$r(t_1, \ldots, t_n)$$

   for a predicate symbol $r \in L$ and terms $t_1, \ldots, t_n$ over L, then

   $$(r(t_1, \ldots, t_n))^{tr(\iota)} = \pi(r)((t_1)^\iota, \ldots, (t_n)^\iota)$$

2. If A is of the form $B|C$, then

   $$(B|C)^{tr(\iota)} = B^{tr(\iota)}|C^{tr(\iota)}$$

   and similarly

   $$(B \& C)^{tr(\iota)} = B^{tr(\iota)} \& C^{tr(\iota)}$$
   $$(B \Rightarrow C)^{tr(\iota)} = B^{tr(\iota)} \Rightarrow C^{tr(\iota)}$$
   $$(B \Leftrightarrow C)^{tr(\iota)} = B^{tr(\iota)} \Leftrightarrow C^{tr(\iota)}$$
   $$(\neg B)^{tr(\iota)} = \neg((B)^{tr(\iota)})$$

3. If A is of the form $\mathbf{A}x^s B$, then

   $$(\mathbf{A}x^s B)^{tr(\iota)} = \mathbf{A}(x^s)^\iota (\rho(s)((x^s)^\iota) \Rightarrow (B)^{tr(\iota)})$$

   where x^s is of sort $s \in S$, and $\rho(s)((x^s)^\iota)$ is used to indicate the relativization predicate $\rho(s)$ corresponding to $s \in S$, with the variables in the tuple $(x^s)^\iota$ as arguments of the predicate.

   Similarly, if A is of the form $\mathbf{E}x^s B$, then

   $$(\mathbf{E}x^s B)^{tr(\iota)} = \mathbf{E}(x^s)^\iota (\rho(s)((x^s)^\iota) \& (B)^{tr(\iota)})$$

Definition: Given ι: $\langle S, L \rangle \rightarrow \langle S', L' \rangle$, we define $()^\iota$: $Form(\langle S, L \rangle) \rightarrow Form(\langle S', L' \rangle)$ as follows. Let A be a formula in $Form(\langle S, L \rangle)$ and let $x_1, \ldots, x_n$ be the free variables in A with corresponding sorts $s_1, \ldots, s_n \in S$. Then

$$(A)^\iota = \rho(s_1)((x_1)^\iota) \& \rho(s_2)((x_2)^\iota) \& \ldots \& \rho(s_n)((x_n)^\iota) \Rightarrow (A)^{tr(\iota)}$$

(Thus we condition or relativize the translation of A to be applicable only if the free variables really represent abstract objects.)

Example
Let t be a variable of sort **set** and m, n variables of sort **nat**. Then:

$$(\mathbf{A}t\mathbf{A}m\mathbf{A}n(ismember(m, remove(n, t)) \Leftrightarrow$$
$$(\neg(m =_{nat} n) \& ismember(m, t))))^\iota$$

$$= \mathbf{A}(t)^{\iota} \ (set\text{-}rep((t)^{\iota})) \Rightarrow (\mathbf{A}m\mathbf{A}n(ismember(m, remove(n, t)))$$
$$\Leftrightarrow (\neg (m =_{nat} n) \ \& \ ismember \ (m, t))))^{tr(\iota)})$$
$$= \mathbf{A}l(set\text{-}rep(l)$$
$$\Rightarrow (\mathbf{A}(m)^{\iota} \ (is\text{-}nat((m)^{\iota})$$
$$\Rightarrow (\mathbf{A}n(ismember(m, remove(n, t)))$$
$$\Leftrightarrow (\neg (m =_{nat} n) \ \& \ ismember(m, t))))^{tr(\iota)})))$$
$$= \mathbf{A}l(set\text{-}rep(l)$$
$$\Rightarrow (\mathbf{A}m(is\text{-}nat(m)$$
$$\Rightarrow (\mathbf{A}(n)^{\iota} \ (is\text{-}nat((n)^{\iota})$$
$$\Rightarrow (ismember(m, remove(n, t)))$$
$$\Leftrightarrow (\neg (m =_{nat} n) \ \& \ ismember \ (m, t)))^{tr(\iota)}))))$$
$$= \mathbf{A}l(set\text{-}rep(l)$$
$$\Rightarrow (\mathbf{A}m(is\text{-}nat(m)$$
$$\Rightarrow (\mathbf{A}n(is\text{-}nat(n)$$
$$\Rightarrow (\pi(ismember)((m)^{\iota}, (remove(n, t))^{\iota})$$
$$\Leftrightarrow ((\neg (m =_{nat} n))^{tr(\iota)} \ \& \ (ismember(m, t))^{tr(\iota)}))))))$$
$$\vdots$$
$$= \mathbf{A}l(set\text{-}rep(l)$$
$$\Rightarrow (\mathbf{A}m(is\text{-}nat(m)$$
$$\Rightarrow (\mathbf{A}n(is\text{-}nat(n)$$
$$\Rightarrow (isin(m, remove'(n, l))$$
$$\Leftrightarrow (\neg (m =_{nat} n) \ \& \ isin(m, l)))))))$$

Definition: Let $\langle S, L \rangle$ be a language in MPC and let $\langle \langle S', L' \rangle, G' \rangle$ be a theory in MPC. An *interpretation* ι of a *language* $\langle S, L \rangle$ in a *theory* $\langle \langle S', L' \rangle, G' \rangle$ is an interpretation $\iota: \langle S, L \rangle \rightarrow \langle S', L' \rangle$ such that:

1. for each sort $s \in S$, the corresponding relativization predicate r_s has the closure property
$$G' \vdash E \xi_{a'} \ldots \xi_{c'} r_s(\xi_{a'}, \ldots, \xi_{c'})$$
where $\phi(s) = \langle a', \ldots, c' \rangle$ and ξ_t stands for a variable sort t;

2. for each constant α_s in L,
$$G' \vdash r_s(\pi(\alpha_s))$$
where α_s is of sort $s \in S$;

3. for each function symbol f in L of sort $\langle \langle a, b, \ldots, c \rangle, s \rangle$
$$G' \vdash r_a(\phi(x_a)) \ \& \ \ldots \ \& \ r_c(\phi(x_c)) \Rightarrow$$
$$r_s(f'(v(x_a), \ldots, v(x_c)), g'(v(x_a), \ldots, v(x_c)), \ldots,$$
$$h'(v(x_a), \ldots, v(x_c)))$$
where
$$\pi(f) = \langle f', g', \ldots, h' \rangle$$
$$\phi(s) = \langle a', b', \ldots, c' \rangle$$

and

$$f' \text{ is of type } \langle \phi(a) \cdot \ldots \cdot \phi(c), a' \rangle$$
$$g' \text{ is of type } \langle \phi(a) \cdot \ldots \cdot \phi(c), b' \rangle$$
$$\vdots$$
$$h' \text{ is of type } \langle \phi(a) \cdot \ldots \cdot \phi(c), c' \rangle$$

This all seems rather intimidating, but (1) tells us that we can derive from G' the fact that the domains of the relativization predicates used to define the interpretation ι are non-empty, while (2) and (3) tell us that the domains defined by the relativization predicates are closed under the operations corresponding to constant and function symbols in L.

Example

Sequences of natural numbers are defined by the axioms (A1)–(A6) (for natural numbers) and the following axioms in which m and n range over natural numbers, while k and l range over sequences:

$$\vdash (cons(m, k) = cons(n, l)) \Rightarrow (m =_{\text{nat}} n \ \& \ k =_{\text{seq}} l) \tag{A21}$$
$$\vdash head(cons(m, l)) = m \tag{A22}$$
$$\vdash tail(cons(m, l)) = l \tag{A23}$$
$$\vdash tail(nil) = nil \tag{A24}$$
$$\vdash set\text{-}rep(l) \Leftrightarrow \mathbf{A}m(isin(m, l) \Rightarrow once(m, l)) \tag{A25}$$
$$\vdash isin(m, l) \Leftrightarrow (\neg(l = nil) \ \& \ ((head(l) = m)$$
$$|isin(m, tail(l)))) \tag{A26}$$
$$\vdash once(m, l) \Leftrightarrow (\neg(l = nil)$$
$$\& \ ((head(l) = m \ \& \ \neg isin(m, tail(l)))$$
$$|(\neg(head(l) = m) \ \& \ once(m, tail(l))))) \tag{A27}$$
$$\vdash is\text{-}nat(m) \tag{A28}$$
$$\vdash insert'(m, k) = l \Leftrightarrow$$
$$((isin(m, k) \ \& \ k = l)|(\neg isin(m, k) \ \& \ l = cons(m, k))) \tag{A29}$$
$$\vdash remove'(m, k) = l$$
$$\Leftrightarrow ((\neg isin(m, k) \ \& \ k = l)$$
$$|(isin(m, k) \ \& \ ((m = head(k) \ \& \ l = tail(k))$$
$$|(\neg(m = head(k)) \ \& \ l = cons(head(k),$$
$$remove'(m, tail(k))))))) \tag{A30}$$
$$\vdash choose'(k) = m \Rightarrow isin(m, k) \tag{A31}$$
$$\vdash (k ='_{\text{set}} l) \Leftrightarrow (\ \forall \ m(isin(m, k) \Leftrightarrow isin(m, l))) \tag{A32}$$

Call these axioms G_{extseq} and let the corresponding language be $\langle S_{\text{extseq}}, L_{\text{extseq}} \rangle$. Then the interpretation between languages

$$\iota: \langle S_{\text{set}}, L_{\text{set}} \rangle \to \langle S_{\text{extseq}}, L_{\text{extseq}} \rangle$$

is an interpretation from a language to a theory

$$\iota: \langle S_{\text{set}}, L_{\text{set}} \rangle \to \langle \langle S_{\text{extseq}}, L_{\text{extseq}} \rangle, G_{\text{extseq}} \rangle$$

The reader is asked to verify for himself that conditions (1)–(3) above are satisfied.

Definition: Let $\langle\langle S, L\rangle, G\rangle$ and $\langle\langle S', L'\rangle, G'\rangle$ be theories in MPC. Then

$$\iota: \langle\langle S, L\rangle, G\rangle \to \langle\langle S', L'\rangle, G'\rangle$$

is an *interpretation between theories* if:

$$\iota: \langle S, L\rangle \to \langle\langle S', L'\rangle, G'\rangle$$

is an interpretation and, further, for formula A over the language L, if $G \vdash A$ then $G' \vdash A^\iota$.

In other words, ι is an interpretation between theories if it is a property-preserving translation from the underlying language $\langle S, L\rangle$ to the theory $\langle\langle S', L'\rangle, G'\rangle$. Thus for any formula derivable from G we can derive its translation from G'. In this way, an interpretation is a faithful translation.

Example

Consider the sets of natural numbers defined by axioms (A1)–(A11). We will refer to this set of axioms as G_{set}. Then

$$\iota: \langle\langle S_{set}, L_{set}\rangle, G_{set}\rangle \to \langle\langle S_{extseq}, L_{extseq}\rangle, G_{extseq}\rangle$$

is an interpretation between theories. We will not ask the reader to verify this as G_{set} has an infinite set of consequences and this checking might prevent the reader from reading the rest of this book.

References

Bauer, F.L. and Wössner, H. (1982) *Algorithmic Language and Program Development*. Springer Verlag, Berlin, Heidelberg, New York.

Barringer, H., Cheng, J.H. and Jones, C.B. (1984) *A Logic Covering Undefinedness in Program Proofs*. Tech. Rep., Dept of Computer Science, University of Manchester.

Barstow, D., Shrobe, H. and Sanderwell, E. (Eds) (1984) *Interactive Programming Environments*. McGraw-Hill, Maidenhead.

Boyer, R. and Moore, S. (1979) *A Computational Logic*. Academic Press, New York.

Broy, M. and Wirsing, M. (1982) Partial abstract data types. *Acta Informatica* **18**, 47–64.

Burstall, R.M. and Goguen, J.A. (1977) Putting theories together to make specifications. In: *Proc. 5th International Joint Conference on Artificial Intelligence*, Cambridge, Mass., pp.1045–1058.

Burstall, R.M. and Goguen, J.A. (1980) Semantics of Clear, a specification language. In: *Abstract Software Specifications. Proc 1979 Copenhagen Winter School*, D. Bjørner (Ed.). LNCS 86. Springer-Verlag, New York, Heidelberg, Berlin.

CIP Language Group (1985) *Report on a Wide Spectrum Language for Program Specification and Development*. LNCS 183. Springer-Verlag, New York, Heidelberg, Berlin.

Correll, C.H. (1978) Proving programs correct through refinement. *Acta Informatica* **9**, 121–132.

Dahl, O.-J., Dijkstra, E.W. and Hoare, C.A.R. (1972) *Structured Programming*. Academic Press, New York.

de Marco, T. (1978) *Structured Analysis and System Specification*. Yourdon Press, New York.

Deussen, P. (1975) A decidability criterion for van Wijngaarden grammars. *Acta Informatica* **5**, 353–375.

Dijkstra, E.W. (1968) The structure of THE multiprogramming system. *CACM* **11**, 341–346.

Dijkstra, E.W. (1976) *A Discipline of Programming*. Prentice-Hall, Englewood Cliffs, NJ.

Ehrich, H.D. (1982) On the theory of specification, implementation and parameterisation of abstract data types. *JACM* **29**, 206–227.

Ehrig, H., Kreowski, H.-J., Mahr, B. and Padawitz, P. (1982) Algebraic implementation of abstract data types. *Theoretical Computer Science* **20**, 209–263.

Enderton, H.B. (1972) *A Mathematical Introduction to Logic*. Academic Press, New York.

Erickson, R. and Musser, D. (1980) The Affirm theorem prover: Proof forests and management of large proofs. In: *5th Conference on Automated Deduction*, W. Bibel and R. Kowalski (Eds.). LNCS87. Springer-Verlag, New York, Heidelberg, Berlin.

Goguen, J.A., Thatcher, J.W. and Wagner, E.G. (1978) An initial algebra approach to the specification correctness and implementation of abstract data types. In: *Current Trends in Programming Methodology*, **IV**, R. Yeh (Ed.). Prentice-Hall, Englewood Cliffs, NJ, 80–149.

Goldblatt, R. (1982) *Axiomatising the Logic of Computer Programming*. LNCS 130. Springer-Verlag, New York, Heidelberg, Berlin.

Gordon, M., Milner, R. and Wadsworth, C. (1979) *Edinburgh LCF*. LNCS 78. Springer-Verlag, New York, Heidelberg, Berlin.

Gries, D. (1981) *The Science of Programming*. Springer-Verlag, New York, Heidelberg, Berlin.

Guttag, J.V. and Horning, J.J. (1978) The algebraic specification of abstract data types. *Acta Informatica* **10**, 27–52.

Guttag, J.V., Horning, J.J. and Wing, J.M. (1985) *Larch in Five Easy Pieces*. DEC Systems Research Centre, Report # 5.

Grzegorczyk, A. (1974) *An Outline of Mathematical Logic*. Reidel, Dordrecht/ Warsaw.

Henderson, P. (Ed.) (1984) ACM SIGSOFT/SIGPLAN Software Engineering Symposium on Practical Software Development Environments. *ACM Software Engineering Notes* **9**, (3).

Hoare, C.A.R. (1972) Proof of correctness of data representations. *Acta Informatica* **1**, 271–281.

Honda, M., Hagino, T. and Shibayama, E. (1983) Proof system. In: *The Iota Programming System*, R. Nakajima and T. Yuasa (Eds). LNCS 160. Springer-Verlag, New York, Heidelberg, Berlin.

Jackson, M.A. (1975) *Principles of Program Design*. Academic Press, New York.

Jacobs, D. and Gries, D. (1985) General correctness: a unification of partial and total correctness. *Acta Informatica* **22**, 67–83.

Jones, C.B (1980) *Software Development: A Rigorous Approach*. Prentice-Hall, Englewood Cliffs, NJ.

Jones, C.B. (1986) *Systematic Software Development using VDM*. Prentice-Hall, Englewood Cliffs, NJ.

Lehman, M.M., Stenning, V. and Turski, W.M. (1984) Another look at software design methodology. *ACM Software Engineering Notes* **9** (2), 38–53.

Liskov, B., Zilles, L.N. (1974) Programming with abstract data types. *ACM SIGPLAN Notices* **9** (4), 50–59.

Maibaum, T.S.E. and Turski, W.M. (1984) On what exactly goes on when software is developed step-by-step. *Proc 7th Int. Conf. on Soft. Eng.*, 528–533.

Maibaum, T.S.E., Veloso, P.A.S. and Sadler, M.R. (1985) A theory of abstract data types for program development: bridging the gap? In: *Formal Methods and Software Development*, **II**. LNCS 186. Springer-Verlag, New York, Heidelberg, Berlin. 214–230.

Myers, G.J. (1975) *Reliable Software Through Composite Design*. Petrocelli/ Charter.

Nakajima, R., Honda, M. and Nakahara, H. (1980) Hierarchical program specification and verification – a many-sorted logical approach. *Acta Informatica* **14**, 135–155.

Naur, P. (1985) Intuition in software development. In: *Formal Methods and*

Software Development, **II**. LNCS 186. Springer-Verlag, New York, Heidelberg, Berlin. 60–79.

Partsch, M. and Steinbruggen, R. (1983) Program transformation systems. *ACM Computing Surveys* **15**, 199–236.

Rosen, B.K. (1973) Tree manipulating systems and Church–Rosser theorems. *JACM* **20**, 160–187.

Ross, D.T. (1977) Structured analysis (SA): a language for communicating ideas. *IEEE Trans. Soft. Eng.* **SE-3**, 16–34.

Shostak, R., Schwartz, R. and Melliar-Smith, M. (1982) STP: a mechanised logic for specification and verification. In: *6th Conference on Automated Deduction*, D. Loveland (Ed.) LNCS 138. Springer-Verlag, New York, Heidelberg, Berlin.

Turski, W.M. (1978) *Computer Programming Methodology*. Heyden, London, Philadelphia, Rheine.

Tyugu, E.H. (1984) *Conceptual Programming*. Russian edition: Nauka, Moscow. English version: *Knowledge-based Programming*. Addison-Wesley, in preparation.

Veloso, P.A.S. and Pequeno, T.H.C. (1978) Interpretations between many-sorted theories, *Proc 2nd Brasilian Colloquium on Logic*. Campinas.

Veloso, P.A.S. (1982) *Divide-and-Conquer via Data Type*. Technical Report PUC/RJ Rio de Janeiro.

Wirth, N. (1971) Program development by stepwise refinement. *CACM* **14**, 221–227.

Würges, H. (1981) A specification technique based on predicate transformer. *Acta Informatica* **15**, 425–446.

Yourdon. E. and Constantine, L.L. (1979) *Structured Design*. Prentice-Hall International, Englewood Cliffs, N.J.

Index

(Page numbers larger than 217, set in italics, refer to the Appendix; as a rule, the material in the Appendix should be consulted before that in the main body of the text.)